D0567695

# The Kingfisher
# REFERENCE ATLAS

## An A-Z Guide to Countries of the World

# The Kingfisher
# REFERENCE ATLAS

*An A-Z Guide to Countries of the World*

Brian Williams
Cartographic consultant    Keith Lye

Kingfisher

NEW YORK

**Yugoslavia**
At the time of going to press the political
situation in the former Yugoslavia was
uncertain. Slovenia, Croatia, and Bosnia
and Hercegovina had been recognized as
independent republics; Serbia and
Montenegro had declared that they formed
the new Yugoslavia, but were not recognized as such; Macedonia had declared
independence but was not completely
recognized as such.

KINGFISHER
Larousse Kingfisher Chambers Inc.
95 Madison Avenue
New York, New York 10016

First American edition 1993
This revised edition published by Larousse plc, 1994, for
Brøderbund Software Inc.
10 9 8 7 6 5 4 3 2

Copyright © Grisewood & Dempsey Ltd. 1992, 1993
This edition copyright © Larousse plc 1994

All rights reserved under International and Pan-American
Copyright Conventions

**LIBRARY OF CONGRESS CATALOGING-IN-PUBLICATION DATA**
Williams, Brian
The Kingfisher reference atlas: an a-z guide to countries of the
world/author, Brian Williams; cartographic consultant, Keith Lye;
[illustrator, Malcolm Porter]. – 1st American ed.
p. cm.
Includes index.
1. Children's atlases. I. Lye, Keith. II. Porter, Malcolm.
III. Title IV. Title: A-z guide to countries of the world.
G1021.W554

ISBN 1-85697-529-0

**Editors** Rachel Pilcher, Pauline Graham, Lee Simmonds, Stuart Cooper
**Cartographic editors** Joan Russell, Andrew Thompson
**Cartographer** Malcolm Porter
**Artwork origination and typesetting** Lovell Johns, Oxford, England

Flags supplied by Lovell Johns, Oxford, England, and authenticated by
the Flag Research Center, Winchester, Mass. 01890

Printed in the USA

# Contents

# Features of this book

In *The Kingfisher Reference Atlas* every page deals with a country or, in a few cases, a small group of neighboring countries. Countries are arranged alphabetically for ease of use. Where necessary, a cross-reference at the top of the page shows where to find a country that is treated as part of a group. Key elements in *The Kingfisher Reference Atlas* are the special features found on all pages. They include an authoritative, concise, introductory text, statistical boxes, and economic, demographic, and climatic data in graphs and charts. To make the most of the atlas, it will help to study these introductory pages, to learn how each key component works, and what information it contains.

This box contains basic statistics: the country's area (in customary and metric units); population; name and population of capital city; names of other important cities; highest point above sea level; official or chief language; religions; currency or money unit; main export products; form of government and per capita gross national product (GNP) in U.S. dollars.

This panel details the country's main economic activities. Under farming, for example, you will find details of which crops are grown and which kinds of domestic animals are reared. Other headings include Fishing, Forestry, and Mining. Under Industry, details of manufactured goods, processes, services, tourism, and other money-earning activities are given.

Each country's national flag is shown in color. Colors, designs, and proportions of the flags have been carefully checked to make sure each is as up-to-date as possible.

The main maps in the atlas are drawn to a scale shown on each map. Each map shows the country in detail. The capital city, other large cities, roads, railroads, mountains, lakes, rivers, deserts, and other important features are clearly shown.

Contour shading indicates height of land above sea level. Darker colors show higher ground. Heights are given (in customary and metric units) on the accompanying key.

The positional map locates each country, showing neighboring states. For a more detailed overview of the whole region, refer to the main continent map.

Climate is the average weather of a place. This graph charts month-by-month rainfall and temperatures at a selected location in the country.

## Poland

**Area:** 120,725 sq. miles (312,677 km²)
**Population:** 38,064,000
**Capital:** Warsaw (pop. 1,649,000)
**Other cities:** Łódź 849,000; Krakow 716,000; Wrocław 637,000; Poznan 575,000
**Highest point:** Rysy Peak 8,199 ft. (2,499 m)
**Official language:** Polish
**Religion:** Roman Catholicism
**Currency:** Zloty
**Main exports:** Machinery and transportation equipment, chemicals, fuel and power, textiles
**Government:** Multiparty republic
**Per capita GNP:** U.S. $7,200

The republic of Poland in eastern Europe is a mostly flat country. Much of it is a large plain, the north of which is either infertile or forested. The central lowlands, where Warsaw, Poznan, and Łódź are situated, are better farmland. In the south the land rises towards the Sudeten and Carpathian mountain ranges. Poland's western border with Germany is formed by the Oder and Neisse rivers. Its other major river is the Vistula. Summers become warmer from north to south. Poland was a kingdom in the 1100s, but its frontiers have changed frequently. In 1795 it was swallowed up by Russia, Prussia, and Austria. Poland reemerged in 1918, but was overrun by Germany in 1939 and again divided. Reunited with new frontiers in 1945 under Communist Party rule, Poland reestablished democratic government in the late 1980s.

**ECONOMIC SURVEY**
**Farming:** Farmland covers 60 percent of Poland. Most farms are small and are privately owned. Cereals, sugarbeet and potatoes are grown. Cattle, pigs, sheep, and poultry are reared. Much of the soil is poor, and methods are old-fashioned by western European standards. **Fishing:** Polish vessels catch fish in the Baltic and North seas, and the North Atlantic Ocean. Cod, hake, and herring are the leading catches. **Mining:** Poland is the world's fifth largest producer of coal. It has reserves of copper, lead, zinc, nickel, and other minerals. **Industry:** Factories produce iron and steel, ships, chemicals, machinery, and textiles.

*Age distribution* — Under 15 / 15 – 60 / Over 60

*miles* 0 50 100
*kilometers* 0 50 100

*Contour map*
- 3,000 ft. (Over 1,000 m)
- 1,500 – 3,000 ft. (500 – 1,000 m)
- 0 – 1,500 ft. (0 – 500 m)

*Climate - Warsaw*

*Population trend* — 1940 1950 1960 1970 1980 1990 2000

*Imports and exports* — Imports / Exports

143

The text introduction explains where the country is, and describes its principal landscape features, (such as mountains, plains, coastlines, and rivers); climate; and population. There is also a summary of the most important events in the country's history.

This bar graph shows the chief goods imported (bought from abroad) and exported (sold to other countries). Comparing these graphs shows how some countries rely on one or two export items, while others produce a wide range of trade goods.

The pie chart shows what proportion of the population is under 15, aged 15 to 60, and over 60. Countries with fast-growing populations tend to have a larger proportion of people under 15 than those with static or slow-growing populations.

The graph shows population growth in modern times, plotted at ten-year intervals. A steeply rising graph means a fast-growing population. A near-level line on the graph indicates that the population is either static or slow-growing.

# How to use the maps

All maps use different styles of lettering, shades of color, and various symbols to convey information. The maps in this book are designed to be easy to read. On the main maps, place names are clearly marked in black type. The capital of a country is shown in bold capitals, for example **WARSAW**, and located by a black square within a square. Smaller type is used for the names of other cities and towns. Bold type (e.g. **Gdansk**) indicates a major city other than the capital. Dams are marked with a thick black dash, and sites of archeological interest are also noted. Rivers, shown in blue, are named in italic type, for example *Vistula*. Main roads are shown in red, railroads in black. A thick red line marks a national frontier. Only the country itself is shaded in color. Neighboring states are named, in black type, on the white surround. Oceans and lakes are shaded blue. The names of oceans and seas are printed in italic type, for example *NORTH SEA*.

Relief (the rise and fall of the land) is shown in an attractive visual style. The names of important mountain ranges are given in bold letters, for example, **Carpathian Mts.** High mountains are marked by a triangle symbol, and the name and height above sea level (in feet) are given alongside.

You will also notice blue lines crisscrossing the main map. These are lines of latitude and longitude, and are marked in degrees. Lines of latitude indicate distance (in degrees) north or south of the equator, which is latitude 0°. These lines run east and west (left to right across the page). Lines of longitude indicate distance east or west of the meridian of Greenwich, which is longitude 0°. The length of a degree of latitude is about 69 land miles (111 km). The length of a degree of longitude is the same at the equator, but gets shorter toward the North and South poles. Lines of latitude and longitude provide a grid that enables you to fix accurately the position of any spot on the Earth's surface.

**Contour map**

| | |
|---|---|
| ■ | Over 3,000 ft. (1,000 m) |
| ▨ | 1,500 - 3,000 ft. (500 - 1,000 m) |
| □ | 0 - 1,500 ft. (0 - 500 m) |

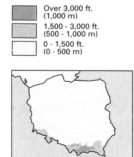

The contour maps use a two- or three-color shading system to show areas of different height above sea level. On the outline map, the paler colors show lowland areas. The key to the map gives the height range (in feet and meters above sea level).

The main map is a close-up view. The positional map locates the country in its immediate geographical context. The country itself is highlighted in color. Neighboring countries are shown in gray, and oceans appear in blue.

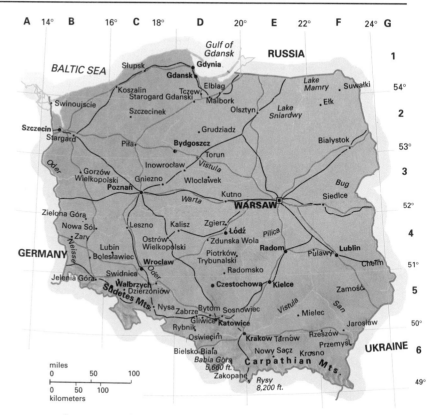

No flat map can be 100 percent accurate because the Earth's surface is curved. However, a flat map can convey three-dimensional information visually, through contour lines and shading. By using the small contour map alongside the main map you will be able to tell at a glance the average height of the land in any part of the country.

All maps are drawn to a scale. This is shown simply by a black line in the corner of the map. The longer length indicates the scale in miles. The shorter length is the scale in kilometers.

The small positional map, colored red and gray, locates the country in relation to its immediate and near neighbors. By identifying these neighboring countries this map also serves as a reference point for those who wish to compare the geography, climate, economy, and other aspects of several countries within a particular region.

# World Climate

Climate is the average weather of a place. The world has a number of climate regions. Climate is related to latitude, since the Sun's heating of the Earth is more intense in the tropics, near the equator, and least intense near the Poles. This explains why tropical areas are generally warmer than regions nearer to the Poles. However, other factors play a part in influencing climate. Altitude, for example, has an important effect on climate. Temperatures fall by about 3.5°F for every 1,000 feet. (6°C for every 1,000 m) of altitude. So mountains in the tropics can have much cooler climates than surrounding lowlands. Nearness to the ocean also affects climate, having a generally moderating influence on coastal climates. This is because although ocean water takes longer to heat up than dry land, the ocean retains heat for much longer. The most extreme climates, with very hot summers and very cold winters, are found in the hearts of continents.

The world climate maps on this page illustrate average temperatures in January (top) and in July (lower map). The key shows how the color shading relates to average temperatures within a given range, in degrees Fahrenheit. The pinker end of the scale indicates highest temperatures, the bluer end of the scale indicates colder climatic conditions.

On the rainfall and temperature charts, the letters along the bottom scale stand for the months of the year. The figures on the scale on the left show temperature in degrees Fahrenheit. The figures on the scale on the right show rainfall in inches.

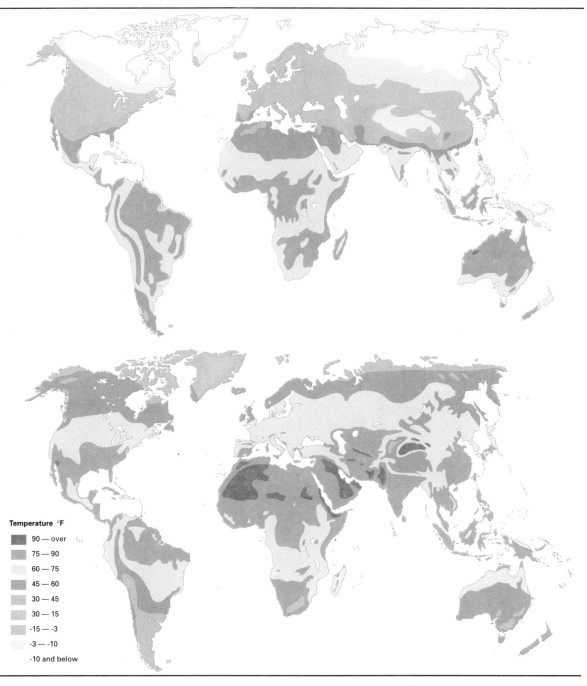

**Temperature °F**

- 90 — over
- 75 — 90
- 60 — 75
- 45 — 60
- 30 — 45
- 30 — 15
- -15 — -3
- -3 — -10
- -10 and below

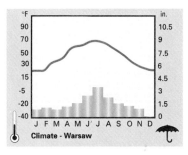

**Climate - Warsaw**

# World Population

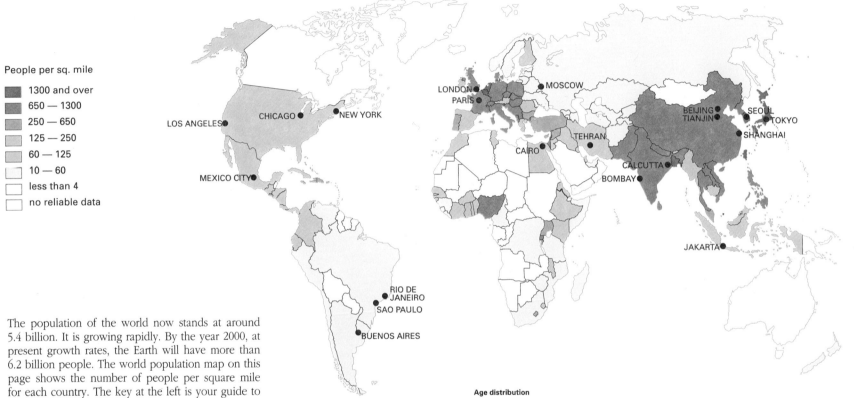

**People per sq. mile**

- 1300 and over
- 650 — 1300
- 250 — 650
- 125 — 250
- 60 — 125
- 10 — 60
- less than 4
- no reliable data

The population of the world now stands at around 5.4 billion. It is growing rapidly. By the year 2000, at present growth rates, the Earth will have more than 6.2 billion people. The world population map on this page shows the number of people per square mile for each country. The key at the left is your guide to the color coding on the map. The map also shows a selection of the world's major cities.

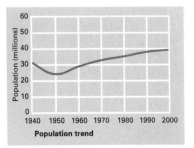

**Population trend**

The population chart shows the population trend, or pattern. The figures on the left show population. The graph is drawn to show growth at ten-year intervals, with a projection, or estimated population, for the year 2000. The red line on the graph indicates growth (rising from left to right) or lack of it (shown by a nearly level line). Compare the graphs of Kenya and Norway. Kenya's population is expected to double in about 17 years. Norway's population is practically static, and will probably not double in the next 100 years.

**Age distribution**

- Under 15
- 15 - 60
- Over 60

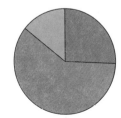

For each country there is also an age-distribution diagram, in the form of a simple pie chart. The pie has three colored pieces. One piece represents the proportion of people under the age of 15; another the proportion in the 15 to 60 age group; and the third shows the proportion of the population aged 60 or over. Countries with fast-growing populations tend to have larger proportions of young people. In Africa, Asia, and Latin America, people tend to have larger families than do people in Europe and North America.

# World Vegetation

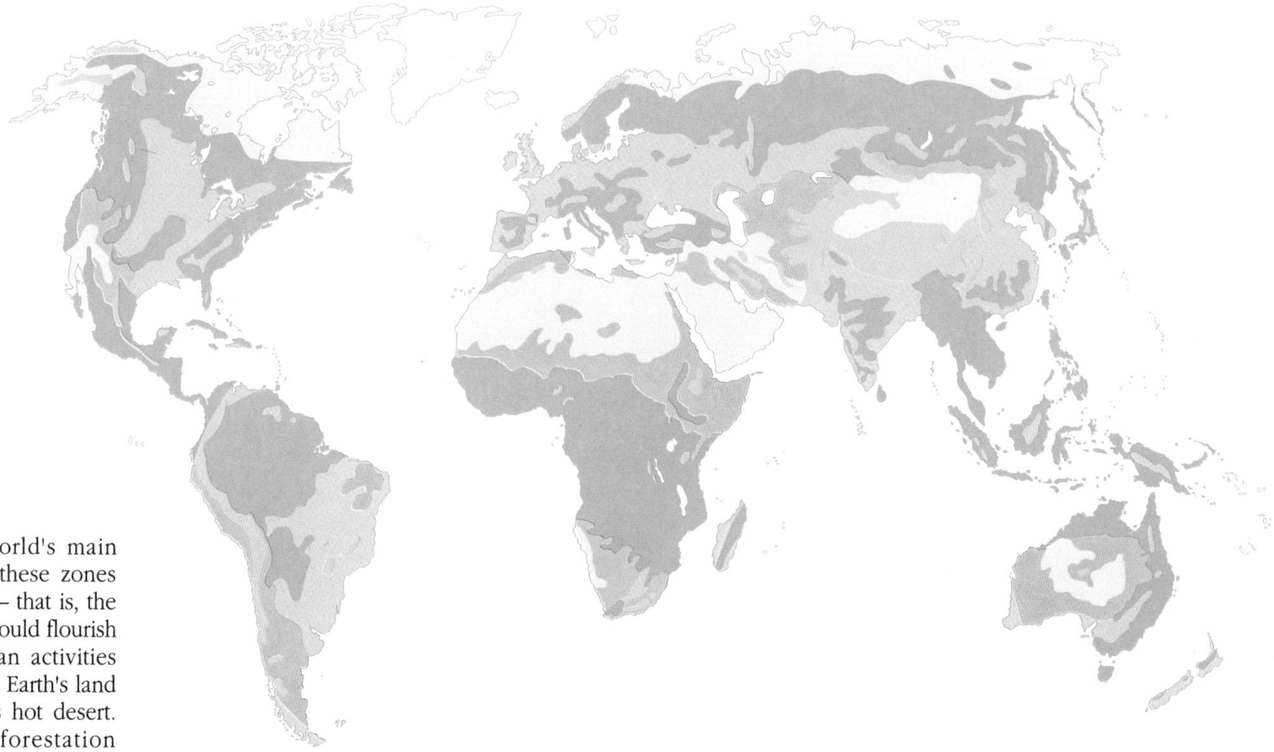

The map on this page shows the world's main vegetation zones. The descriptions of these zones (see key) refer to the *climax* vegetation – that is, the vegetation natural to the region, which would flourish if the land were undisturbed by human activities (such as farming). About a quarter of the Earth's land surface is forested, and about a fifth is hot desert. About a tenth is ice-covered. Deforestation (destruction of forests, especially in the tropics) is a major environmental threat. Only about half of the Earth's great natural tropical forests remain. They include the cold forests of Siberia and Canada and the tropical rain forests of South America, West Africa, and Southeast Asia. Recent surveys suggest that an area roughly twice the size of Austria is still being lost each year, despite efforts by conservationists to persuade governments to adopt forest-management policies. Forestry, urban sprawl, farming, road development, pollution, and climatic change have major impacts on the world's vegetation patterns.

**Physical zones**

- ice and snow
- tundra
- mountains/barren land
- forest
- grassland
- semidesert
- desert

# World Political Map

**THE AMERICAS**

1. HAITI
2. BELIZE
3. GUATEMALA
4. EL SALVADOR
5. HONDURAS
6. JAMAICA
7. DOMINICAN REPUBLIC
8. PUERTO RICO
9. NICARAGUA
10. COSTA RICA
11. PANAMA
12. ECUADOR
13. VENEZUELA
14. GUYANA
15. SURINAM
16. FRENCH GUYANA
17. PARAGUAY
18. URUGUAY
19. CHILE

**EUROPE**

1. IRELAND
2. BELGIUM
3. NETHERLANDS
4. SWITZERLAND
5. GERMANY
6. LUXEMBOURG
7. ITALY
8. AUSTRIA
9. CZECH REPUBLIC
10. POLAND
11. DENMARK
12. NORWAY
13. SWEDEN
14. FINLAND
15. ESTONIA
16. LATVIA
17. LITHUANIA
18. RUSSIA
19. HUNGARY
20. FORMER YUGOSLAVIA
21. ALBANIA
22. ROMANIA
23. BULGARIA
24. GREECE
25. BELARUS
26. UKRAINE
27. MOLDOVA
28. SLOVAKIA

**THE MIDDLE EAST
AND ASIA**

1. GEORGIA
2. ARMENIA
3. AZERBAIJAN
4. TURKMENISTAN
5. UZBEKISTAN
6. KYRGYZSTAN
7. TAJIKISTAN
8. LEBANON
9. ISRAEL
10. JORDAN
11. SYRIA
12. KUWAIT
13. QATAR
14. UNITED ARAB
   EMIRATES
15. OMAN
16. YEMEN
17. AFGHANISTAN
18. NEPAL
19. BHUTAN
20. BANGLADESH
21. MYANMAR
22. LAOS
23. VIETNAM
24. THAILAND
25. CAMBODIA
26. NORTH KOREA
27. SOUTH KOREA
28. BRUNEI

**AFRICA**

1. MOROCCO AND
   WESTERN SAHARA
2. TUNISIA
3. SENEGAL
4. GAMBIA
5. GUINEA-BISSAU
6. GUINEA
7. SIERRA LEONE
8. LIBERIA
9. CÔTE D'IVOIRE
10. BURKINA FASO
11. GHANA
12. TOGO
13. BENIN
14. NIGERIA
15. CAMEROON
16. CENTRAL AFRICAN
   REPUBLIC
17. UGANDA
18. KENYA
19. DJIBOUTI
20. SOMALIA
21. GABON
22. CONGO
23. RWANDA
24. BURUNDI
25. TANZANIA
26. MALAWI
27. MOZAMBIQUE
28. ZIMBABWE
29. BOTSWANA
30. NAMIBIA
31. LESOTHO
32. SWAZILAND
33. ERITREA

# World Relief Map

Arctic Circle

NORTH
AMERICA

EUROPE

ASIA

ATLANTIC OCEAN

PACIFIC OCEAN

Tropic of Cancer

PACIFIC OCEAN

AFRICA

Equator

INDIAN OCEAN

SOUTH
AMERICA

OCEANIA

Tropic of Capricorn

Mountains

Tundra

Forest

Hills

Crop/Grazing
land

Dry scrub

Desert

# Afghanistan

**Area:** 250,000 sq. miles (647,497 km²)
**Population:** 18,136,000
**Capital:** Kabul (pop. 1,424,000)
**Other cities:** Kandahar 225,000; Herat 177,000; Mazar-i-Sharif 115,000
**Highest point:** Nowshak 24,557 ft. (7,485 m)
**Official languages:** Pashto (Pushto), Dari
**Religion:** Islam
**Currency:** Afghani
**Main exports:** Natural gas, dried fruit and nuts, carpets
**Government:** Single-party republic
**Per capita GNP:** Under U.S. $500

Afghanistan is largely mountainous and completely landlocked. Major mountain ranges include the Hindu Kush, with peaks of 23,000 feet (7,000 metres). The climate is hot in summer, but severely cold in winter in the mountains. Most of the people are Pashtuns, but there are Tadzhik, Uzbek, Hazara, and other tribal groups. Almost all Afghans are Muslims. Afghanistan was created in the 1700s by Ahmad Shah Abdali, who united warring tribes and invaded India. Britain and Russia were rivals for influence in Afghanistan. The country became a constitutional monarchy in 1964, but the king was deposed in 1973 and Afghanistan became a republic. Communists seized power in 1978. In 1979 Soviet forces invaded Afghanistan to support the communist government against Islamic guerrillas. The last Soviet troops pulled out in 1989, but internal fighting continued.

## ECONOMIC SURVEY

**Farming:** Only 10 percent of the land is suitable for crops, mostly in irrigated valleys. Cereals, including barley, corn, and wheat, fruit such as grapes, and a variety of vegetables are grown. Cotton is a major cash crop. Many Afghans are nomads, keeping sheep, cattle, goats, horses, and camels.

**Mining:** Natural gas is extracted, but the rich deposits of minerals such as iron, chrome, silver, gold, rubies, lapis lazuli, lead, and coal are largely untapped.

**Industry:** In a country with few urban areas, manufacturing is still on a small scale. Afghanistan produces many craft items such as carpets and rugs, and woolen and leather goods.

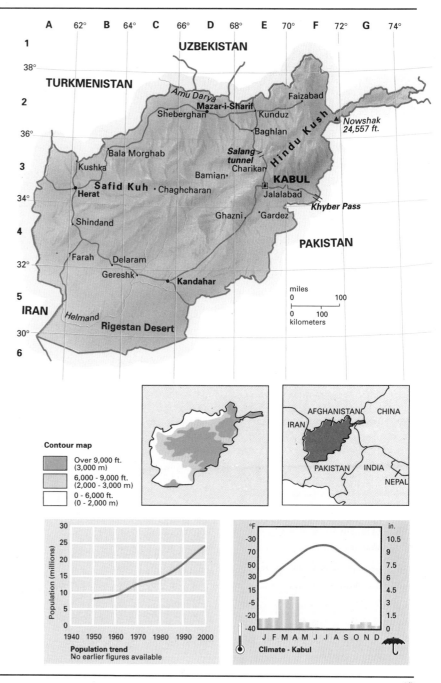

Contour map

- Over 9,000 ft. (3,000 m)
- 6,000 - 9,000 ft. (2,000 - 3,000 m)
- 0 - 6,000 ft. (0 - 2,000 m)

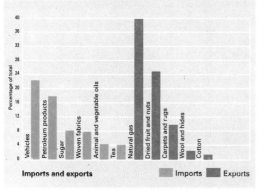

**Imports and exports**
Imports / Exports

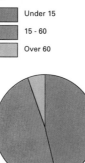

**Age distribution**
- Under 15
- 15 - 60
- Over 60

**Population trend**
No earlier figures available

**Climate - Kabul**

# AFRICA

**Area:** 11,703,915 sq. miles (30,313,000 km²)
**Population:** 655,700,000
**Major cities:** Cairo (Egypt) 6,325,000;
Alexandria (Egypt) 2,893,000; Kinshasa (Zaire)
2,654,000; Casablanca (Morocco) 2,139,000;
Abidjan (Côte d'Ivoire) 1,850,000
**Number of independent countries:** 53,
including the islands of Cape Verde and São
Tomé and Príncipe in the Atlantic Ocean; and
the Comoros, Mauritius, and the Seychelles in
the Indian Ocean
**Largest country:** Sudan
**Smallest independent country:** Seychelles
**Highest mountain:** Mt. Kilimanjaro, in
Tanzania, 19,340 ft. (5,895 m)
**Longest river:** Nile 4,145 miles (6,670 km)
**Largest lake:** Lake Victoria 26,828 sq. miles
(69,484 km²)

Africa covers about a fifth of the Earth's land area,
making it the second largest continent after Asia. Its
countries range in size from huge (Sudan) to tiny
(Gambia). Its landscapes also vary greatly. They
include the world's biggest desert, the Sahara, tropical
forests, bush, and savanna grassland. Africa has the
world's longest river, the Nile, and large lakes in the
Great Rift Valley. Arabs and Berbers live north of the
Sahara, black Africans south of the Sahara. There are
more than 800 ethnic and language groups, including
people of European origin. Egypt's ancient civilization
flourished from 3000 B.C. Other empires rose and fell,
before Islamic and European trade and colonization.
Africa was almost entirely colonized by 1900. A
different Africa emerged during the 1960s as newly-
independent states developed fresh identities. The
present political boundaries were largely drawn up by
the colonial powers, who took no notice of traditional
tribal territories. These boundary problems have led to
unrest, and even civil war, in a number of nations.
South Africa, long isolated by its white-dominated
government's policy of apartheid – racial separation –
has begun moving toward reform. Three countries
which politically are part of Africa, Mauritius,
Comoros, and Seychelles, are treated in their
geographical location, the Indian Ocean: see page 92.

**Contour map**

- 6,000 ft. (Over 2,000 m)
- 3,000 - 6,000 ft. (1,000 - 2,000 m)
- 0 - 3,000 ft. (0 - 1,000 m)

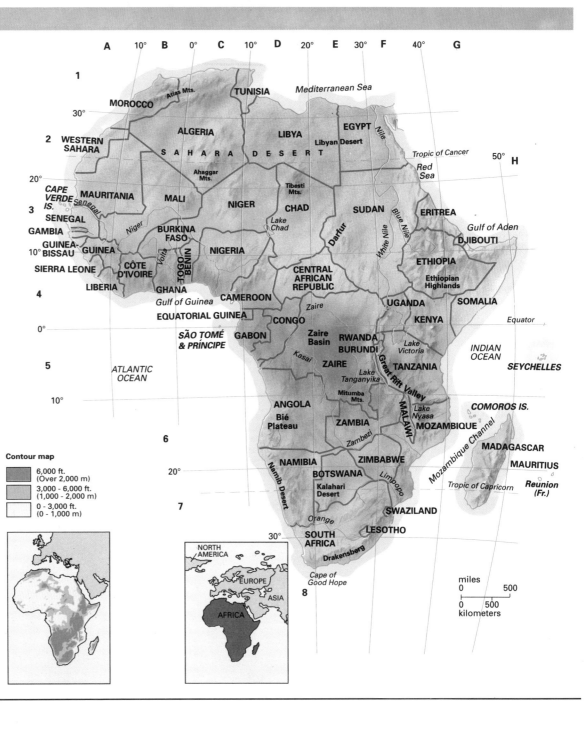

# Albania

**Area:** 11,100 sq. miles (28,748 km²)
**Population:** 3,278,000
**Capital:** Tirana (pop. 206,000)
**Other cities:** Durresi 72,000; Shkodra 71,000
**Highest point:** Mount Jezerce 8,835 ft. (2,693 m)
**Official language:** Albanian
**Religions:** Eastern Orthodoxy, Islam, Roman Catholicism
**Currency:** Lek
**Main exports:** Minerals including chrome, nickel, copper and oil, food products
**Government:** Multiparty republic
**Per capita GNP:** U.S. $930

A small country bordering the Adriatic Sea, Albania is mostly mountainous, with several peaks over 7,546 ft. (2,300 metres) high. The coast is dry with a Mediterranean climate, while in the wetter uplands rainfall averages 70 inches (1,800 mm) a year. Scrub and forest cover more than 40 percent of the land. The chief rivers are the Drini and Vjosa. The Albanian language has two main dialects, Gheg in the north and Tosk in the south. Many times conquered during its history, Albania was created from the ruins of the Turkish empire in 1912, and became a kingdom in 1928. Italy occupied the country in 1939. In 1946 Albania became a communist republic under a Stalinist regime. Long regarded as the most backward state in Europe, Albania moved toward democratic reform and Westernization in the early 1990s.

## ECONOMIC SURVEY

**Farming:** Forests and scrub cover nearly half the country. Farmers grow corn, vegetables, fruit including grapes and olives, sunflower seeds, and tobacco. Cattle, sheep, goats, and pigs are raised. Farm methods are often primitive, and mules and horses are used as working animals. Farms were collectivized by the communists, and more than half the work force remains on the land.
**Mining:** Albania has large reserves of iron, chromite, copper, and other minerals, and produces oil and natural gas.
**Industry:** State-run factories produce cement, textiles, fertilizers, food products, beer, and cigarettes.

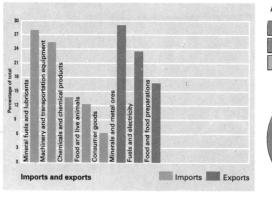

**Imports and exports**

Imports | Exports

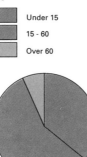

**Age distribution**

- Under 15
- 15 - 60
- Over 60

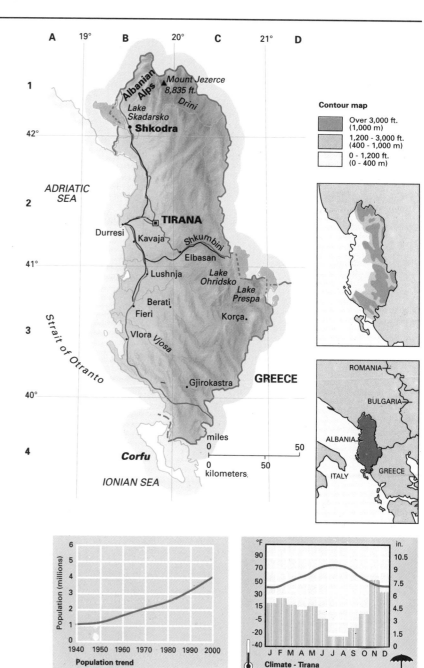

**Contour map**

- Over 3,000 ft. (1,000 m)
- 1,200 - 3,000 ft. (400 - 1,000 m)
- 0 - 1,200 ft. (0 - 400 m)

**Population trend**

**Climate - Tirana**

# Algeria

**Area:** 919,595 sq. miles (2,381,741 km²)
**Population:** 25,337,000
**Capital:** Algiers (1,483,000)
**Other cities:** Oran 590,000; Constantine 438,000; Annaba 348,000
**Highest point:** Mount Tahat 9,852 ft. (3,003 m)
**Official language:** Arabic
**Religion:** Islam
**Currency:** Dinar
**Main exports:** Petroleum and natural gas, petroleum products, wine
**Government:** Multiparty republic
**Per capita GNP:** U.S. $2170

Algeria is largely desert, because 85 percent of the country lies within the Sahara. The narrow Mediterranean coastal strip has a pleasant climate and rich farmland. Known as the Tell (meaning "hill" in Arabic), this region has plains and hills, rising in the southeast to the Saharan Atlas Mountains. Most Algerians are Arabs and live in the north. A minority inhabit the high plateaus south of the Tell Atlas Mountains. The Sahara is largely uninhabited except by nomads moving between oases, and oil workers. The first Algerians were Berbers. Later conquerors were the Romans and the Vandals. Arabs introduced Islam and Arabic in the late 600s. Ottoman Turkish rule lasted from the early 1500s to the 1800s, when France took over. Algeria became independent in 1962 after a seven-year war between nationalists and the French.

## ECONOMIC SURVEY

**Farming:** Most farmers have small plots, and engage in subsistence farming. There are some large state-run farms, but many have been broken up under a reform plan. Crops include wheat, barley, dates, grapes, olives, potatoes, and fruit. Cattle, goats, and sheep are kept.

**Mining:** Natural gas and petroleum make up almost all Algeria's exports by value. There are deposits of iron ore, gypsum, phosphates, and barite.

**Industry:** The state controls the textile, vehicle-assembly, steel-making and building-materials industries. Private firms run factories producing flour, semolina, edible oils, and other foodstuffs.

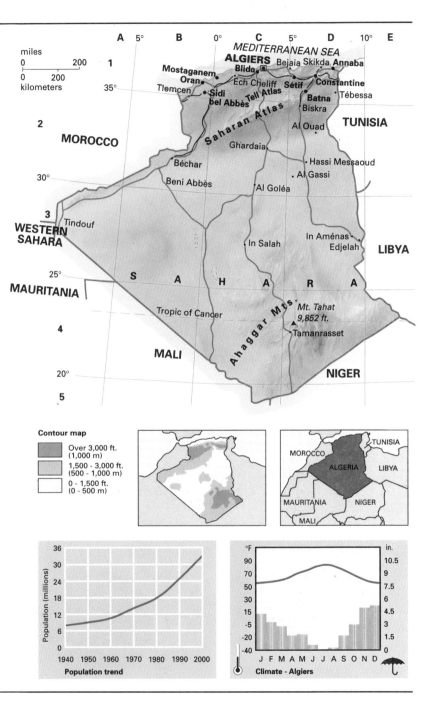

### Contour map
- Over 3,000 ft. (1,000 m)
- 1,500 - 3,000 ft. (500 - 1,000 m)
- 0 - 1,500 ft. (0 - 500 m)

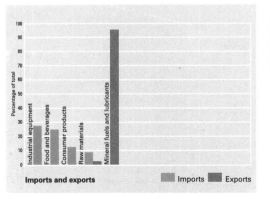

**Imports and exports**

Imports · Exports

**Age distribution**
- Under 15
- 15 - 60
- Over 60

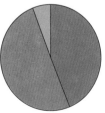

**Population trend**

**Climate - Algiers**

# Angola

**Area:** 481,354 sq. miles (1,246,700 km²)
**Population:** 10,002,000
**Capital:** Luanda (pop. 1,134,000)
**Other cities:** Huambo 203,000
**Highest point:** Moco 8,592 ft. (2,619 m)
**Official language:** Portuguese
**Religions:** Christianity, various traditional beliefs
**Currency:** Kwanza
**Main exports:** Petroleum and petroleum products, vegetable and animal products
**Government:** Republic
**Per capita GNP:** U.S. $620

Angola includes the enclave of Cabinda in the northwest. Most of the land is hilly and grass covered, with rocky desert in the south. There is a narrow coastal plain. The climate is generally warmest and wettest in the north. Angola has numerous rivers, flowing either into the Zaire (Congo) or the Atlantic Ocean. The people belong to several ethnic groups, including the Ovimbundu, Mbundu, Kongo, and Luanda-Chokwe. There are also people of mixed African and European ancestry. Angola was settled over 50,000 years ago. Bantu speakers moved into the area some 2,000 years ago. In the 1500s Portugal set up bases along the coast. Portuguese settlement was substantial by the 1930s. A nationalist guerrilla war brought independence in 1975, but civil war against the new left-wing government raged into the 1990s.

## ECONOMIC SURVEY

**Farming:** Angola produces coffee, corn, palm oil, and sisal as cash crops. Sugarcane, bananas, and cotton are also grown, while the main food crops are cassava, corn, sweet potatoes, groundnuts (peanuts), and beans. Cattle are the chief livestock.
**Fishing:** Coastal fishing produces fish for overseas sale.
**Forestry:** Angola's timber includes mahogany and other hardwoods.
**Mining:** Petroleum is the single most valuable export. Angola also has diamonds, copper, phosphates, iron ore, and manganese.
**Industry:** Factory products include bricks, foodstuffs, beverages, steel, shoes, and textiles.

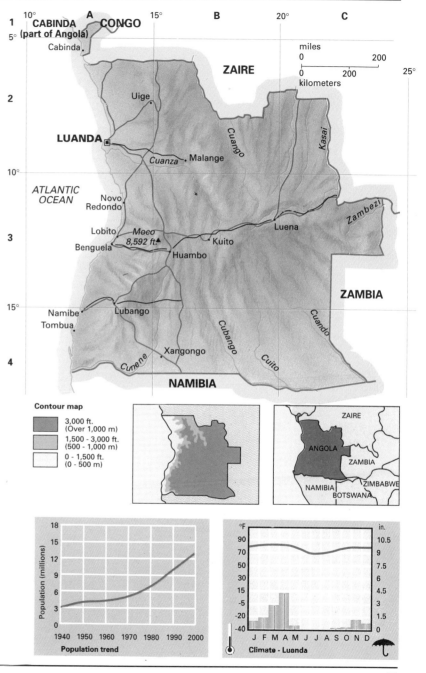

**Contour map**

- 3,000 ft. (Over 1,000 m)
- 1,500 - 3,000 ft. (500 - 1,000 m)
- 0 - 1,500 ft. (0 - 500 m)

**Population trend**

**Climate - Luanda**

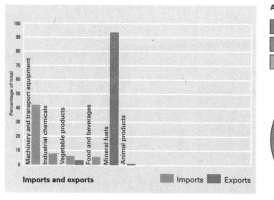

**Imports and exports**
Imports  Exports

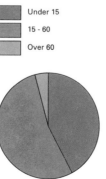

**Age distribution**

- Under 15
- 15 - 60
- Over 60

# Antarctica

**Area:** About 5,400,000 sq. miles
(14,000,000 km²)
**Population:** No permanent population
**Highest point:** Vinson Massif 16,860 ft.
(5,139 m)
**Ice cover:** Ice and snow cover 98 percent of
Antarctica; the ice sheet has a volume of about
7 million cubic miles (about 30 million km³)
**Deepest part of ice sheet:** About 15,700 ft.
(4,800 m)

The Antarctic continent is 98 percent covered with ice
and snow. Beneath the ice, which in places is up to
3 miles (4,800 m) thick, are mountains and valleys.
High peaks of the Transantarctic Mountains rise above
the icecap. The east-central region is a windswept
plateau, and includes the South Pole. Western
Antarctica has younger rocks than in the east,
suggesting more recent volcanic activity. The plateau is
cold and dry, the coast is milder and moister. Icy winds
intensify the cold. Few plants survive the extreme
climate. They include lichens, mosses and two
flowering plants. Animal life includes a few insects, and
around the coasts seals and penguins. There are no
native human inhabitants. The only permanent human
settlements are scientific bases. The Antarctic was
discovered by European sailors in the 1700s and 1800s.
It was explored by land and air in the 1900s. No
territorial claims are recognized and by treaty it is
reserved for peaceful, non-exploitative uses.

**ECONOMIC SURVEY**
**Farming:** In the ice-
bound Antarctic
continent, where the
world's record low
temperature (-128.6°F)
has been recorded, no
farming is possible.
**Fishing and whaling:**
The Antarctic seas are
rich in fish and
shellfish, especially
krill, and whales.
Commercial whaling
(now controlled) has

severely reduced the
numbers of several
species. Fur seals are
now protected.
**Mining:** Antarctica has
deposits of coal,
copper, chromium,
gold, iron ore, lead,
manganese, and other
minerals. There are at
present no plans to
exploit these minerals.
But ice may one day
be taken to provide
fresh water.

**Contour map**
- Over 12,000 ft. (4,000 m)
- 6,000 - 12,000 ft. (2,000 - 4,000 m)
- 0 - 6,000 ft. (0 - 2,000 m)

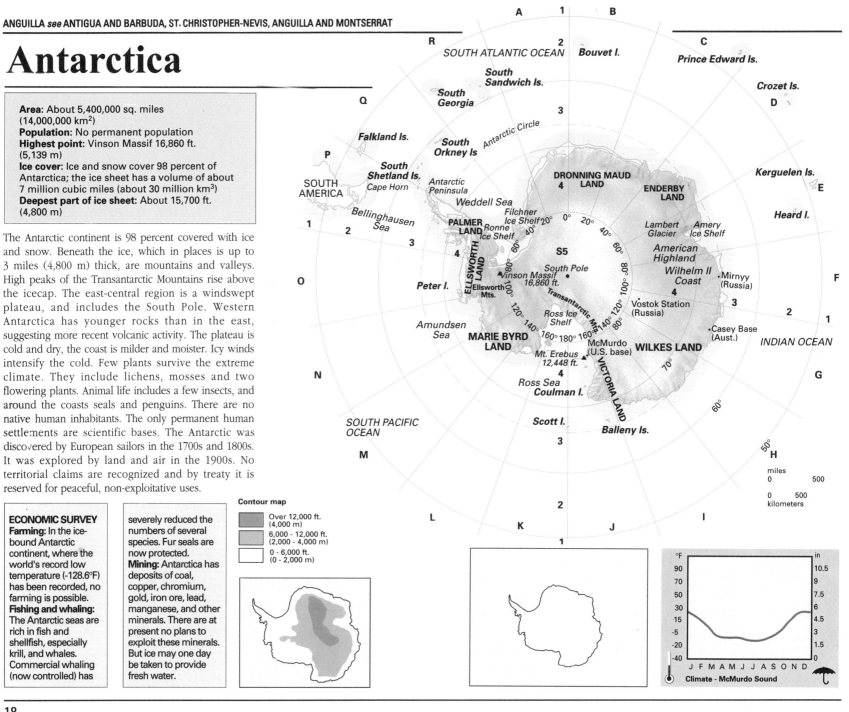

Climate - McMurdo Sound

# Antigua and Barbuda, St. Christopher-Nevis, Anguilla, and Montserrat

**ANTIGUA and BARBUDA: Area:** 170 sq. miles (440 km²)
**Population:** 79,000
**Capital:** Saint Johns (pop. 30,000)
**Government:** Constitutional monarchy
**ST. CHRISTOPHER-NEVIS: Area:** 101 sq. miles (261 km²)
**Population:** 44,000
**Capital:** Basseterre (pop. 18,000)
**Government:** Constitutional monarchy
**ANGUILLA: Area:** 37 sq. miles (96 km²)
**Population:** 7,000
**Capital:** The Valley
**Government:** British dependency
**MONTSERRAT: Area:** 35 sq. miles (98 km²)
**Population:** 12,000
**Capital:** Plymouth (pop. 3,500)
**Government:** British colony

Two small independent countries, Antigua and St. Christopher-Nevis, form part of the Leeward Islands. The islands have a warm, tropical climate. Most of their inhabitants are descendants of slaves brought from Africa. Antigua and Barbuda achieved independence in 1981 and St. Christopher-Nevis became fully independent in 1983.

**ECONOMIC SURVEY**
**Farming:** The islands' main cash crop is sugarcane. Cotton and corn are also grown, as well as fruit such as mangoes and limes. Fruit and herbal teas grown (on Montserrat) are packaged for export. Cattle, sheep, goats, and poultry are kept.
**Fishing:** The waters around the islands provide fish for local consumption, and spiny lobsters are sold overseas.
**Industry:** Tourism is important on the larger islands, such as Antigua and St. Christopher-Nevis. Clothing, paint, refrigerators, and machinery are made.

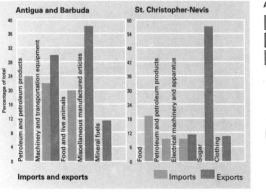

Imports and exports — Antigua and Barbuda / St. Christopher-Nevis

Age distribution - Antigua
- Under 15
- 15 - 60
- Over 60

Population trend - Antigua

Population trend - St. Christopher-Nevis

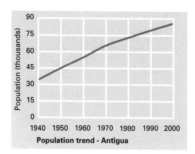

Contour map
Over 600 ft. (200 m)
0 - 600 ft. (0 - 200 m)

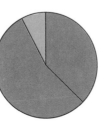

Climate - Antigua

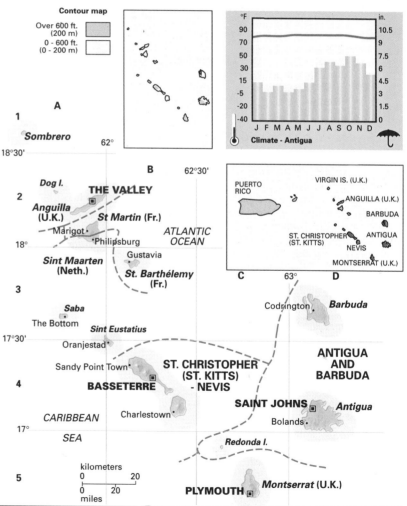

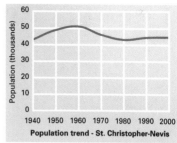

# The Arctic

**Area (Arctic Ocean):** About 4,700,000 sq. miles (12,173,000 km²)
**Land area:** The Arctic includes the northern parts of Europe, Asia, and North America, but the region has no agreed southern boundaries
**Average depth of Arctic Ocean:** 3,250 ft. (990 m)
**Greatest depth:** 15,091 ft. (4,600 m)
**Resources:** Petroleum and natural gas

The main part of the Arctic is the frozen Arctic Ocean. The land areas include the northernmost parts of Europe, Asia, and North America. The polar ice cap also extends over Greenland. South of the Arctic lie the subarctic regions, which are almost as cold in winter but have warmer summers. The coldest region is northeast Siberia. North of the tree line, the vegetation includes mosses, lichens, and shrubs. Wildlife includes reindeer and their relatives the caribou, polar bears, Arctic foxes and hares, musk ox, and lemmings. Native Arctic peoples include the Lapps of Scandinavia and the so-called Eskimos; Inupiat and Yupik in Alaska, Inuit in Canada and Greenland, and Yuit in Siberia. Also in Siberia are peoples similar to Native Americans, such as the Chukchi and the Koryaks, and Asians such as the Yakuts and Tungus. The traditional ways of life of these Arctic peoples were based on hunting (mostly reindeer, musk ox, whales, and seals) and fishing. Some people herded reindeer. These traditional ways have now almost wholly vanished.

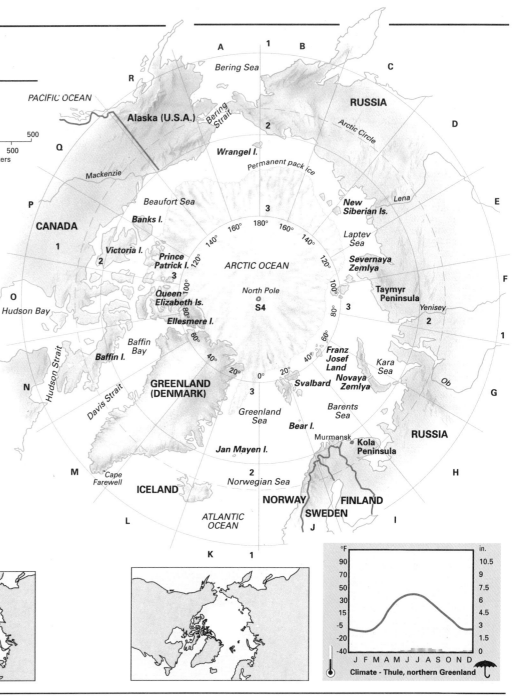

## ECONOMIC SURVEY

**Farming:** Although plants grow in the Arctic, the harsh climate and frozen subsoil (permafrost) have prevented crop-growing. Some of the people herd reindeer or caribou.

**Fishing and Hunting:** Arctic peoples have traditionally lived by fishing and hunting. Several whaling and fishing fleets operate in the Arctic Ocean in summer.

**Mining:** The Arctic and subarctic regions have rich mineral deposits. These include petroleum, natural gas, coal, uranium, iron ore, lead, nickel, gold, copper, tin, and cryolite.

**Industry:** There is little industry in the Arctic region. Tourism is growing.

**Contour map**

- Over 12,000 ft. (4,000 m)
- 6,000 - 12,000 ft. (2,000 - 4,000 m)
- 0 - 6,000 ft. (0 - 2,000 m)

Climate - Thule, northern Greenland

# Argentina

**Area:** 1,068,302 sq. miles (2,766,889 km²)
**Population:** 32,880,000
**Capital:** Buenos Aires (pop. with suburbs 9,968,000)
**Other cities:** Córdoba 969,000; Rosario 876,000
**Highest point:** Mt. Aconcagua 22,831 ft. (6,960 m)
**Official language:** Spanish
**Religion:** Christianity
**Currency:** Peso
**Main exports:** Wheat, corn, meat, vegetable oils, hides and skins, wool
**Government:** Federal republic
**Per capita GNP:** U.S. $2,160

Argentina is the second largest South American country. The tropical north is thinly populated. The dry west has occasional settlements, such as San Juan and Mendoza, and rises to the Andes Mountains. On the border with Chile is Mount Aconcagua, the highest point in the western hemisphere. The wild plateaus of Patagonia, in southern Argentina, are semi-arid and windswept. In the far south is half of the barren and cold archipelago, Tierra del Fuego. Most people live on the central pampas or plains, where soils are fertile and the climate mild. They are nearly all of European origin. The rest are Native Americans or of mixed descent. Argentina was ruled by Spain from 1535 until independence in 1816. Since 1955 it has experienced military rule, war with Britain over the Falkland (Malvinas) Islands in 1982, and economic turmoil.

## ECONOMIC SURVEY

**Farming:** Ranches, often huge in extent, support more than 50 million beef cattle and some 29 million sheep. Crops include corn, wheat, alfalfa, fruit, cotton, flax, potatoes, sorghum, sugarcane, sunflower seeds, soy beans, olives, and peanuts.
**Forestry:** In the Gran Chaco quebracho trees grow, yielding a very tough timber that is used for railroad sleepers.
**Mining:** Argentina produces natural gas and oil, and also mines coal, copper, iron ore, lead, zinc, gold, silver, antimony, and uranium.
**Industry:** Factories process food especially meat, refine oil, produce chemicals, and make electrical equipment and vehicles.

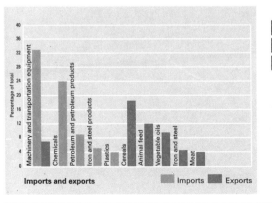

**Imports and exports**

Imports | Exports

**Age distribution**

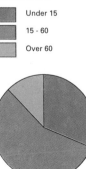

Under 15
15 - 60
Over 60

miles
0 — 500

0 — 500
kilometers

**Contour map**

Over 6,000 ft. (2,000 m)

3,000 - 6,000 ft. (1,000 - 2,000 m)

0 - 3,000 ft. (0 - 1,000 m)

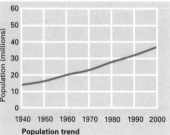

**Population trend**

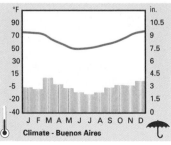

**Climate - Buenos Aires**

# ASIA

**Area:** 17,135,370 sq. miles (44,380,400 km²), including about 75 percent of the former U.S.S.R. and 97 percent of Turkey
**Population:** 3,202,900,000
**Major cities:** Tokyo (Japan) 11,719,000; Seoul (South Korea) 10,513,000; Calcutta (India) 9,166,000; Bombay (India) 8,243,000; Jakarta (Indonesia) 7,829,000
**Number of independent countries:** 49
**Largest country:** Russia
**Smallest independent country:** Maldives
**Highest mountain:** Mount Everest 29,028 ft. (8,848 m)
**Longest river:** Chang Jiang (Yangtze) 3,915 miles (6,300 km)
**Largest lake:** Caspian Sea, on the Asia-Europe border, 169,381 sq. miles (438,695 km²)

Of the continents, Asia is unmatched in size and population. About 60 percent of the Earth's people live there. Its natural features are astonishingly varied, and include the world's highest mountains, long rivers, wide deserts, plains and plateaus, polar wastes, forests, and tropical jungles. Asia includes China and India, the most populous nations, and most of the former Soviet Union's land area. There are many ethnic groups. The world's great religions began in Asia. So too did important early civilizations: in the Tigris-Euphrates valley in Iraq, the Indus Valley of Pakistan, and China. Western contact increased from the 1500s. By the 1800s much of Asia had come under European colonial rule, including India, Indochina, and Indonesia. Japan and China, while still independent, felt obliged to "Westernize." In the 1900s Asia saw the growth of nationalist movements, leading to the independence of former European colonies by the 1960s. China moved from autocratic empire to republic, was devastated by invasion and civil war, and became the world's largest communist state. Japan emerged from defeat in World War II to become the richest Asian nation and the most successful manufacturer in the world. Smaller states also prospered through trade (Singapore) or oil (the Gulf states). Since World War II Asia has seen ideological and territorial wars (the Middle East, Korea, Vietnam), and poverty and natural disaster on a huge scale (Bangladesh).

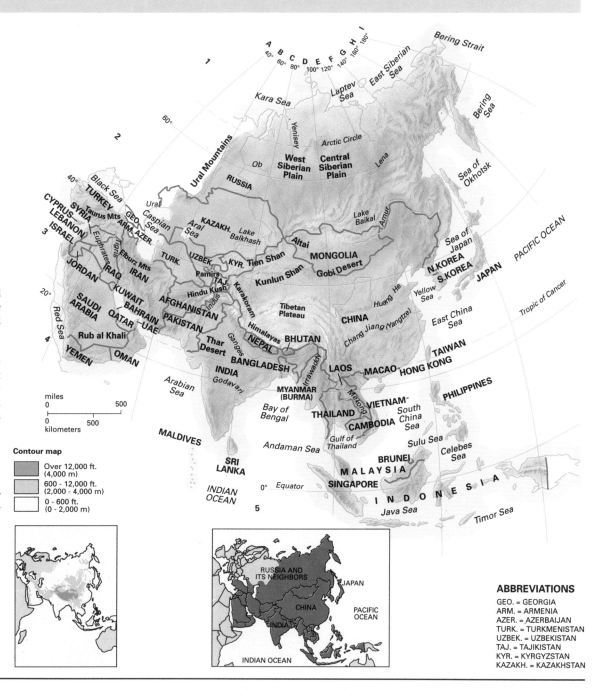

miles
0        500

0        500
kilometers

**Contour map**

Over 12,000 ft. (4,000 m)

600 - 12,000 ft. (2,000 - 4,000 m)

0 - 600 ft. (0 - 2,000 m)

**ABBREVIATIONS**

GEO. = GEORGIA
ARM. = ARMENIA
AZER. = AZERBAIJAN
TURK. = TURKMENISTAN
UZBEK. = UZBEKISTAN
TAJ. = TAJIKISTAN
KYR. = KYRGYZSTAN
KAZAKH. = KAZAKHSTAN

# Atlantic Ocean

**CAPE VERDE Area:** 1557 sq. miles (4033 km²)
**Population:** 339,000
**Capital:** Praia (pop. 50,000)
**Government:** Multiparty republic
**Per capita GNP:** U.S. $760

**SÃO TOMÉ AND PRÍNCIPE Area:** 372 sq. miles (964 km²)
**Population:** 121,000
**Capital:** São Tomé (pop. 35,000)
**Government:** Multiparty republic
**Per capita GNP:** U.S. $360

**FALKLAND ISLANDS Area:** 4700 sq. miles (12,173 km²)
**Population:** 1900
**Government:** British dependency

**ST. PIERRE AND MIQUELON Area:** 93 sq. miles (242 km²)
**Population:** 6400
**Government:** French dependency

**BERMUDA Area:** 20 sq. miles (53 km²)
**Population:** 59,000
**Government:** British dependency

**ST. HELENA Area:** 47 sq. miles (122 km²)
**Population:** 5600
**Government:** British dependency

**ECONOMIC SURVEY**
**Farming:** Few Atlantic islands have conditions suitable for agriculture. Cape Verde's warm, dry climate makes most of its land too dry for agriculture, but farmers manage to grow coffee, sugarcane, vegetables, and fruit. People on St. Helena and the Falklands raise sheep, and St. Helena farmers grow flax and coffee.
**Fishing:** Cape Verde has an active fishing fleet, as does the St. Helena dependency of Tristan da Cunha.
**Mining:** Cape Verde produces raw materials for cement.
**Industry:** There is little manufacturing on any of the Atlantic islands. Cape Verde's industries are small and produce goods for home use. Bermuda's economy is based on tourism, and it is a tax haven for overseas businesses.

The Atlantic Ocean is the second largest ocean on Earth, but it is only half the size of the Pacific. Its coastal waters include the North, Baltic, and Mediterranean seas in the east, and the Gulf of St. Lawrence, Gulf of Mexico, and Caribbean and Sargasso seas in the west.

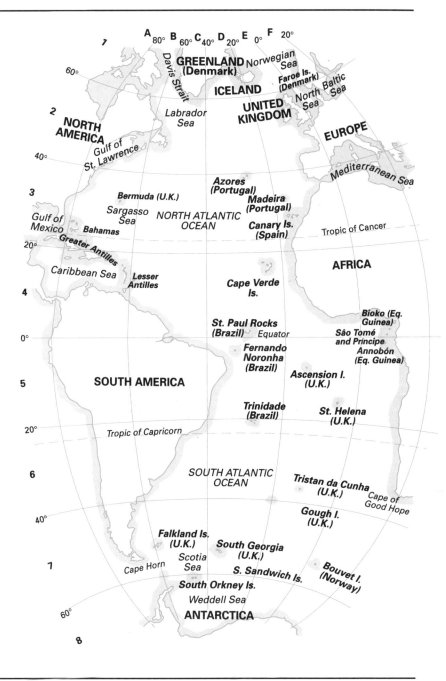

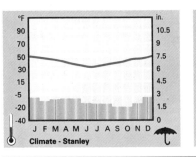

Climate - Stanley

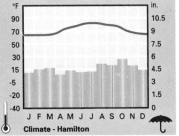

Climate - Hamilton

# Australia

**Area:** 2,967,909 sq. miles (7,686,848 km²)
**Population:** 17,076,000
**Capital:** Canberra (pop. 289,000)
**Other cities:** Sydney 3,531,000; Melbourne 2,965,000; Brisbane 1,215,000
**Highest point:** Mount Kosciusko 7316 ft. (2230 m)
**Official language:** English
**Religion:** Christianity
**Currency:** Australian dollar
**Main exports:** Metal ores and scrap, textile fibres, coal, cereals, meat
**Government:** Federal constitutional monarchy
**Per capita GNP:** U.S. $14,440

Australia, the world's sixth largest country, is also the smallest of the Earth's seven continents. Two-thirds of the land, in the vast western plateau region, is desert or semi-desert. The flat landscape is broken by low mountains. It includes salt lakes, usually dry, such as Lake Eyre. The Great Artesian Basin in the central lowlands is suitable for livestock grazing because of water from artesian wells. The water comes from rain falling on the Eastern Highlands, or Great Dividing Range. Australia's longest rivers, the Murray and Darling, rise in this range, and most people live east of it. Along the east coast of Australia is the Great Barrier Reef, the world's largest coral reef, 1260 miles (2027 km) long. The climate ranges from hot and wet in the north to warm temperate in the southeastern coastlands.

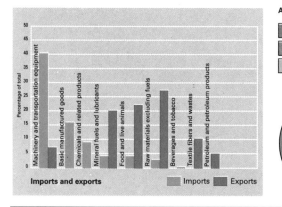

**Imports and exports**

*Percentage of total*

Machinery and transportation equipment · Basic manufactured goods · Chemicals and related products · Mineral fuels and lubricants · Food and live animals · Raw materials excluding fuels · Beverages and tobacco · Textile fibers and wastes · Petroleum and petroleum products

Imports · Exports

**Age distribution**

Under 15
15 - 60
Over 60

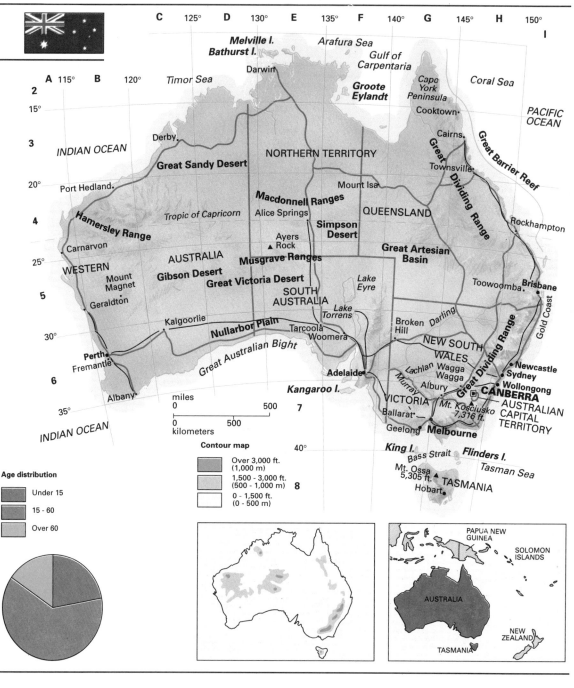

**Contour map**

Over 3,000 ft. (1,000 m)
1,500 - 3,000 ft. (500 - 1,000 m)
0 - 1,500 ft. (0 - 500 m)

miles 0 — 500
kilometers 0 — 500

AUSTRALIAN HISTORY. The first people in Australia reached there about 40,000 years ago. They were probably the Tasmanians. They were driven into Tasmania by later migrants from Asia, the Australian Aborigines. European contact began in the 1600s. British settlement started in 1788 with the arrival of the First Fleet to found a convict settlement on the site of modern-day Sydney. Immigration from Britain accelerated following the gold rushes of the mid-1800s. The numbers of Aborigines declined, and the Tasmanians had died out altogether by 1876. Today some 100,000 Aborigines remain, many of mixed ancestry. About 80 out of every 100 Australians are of British or Irish origin. Since the 1950s many new settlers have come from other parts of Europe and Southeast Asia. Australia became united and independent in 1901 as the Commonwealth of Australia, with a federal constitution. In 1911 the Australian Capital Territory (ACT) was set up and Northern Territory (formerly part of South Australia) became a separate territory. Australia thus had six states: New South Wales, Victoria, South Australia, Tasmania (the name given to Van Diemen's Land in 1855), Western Australia, and Queensland; and the two territories. In both world wars (1914-1918 and 1939-1945) Australia fought alongside Britain. Australian forces also took part in the Korean and Vietnam wars. From the 1970s, Aborigines campaigned for greater rights and the return of tribal lands. Ties with Britain began to weaken, following Britain's membership of the European Community, though sporting, cultural, and family links were still strong. Some Australians called for the country to become a republic, to end the link with the British monarch, who is Australia's head of state. Non-European immigration increased and Australia turned to the Pacific for its main trading partners.

## ECONOMIC SURVEY

**Farming:** Farming, particularly stock rearing, is a major activity though less important than formerly in terms of employment and contribution to the national economy. Australia is the world's leading wool producer, with more than 160 million sheep. It also produces beef, butter, and cheese. Crops include sugar, wheat, barley, rice, bananas, apples, pineapples, oranges, grapes, and vegetables.

**Fishing:** Main catches include shellfish, tuna, mullet, and salmon.

**Mining:** There are large deposits of uranium, bauxite, diamonds, iron ore, lead, coal, manganese, tin, tungsten, oil, and natural gas.

**Industry:** Service industries have grown while manufacturing is declining. Factory goods include steel, farm products, vehicles, chemicals, textiles, and light engineering.

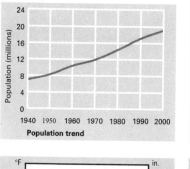

Population trend

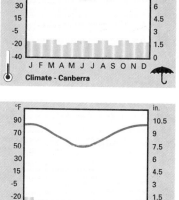

Climate - Canberra

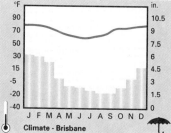

Climate - Brisbane

Climate - Alice Springs

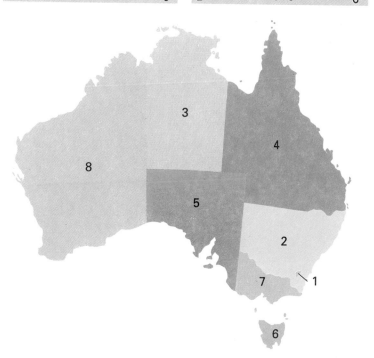

### STATES AND TERRITORIES OF AUSTRALIA (with capitals)

| | | Area (sq. miles) | Area (km²) | Population (1989) |
|---|---|---|---|---|
| 1 | **Australian Capital Territory** (Canberra) | 927 | 2,400 | 278,000 |
| 2 | **New South Wales** (Sydney) | 309,500 | 801,600 | 5,762,000 |
| 3 | **Northern Territory** (Darwin) | 519,887 | 1,346,200 | 156,000 |
| 4 | **Queensland** (Brisbane) | 666,876 | 1,727,200 | 2,830,000 |
| 5 | **South Australia** (Adelaide) | 379,925 | 984,000 | 1,423,000 |
| 6 | **Tasmania** (Hobart) | 26,178 | 67,800 | 451,000 |
| 7 | **Victoria** (Melbourne) | 87,877 | 227,600 | 4,315,000 |
| 8 | **Western Australia** (Perth) | 975,101 | 2,525,500 | 1,591,000 |

# Austria

**Area:** 32,374 sq. miles (83,849 km²)
**Population:** 7,614,000
**Capital:** Vienna (pop. 1,483,000)
**Other cities:** Graz 243,000; Linz 200,000; Salzburg 138,000
**Highest point:** Gross Glockner 12,460 ft. (3,798 m)
**Official language:** German
**Religions:** Roman Catholicism, Protestantism
**Currency:** Schilling
**Main exports:** Machinery and transportation equipment, chemicals, iron and steel
**Government:** Constitutional republic
**Per capita GNP:** U.S. $17,360

This federal republic in central Europe is a country of pastures, mountains, and swift-flowing rivers. About 75 percent of Austria is mountainous. The Austrian Alps are a center for winter sports and tourism. Forests cover about 40 percent of the land. In the north is the valley of the Danube River, a farming region. More than half the Austrian people live in towns. Austrian history began in the late A.D. 700s under the Frankish emperor, Charlemagne. From 955 it came under the rule of Otto I, who became the emperor of the Holy Roman (German) empire. During the rule of the Habsburg family from 1282 Austria became a leading power, controlling much of central Europe. It declined in the 1800s. It became a republic in 1918. In 1938 Germany annexed Austria. It regained its independence in 1955 after Allied occupation following World War II.

## ECONOMIC SURVEY

**Farming:** The Danube River valley in the north is Austria's chief farming region. Crops include cereals (barley, corn, wheat and rye), sugar beet, potatoes, and fruits. Farmers raise dairy cattle and pigs.
**Forestry:** Almost 40 percent of Austria is forested. Timber and paper are produced.
**Mining:** Austria has important deposits of graphite and magnesite, and small quantities of iron ore, lignite, oil, and natural gas.
**Industry:** Factories produce iron and steel, machinery, transportation equipment, food products, chemicals, and electrical goods. Winter sports, such as skiing, and other forms of tourism are money earners.

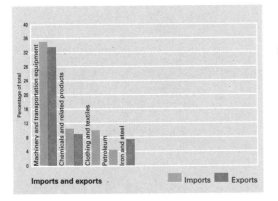

**Imports and exports**
Imports   Exports

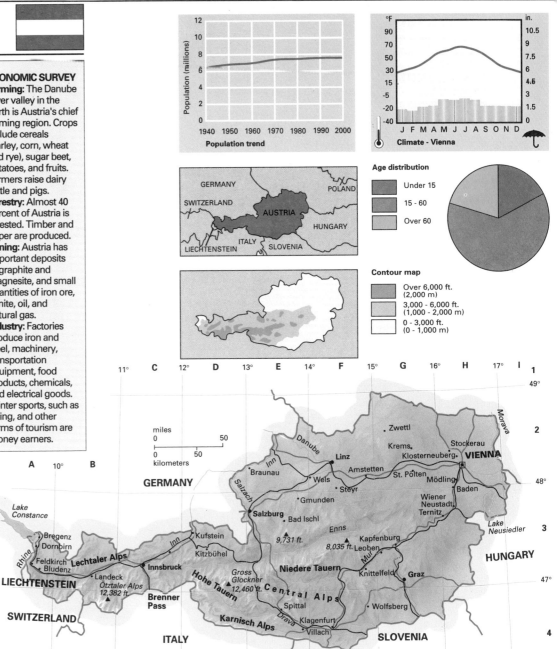

**Population trend**

**Climate - Vienna**

**Age distribution**
Under 15
15 - 60
Over 60

**Contour map**
Over 6,000 ft. (2,000 m)
3,000 - 6,000 ft. (1,000 - 2,000 m)
0 - 3,000 ft. (0 - 1,000 m)

# Bahamas and Turks and Caicos Islands

**BAHAMAS: Area:** 5,387 sq. miles (13,953 km²)
**Population:** 253,000
**Capital:** Nassau (pop. 135,000)
**Currency:** Bahamian dollar
**Government:** Constitutional monarchy
**Per capita GNP:** U.S. $11,370
**TURKS AND CAICOS ISLANDS: Area:** 166 sq. miles (430 km²)
**Population:** 14,000
**Capital:** Grand Turk
**Government:** British dependency

The Bahamas lie southeast of Florida. They consist of 4 large islands and about 700 small, mainly coral, islands. There are many lagoons and mangrove swamps, but no rivers. Hurricanes occur during July-November, but overall the climate is mild. To the southeast are the Turks and Caicos Islands, two island groups geographically part of the Bahamas. Most Bahamians are descendants of African slaves. The original inhabitants were Arawak Native Americans. Christopher Columbus discovered the Bahamas in 1492. Britain governed them as a colony from 1717 until 1973, when the Bahamas became fully independent. The Turks and Caicos Islands then became a British dependency.

## ECONOMIC SURVEY

**Farming:** Most foods have to be imported. Sugarcane is grown and small farms produce fruit such as bananas, oranges, and pineapples, and cucumbers, tomatoes, and vegetables. Poultry and a few cattle, sheep, and goats are kept.
**Fishing:** Red fish and shrimps are found locally, and lobster and snapper are also caught. Crayfish and conch (a shellfish) are caught off the Turks and Caicos Islands.
**Mining:** Limestone and salt are mined.
**Industry:** Tourism is the major source of revenue. The Bahamas are a base for many international finance houses.

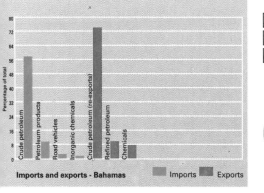

**Imports and exports - Bahamas**

Crude petroleum; Petroleum products; Road vehicles; Inorganic chemicals; Crude petroleum (re-exports); Refined petroleum; Chemicals

Percentage of total

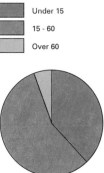

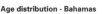

**Age distribution - Bahamas**
- Under 15
- 15 - 60
- Over 60

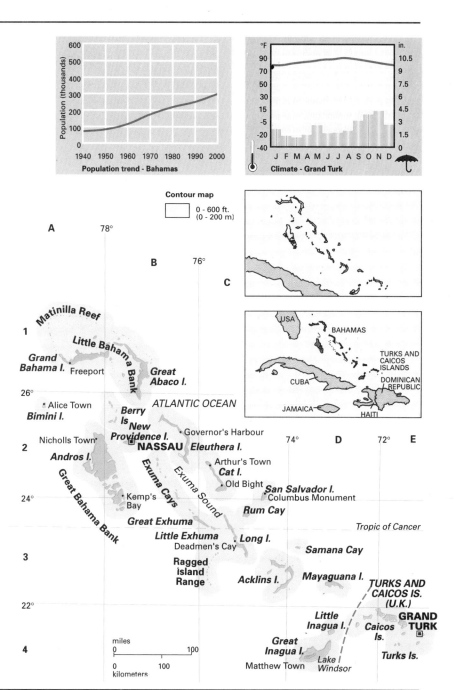

**Population trend - Bahamas**

**Climate - Grand Turk**

**Contour map**
0 - 600 ft. (0 - 200 m)

ATLANTIC OCEAN

Matinilla Reef
Little Bahama Bank
Grand Bahama I.   Freeport
Great Abaco I.
Alice Town
Bimini I.
Berry Is
New Providence I.
NASSAU
Governor's Harbour
Eleuthera I.
Nicholls Town
Andros I.
Arthur's Town
Cat I.
Old Bight
San Salvador I.
Columbus Monument
Great Bahama Bank
Exuma Cays
Exuma Sound
Rum Cay
Kemp's Bay
Great Exhuma
Little Exhuma
Deadmen's Cay
Long I.
Samana Cay
Ragged Island Range
Acklins I.
Mayaguana I.
TURKS AND CAICOS IS. (U.K.)
Little Inagua I.
Caicos Is.
GRAND TURK
Great Inagua I.
Lake Windsor
Turks Is.
Matthew Town

Tropic of Cancer

USA
BAHAMAS
TURKS AND CAICOS ISLANDS
CUBA
DOMINICAN REPUBLIC
JAMAICA
HAITI

miles 0 — 100
kilometers 0 — 100

*see* CENTRAL AMERICA & THE CARIBBEAN, page 48   **27**

# Bahrain

**Area:** 240 sq. miles (622 km²)
**Population:** 503,000
**Capital:** Al Manamah (pop. 147,000)
**Other cities:** Al Muharraq 76,000
**Highest point:** Jabal ad Dukhan 443 ft. (135 m)
**Official language:** Arabic
**Religion:** Islam
**Currency:** Dinar
**Main exports:** Refined petroleum and aluminum products
**Government:** Monarchy (the head of state is an emir)
**Per capita GNP:** U.S. $6360

Bahrain is a nation of small islands in the Arabian Gulf. Bahrain Island itself is only 30 miles (48 km) long, and the other islands are much smaller. A road causeway links Bahrain with Al Muharraq Island, and another links Bahrain to Saudi Arabia. Sitrah Island, which has a deep-water anchorage, also has a road causeway. The climate is mostly hot, though cooler in winter (November-March). Little rain falls, and marine desalination plants provide fresh water. Almost 70 percent of the people are Bahrainis, who are Arabs and Muslims. The rest are Iranian, Indian, Pakistani, and European. Bahrain came under Arab rule in the A.D. 700s. In 1861, it became a British protectorate, and gained independence in 1971. Its national assembly was dissolved in 1975 by the emir, who rules through an appointed cabinet.

## ECONOMIC SURVEY

**Farming:** Farmers in Bahrain grow dates, tomatoes, and other fruit and vegetables on irrigated land. Goats and chickens are the most numerous animals raised, with smaller numbers of sheep and cattle.

**Fishing:** Shrimps and fish are caught in the coastal waters of the Persian Gulf.

**Industry:** The oil industry, dating from the 1930s, relies on refining rather than extraction. The main refinery is on Sitrah Island. Seventy percent of the oil refined is piped there from Saudi Arabia. Bahrain also has natural gas reserves. Banking, ship repairing, petroleum products, and aluminum processing contribute to Bahrain's economy.

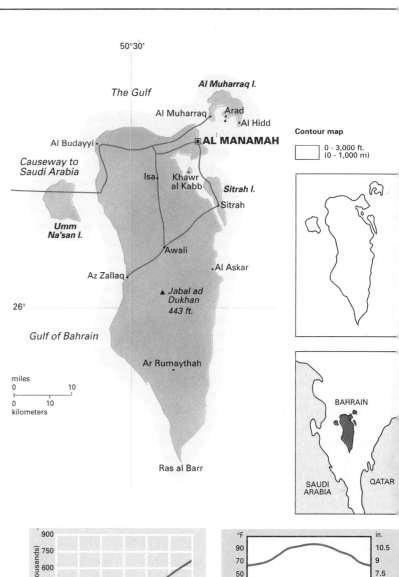

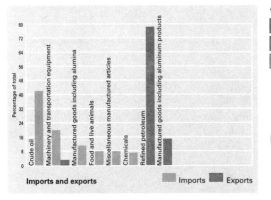

Imports and exports

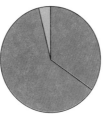

**Age distribution**
- Under 15
- 15 - 60
- Over 60

Population trend

Climate - Bahrain

# Baltic States

**LATVIA Area:** 24,711 sq. miles (64,000 km²)
**Population:** 2,681,000
**Capital:** Riga (pop. 915,000)
**Highest Point:** 1,024 ft. (312 m)
**Government:** Republic
**Official languages:** Latvian, Russian
**Religions:** Lutheran Church, Roman Catholicism
**Currency:** Lat

**LITHUANIA Area:** 25,097 sq. miles (65,000 km²)
**Population:** 3,690,000
**Capital:** Vilnius (580,000)
**Highest Point:** 945 ft. (285 m)
**Government:** Republic
**Official languages:** Lithuanian, Russian
**Religion:** Roman Catholicism
**Currency:** Litas

**ESTONIA Area:** 17,375 sq. miles (45,000 km²)
**Population:** 1,573,000
**Capital:** Tallinn (pop. 482,000)
**Highest Point:** 1,043 ft. (318 m)
**Government:** Republic
**Official languages:** Estonian, Russian
**Religions:** Lutheran Church, Eastern Orthodox
**Currency:** Kroon

## ECONOMIC SURVEY

**Farming:** Potatoes, rye, oats, sugar beet and flax are grown. Farmers keep pigs, cattle, sheep, and geese. Under Soviet rule, farms were collectivized but will now be reformed.
**Forestry:** Forests yield timber and wood pulp.
**Mining:** There are few useful minerals. Estonia has oil and gas reserves.
**Industry:** The Soviets shifted the Baltics' economies from farming to industry. Estonian industries include engineering, shipbuilding, textiles, and chemicals. Tallinn is a busy port. Latvia makes electronics, consumer goods, and machinery. Lithuania produces chemicals, foods, machinery, and domestic appliances.

Estonia, Latvia, and Lithuania are three neighboring states bordering the Baltic Sea. Estonia is the most northerly, Lithuania the southernmost. The land is mostly flat, with marshes, lakes, and coniferous forests. Sand dunes edge the Baltic Sea. Winters are long and cold, and summers short. The populations include Russians as well as Estonians, Latvians, and Lithuanians. The Estonian language is related to Finnish; Latvian (or Lettish) and Lithuanian form a separate Baltic language group. The three countries have a long history of foreign rule by Danes, Poles, Swedes, and most recently Russians. All three declared independence after the Russian Revolution during World War I, but came under communist control as Soviet republics following World War II. Many people were imprisoned for political opposition, others fled. The Baltic states achieved independence from the Soviet Union in 1991.

**Imports and Exports**
Since the Baltic States only became independent in 1991, there were no import and export figures available for the individual countries when this book went to press.

Estonia

Latvia

Lithuania

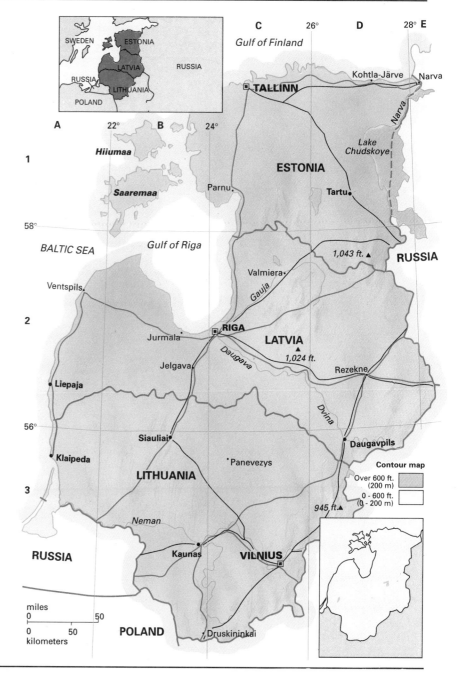

# Bangladesh

**Area:** 55,598 sq. miles (143,998 km$^2$)
**Population:** 113,005,000
**Capital:** Dhaka (pop. 4,770,000)
**Other cities:** Chittagong 1,840,000; Khulna 860,000
**Highest point:** Mount Keokradong, near Chittagong 4,034 ft. (1,230 m)
**Official language:** Bengali
**Religions:** Islam, Hinduism
**Currency:** Taka
**Main exports:** Clothing, jute, leather, shrimps
**Government:** Multiparty republic
**Per capita GNP:** U.S. $180

One of the world's poorest countries, Bangladesh has an almost entirely flat landscape. Much of the land is only a number of feet above sea level, and flooding is frequent and severe, particularly when cyclones (tropical storms) drive the sea inland. The major river system is that of the Jamuna-Ganges which flows into the Bay of Bengal, forming a vast delta. There are forests in the Chittagong Hills of the southeast and the Sundarbans in the southwest. The climate is warm and humid. The country is densely populated. Bangladesh was formerly part of Bengal, an Indian province. When British India was partitioned in 1947, East Bengal became part of the Muslim nation of Pakistan, as East Pakistan. Popular discontent with control from West Pakistan led to civil war in 1971, and the creation of the independent republic of Bangladesh.

## ECONOMIC SURVEY

**Farming:** Bangladesh has one vital natural resource: fertile soil. Most farms are very small. Rice is the main crop. Bangladesh is a major producer of jute, and also grows wheat, sugarcane, tea and tobacco. Food production has not kept pace with population growth. Livestock, mainly cattle, is of poor quality.
**Fishing:** Catches are made both at sea and in rivers and canals. Shrimps are exported.
**Industry:** Jute processing is the main industry. Small factories make agricultural goods. Lack of raw materials has hindered development. Many people make craft goods, such as textiles, leather, and metal products.

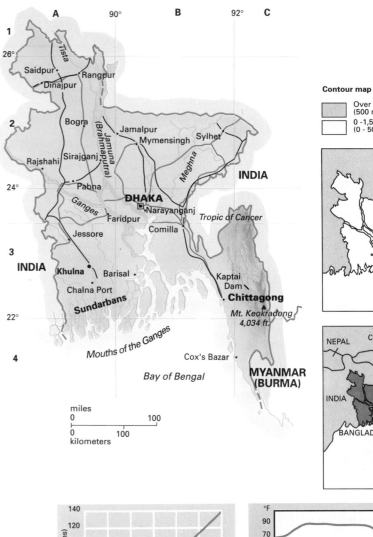

**Contour map**
- Over 1,500 ft. (500 m)
- 0 -1,500 ft. (0 - 500 m)

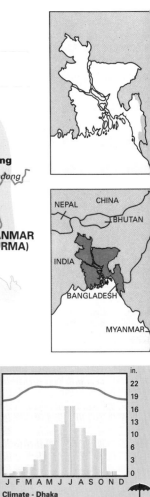

miles
0 — 100
0 — 100
kilometers

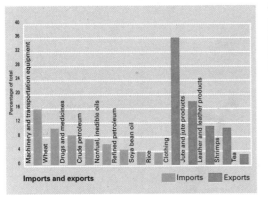

**Imports and exports** — Imports / Exports

**Age distribution**
- Under 15
- 15 - 60
- Over 60

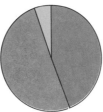

Population (millions) — 1940 1950 1960 1970 1980 1990 2000
**Population trend**

°F / in. — J F M A M J J A S O N D
**Climate - Dhaka**

# Belgium

**Area:** 11,781 sq. miles (30,513 km²)
**Population:** 9,881,000
**Capital:** Brussels (pop. with suburbs 970,000)
**Other cities:** Antwerp 476,000; Ghent 236,000
**Highest point:** Botrange Mt. 2,277 ft. (694 m)
**Official languages:** Dutch, French
**Religions:** Roman Catholicism, Protestantism
**Currency:** Belgian franc
**Main exports:** Machinery and transportation equipment, chemicals, food and live animals, iron and steel, cut diamonds, textiles
**Government:** Constitutional monarchy
**Per capita GNP:** U.S. $16,390

Belgium is a small country in western Europe. The land is mainly flat, with the forests of the Ardennes rising in the southeast. The main rivers are the Meuse and Schelde. Summers are warm and winters mild. Most Belgians live in towns and work in industry. There are major industrial areas around Antwerp and Brussels. There is continuing tension between the Flemings of Flanders, in northern Belgium, and the Walloons of Wallonia in southern Belgium. The country was ruled by Austrian and Spanish kings in the 1400s and 1500s, and later by France and the Netherlands. In 1830 it declared its independence from the Netherlands. Belgium was occupied by Germany in both World Wars. It was a founder member of the European Community in 1957, and with the Netherlands and Luxembourg formed the Benelux group.

**ECONOMIC SURVEY**

**Farming:** Lowlands are intensely cultivated. Many farmers also have industrial jobs. They grow barley, wheat, flax, potatoes, and sugar beet.
**Fishing:** Flatfish and cod are the chief catches.
**Industry:** The mining of coal is important in northeast Belgium. The older industrial areas in the Sambre-Meuse valley have declined. Brussels is the heart of the European Community's administration, and is also a nucleus for industries making luxury goods such as lace and chocolates. Ghent is important for textiles. Antwerp is a major industrial center, where work includes making plastics.

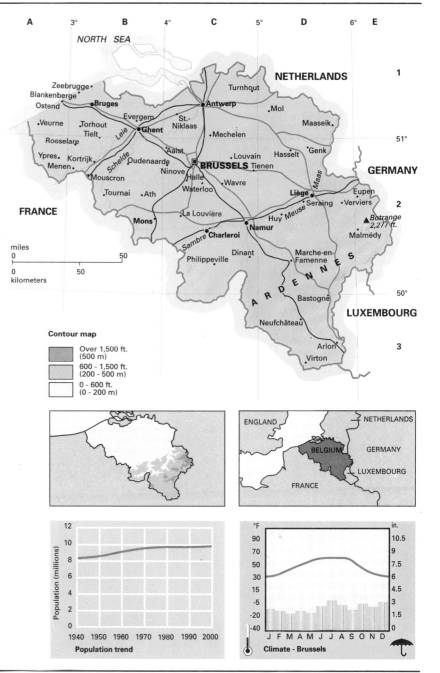

**Contour map**

Over 1,500 ft. (500 m)
600 - 1,500 ft. (200 - 500 m)
0 - 600 ft. (0 - 200 m)

**Age distribution**

Under 15
15 - 60
Over 60

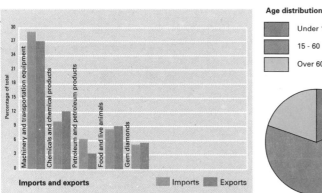

**Imports and exports**

Imports  Exports

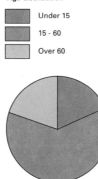

**Population trend**

**Climate - Brussels**

*see* EUROPE, page 70  **31**

# Belize

**Area:** 8,867 sq. miles (22,965 km²)
**Population:** 190,000
**Capital:** Belmopan (pop. 3500)
**Other cities:** Belize City 50,000
**Highest point:** Victoria Peak 3,681 ft. (1,122 m)
**Official language:** English (Spanish and some Mayan languages are also spoken)
**Religion:** Christianity
**Currency:** Belize dollar
**Main exports:** Sugar, clothes, citrus products, bananas
**Government:** Constitutional monarchy
**Per capita GNP:** U.S. $1600

Belize is a land of mountains, swamps, and tropical forests. It is hot and wet, with little annual variation in temperature. The forests are luxuriant, but have been reduced by logging. Reforestation programs have been encouraged by the government. All main towns and villages are linked by road to the principal cities of Belmopan and Belize City. More than half the people are Creoles, descendants of early Spanish settlers. Most of the others are of other European, Mayan, or Carib descent. From about 300 B.C. to A.D. 900 the Mayans ruled the region. Ruins of some of their ceremonial centers can be seen at Caracol and Xunantunich. As British Honduras, Belize became a British colony in 1862, despite a long-standing claim to sovereignty over the country by Guatemala. It became fully independent as Belize in 1981.

## ECONOMIC SURVEY

**Farming:** Sugarcane and citrus fruits (oranges and grapefruit) are grown as cash crops. Other major crops include bananas, mangoes, corn, rice, beans, and root crops. Cattle, pigs, and poultry are reared.
**Forestry:** Forests cover 44 percent of the land. Valuable trees include cedar, pine, mahogany, and rosewood.
**Fishing:** Lobster, shrimps, and fish are caught for export.
**Mining:** Belize has few minerals, but some oil has been discovered.
**Industry:** Food and wood products are processed. Small factories produce garments, molasses, cigarettes, fertilizers, and soft drinks. Much of the industry is seasonal.

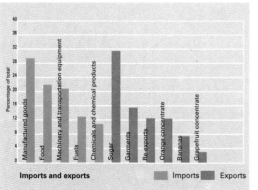

Imports and exports

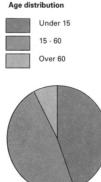

**Age distribution**
Under 15
15 - 60
Over 60

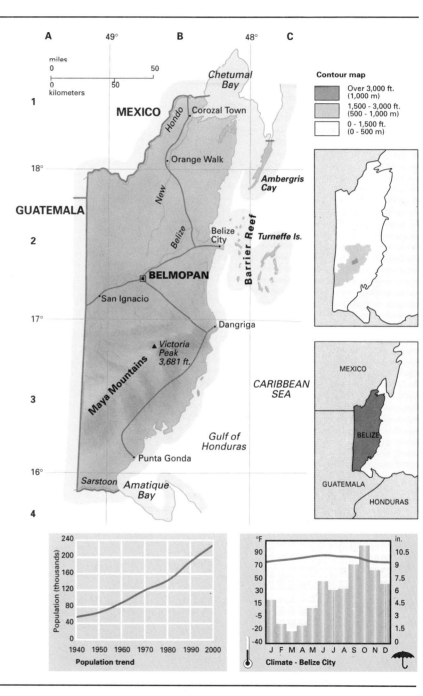

**Contour map**
Over 3,000 ft. (1,000 m)
1,500 - 3,000 ft. (500 - 1,000 m)
0 - 1,500 ft. (0 - 500 m)

**Population trend**

**Climate - Belize City**

# Benin

**Area:** 43,484 sq. miles (112,622 km²)
**Population:** 4,741,000
**Capital:** Porto-Novo (pop. 208,000)
**Other cities:** Cotonou 487,000
**Highest point:** Atacora Mountains 2,103 ft. (641 m )
**Official language:** French
**Religions:** Traditional beliefs, Christianity, Islam
**Currency:** Franc CFA
**Main exports:** Petroleum products, cotton, cocoa, sugar, palm products
**Government:** Multiparty republic
**Per capita GNP:** U.S. $380

Benin, formerly called Dahomey, is a country extending northward from the Bight of Benin. It has a sandy coastal region, behind which are forested plateaus. There is higher ground in the Atacora range in the northwest. About 50 miles (80 km) inland is a marshy area. The longest river is the Ouémé. The south has a hot, humid climate, with two rainy seasons. Winters are dry in the northern savanna. The people are Black Africans in some 50 ethnic-linguistic groups, the largest being the Fon, Adja, Bariba, and Yoruba. From the 1100s the region was the center of several kingdoms, with Dahomey dominating local trade in slaves in the 1600s. European contact began at this time. France took control of Dahomey in 1904. The country became self-governing in 1958, and independent in 1960. It took the name Benin in 1975.

## ECONOMIC SURVEY

**Farming:** Palm trees are an important source of wealth, yielding palm oil and kernels as cash crops. Other cash crops include cotton, cocoa beans, coffee, groundnuts (peanuts), and shea nuts. For food, Benin's farmers grow beans, cassava, corn, millet, rice, sorghum, and yams. Cattle, goats, sheep, and pigs are reared.
**Fishing:** Coastal fishing supplies local needs.
**Mining:** Benin has deposits of chromite, iron ore, titanium ore, and ilmenite, but they have been little exploited. Some oil and limestone are produced.
**Industry:** Benin's industry is small, but developing. It is an important regional trade center.

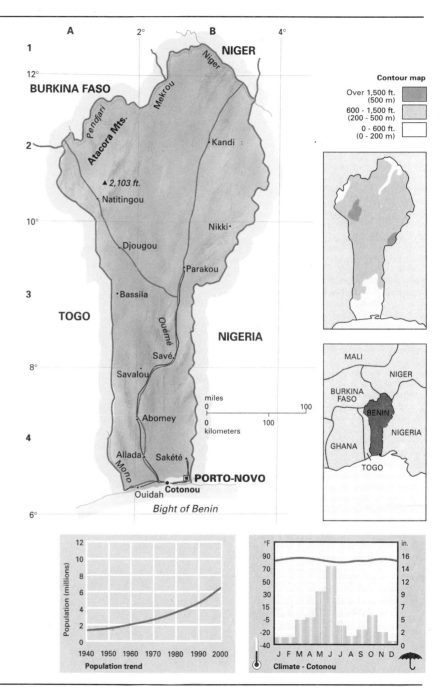

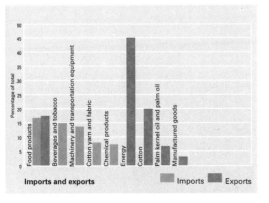

**Imports and exports**

Imports  Exports

**Age distribution**

Under 15
15 - 60
Over 60

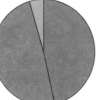

**Population trend**

**Climate - Cotonou**

# Bhutan

**Area:** 18,147 sq. miles (47,000 km²)
**Population:** 1,442,000
**Capital:** Thimphu (pop. 20,000)
**Highest point:** Kula Kangri 24,783 ft. (7,554 m)
**Official language:** Dzongkha (a Tibetan dialect);
25 percent of the people speak Nepali
**Religions:** Buddhism, Hinduism
**Currency:** Ngultrum
**Main exports:** Timber and wood products, coal,
rice, and other foods
**Government:** Constitutional monarchy
**Per capita GNP:** U.S. $190

Bhutan lies in the eastern Himalaya Mountains, between India and Tibet. The country is extremely rugged, with high snow-topped mountains, dense forests, and isolated valleys. Near the border with India there are plains and river valleys. The climate ranges from bitter cold in the mountains to intense heat in the foothills and plains. The summer monsoon brings most of the yearly rainfall. The Bhutanese are mainly of Tibetan or Indian origin. Most of them live in the upland valleys, where the best farmland is located. Bhutan was settled by Tibetans in the A.D. 800s, and became a separate state in the 1600s. The country's first king was Ugyen Wangchuk in 1907. First Britain, then India assumed control of Bhutan's foreign affairs. Bhutan maintains close political links with India. As chairman of the council of ministers, the king retains considerable powers.

## ECONOMIC SURVEY

**Farming:** Nine out of every ten workers are in agriculture. Most grow crops in valleys or on terraced hillsides, including wheat, rice, millet, corn, barley, and the spice cardamom. Herders in the mountains keep cattle and yaks.
**Forestry:** Ash, poplar, and oak grow in the Himalayan foothills.
**Mining:** A small amount of coal is mined in the south of the country.
**Industry:** Bhutan has only small industries, including cement-making, food processing, and factories making timber products. India has encouraged industrial development since 1959, when Bhutan began programs of modernization.

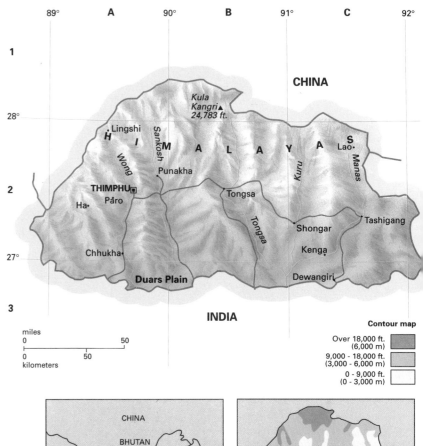

Contour map

Over 18,000 ft. (6,000 m)
9,000 - 18,000 ft. (3,000 - 6,000 m)
0 - 9,000 ft. (0 - 3,000 m)

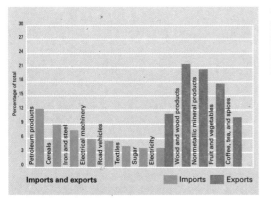

**Imports and exports**
Imports   Exports

**Age distribution**
Under 15
15 - 60
Over 60

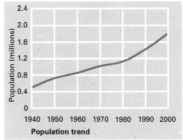

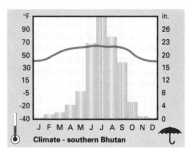

**Population trend**

**Climate - southern Bhutan**

# Bolivia

**Area:** 424,165 sq. miles (1,098,581 km²)
**Population:** 7,400,000
**Capital:** La Paz (pop. 1,033,000)
**Other cities:** Santa Cruz 458,000; Cochabamba 282,000
**Highest point:** Sajama 21,463 ft. (6,542 m)
**Official languages:** Spanish, Aymara, Quechua
**Religion:** Christianity
**Currency:** Boliviano
**Main exports:** Natural gas, tin, zinc, silver, gold, antimony
**Government:** Republic
**Per capita GNP:** U.S. $600

Bolivia has no sea coast. The Andes Mountains in the southwest contain a central plateau, the Altiplano, where most Bolivians live. The climate there is cool, contrasting with the hot Amazon rain forests in the northeast. On the border with Peru is Lake Titicaca. More than half the people are Native Americans, and a third are of mixed Native American and European origin. There are marked social and wealth divisions between Native Americans and whites. A civilization in Bolivia existed about 2,000 years ago. The Aymaras, and then the Incas, ruled the region. Spain conquered Bolivia in the 1530s, calling it Upper Peru. It gained independence in 1825, its present name honoring the Venezuelan general and liberator Simón Bolívar. It lost territory during wars in the 1800s. Bolivia has frequently been under military rule in modern times.

## ECONOMIC SURVEY

**Farming:** On the high Altiplano farmers grow potatoes and wheat, and they herd llamas and alpacas for their wool. Other regions produce bananas and plantains, cassava, beans, cocoa, soya beans, coffee, corn, cotton, rice, barley, oats, and sugar. Some farmers cultivate medicinal herbs and coca.
**Forestry:** Bolivia is beginning to exploit the rain forests of the northern Oriente.
**Mining:** The chief mineral is tin. The Andes region yields antimony, copper, lead, silver, tungsten, and zinc. From the lowlands come gold, oil, and natural gas.
**Industry:** There are small food, chemical, textile, and leather industries.

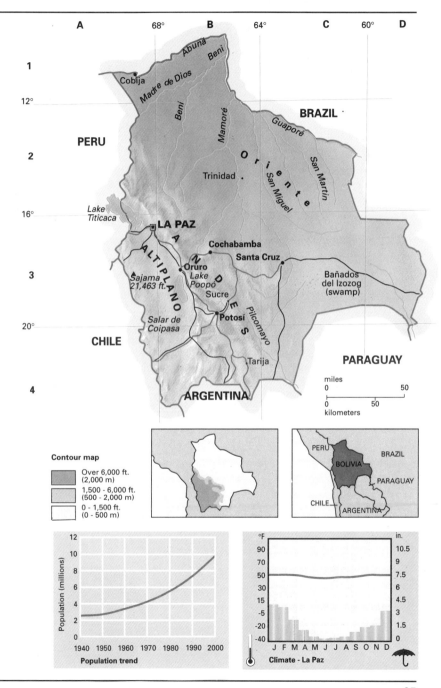

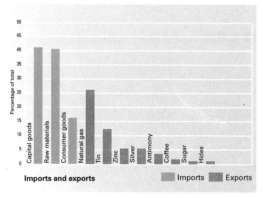

**Imports and exports**

**Age distribution**
- Under 15
- 15 - 60
- Over 60

**Contour map**
- Over 6,000 ft. (2,000 m)
- 1,500 - 6,000 ft. (500 - 2,000 m)
- 0 - 1,500 ft. (0 - 500 m)

**Population trend**

**Climate - La Paz**

*see* SOUTH AMERICA, page 159 **35**

# Botswana

**Area:** 224,607 sq. miles (581,730 km²)
**Population:** 1,295,000
**Capital:** Gaborone (pop. 120,000)
**Other cities:** Mahalapye 104,000; Serowe 95,000
**Highest point:** Otse Mountain, near Gaborone 4,885 ft. (1,489 m)
**Official languages:** Tswana, English
**Religions:** Christianity, traditional beliefs
**Currency:** Pula
**Main exports:** Diamonds, copper-nickel, meat
**Government:** Multiparty republic
**Per capita GNP:** U.S. $940

Most of Botswana lies on a vast plateau about 3,300 ft. (1,000 m) above sea level. It has hills in the east and flat or rolling landscapes elsewhere. The east is the most fertile region. There are forests in part of the north. The central and southwestern regions lie within the Kalahari Desert, some of which is sandy, though bushes and grasses grow in most parts. The Okavango River forms marshland in the northwest. The climate is dry with hot summers and cool winters. The people include Bantu Tswana, who form the majority, and the San (Bushmen), the original inhabitants. There are also people of European origin. The Tswana settled the region about 1,000 years ago. Britain made the area into the protectorate of Bechuanaland in the 1800s. It became an independent republic as Botswana in 1966. Income per head is one of the highest in Africa.

## ECONOMIC SURVEY

**Farming:** Livestock rearing, chiefly of cattle, is the main occupation. Beef is exported to the European Community. Goats, sheep, and chickens are also kept. Food crops include such staples as sorghum, corn, millet, beans, and vegetables. The variable rainfall affects crop growing.
**Fishing:** There is some river fishing.
**Mining:** Botswana's leading export is diamonds. The country also has deposits of copper-nickel, coal, salt, and soda ash.
**Industry:** There is little local manufacturing, and communications are poor. But there are close links with South Africa and migrant workers send home money.

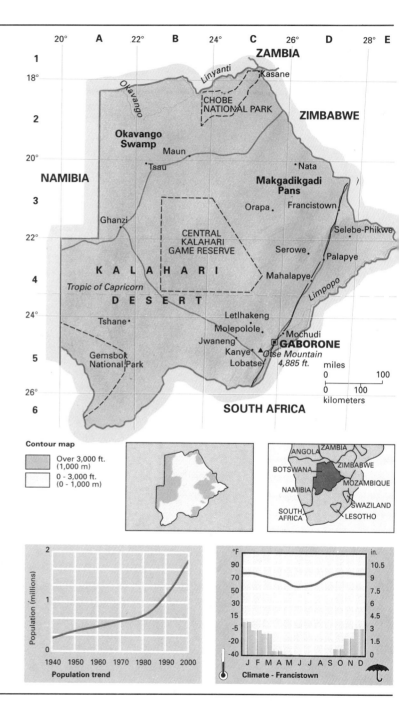

Contour map
Over 3,000 ft. (1,000 m)
0 - 3,000 ft. (0 - 1,000 m)

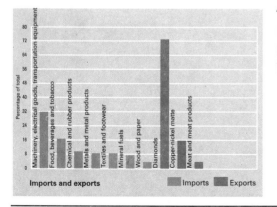

**Imports and exports**
Imports  Exports

**Age distribution**
Under 15
15 - 60
Over 60

**Population trend**

**Climate - Francistown**

# Brazil

**Area:** 3,286,488 sq. miles (8,511,965 km²)
**Population:** 150,368,000
**Capital:** Brasília (pop. with suburbs 1,568,000)
**Other cities:** São Paulo 16,832,000; Rio de Janeiro 11,141,000; Belo Horizonte 3,446,000
**Highest point:** Neblina 9,888 ft. (3,014 m)
**Official language:** Portuguese
**Religion:** Christianity
**Currency:** Cruzeiro
**Main exports:** Coffee, soya beans, fruit, iron and steel, vehicles
**Government:** Multiparty federal republic
**Per capita GNP:** U.S. $2550

Brazil occupies almost half of South America. It has three main regions. The Amazon River basin in the north contains lowland, jungle, highlands, and the world's biggest rain forest with over 40,000 plant varieties known. In the northeast is a fertile coastal plain, and interior plateaus and hills known as the Sertâo, where the soil is poor. The central and southern plateau region includes most of the Brazilian Highlands, and is the nation's economic core. The major industrial cities of São Paulo and Rio de Janeiro are there, as well as some of Brazil's best farmland and mineral-producing areas. The climate ranges from tropical in the north to temperate in the plateau region. About 75 percent of the people are of Portuguese or other European origin. Others are of mixed European/Native American/African origin.

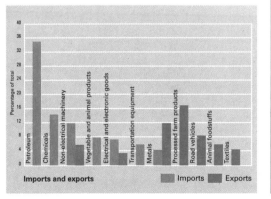

Imports and exports — Imports, Exports

## ECONOMIC SURVEY

**Farming:** Brazil is the world's leading producer of coffee, bananas, cassava, oranges, papayas, and sugarcane. Cattle, poultry, pigs, horses, and sheep are reared.
**Forestry:** Brazil is the third largest producer of forest products, including timber - especially parana pine - nuts, resins, rubber, oils, and medicines.
**Fishing:** Catches include lobsters and shrimps, and bony fish.
**Mining:** Minerals include quartz (the world's chief source), diamonds, gold, iron ore, lead, magnesium, copper, manganese, mica, uranium, and oil.
**Industry:** Products include vehicles, aircraft, cement, chemicals, machinery, textiles, foods, and pharmaceuticals.

### Contour map

Over 3,000 ft. (1,000 m)
1,500 - 3,000 ft. (500 - 1,000 m)
0 - 1,500 ft. (0 - 500 m)

BRAZILIAN HISTORY. The first Brazilians, the Native Americans, arrived in the area many thousands of years before the first Europeans. They included the Guarani and Tupinamba peoples. In 1500 European contact began when the navigator Pedro Cabral landed in Brazil and Portugal claimed possession. This followed a treaty with Spain in which the Americas were divided between the two Iberian nations, then Europe's leading sea powers. Colonists began to settle from the 1530s. In the 1600s the Dutch tried to seize Brazil but were driven out. In 1822 Brazil, then ruled by Pedro I, the son of Prince John of Portugal, declared its independence. Slavery was abolished in 1888 by Pedro II. Brazil was ruled as an empire until 1889 when it became a republic. In 1960 the capital was moved from Rio de Janeiro to the newly built interior city of Brasília. Brazil's modern history has included dictatorships and military rule, but civilian democracy was restored in 1985 with free presidential elections in 1989. Despite severe economic problems, Brazil has become a major industrial nation.

**INDUSTRIAL PROFILE**
Brazil is South America's awakening giant. Its farmland, vast forests, and mineral diversity are potentially of enormous value. Industry has developed rapidly since the 1940s. Most of Brazil's energy comes from hydroelectric schemes. The environmental effects of such schemes, and of the destruction of the Amazon rain forest by mining and ranching, aroused great international concern. Moves to protect forests began in 1990.

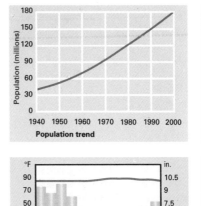

**Population trend**

**Climate - Goiânia**

**Climate - Manaus**

**Climate - Rio de Janeiro**

**AREA AND POPULATION**

| | State (Capital) | Area (sq. miles) | Area (km²) | Population |
|---|---|---|---|---|
| 1 | **Acre** (Rio Branco) | 59,343 | 153,698 | 417,200 |
| 2 | **Alagoas** (Maceió) | 11,238 | 29,107 | 2,420,400 |
| 3 | **Amapá** (Macapá) | 54,965 | 142,359 | 256,100 |
| 4 | **Amazonas** (Manaus) | 605,390 | 1,567,954 | 2,001,800 |
| 5 | **Bahia** (Salvador) | 218,912 | 566,979 | 11,738,000 |
| 6 | **Ceará** (Fortaleza) | 56,253 | 145,694 | 6,471,800 |
| 7 | **Distrito Federal** (Brasília) | 2237 | 5794 | 1,864,200 |
| 8 | **Espírito Santo** (Vitória) | 17,658 | 45,733 | 2,523,900 |
| 9 | **Fernando de Noronha** (Federal Territory) | 10 | 25 | 1,266 |
| 10 | **Goiás** (Goiânia) | 131,339 | 340,166 | 3,983,300 |
| 11 | **Maranhão** (São Luis) | 127,242 | 329,556 | 5,181,800 |
| 12 | **Mato Grosso** (Cuibá) | 348,040 | 901,421 | 1,727,100 |
| 13 | **Mato Grosso do Sul** (Campo Grande) | 138,021 | 357,472 | 1,797,000 |
| 14 | **Minas Gerais** (Belo Horizonte) | 226,497 | 586,624 | 15,831,800 |
| 15 | **Pará** (Belém) | 481,405 | 1,246,833 | 5,001,800 |
| 16 | **Paraíba** (João Pessoa) | 20,833 | 53,958 | 3,247,600 |
| 17 | **Paraná** (Curitiba) | 76,959 | 199,324 | 9,137,700 |
| 18 | **Pernambuco** (Recife) | 39,005 | 101,023 | 7,360,900 |
| 19 | **Piauí** (Teresina) | 97,017 | 251,273 | 2,666,100 |
| 20 | **Rio de Janeiro** (Rio de Janeiro) | 16,855 | 43,653 | 14,133,300 |
| 21 | **Rio Grande do Norte** (Natal) | 20,528 | 53,167 | 2,318,900 |
| 22 | **Rio Grande do Sul** (Pôrto Alegre) | 108,369 | 280,674 | 9,163,200 |
| 23 | **Rondônia** (Pôrto Velho) | 92,039 | 238,379 | 1,095,600 |
| 24 | **Roraima** (Boa Vista) | 86,880 | 225,017 | 120,400 |
| 25 | **Santa Catarina** (Florianópolis) | 36,803 | 95,318 | 4,461,400 |
| 26 | **São Paulo** (São Paulo) | 95,852 | 248,256 | 33,069,900 |
| 27 | **Sergipe** (Aracajú) | 8441 | 21,863 | 1,416,600 |

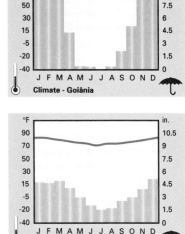

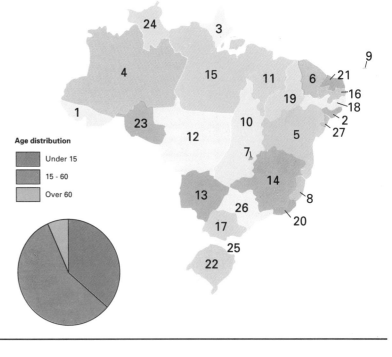

**Age distribution**

Under 15
15 - 60
Over 60

# Brunei

| Area: | 2,226 sq. miles (5,765 km²) |

**Area:** 2,226 sq. miles (5,765 km²)
**Population:** 258,000
**Capital:** Bandar Seri Begawan (pop. 52,000)
**Other cities:** Seria 23,000
**Highest point:** Pagon 6,070 ft. (1,850 m)
**Official language:** Malay
**Religions:** Islam, Christianity, Buddhism
**Currency:** Brunei dollar
**Main exports:** Natural gas, petroleum, petroleum products
**Government:** Absolute monarchy
**Per capita GNP:** U.S. $15,400

Brunei is a small, oil-rich independent sultanate on the north coast of Borneo. There are two main areas, separated by a tongue of land belonging to Sarawak, which is part of Malaysia. Offshore lie the oil and gas fields that have made Brunei rich. A narrow coastal plain is washed by the South China Sea. The interior is rugged and thickly forested. Several rivers flow through it. The climate is tropical. Two thirds of the population are Malays, with the remainder mostly Chinese. Most of the Malays are Muslims, and most of the Chinese are Christians, although some are Buddhists. Brunei was an important trading center in the Middle Ages, and larger than the modern state. The first sultan ruled in the 1200s. In 1888 Britain made Brunei a protectorate, which ended in 1971 and Brunei became an independent state in 1984. It remained an absolute monarchy under the ruling sultan.

## ECONOMIC SURVEY

**Farming:** Coconuts are the main farm product. Rice, bananas, and other fruit and vegetables are grown. Cattle, buffaloes, pigs, and chickens are reared. Forestry is small scale but developing. There is some offshore fishing.

**Industry:** Brunei depends almost wholly on its petroleum and natural gas products, most of which are exported to Japan and other Asian countries. There are no other minerals, apart from sand and gravel. About half the work force is employed by the government. New industries are being developed because the deposits of oil and natural gas are expected to run out in about 2025.

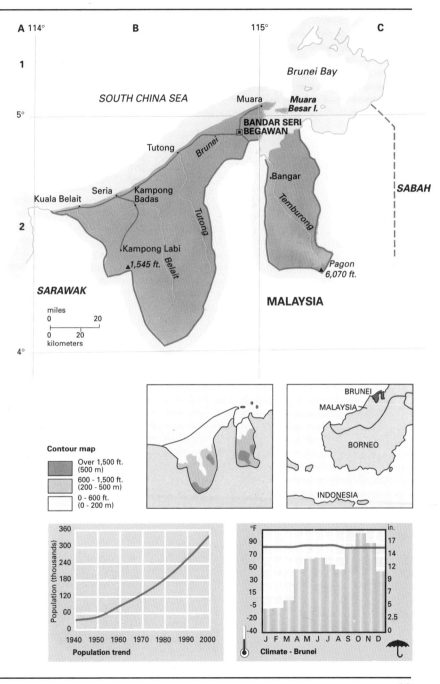

Contour map
- Over 1,500 ft. (500 m)
- 600 - 1,500 ft. (200 - 500 m)
- 0 - 600 ft. (0 - 200 m)

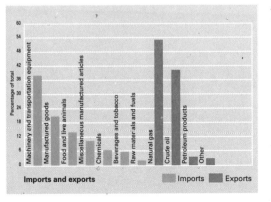

**Imports and exports**

Percentage of total

Machinery end transportation equipment · Manufactured goods · Food and live animals · Miscellaneous manufactured articles · Chemicals · Beverages and tobacco · Raw materials and fuels · Natural gas · Crude oil · Petroleum products · Other

Imports | Exports

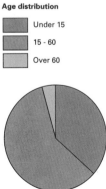

**Age distribution**
- Under 15
- 15 - 60
- Over 60

**Population trend**
1940 1950 1960 1970 1980 1990 2000
Population (thousands)

**Climate - Brunei**
J F M A M J J A S O N D

# Bulgaria

**Area:** 42,823 sq. miles (110,912 km²)
**Population:** 8,995,000
**Capital:** Sofia (pop. 1,129,000)
**Other cities:** Plovdiv 357,000; Varna 306,000
**Highest point:** Musala Peak 9,596 ft. (2,925 m)
**Official language:** Bulgarian
**Religions:** Eastern Orthodox, Roman Catholicism, Protestantism, Islam
**Currency:** Lev
**Main exports:** Machinery, consumer goods, fuels and raw materials, food and tobacco
**Government:** Multiparty republic
**Per capita GNP:** U.S. $7510

Bulgaria has a Black Sea coast and a climate that varies from Mediterranean to continental. The mountains include the Balkans in the north and the higher Rhodope Mountains on the southern border with Greece. The capital, Sofia, lies in a fertile basin. The Danube River plain is in the north, but the central plains form the main farming region. The Bulgarians are Slavs, speaking a language related to Serbo-Croatian and Russian. From 1396 Bulgaria was ruled by Islamic Turks, but its people remained Christian. In 1878 Bulgaria became an independent kingdom. It was an ally of Germany during World War I. After World War II the monarchy was abolished in favor of communist rule. Bulgaria moved away from strict communism toward a more liberal and democratic form of government in the late 1980s and early 1990s.

## ECONOMIC SURVEY

**Farming:** Bulgarian agricultural land is organized mainly into state and collective farms. Farmers grow corn, barley, fruit including grapes and melons, potatoes, and other vegetables, and sugar beet. Attar of roses, used in perfume-making, is a famous Bulgarian export. Sheep are the main livestock.
**Mining:** Lignite, copper, iron, and oil are extracted, with other minerals such as sulfur and zinc.
**Industry:** About one third of the work force is engaged in industry. Factories make cement, iron, and steel products, textiles and machinery. Bulgaria is hampered by an energy shortage. Until the 1990s most of its trade was with the former USSR.

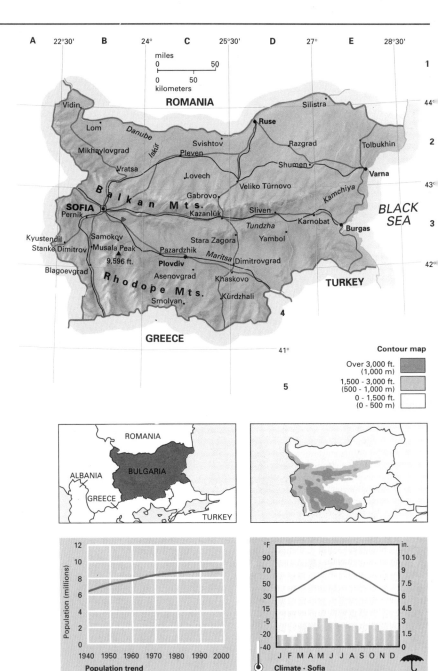

**Contour map**

Over 3,000 ft. (1,000 m)
1,500 - 3,000 ft. (500 - 1,000 m)
0 - 1,500 ft. (0 - 500 m)

**Age distribution**

- Under 15
- 15 - 60
- Over 60

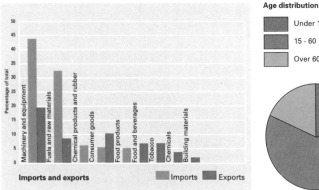

Imports and exports

Imports    Exports

**Population trend**

**Climate - Sofia**

# Burkina Faso

**Area:** 105,869 sq. miles (274,200 km²)
**Population:** 8,948,000
**Capital:** Ouagadougou (pop. 442,000)
**Other cities:** Bobo Dioulasso 231,000
**Highest point:** Aiguille de Sindou 2,352 ft. (717 m )
**Official language:** French
**Religions:** Traditional beliefs, Islam, Christianity
**Currency:** Franc CFA
**Main exports:** Cotton, livestock, millet, sorghum, groundnuts (peanuts)
**Government:** Military regime
**Per capita GNP:** U.S. $310

Known as Upper Volta until 1984, Burkina Faso is a West African country which consists mainly of low plateaus. Its eastern part lies in the basin of the Niger River. The central and western regions are drained by the Black, Red, and White Volta rivers. The climate is hot and tropical. The main rainy season is from July to October, but droughts are frequent. The people are blacks, the largest ethnic group being the Mossi (just under half the population). Upper Volta was created as a separate French colony in 1919, having come under French control in the late 1800s. In 1932 the colony was abolished, most of Upper Volta being transferred to the Côte d'Ivoire, but it was reconstituted in 1947. It became self-governing in 1958 and fully independent in 1960. Several military coups took place during the 1970s and 1980s.

## ECONOMIC SURVEY

**Farming:** Most of Burkina Faso's good farmland is in river valleys. There farmers grow beans, corn, millet, sorghum, and a local cereal, fonio. Groundnuts (peanuts) and shea nuts (used to make soap) are also grown. Cotton is the most valuable cash crop. Cattle, sheep, and goats are herded in large numbers.
**Fishing:** Fish for food are kept in the small lakes created to water stock.
**Mining:** Deposits of manganese, gold, and other minerals await development.
**Industry:** Textiles and metal goods are the main products. Migrant Burkinans who work in Ghana and Côte d'Ivoire contribute to the economy by sending money home.

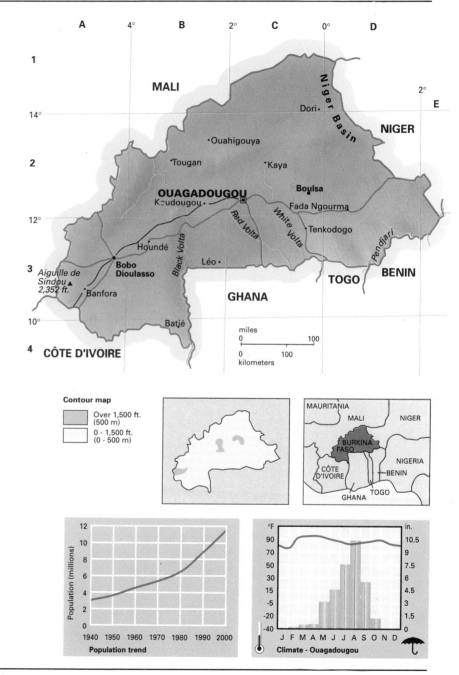

### Contour map

Over 1,500 ft. (500 m)

0 - 1,500 ft. (0 - 500 m)

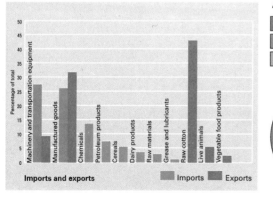

**Imports and exports**

Machinery and transportation equipment / Manufactured goods / Chemicals / Petroleum products / Cereals / Dairy products / Raw materials / Grease and lubricants / Raw cotton / Live animals / Vegetable food products

Imports  Exports

### Age distribution

Under 15
15 - 60
Over 60

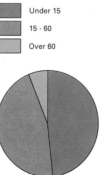

**Population trend**

**Climate - Ouagadougou**

# Burundi

**Area:** 10,747 sq. miles (27,834 km$^2$)
**Population:** 5,439,000
**Capital:** Bujumbura (pop. 273,000)
**Other cities:** Gitega 95,000
**Highest point:** Northeast of Bujumbura, 8,858 ft. (2,700 m)
**Official languages:** Kirundi, French
**Religions:** Christianity, various traditional beliefs
**Currency:** Burundi franc
**Main exports:** Coffee, tea, cotton
**Government:** Military regime
**Per capita GNP:** U.S. $220

Small but densely populated, Burundi is a country with highlands and plateaus in the east. In the west is the Great Rift Valley, with part of Lake Tanganyika on Burundi's border. The climate is cool and pleasant, with two wet seasons. Most of western Burundi is made up of heavily eroded volcanic rock. The plateaus have steep slopes ending in swamps. The forest on the plateaus has been largely cleared by farmers. Most of the people are from three groups: the Hutu (about 80 percent), the Tutsi (under 15 percent) and the Twa or pygmies. A Tutsi-dominated kingdom existed from the 1400s. In 1897 Germany made the region part of its East Africa colony. From 1919 it was part of Ruanda-Urundi, a Belgian trust territory. The country became independent as Burundi in 1962. The monarchy was violently replaced by a republic in 1966.

## ECONOMIC SURVEY

**Farming:** Coffee is Burundi's main cash crop (more than 70 percent by value). Tea is also grown for export. Food crops include bananas, beans, sorghum, cassava, corn, yams, and sweet potatoes. Goats are the most numerous livestock. Sheep, cattle, and chickens are also reared.

**Fishing:** There is a commercial fishery on Lake Tanganyika, making a contribution to the food supply.

**Mining:** Burundi has small undeveloped reserves of nickel and vanadium.

**Industry:** Small-scale development includes factories processing coffee and cotton, and making cement, shoes, soap, and textiles for local consumption.

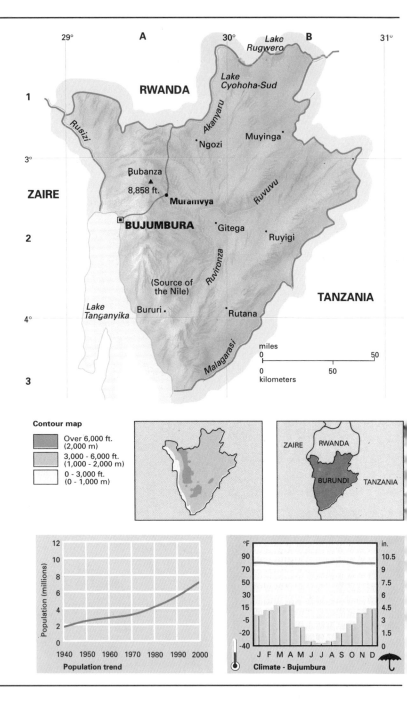

**Contour map**

- Over 6,000 ft. (2,000 m)
- 3,000 - 6,000 ft. (1,000 - 2,000 m)
- 0 - 3,000 ft. (0 - 1,000 m)

**Population trend**

**Climate - Bujumbura**

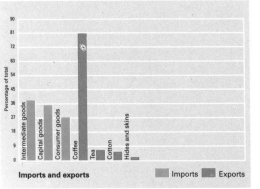

**Imports and exports**

Imports / Exports

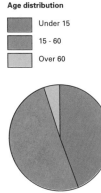

**Age distribution**

- Under 15
- 15 - 60
- Over 60

# Cambodia

**Area:** 69,898 sq. miles (181,035 km²)
**Population:** 8,246,000
**Capital:** Phnom Penh (pop. 750,000)
**Other cities:** Kompong Cham 35,000
**Highest point:** Phnum Aoral, in the Cardamomes Range 5,948 ft. (1,813 m)
**Official language:** Khmer
**Religions:** Buddhism, Islam
**Currency:** Riel
**Main export:** Rubber
**Government:** Republic
**Per capita GNP:** Under U.S. $500

Cambodia has reverted to its original name, having for a time been known as the Khmer Republic and then as Kampuchea. Much of the country is low lying. The Mekong River drains a flat plain which is surrounded by hills. Most people live on this fertile plain or around the Tonle Sap or Great Lake. Cambodia has a tropical monsoon climate. Dense forests cover about half of the land. Khmers make up 90 percent of the population. They have their own language and alphabet. There are Chinese and Vietnamese minorities. The Khmer empire of the 800s–1400s produced the magnificent temple of Angkor Wat. From 1863 the French controlled the region. Cambodia became independent in 1953. During the 1970s and 1980s there was civil war, and millions of people are thought to have lost their lives under the rule of the communist Khmer Rouge. A new regime took over in 1991.

## ECONOMIC SURVEY

**Farming:** Cambodia's economy is based on agriculture, chiefly on growing rice and corn. Production was adequate before the 1970s, but collapsed during the civil war period. Farms and rubber plantations were destroyed. Most of the people are subsistence farmers. Cattle, buffaloes, pigs, and chickens are raised.
**Forestry:** At least 50 percent of the land is forested. In normal times much timber is produced.
**Industry:** A modest industrial base has suffered from the upheaval of the 1970s and 1980s. Small factories produce cotton textiles, rubber tyres, plywood, and other goods. Foreign trade is struggling to recover.

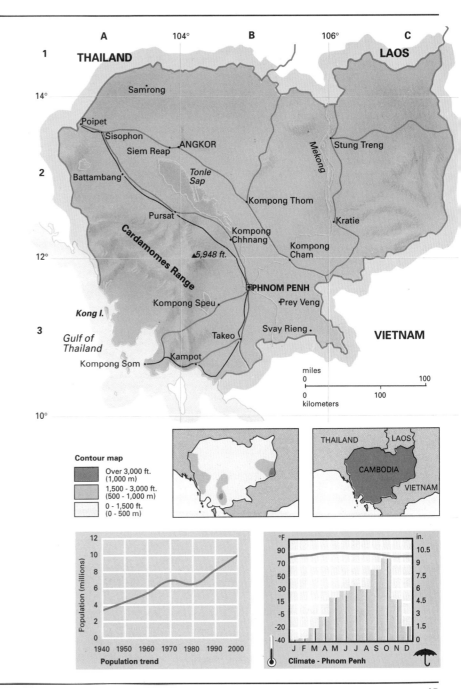

Contour map
Over 3,000 ft. (1,000 m)
1,500 - 3,000 ft. (500 - 1,000 m)
0 - 1,500 ft. (0 - 500 m)

Climate - Phnom Penh

Population trend

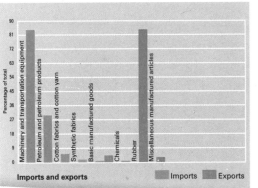

Imports and exports

Imports    Exports

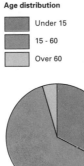

Age distribution
Under 15
15 - 60
Over 60

# Cameroon

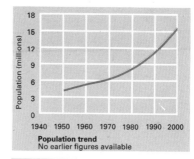

**Area:** 183,569 sq. miles (475,442 km²)
**Population:** 11,742,000
**Capital:** Yaoundé (pop. 654,000)
**Other cities:** Douala 1,030,000
**Highest point:** Mt Cameroon 13,353 ft. (4,070 m)
**Official languages:** French, English
**Religions:** Christianity, various traditional beliefs, Islam
**Currency:** Franc CFA
**Main exports:** Petroleum, coffee, cocoa, aluminum, wood
**Government:** Single-party republic
**Per capita GNP:** U.S. $1010

This country in west-central Africa is on the Gulf of Guinea. In the west are mountains, while in the center is a forested plateau which separates the northern savanna grasslands from the coastal, tropical lowlands. The climate is hot and dry in the north, cooler on the plateau and hot and humid near the coast. The people are Black Africans, mainly of the Bamileké, Fulani, Douala, Ewondo, and Fang ethnic groups. People have lived in the region since prehistoric times. About A.D. 800 it formed part of the empire of Kanem. Portuguese explorers arrived in the 1400s, followed by other Europeans. Cameroon became a German protectorate in 1884, but was divided between France and Britain after World War I. French Cameroon gained its independence in 1960, and was joined by the southern part of British Cameroon in 1961.

## ECONOMIC SURVEY

**Farming:** Coffee and cocoa beans are grown as the main cash crops. Other products are bananas, cotton, palm oil, and groundnuts (peanuts). Rubber and sugar are also produced. Food items include cassava, corn, millet, and yams. Cattle, pigs, sheep, and goats are reared.
**Forestry:** Hardwoods include mahogany, ebony, and sapele.
**Fishing:** There are small coastal and freshwater fishing industries.
**Mining:** Petroleum is the major export. There are deposits of bauxite and kyanite.
**Industry:** Most important is aluminum smelting, followed by the manufacture of soap, cement, palm oil, shoes, and beer.

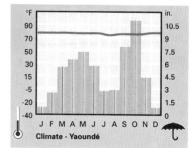

**Population trend**
No earlier figures available

**Climate - Yaoundé**

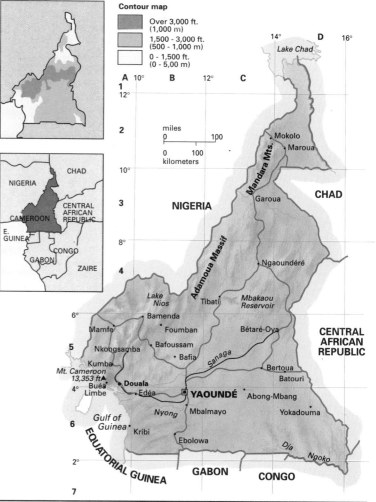

**Contour map**

- Over 3,000 ft. (1,000 m)
- 1,500 - 3,000 ft. (500 - 1,000 m)
- 0 - 1,500 ft. (0 - 5,00 m)

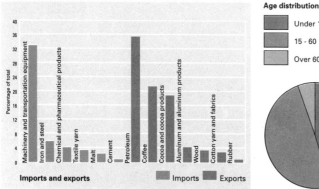

**Imports and exports**

Machinery and transportation equipment · Iron and steel · Chemical and pharmaceutical products · Textile yarn · Malt · Cement · Petroleum · Coffee · Cocoa and cocoa products · Aluminum and aluminum products · Wood · Cotton yarn and fabrics · Rubber

Imports · Exports

**Age distribution**

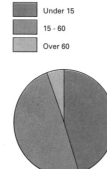

- Under 15
- 15 - 60
- Over 60

# Canada

**Area:** 3,851,809 sq. miles (9,976,139 km²)
**Population:** 26,442,000
**Capital:** Ottawa (pop. 301,000)
**Other cities:** Toronto 3,427,000; Montreal 2,921,000; Vancouver 1,381,000
**Highest point:** Mount Logan 19,524 ft. (5,951 m)
**Official languages:** English, French
**Religion:** Christianity
**Currency:** Canadian dollar
**Main exports:** Cars, trucks, wood pulp, newsprint, timber, petroleum, aluminum
**Government:** Constitutional monarchy
**Per capita GNP:** U.S. $19,020

In area, Canada is the second largest country in the world, after Russia. Western Canada is dominated by the Rocky Mountains. In the far north are the bleak Arctic islands. In the midwest are vast prairies, now given over to grain farming. Curving around Hudson Bay is the Canadian Shield, a rocky region with numerous lakes and rivers, covering half the country. Canada has very cold winters, especially in the far north. Summers in the south are warm and moist. Forests cover more than a third of the country. Canada is thinly populated. Most Canadians live in the central-southeast region, close to the Great Lakes and the St. Lawrence River. Canada's original inhabitants were the Inuit and the Native Americans, but today most Canadians are descendants of British, French, and other European immigrants.

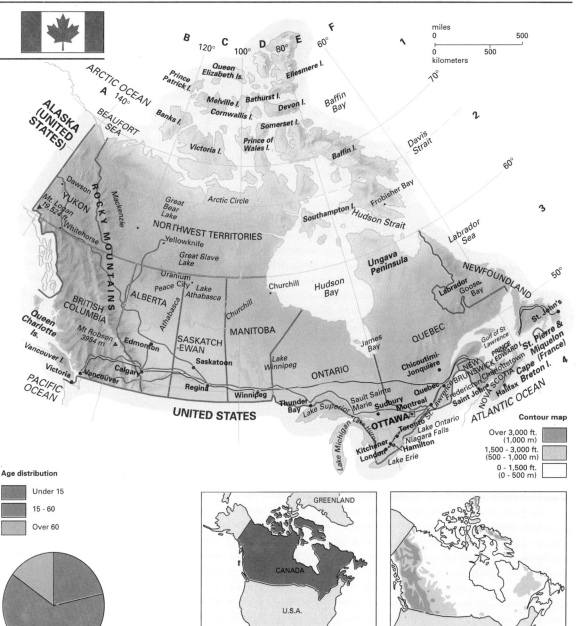

**Contour map**

Over 3,000 ft. (1,000 m)
1,500 - 3,000 ft. (500 - 1,000 m)
0 - 1,500 ft. (0 - 500 m)

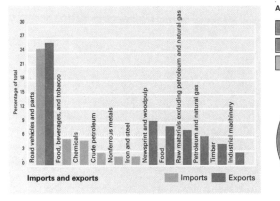

**Imports and exports**

Imports    Exports

Road vehicles and parts; Food, beverages, and tobacco; Chemicals; Crude petroleum; Nonferrous metals; Iron and steel; Newsprint and woodpulp; Food; Raw materials excluding petroleum and natural gas; Petroleum and natural gas; Timber; Industrial machinery

**Age distribution**

Under 15
15 - 60
Over 60

CANADIAN HISTORY. The first people in Canada were the Native Americans, who migrated from Asia at least 30,000 years ago. After them came the Inuit, or Eskimos. Europeans discovered fishing grounds off eastern Canada in the late 1400s, and slowly explored the coast and rivers. Montreal was founded by French missionaries in 1642. Fur traders traveled westward. France and Britain were rivals for control of Canada in the 1700s, Britain eventually conquering the French territory of New France in 1763. French influence and culture has remained powerful in Quebec to this day. The Dominion of Canada, comprising Quebec, Ontario, Nova Scotia and New Brunswick, was set up in 1867. The vast Northwest Territories and Rupert's Land later became part of Canada. In 1885 the Canadian Pacific Railway was completed. Immigrants came to Canada in increasing numbers, mostly from Europe, and by 1905 Canada had more or less its present look, with nine provinces and two territories. Newfoundland remained a separate British colony (until 1949, when it became the tenth province). In 1931 Canada became an independent nation, with a federal system of government. There was a further wave of emigration from Europe after World War II (1939-1945), in which Canadian forces took a leading part on the Allied side. Quebec separatist movements and concern about economic dependence on the United States have been Canada's chief problems since 1970. An attempt to reconcile the federal state and Quebec's ideas failed narrowly in 1990. The same year there was unrest among the Mohawks of Quebec over a threat to develop land they regarded as theirs. It ended only after federal troops were brought in.

## ECONOMIC SURVEY

**Farming:** Large amounts of cereals, including wheat and barley, are grown on the prairies, and fruit, vegetables, dairy produce, and beef are important. Flax and rape are grown.

**Forestry:** Large quantities of timber, wood pulp, and paper are produced.

**Fishing:** The Grand Banks in the Atlantic yield cod, and salmon is the main catch in the Pacific. Perch and white fish are caught in the lakes.

**Mining:** Canada has vast energy and mineral resources. It produces petroleum, natural gas, copper, gold, iron ore, zinc, nickel, and uranium. Hydroelectric schemes produce about 65 percent of Canada's electric power.

**Industry:** Factories produce processed food, vehicles, aircraft, machinery, chemicals, paper, and steel.

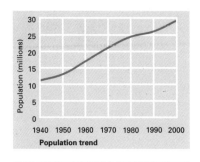

**Population trend**

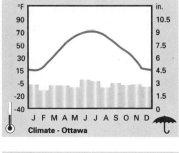

**Climate - Ottawa**

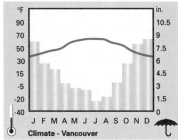

**Climate - Vancouver**

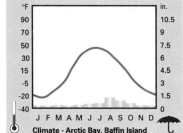

**Climate - Arctic Bay, Baffin Island**

**PROVINCES AND TERRITORIES OF CANADA** (with capitals)

| | | Area (sq. miles) | Area (km²) | Population (1989) |
|---|---|---|---|---|
| 1 | **Alberta** (Edmonton) | 248,800 | 644,390 | 2,423,000 |
| 2 | **British Colombia** (Victoria) | 358,971 | 929,730 | 3,044,000 |
| 3 | **Manitoba** (Winnipeg) | 211,723 | 548,360 | 1,083,000 |
| 4 | **New Brunswick** (Fredericton) | 27,834 | 72,090 | 718,000 |
| 5 | **Newfoundland** (St. John's) | 143,510 | 371,690 | 569,000 |
| 6 | **Northwest Territories** (Yellowknife) | 1,271,442 | 3,293,020 | 53,000 |
| 7 | **Nova Scotia** (Halifax) | 20,402 | 52,840 | 886,000 |
| 8 | **Ontario** (Toronto) | 344,090 | 891,190 | 9,546,000 |
| 9 | **Prince Edward Island** (Charlottetown) | 2,185 | 5,660 | 130,000 |
| 10 | **Quebec** (Quebec) | 523,859 | 1,356,790 | 6,679,000 |
| 11 | **Saskatchewan** (Regina) | 220,348 | 570,700 | 1,007,000 |
| 12 | **Yukon** (Whitehorse) | 184,931 | 478,970 | 26,000 |

# Central African Republic

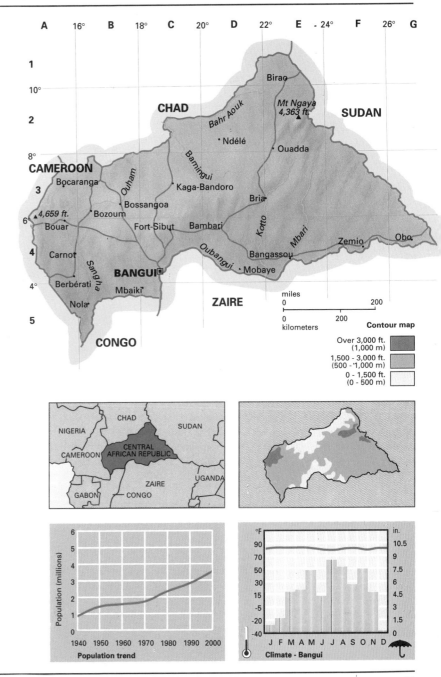

**Area:** 240,535 sq. miles (622,984 km²)
**Population:** 2,875,000
**Capital:** Bangui (pop. 597,000)
**Other cities:** Bambari 52,000
**Highest point:** 4,659 ft. (1,420 m)
**Official language:** French
**Religions:** Christianity, various traditional beliefs, Islam
**Currency:** Franc CFA
**Main Exports:** Coffee, diamonds, wood
**Government:** Single-party republic
**Per capita GNP:** U.S. $390

The country consists largely of a high, rolling plateau crossed by river valleys. The vegetation is mostly grass with scattered trees. The highest ground is in the northeast and in the west along the border with Cameroon. Although the country is in the tropics, its altitude keeps the climate not too hot. The heaviest rainfall is in the southwest. Most of the people are black Africans belonging to many ethnic groups and speaking many languages. In 1894 France created the territory of Ubangi-Shari, making it part of the colony of French Equatorial Africa in 1910. In 1960 it became independent as a republic. From 1976 to 1979 it was called the Central African Empire.

## ECONOMIC SURVEY

**Farming:** Coffee is the principal cash crop, followed by tobacco and cotton. More than 80 percent of the people are subsistence farmers, growing cassava, groundnuts (peanuts), plantains, bananas, millet, corn, and rice. Cattle are reared in those regions that are free from tsetse fly, and people also keep sheep, goats, and pigs.
**Forestry:** More than half the land is forested. Hardwoods include mahogany, obeche, and limba.
**Mining:** Gem and industrial diamonds are produced. There is some gold mining.
**Industry:** A few small factories make textiles, shoes, and radios.

**Age distribution**
- Under 15
- 15 - 60
- Over 60

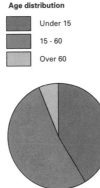

**Imports and exports**
Imports / Exports

Food, Chemicals and plastics, Fuels and lubricants, Machinery and transportation equipment, Building materials, Coffee, Diamonds, Wood, Tobacco, Cotton

Percentage of total

**Population trend**
Population (millions)
1940 1950 1960 1970 1980 1990 2000

**Climate - Bangui**
J F M A M J J A S O N D

**Contour map**
- Over 3,000 ft. (1,000 m)
- 1,500 - 3,000 ft. (500 - 1,000 m)
- 0 - 1,500 ft. (0 - 500 m)

# CENTRAL AMERICA & THE CARIBBEAN

**Area:** 292,665 sq. miles (758,000 km²)
**Population:** 61,280,000
**Major cities:** Havana (Cuba) 2,015,000;
Guatemala City 2,000,000; Santo Domingo
(Dominican Republic) 1,600,000; San Salvador
(El Salvador) 973,000
**Number of independent countries:** 20
**Largest country:** Nicaragua
**Smallest independent country:** St. Christopher
-Nevis
**Highest mountain:** Volcán Tajumulco (in
Guatemala) 13,845 ft. (4,220 m)
**Longest river:** Rio Usumacinta (in Guatemala
and Mexico) 688 miles (1,107 km)
**Largest lake:** Lake Nicaragua 3,060 sq. miles
(7,925 km²)

The narrow, tapering land linking North and South America contains the small countries of Central America. To the east in the Caribbean Sea are groups of islands: the Greater Antilles (including Cuba, Haiti, and Dominican Republic) and the Lesser Antilles (the Leeward and Windward Islands). Central America's rugged, forested interior hampers efficient road communications. There are several volcanoes, and earthquakes are not uncommon. The first inhabitants of the mainland and islands were Native Americans, among them the Aztecs, Caribs, and Maya. Some of these peoples developed impressive civilizations, building stone cities and temples. After Columbus 'discovered' the Americas in 1492, European explorers arrived. Spain was foremost in colonizing Central America, where native peoples and cultures were often wiped out with savage swiftness. Britain, France, and the Netherlands colonized several Caribbean islands. Plantations were set up, and plantation owners brought black slaves from Africa. In the 1800s Spain's Central American colonies gained independence as republics. Most of the Caribbean islands had become independent by the 1980s. Puerto Rico passed from Spanish to United States control in 1898. It is self-governing but its people are American citizens.

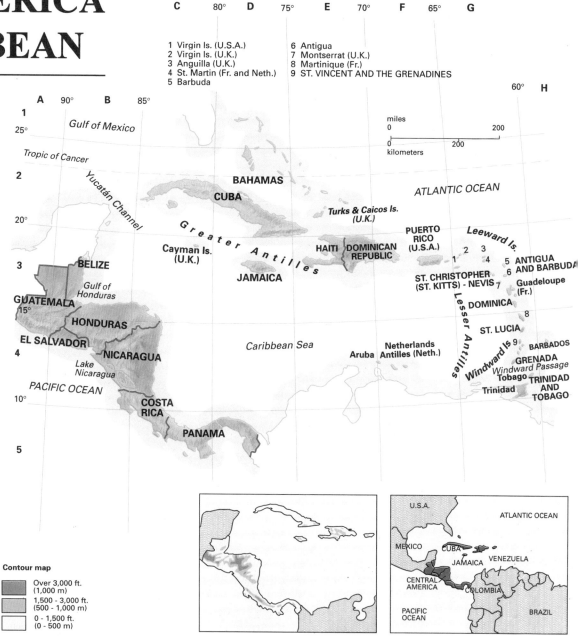

1 Virgin Is. (U.S.A.)
2 Virgin Is. (U.K.)
3 Anguilla (U.K.)
4 St. Martin (Fr. and Neth.)
5 Barbuda
6 Antigua
7 Montserrat (U.K.)
8 Martinique (Fr.)
9 ST. VINCENT AND THE GRENADINES

**Contour map**

Over 3,000 ft. (1,000 m)
1,500 - 3,000 ft. (500 - 1,000 m)
0 - 1,500 ft. (0 - 500 m)

# Chad

**Area:** 495,755 sq. miles (1,284,000 km²)
**Population:** 5,678,000
**Capital:** N'Djamena (pop. 512,000)
**Other cities:** Sarh 124,000
**Highest point:** Emi Koussi 11,204 ft. (3,415 m)
**Official languages:** Arabic, French
**Religions:** Islam, Christianity, various traditional beliefs
**Currency:** Franc CFA
**Main exports:** Raw cotton, live animals, meat, hides
**Government:** Republic
**Per capita GNP:** U.S. $190

The north of Chad is mostly desert with bare rocky highlands, notably the Tibesti Mountains. The southernmost strip is fertile. Savanna covers the central region. In the west is Lake Chad, whose level varies greatly between the wet and dry seasons. The largest rivers are the Chari and Logone. Temperatures in the desert can be extremely high. Black Africans make up most of the population, with Arabs and Berbers in the north. Rock paintings provide evidence of prehistoric settlement. Islam came to the region about A.D. 1000. Local kingdoms traded in slaves, and the northern peoples exploited those of the south. France claimed Chad in the late 1800s. Chad became a colony in 1920 as part of French Equatorial Africa, but gained independence in 1960. A long civil war between north and south, with French and Libyan involvement, began in the 1960s.

## ECONOMIC SURVEY

**Farming:** More than 80 percent of Chad's work force is engaged in agriculture. Farmers grow cassava, sugarcane, millet, yams, groundnuts (peanuts), beans, rice, sweet potatoes, and other food crops. Cotton is the major cash crop. A lesser one is groundnuts. Cattle, goats, sheep, camels, donkeys, and chickens are reared. Meat and hides are exported.

**Fishing:** Lake Chad is fished, and so are the Chari and Logone rivers.

**Minerals:** Oil production has been disrupted by civil war. Salt is produced around Lake Chad.

**Industry:** Cotton ginning is the main industry. Factories also refine sugar, make textiles, and process meat.

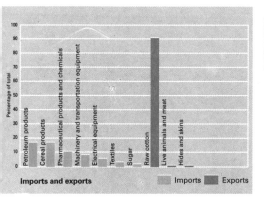

Imports and exports

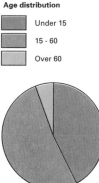

Age distribution
- Under 15
- 15 - 60
- Over 60

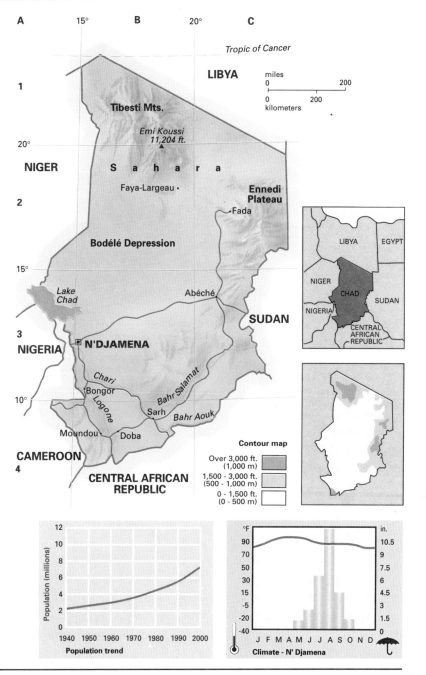

Contour map
- Over 3,000 ft. (1,000 m)
- 1,500 - 3,000 ft. (500 - 1,000 m)
- 0 - 1,500 ft. (0 - 500 m)

Population trend

Climate - N' Djamena

# Chile

**Area:** 292,258 sq. miles (756,945 km²)
**Population:** 13,173,000
**Capital:** Santiago (pop. 4,858,000)
**Other cities:** Vina del Mar 297,000; Concepción 294,000
**Highest point:** Ojos del Salado 22,539 ft. (6,870 m)
**Official language:** Spanish
**Religion:** Christianity
**Currency:** Peso
**Main exports:** Copper, fruit, fish meal, paper
**Government:** Republic
**Per capita GNP:** U.S. $1770

Chile has three main land regions, from west to east: coastal uplands, central lowland basins and valleys, and the high Andes Mountains. The country is long and narrow and the climate changes from north to south. The north is hot and dry, and includes the almost rainless Atacama Desert. Central Chile has hot summers and mild winters. The forested south has a beautiful fjord coastline and is cool with heavy rain. People of mixed Native American and European origin make up 68 percent of the population, Europeans form 30 percent and Araucanians 2 percent. The Incas conquered Chile in the 1400s. Spanish rule began in the mid-1500s. In 1818 Chilean patriots led by General Bernardo O'Higgins won independence. A military government seized power in 1973, but Chile returned to a democracy with an elected president in 1990.

## ECONOMIC SURVEY

**Farming:** Important crops include wheat, barley, rice, corn, potatoes, sugar beet, and fruit such as apples, grapes, and peaches. Most farms are small. Cattle and sheep are reared on ranches in central and southern Chile.
**Fishing:** Catches include more than 200 kinds of fish, mainly anchovetas, mackerel, and sardines.
**Mining:** Chile is currently the world's leading copper producer. Other minerals include molybdenum, sodium nitrate, oil, gold, manganese, iron ore, and lithium.
**Industry:** Consumer goods and foodstuffs are the principal output, together with timber and paper products, machinery, steel, and chemicals.

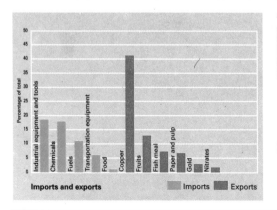

Imports and exports

**Age distribution**

- Under 15
- 15 - 60
- Over 60

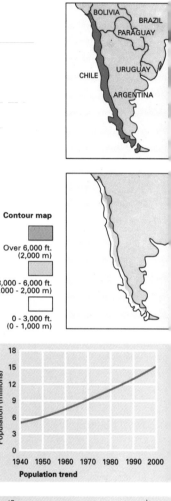

**Contour map**

Over 6,000 ft. (2,000 m)

3,000 - 6,000 ft. (1,000 - 2,000 m)

0 - 3,000 ft. (0 - 1,000 m)

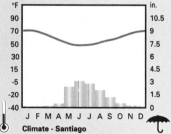

Climate - Santiago

# China

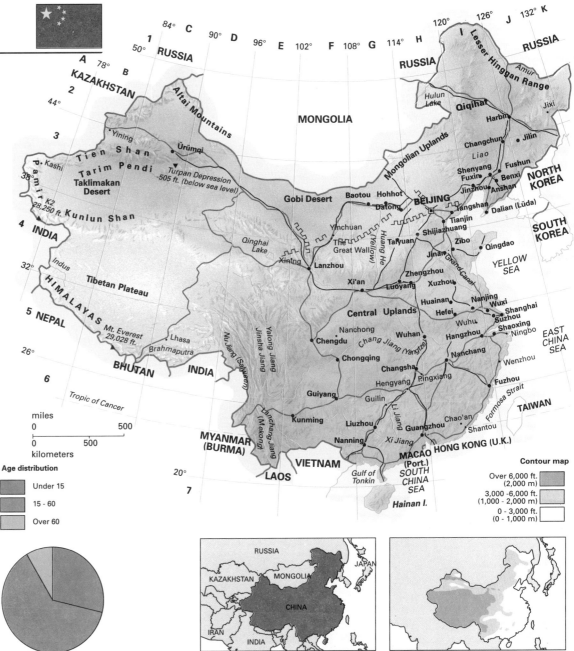

**Area:** 3,705,408 sq. miles (9,596,961 km²)
**Population:** 1,121,544,000
**Capital:** Beijing (pop. 5,970,000)
**Other cities:** Shanghai 7,100,000; Tianjin 5,460,000; Shenyang 4,290,000 Wuhan 3,490,000
**Highest point:** Mt. Everest 29,028 ft. (8,848 m)
**Official language:** Mandarin (Northern Chinese)
**Religions:** Taoism, Buddhism, Christianity
**Currency:** Yuan
**Main exports:** Textiles, electronic products, farm products, metal and plastic products
**Government:** Single-party people's republic
**Per capita GNP:** U.S. $360

China is the third largest country in the world. The land is varied. In the north is the highly fertile basin of the Huang He or Yellow River. This river became known as "China's sorrow" because of its frequent destructive floods. In the northeast are the central plain and eastern highlands of Manchuria. To the south is a basin drained by the Chang Jiang (Yangtze), Asia's longest river. A third river basin is that of the Xi Jiang in the southeast. Western China contains the vast Tibetan plateau, with the towering peaks of the Himalaya, Pamir, and Tien Shan ranges. In northwest China are deserts, such as the Tarim. Northern China has cold winters and warm summers. There is a milder, moister climate in central China, and a subtropical monsoon climate in the southeast.

miles
0 — 500
0 — 500
kilometers

**Age distribution**
- Under 15
- 15 - 60
- Over 60

**Contour map**
- Over 6,000 ft. (2,000 m)
- 3,000 -6,000 ft. (1,000 - 2,000 m)
- 0 - 3,000 ft. (0 - 1,000 m)

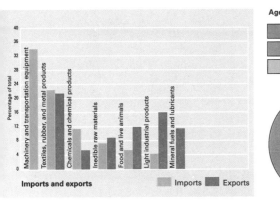

Imports and exports — Imports — Exports

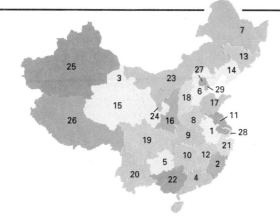

## PROVINCES OF CHINA

| Province (Capital) | Area (sq. miles) | Area (km²) | Population (1981) |
|---|---|---|---|
| 1 **Anhui** (Hefei) | 54,000 | 139,900 | 52,866,000 |
| 2 **Fujian** (Fuzhou) | 47,500 | 123,100 | 28,005,000 |
| 3 **Gansu** (Lanzhou) | 141,500 | 366,500 | 21,034,000 |
| 4 **Guangdong** (Guangzhou) | 89,300 | 231,400 | 63,640,000 |
| 5 **Guizhou** (Guiyang) | 67,200 | 174,000 | 30,514,000 |
| 6 **Hebei** (Shijiazhuang) | 78,200 | 202,700 | 56,958,000 |
| 7 **Heilongjiang** (Harbin) | 179,000 | 463,600 | 33,640,000 |
| 8 **Henan** (Zhengzhou) | 64,500 | 167,000 | 79,335,000 |
| 9 **Hubei** (Wuhan) | 72,400 | 187,500 | 50,581,000 |
| 10 **Hunan** (Changsha) | 81,300 | 210,500 | 57,826,000 |
| 11 **Jiangsu** (Nanjing) | 39,600 | 102,600 | 63,480,000 |
| 12 **Jiangxi** (Nanchang) | 63,600 | 164,800 | 35,590,000 |
| 13 **Jilin** (Changchun) | 72,200 | 187,000 | 23,364,000 |
| 14 **Liaoning** (Shenyang) | 58,300 | 151,000 | 37,774,000 |
| 15 **Qinghai** (Xining) | 278,400 | 721,000 | 4,175,000 |
| 16 **Shaanxi** (Xi'an) | 75,600 | 195,800 | 30,882,000 |
| 17 **Shandong** (Jinan) | 59,200 | 153,300 | 78,895,000 |
| 18 **Shanxi** (Taiyuan) | 60,700 | 157,100 | 26,908,000 |
| 19 **Sichuan** (Chengdu) | 219,700 | 569,000 | 104,584,000 |
| 20 **Yunnan** (Kunming) | 168,400 | 436,200 | 35,130,000 |
| 21 **Zhejiang** (Hangzhou) | 39,300 | 101,800 | 41,212,000 |

### Autonomous regions

| | | | |
|---|---|---|---|
| 22 **Guangxi** (Nanning) | 85,100 | 220,400 | 40,164,000 |
| 23 **Inner Mongolia** (Hohhot) | 454,600 | 1,177,500 | 20,536,000 |
| 24 **Ningxia** (Yinchuan) | 25,600 | 66,400 | 4,352,000 |
| 25 **Xinjiang** (Urümqi) | 635,900 | 1,646,900 | 14,.63,000 |
| 26 **Xizang** (Tibet, Lhasa) | 471,700 | 1,221,600 | 2,079,000 |

### Special municipalities

| | | | |
|---|---|---|---|
| 27 **Beijing** | 6,870 | 17,800 | 9,926,000 |
| 28 **Shanghai** | 2,240 | 5,800 | 12,495,000 |
| 29 **Tianjin** | 1,640 | 4,250 | 8,324,000 |

CHINESE HISTORY. The Han, or true Chinese, make up 94 percent of the population. There are about 55 minority groups including Manchu, Mongol, Tibetan, and Uighur. Since the 1950s the government has reformed written Chinese by simplifying the written characters and teaching a common standard language (Mandarin). China's written history goes back 3,500 years. The first imperial dynasty was the Shang (about 1766 to 1122 B.C.). In 221 B.C. the Qin dynasty set up a strong central government, and the Han dynasty (202 B.C. to A.D. 220) established the Chinese empire. After a period of unrest, the Tang and Sung dynasties (618 to 1279) gave China prosperity and great artistic and technological accomplishments. The Venetian Marco Polo visited China between 1275 and 1292. The Mongols controlled China until the 1300s. The Ming dynasty (1368-1644) was a further period of prosperity. The Manchu or Qing dynasty ruled from 1644 until 1912, when a republic was set up. China was devastated by Japanese attacks and by civil war in the 1930s and 1940s. In 1949 the communists took power. Under Mao Zedong (1949-1976) China was modernized and efforts made to destroy traditional culture. Under Mao's successors, contacts with the West increased, but pro-democracy movements were quashed.

**ECONOMIC SURVEY**
**Farming:** China is the world leader in millet, rice, and tobacco. Barley, cotton, peanuts, corn, tea, sorghum, and wheat are grown in quantity. More pigs are reared than in any other country; cattle, sheep, goats, and camels are also kept.
**Mining:** Antimony, coal, iron ore, mercury, natural gas, oil, tin, and tungsten are produced.
**Industry:** Iron and steel, machinery, fertilizers, clothes, toys, ships, and vehicles are manufactured. Heavy industry has caused serious air and water pollution in some areas. Most concerns are state-run.

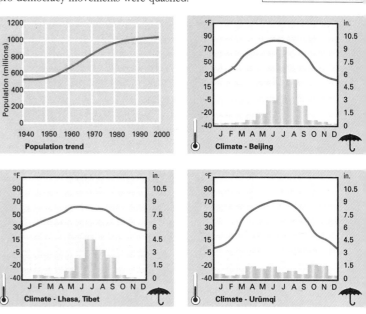

**Population trend**

**Climate - Beijing**

**Climate - Lhasa, Tibet**

**Climate - Urümqi**

# Hong Kong

**Area:** 403 sq. miles (1,045 km²)
**Population:** 5,841,000
**Capital:** Central district, Hong Kong Island
**Highest point:** Tai Mo Shan 3,140 ft. (957 m)
**Official languages:** English, Chinese
**Religions:** Buddhism, Taoism, Christianity
**Currency:** Hong Kong dollar
**Main exports:** Textiles and clothing, electronics, metal and plastic goods
**Government:** British dependency
**Per capita GNP:** U.S. $10,320

Hong Kong is a small, densely populated British colony. It consists of Hong Kong island, some 200 smaller islands, and a strip of the mainland known as the New Territories, leased from China. Because land is so scarce, tall buildings cluster together in the Central district of Hong Kong Island. The people are mostly Chinese. Hong Kong was ceded to Britain by treaty in 1842, and developed a booming trade as a port and trading center. It has a thriving financial business, and a range of manufacturing industries including textiles, electronics, optical goods, plastics, and toys. Britain has agreed to restore Hong Kong to China in 1997. A joint declaration signed in 1984 stated that China would set up a special administrative region for Hong Kong, Kowloon, and the New Territories, retaining the existing free enterprise economic system for 50 years.

**Contour map**

0 -3,000 ft.
(0 - 1,000 m)

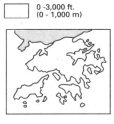

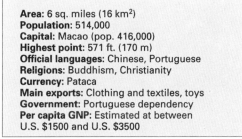

**Age distribution**

Under 15

15 - 60

Over 60

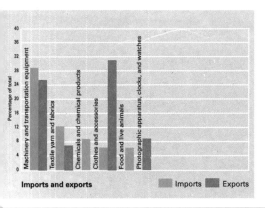
**Imports and exports**
Imports  Exports

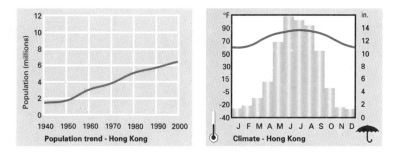

**Population trend - Hong Kong**

**Climate - Hong Kong**

# Macao

**Area:** 6 sq. miles (16 km²)
**Population:** 514,000
**Capital:** Macao (pop. 416,000)
**Highest point:** 571 ft. (170 m)
**Official languages:** Chinese, Portuguese
**Religions:** Buddhism, Christianity
**Currency:** Pataca
**Main exports:** Clothing and textiles, toys
**Government:** Portuguese dependency
**Per capita GNP:** Estimated at between U.S. $1500 and U.S. $3500

Macao is a Portuguese colony on the south coast of China, at the mouth of the Canton (Pearl) River. Macao is a peninsula, just over 3.7 miles (6 kilometers) long. It is linked to the Chinese mainland by a narrow isthmus, on which stands the city of Santa Nome de Deus de Macao. The territory also includes the small islands of Taipa and Coliane, which are linked with Macao by a bridge and causeway respectively. Portuguese traders began visiting Macao in 1513 and the territory became a Portuguese colony in 1557. Since 1974 it has officially been Chinese territory under Portuguese administration. The colony has a Portuguese governor and a legislative assembly, part-elected and part-appointed. The official language is Portuguese but almost all the inhabitants speak Cantonese. Ninety percent of the people live in the city of Macao. Macao is known mostly as a tourist resort. Its attractions include gambling casinos, which are forbidden in neighboring Hong Kong as well as in mainland China. Like Hong Kong, Macao is destined to be returned to Chinese rule, at the end of 1999.

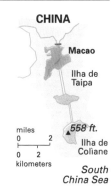

**Contour map**

0 - 600 ft.
(0 - 200 m)

*see* ASIA, page 22

# Colombia

**Area:** 439,737 sq. miles (1,138,914 km²)
**Population:** 32,961,000
**Capital:** Bogotá (pop. 4,185,000)
**Other cities:** Medellin 1,506,000; Cali 1,397,000
**Highest point:** Pico Cristóbal Colón 18,947 ft. (5,775 m)
**Official language:** Spanish
**Religion:** Christianity
**Currency:** Peso
**Main exports:** Coffee, petroleum, and petroleum products
**Government:** Multiparty republic
**Per capita GNP:** U.S. $1190

## ECONOMIC SURVEY

**Farming:** Conditions and climate vary with altitude. Coffee, which is the main cash crop, is grown on thousands of small farms. Farmers also grow bananas, rice, cassava, corn, cotton, potatoes, and sugarcane. Flowers are exported. Cattle are the chief livestock. Most land not used for coffee is held by large landowners. Rubber trees grow wild.
**Mining:** Minerals include salt, coal, iron ore, petroleum, gold, and emeralds (in which Colombia is the world leader).
**Industry:** Most of the country's factories are small. They make textiles, processed foods, pop-up books for children, chemicals, metal goods, and building materials.

In the southwest of Colombia are the Andes Mountains, where about three-fourths of the people live in the high, fertile mountain valleys. In the east are the llanos — hot, flat, grassy plains. In the south, the grasslands merge into the forests of the upper Amazon and Orinoco river basins. The coastal lowlands border the Caribbean Sea and Pacific Ocean, and are hot and wet. The highlands are cooler and drier, and the grasslands wet in summer but dry in winter. Most people are of mixed Native American, European, or African ancestry. Spanish settlement began in 1525, when the area was named New Granada. In 1819 Simón Bolívar liberated Colombia, which until 1830 included Ecuador and Venezuela. The modern republic has a tradition of elected governments, but is troubled by poverty and major drug-related crime.

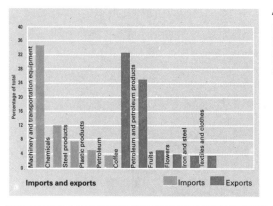

**Imports and exports**

**Age distribution**

- Under 15
- 15 - 60
- Over 60

Population trend

Climate - Bogotá

**Contour map**

- Over 6,000 ft. (2,000 m)
- 3,000 - 6,000 ft. (1,000 - 2,000 m)
- 0 - 3,000 ft. (0 - 1,000 m)

miles
0        200

0        200
kilometers

# Congo

**Area:** 132,047 sq. miles (342,000 km²)
**Population:** 2,326,000
**Capital:** Brazzaville (pop. 596,000)
**Other Cities:** Pointe-Noire 298,000
**Highest point:** Monts de la Lékéti, near Djambala, 3,412 ft. (1,040 m)
**Official language:** French
**Religions:** Christianity, traditional beliefs
**Currency:** Franc CFA
**Main exports:** Petroleum, crude and refined, wood, diamonds
**Government:** Single-party republic
**Per capita GNP:** U.S. $930

Congo is a country with a narrow coastal plain, behind which are uplands. The north is flat swampland, drained by the Congo (Zaire) and Oubangui rivers. In the south is higher ground cut by several river valleys. The valley of the Niari River is a good farming region. Rain forest and wooded savanna are the main vegetation types. The climate is hot all year round, with heavy rainfall except on the coast. The people belong to four main ethnic groups – Babonko, Teke, Bobangi, and Gabonais. About 40 percent speak dialects of the Bantu language, Kongo. Part of what is now Congo may have belonged to the medieval Kongo kingdom. European slave trading started in the late 1400s. Inland exploration took place in the 1800s. Congo was part of French Equatorial Africa until it became independent in 1960. It has had communist and military governments.

## ECONOMIC SURVEY

**Farming:** Most farmers grow subsistence crops – bananas, plantains, corn, rice, and cassava. Sugarcane and pineapples are also grown. Goats and poultry are kept, and also some cattle and sheep.
**Forestry:** There is a rich potential, with hardwoods such as okoumé, sapele, and mahogany exported.
**Fishing:** A fleet is being developed at Pointe-Noire.
**Mining:** Oil production offshore is Congo's major revenue source and there is a local refinery. Diamonds, lead, copper, zinc, and gold are produced.
**Industry:** Congo's industries are growing in processed foods (sugar, flour), textiles, cement, metal goods, and chemicals.

**Population trend**
No further figures available

**Climate - Brazzaville**

Contour map
- Over 1,500 ft. (500 m)
- 600 - 1,500 ft. (200 - 500 m)
- 0 - 600 ft. (0 - 200 m)

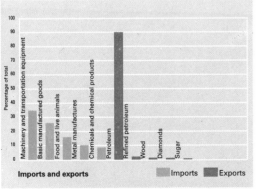

**Imports and exports**

Age distribution
- Under 15
- 15 - 60
- Over 60

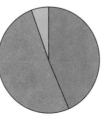

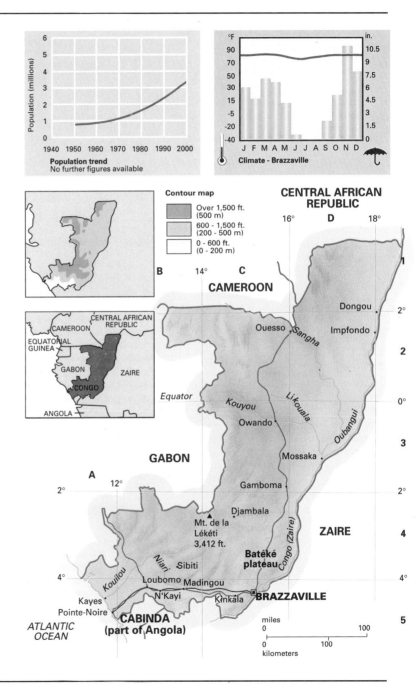

# Costa Rica

**Area:** 19,575 sq. miles (50,700 km²)
**Population:** 3,015,000
**Capital:** San José (pop. with suburbs 692,000)
**Other cities:** Limón 34,000
**Highest point:** Chirripó Grande 12,529 ft. (3,819 m)
**Official language:** Spanish (some people speak a dialect of English)
**Religion:** Christianity
**Currency:** Colón
**Main exports:** Textiles, coffee, bananas, sugar
**Government:** Multiparty republic
**Per capita GNP:** U.S. $1790

## ECONOMIC SURVEY

**Farming:** Agriculture is the chief economic activity. The main cash crops are coffee and bananas, plus ornamental plants and cut flowers. Farmers also grow cocoa, sugar, corn, rice, oranges, pineapples, and vegetables. Cattle and pigs are the chief livestock.

**Fishing:** Shrimps are the most important catch, together with turtles and tuna.

**Forestry:** Timber from the forests of oak, pine, mahogany, and other hardwoods is a major money earner.

**Industry:** Manufacturing is growing. Products include cement, clothes, cosmetics, fertilizers, foods, textiles, drugs, and medicines, and petroleum and wood products.

The narrow Pacific coast of Costa Rica rises abruptly into central highlands. There are active volcanoes in these uplands. The country is thickly forested in its lowland areas along the Caribbean coast, and the climate is hot and humid. The people have a mixture of Spanish, Native American, and African ancestry. Blacks living in the eastern Caribbean lowlands are descended from slaves brought from the West Indies. Christopher Columbus was the first European to visit Costa Rica, landing in 1502 at Limón. In 1822 Costa Rica joined a short-lived Mexican empire and the next year formed part of the United Provinces of Central America. In 1838 it became independent. In 1890 the first free elections in Central America established Costa Rican democracy. The country has a recent record of stability unrivaled in Central America.

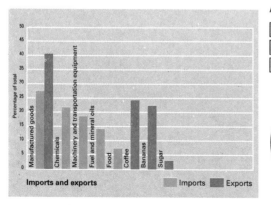

**Imports and exports**

Imports · Exports

**Age distribution**

Under 15
15 - 60
Over 60

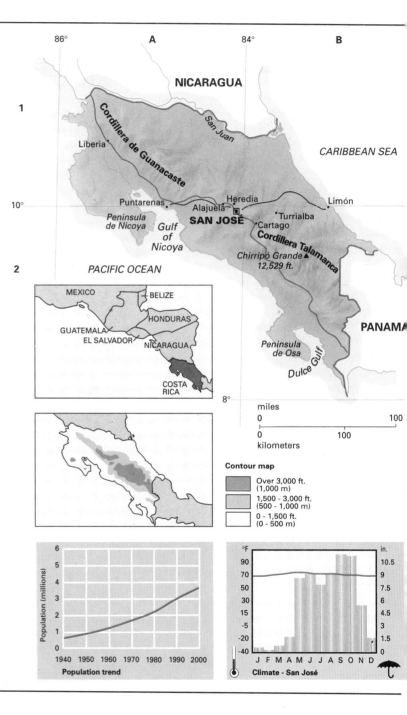

**Contour map**

Over 3,000 ft. (1,000 m)
1,500 - 3,000 ft. (500 - 1,000 m)
0 - 1,500 ft. (0 - 500 m)

**Population trend**

**Climate - San José**

# Côte d'Ivoire

**Area:** 124,504 sq. miles (322,463 km²)
**Population:** 12,657,000
**Capital:** Abidjan (pop. 1,850,000);
Yamoussoukro (capital designate)
**Other cities:** Bouaké 220,000
**Highest point:** Mount Nimba 5,800 ft. (1,768 m)
**Official language:** French
**Religions:** Traditional beliefs, Islam, Christianity
**Currency:** Franc CFA
**Main exports:** Cocoa, coffee, petroleum
products, timber, fruit
**Government:** Multiparty republic
**Per capita GNP:** U.S. $790

The Côte d'Ivoire (formerly often known by the English version of its name as the Ivory Coast) is a West African country with a south-facing coast on the Gulf of Guinea. Behind its broad coastal lowlands are high plains. The main highlands are in the northwest. The south has an equatorial climate. The north is often scorched by the harmattan wind from the Sahara. Savanna is the chief vegetation, although there is some forest in the south. The people are mainly black Africans belonging to several ethnic groups. They speak about 60 local languages. French traders began buying ivory and slaves in the region in the 1500s. The French made the Côte d'Ivoire a colony in 1893, and made it part of French West Africa in 1904. It became self-governing in 1958, and a fully independent republic in 1960, keeping trade links with France.

## ECONOMIC SURVEY

**Farming:** The cash crops used to be mainly coffee and cocoa beans, but now also include palm oil, bananas, pineapples, and rubber. Cocoa is still an important export crop. Cassava, corn, rice, and yams are the principal food crops. Sheep, goats, and cattle are reared.
**Forestry:** The tropical rain forests contain valuable hardwoods such as teak, ebony, and mahogany.
**Mining:** The country has offshore oil deposits, and mines diamonds, gold, and iron ore.
**Industry:** Food processing, textiles, electrical goods and plastics production, sawmills and palm-oil processing are the leaders in this developing sector of the economy.

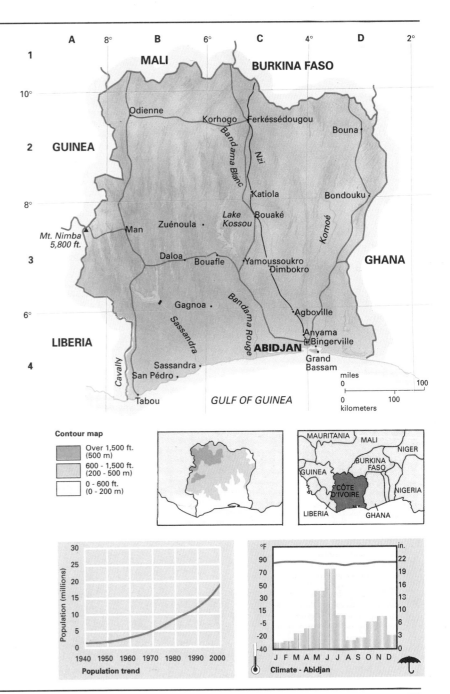

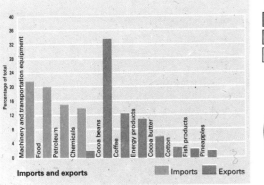

**Imports and exports**

**Age distribution**
- Under 15
- 15 - 60
- Over 60

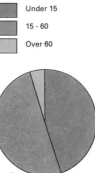

**Population trend**

**Climate - Abidjan**

**Contour map**
- Over 1,500 ft. (500 m)
- 600 - 1,500 ft. (200 - 500 m)
- 0 - 600 ft. (0 - 200 m)

see AFRICA, page 14

# Cuba

**Area:** 42,804 sq. miles (110,861 km²)
**Population:** 10,683,000
**Capital:** Havana (pop. 2,015,000)
**Other cities:** Santiago de Cuba 359,000;
Camagüey 245,000; Cienfuegos 103,000
**Highest point:** Mt. Turquino 6,578 ft. (2,005 m)
**Official language:** Spanish
**Religion:** Christianity
**Currency:** Peso
**Main exports:** Sugar, refined minerals, fruit, fish, cigars, rum
**Government:** Socialist republic
**Per capita GNP:** U.S. $2690

This West Indian country consists of one large island and several small islands. About a third of the land area is mountainous, the rest is made up of plains and basins. The climate is semi-tropical, and there are forests containing valuable wood. The Native Americans of Cuba are now virtually extinct. The modern population includes mulattoes (people of mixed black and white ancestry), blacks descended from African slaves, and whites, many of whose forebears settled in Cuba in the early 1900s. Christopher Columbus claimed Cuba for Spain in 1492. In the 1600s European powers struggled to control the country. Slavery was abolished in 1855. After two wars of independence, Cuba won its freedom from Spanish rule in 1899. In 1958 a communist revolution was led by Fidel Castro, who ruled Cuba into the 1990s.

## ECONOMIC SURVEY

**Farming:** All major farms are state-run, and private farmers have to sell their produce to the state. Sugarcane and tobacco are the chief products. Other crops include bananas, corn, cassava, fruit, coffee, rice, potatoes, and tomatoes. Cattle rearing has been encouraged. Pigs, horses, sheep, and goats are also kept.
**Fishing:** Cuba's state-owned fishing fleet is an important revenue earner.
**Mining:** Cuba has large nickel reserves, and also deposits of limestone, chromium, copper, and iron.
**Industry:** Textiles, cement, shoes, and clothing are made. Food processing and refining of imported petroleum are the major industries.

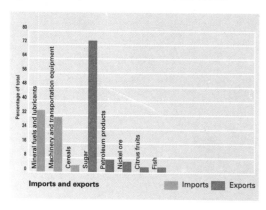

**Imports and exports** — Imports / Exports

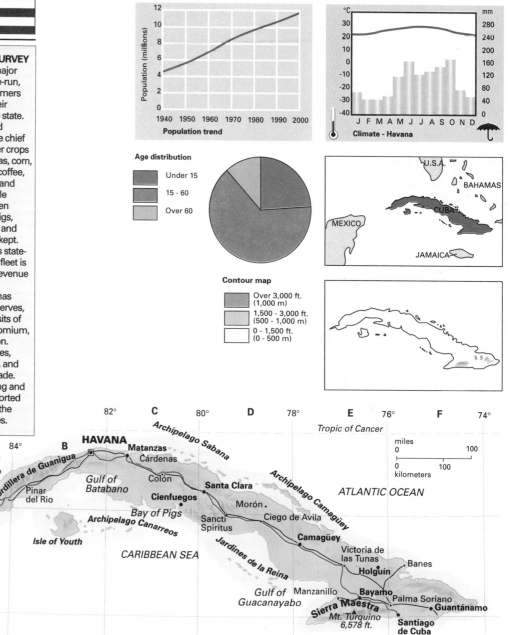

Population trend

Climate - Havana

Age distribution
- Under 15
- 15 - 60
- Over 60

Contour map
- Over 3,000 ft. (1,000 m)
- 1,500 - 3,000 ft. (500 - 1,000 m)
- 0 - 1,500 ft. (0 - 500 m)

# Cyprus

**Area:** 3,572 sq. miles (9,251 km²)
**Population:** 742,000
**Capital:** Nicosia (pop. 167,000)
**Other cities:** Limassol 120,000
**Highest point:** Mt. Olympus 6,407 ft. (1,953 m)
**Official languages:** Greek, Turkish
**Religions:** Greek Orthodox (Greek area), Islam (Turkish area)
**Currency:** Cyprus pound
**Main exports:** Clothing and footwear, potatoes, citrus fruits, grapes
**Government:** Constitutional republic
**Per capita GNP:** U.S. $7050

This island at the eastern end of the Mediterranean has broad, fertile coastal plains, and a wide central plain, the Mesaoria. In the north are the Kyrenia and Karpas Mountains, while in the south are the Troödos Mountains. The climate is Mediterranean. Cyprus is culturally a European country, but part of an Asian geological formation. The Turks ruled Cyprus from the 1570s. Britain took over in 1878, ruling Cyprus until 1960, when it gained independence. The island has Greek-speaking and Turkish-speaking communities, Greeks forming the majority of the people. There was fighting between the two groups in the 1960s and 1970s. In 1974 Turkish forces occupied the northern 40 percent of the island, which was declared the Turkish Republic of Northern Cyprus. All countries except Turkey recognize Cyprus as one nation.

## ECONOMIC SURVEY

**Farming:** About 60 percent of the island is cultivated, and 33 percent of the labor force works on the land. Crops include grapes, potatoes, barley, wheat, grapefruit, and other citrus fruits. Sheep, goats, and pigs are kept. Food and live animals are exported, particularly from the Turkish region.
**Mining:** Cyprus has copper and chromium ore, and asbestos.
**Industry:** The Greek part of the island is more industrialized than the Turkish part. Products of Cypriot factories include chemicals, clothes, leather goods, and shoes. Tourism is important. Cyprus's main trading partners are the United Kingdom, Greece, and Turkey.

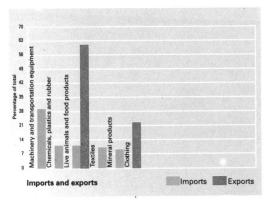

Imports and exports

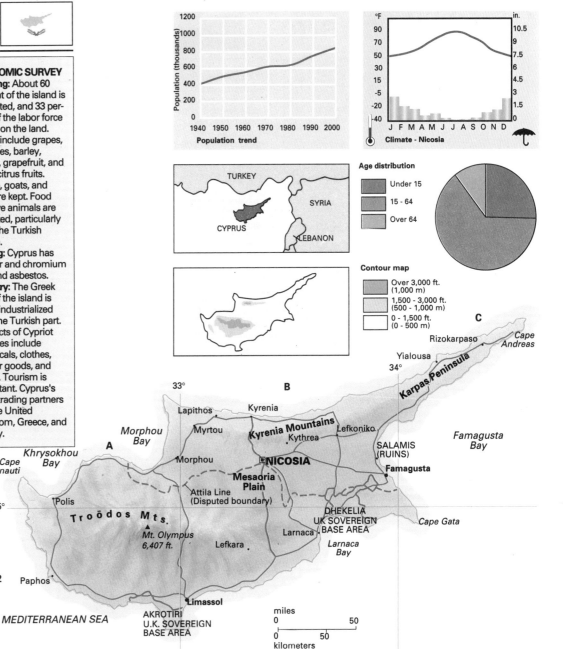

Population trend

Climate - Nicosia

Age distribution
- Under 15
- 15 - 64
- Over 64

Contour map
- Over 3,000 ft. (1,000 m)
- 1,500 - 3,000 ft. (500 - 1,000 m)
- 0 - 1,500 ft. (0 - 500 m)

see ASIA, page 22

# Czech Republic

**Area:** 30,450 sq. miles (78,864 km²)
**Population:** 10,404,000
**Capital:** Prague (pop. 1,215,000)
**Other cities:** Brno (391,000), Ostrava (331,000)
**Highest point:** Sněžka, 5,256 ft. (1,602 m)
**Official language:** Czech
**Religions:** Roman Catholicism, Protestantism
**Currency:** Koruna

**ECONOMIC SURVEY**
**Farming:** Farmland covers 55 percent of Czechoslovakia. Crops include barley, rye, wheat, sugar beet, and hops. Pigs are the most numerous livestock, but farmers also raise cattle, poultry, and sheep. The best agricultural land is in Moravia.

The area of the former Czechoslovakia has three main regions. The Bohemian plateau in the northwest is drained by the Vltava River. Moravia, the central region, is lowland, with rivers draining to the Danube. The eastern region, Slovakia, is the most mountainous, with some plains in the south. The region has cold winters and mild summers. The population is made up of Czechs (65 percent), Slovaks (30 percent), and various minorities.

# Slovakia

**Mining:** The country is rich in coal and lignite, and has lead, tin, zinc, and other valuable ores, oil, and natural gas reserves.
**Industry:** More than 37 percent of the work force is in industry. Products include steel, machinery, cement, chemicals, plastics, fertilizers, alcoholic drinks including beer, transportation equipment, paper, ceramics, and textiles. Bohemia has a long tradition of glassmaking.

**Area:** 18,933 sq. miles (49,035 km²)
**Population:** 5,287,000
**Capital:** Bratislava (pop. 440,000)
**Other cities:** Kosice (236,000)
**Highest point:** Gerlachovský Štit, 8,714 ft. (2,656 m)
**Official language:** Slovak
**Religions:** Roman Catholicism, Protestantism
**Currency:** Koruna

Czechs and Slovaks have shared a common Slav culture since the early Middle Ages. Prague became one of the great cities of Europe, within the Holy Roman and Austrian empires. Czechoslovakia became independent in 1918. It was Communist-ruled from 1948 until the democratic revolution of 1989. On January 1, 1993, Czechoslovakia split into two self governing states the Czech Republic and Slovakia, with respective capitals Prague and Bratislava.

**Age distribution**
- Under 15
- 15 - 60
- Over 60

**Population trend** (1940–2000, Population in millions)

**Climate - Prague** (°F, in., J F M A M J J A S O N D)

*The charts, graphs, and text apply to the area of the former Czechoslovakia before it split into two independent states.*

**Contour map**
- Over 3,000 ft. (1,000 m)
- 1,500 - 3,000 ft. (500 - 1,000 m)
- 0 - 1,500 ft. (0 - 500 m)

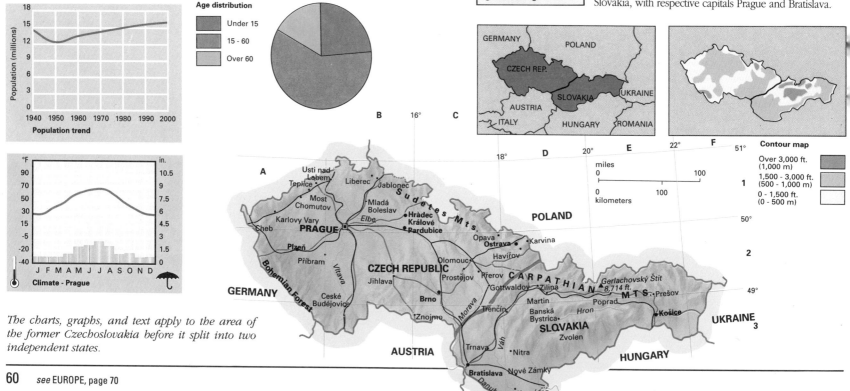

# Denmark

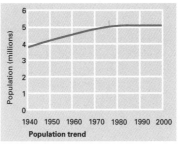

**Area:** 16,629 sq. miles (43,069 km²); the Faeroe Islands cover 540 sq. miles (1399 km²)
**Population:** 5,141,000 (Faeroe Islands 48,000)
**Capital:** Copenhagen (pop. 1,339,000)
**Other cities:** Århus 259,000; Odense 175,000
**Highest point:** Yding Skovhøj 568 ft. (173 m)
**Official language:** Danish
**Religion:** Protestantism
**Currency:** Krone
**Main exports:** Machinery and instruments, farm products, chemicals, transportation equipment
**Government:** Constitutional monarchy
**Per capita GNP:** U.S. $20,510

Denmark consists of the low-lying Jutland peninsula and 482 islands. All but about 100 of the islands are uninhabited. Copenhagen, the capital city, stands on the largest island, Sjælland. Almost surrounded by sea, Denmark has a mild climate, with moderate rainfall. The land is flat, and about two-thirds of the country is fertile farmland. Agriculture is important, though few people work on the land. Manufacturing is the leading sector of the Danish economy. Denmark was a major power from the A.D. 800s to the 1200s. For a time it was in a union with Norway and Sweden, which finally broke up in 1523. Neutral in World War I, Denmark was occupied by Germany in World War II. It joined the European Community in 1973. Greenland, self-governing since 1979, and the Faeroe Islands (see the Atlantic Ocean) are parts of Denmark.

## ECONOMIC SURVEY

**Farming:** Many farmers belong to co-operatives. About half the farmland is used for growing cereals such as barley and wheat. Much of the cereal crop is used for animal feed. Flowers are grown for sale. Farmers rear pigs and dairy cattle. Denmark's food products include butter, cheese, eggs, and bacon.

**Fishing:** Sea fishing is economically important. Catches include cod, herring, mackerel, flatfish, and shrimps.

**Industry:** Denmark's manufactured goods include silverware, furniture, engineering goods, machinery, electrical equipment such as television sets, and chemicals. Oil and gas come from the North Sea.

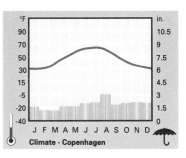

**Population trend**

**Climate - Copenhagen**

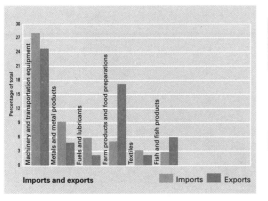

**Imports and exports**

Imports   Exports

**Age distribution**

Under 15

15 - 60

Over 60

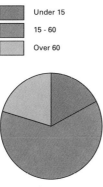

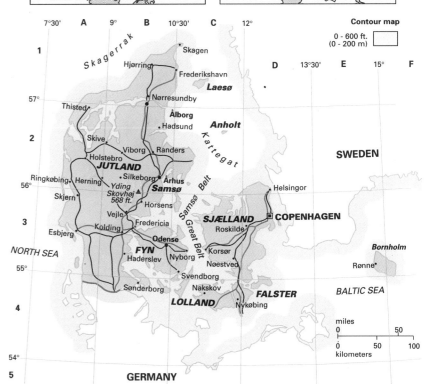

Contour map

0 - 600 ft.
(0 - 200 m)

miles
0    50

0    50    100
kilometers

# Djibouti

**Area:** 8,494 sq. miles (22,000 km²)
**Population:** 528,000
**Capital:** Djibouti (pop. 290,000)
**Highest point:** Mousaali 6,768 ft. (2,063 m)
**Official languages:** Arabic, French
**Religions:** Islam, Christianity
**Currency:** Djibouti franc
**Main exports:** Live animals including camels, food, and food products
**Government:** Single-party republic
**Per capita GNP:** U.S. $740

This small republic on the Red Sea coast of northeast Africa is covered mostly by desert. On either side of the Gulf de Tadjoura, which partly divides Djibouti, are dry, volcanic plateaus, where the only vegetation is scrub. In the north are mountains. The climate is one of the hottest and driest in the world. Most of the people belong to two groups, the Issas (Somalis) and the Afars (who have traditional links with Ethiopia). There are some Europeans and Arabs. The people of the region became Muslims in the 800s. Wars with Christian Ethiopia were frequent. French influence began in 1862, and the town of Djibouti became the port for Ethiopia's trade. The area became part of the colony of French Somaliland which was formed in the 1880s. In 1967 the country was renamed the Territory of the Afars and Issas, remaining in association with France. In 1977 it became fully independent as the Republic of Djibouti, but France retains military bases.

## ECONOMIC SURVEY

**Farming:** Djibouti is a poor country, with very few natural resources. The climate and soil conditions make agriculture difficult. Less than 10 percent of the land is farmed. Vegetables, including tomatoes and eggplants are grown. Livestock rearing is the main activity. Goats, sheep, camels, and cattle are raised. **Fishing:** Species such as grouper and snapper are caught.
**Mining:** There are unexploited deposits of copper and gypsum.
**Industry:** The port of Djibouti serves Ethiopia and contributes largely to the economy. Small factories produce soft drinks and light electro-mechanical goods.

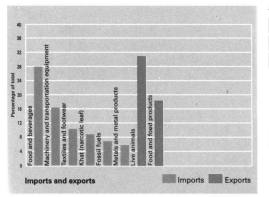

**Imports and exports**
Imports  Exports

**Age distribution**
Under 15
15 - 60
Over 60

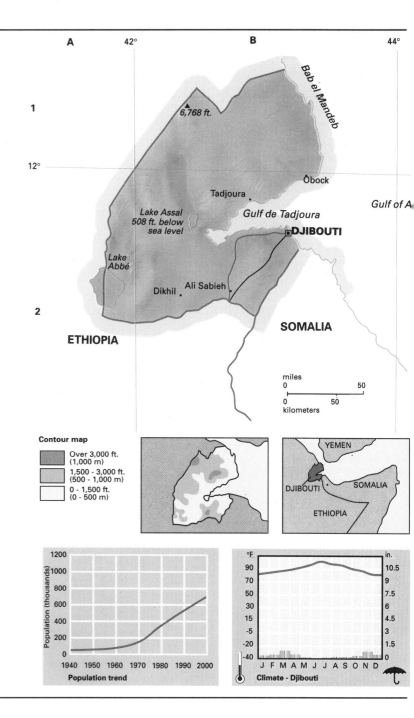

**Contour map**
Over 3,000 ft. (1,000 m)
1,500 - 3,000 ft. (500 - 1,000 m)
0 - 1,500 ft. (0 - 500 m)

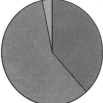
**Population trend**

**Climate - Djibouti**

# Dominica, Guadeloupe, and Martinique

**DOMINICA: Area:** 290 sq. miles (751 km²)
**Population:** 84,000
**Capital:** Roseau (pop. 22,000)
**Government:** Republic
**Per capita GNP:** U.S. $1670
**GUADELOUPE: Area:** 687 sq. miles (1,779 km²)
**Population:** 344,000
**Capital:** Basse-Terre (pop. 14,000)
**Government:** French overseas department
**MARTINIQUE: Area:** 425 sq. miles (1,102 km²)
**Population:** 338,000
**Capital:** Fort-de-France (pop. 97,000)
**Government:** French overseas department

## ECONOMIC SURVEY

**Farming:** The economies of these islands are based on agriculture. Bananas are the chief cash crop, followed by coconuts, sugar, and pineapples. Some timber is exported.
**Fishing:** Shrimps are an important export from Guadeloupe.
**Mining:** There are few minerals, although pumice is mined on Dominica.
**Industry:** Coconuts are processed to make soap. Most of Dominica's trade is with the U.K., most of Martinique's and Guadeloupe's is with France. Rum is a leading product in Guadeloupe and Martinique. Tourism is small-scale.

Dominica, Guadeloupe, and Martinique are three Caribbean island territories in the Lesser Antilles group. Only Dominica is an independent nation; the other two are overseas departments of France, but with considerable powers of self-government. The Guadeloupe department includes five other islands, one of which, St. Martin, is partly Dutch. All the islands are volcanic in origin, and Mont Pelée on Martinique erupted in 1902 claiming 30,000 lives. All the islands have a tropical climate, and have some rain forests. The French and British argued over ownership of the islands. Dominica became independent in 1978.

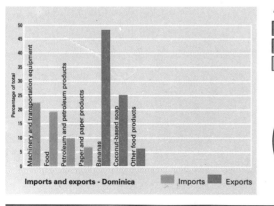

**Imports and exports - Dominica**
Imports  Exports

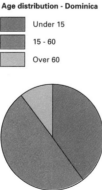

**Age distribution - Dominica**
Under 15
15 - 60
Over 60

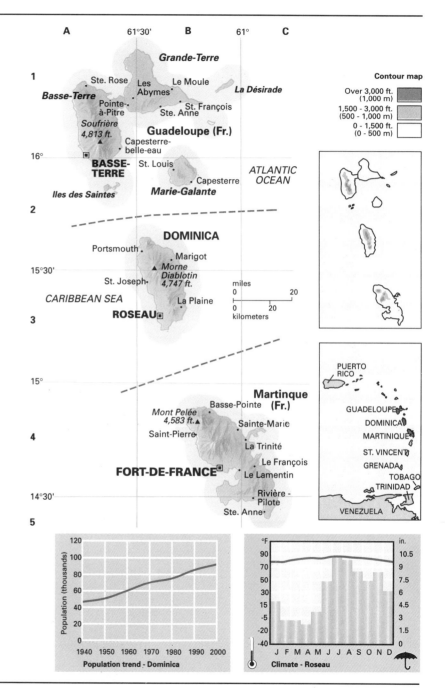

**Population trend - Dominica**

**Climate - Roseau**

# Dominican Republic

**Area:** 18,816 sq. miles (48,734 km²)
**Population:** 7,170,000
**Capital:** Santo Domingo (pop. 1,600,000)
**Other cities:** Santiago de los Caballeros 308,000; La Vega 300,000
**Highest point:** Pico Duarte 10,420 ft. (3,175 m)
**Official language:** Spanish
**Religion:** Christianity
**Currency:** Peso
**Main exports:** Sugar, ferro-nickel, gold, coffee
**Government:** Multiparty republic
**Per capita GNP:** U.S. $790

The Dominican Republic is Haiti's eastern neighbor on the island of Hispaniola. The land is mountainous and the climate is tropical. Rain forests are widespread and the valleys are fertile. Three-fourths of the people are of mixed black and white descent, about 15 percent are whites and about 10 percent are blacks. Christopher Columbus discovered Hispaniola in 1492. Spain gave up the territory to France in 1795, but regained it from 1809 to 1821. From 1822 to 1844 Haiti took over the whole island. There was a rebellion against Haiti, and the Dominican Republic was founded. Occupation by U.S. marines, dictatorships, and civil wars have been features of the country's subsequent history.

## ECONOMIC SURVEY

**Farming:** The best farmland is on the plains. Sugarcane is the chief cash crop, followed by coffee and cocoa. Avocados, beans, peanuts, corn, plantains, rice, mangoes, oranges, tomatoes, and vegetables are also grown. The growing of bananas and tobacco is being encouraged.
**Mining:** Ferro-nickel and gold are the republic's leading mineral resources and export items. Other minerals include bauxite, platinum, silver, gypsum, and limestone.
**Industry:** Sugar refining, foods, rum, textiles, and cement are important.

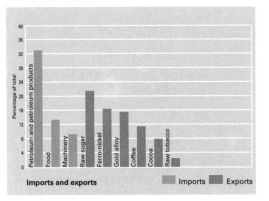

**Imports and exports**

**Age distribution**

- Under 15
- 15 - 60
- Over 60

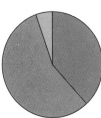

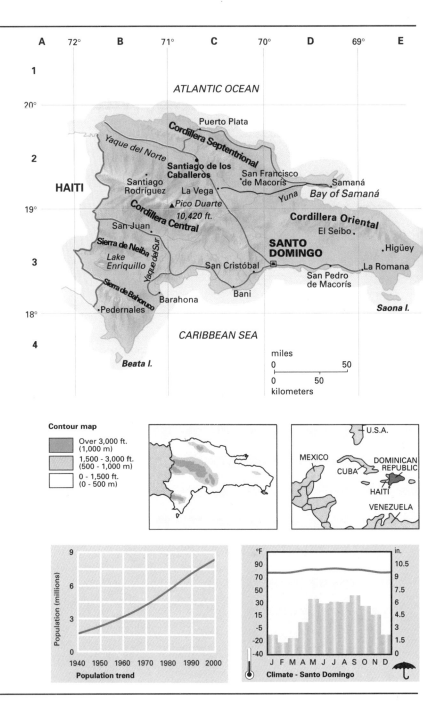

**Contour map**

- Over 3,000 ft. (1,000 m)
- 1,500 - 3,000 ft. (500 - 1,000 m)
- 0 - 1,500 ft. (0 - 500 m)

**Population trend**

**Climate - Santo Domingo**

# Ecuador

**Area:** 109,484 sq. miles (283,561 km²); Galápagos Islands 3,029 sq. miles (7,844 km²)
**Population:** 10,782,000
**Capital:** Quito (pop. 1,234,000)
**Other cities:** Guayaquil 1,699,000; Cuenca 152,000; Machala 106,000; Portoviejo 103,000
**Highest point:** Chimborazo 20,561 ft. (6,267 m)
**Official language:** Spanish
**Religion:** Christianity
**Currency:** Sucre
**Main exports:** Petroleum, shrimps, bananas
**Government:** Multiparty republic
**Per capita GNP:** U.S. $1040

Ecuador has two lowland regions, one along the Pacific coast, the other, known as the Oriente, covering almost half the country in the east. The coastal lowland includes swamps and tropical forests. The Oriente is thickly forested around the Amazon basin and the foothills of the Andes Mountains. Many rivers flow through the Oriente. Plateaus and active volcanoes are a feature of the high Andes or Sierra. Ecuador also includes the 15 Galápagos Islands to the west. The lowlands are hot and wet, the highlands are cooler. More than half the people are Native Americans. The others are of European, African, and mixed descent. The Incas ruled the region from about 1470 until the Spanish conquest of 1533. Ecuador became independent, within Gran Colombia, in 1822 and has been a separate republic since 1830.

## ECONOMIC SURVEY

**Farming:** Bananas, cocoa, coffee, and sugarcane are grown on large plantations. Near the coast oranges and rice are grown. The Andes highlands yield beans, corn, potatoes, and wheat. Beef and dairy cattle are reared.
**Forestry:** Ecuador is the world's leading producer of balsa wood, and also has tropical hardwoods such as mahogany.
**Fishing:** Coastal waters are rich in shrimps, herring, mackerel, tuna, and other fish.
**Mining:** Petroleum is the mainstay of the economy. Ecuador also has deposits of silver, gold, copper, and zinc.
**Industry:** Factories produce cement, drugs, Panama hats, foods, and textiles.

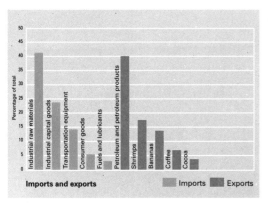

**Imports and exports**

Imports · Exports

**Age distribution**

Under 15
15 - 60
Over 60

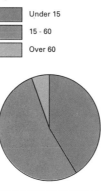

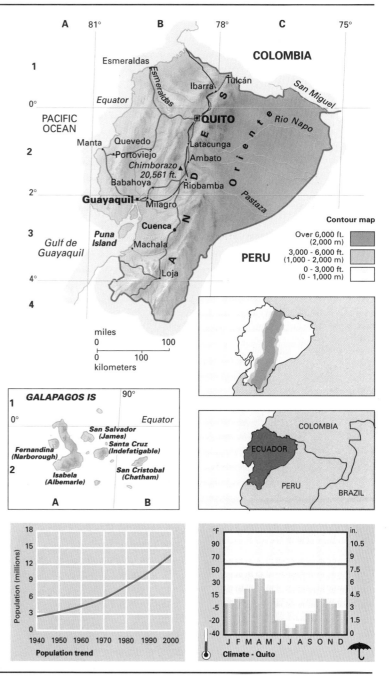

**Contour map**

Over 6,000 ft. (2,000 m)
3,000 - 6,000 ft. (1,000 - 2,000 m)
0 - 3,000 ft. (0 - 1,000 m)

miles
0 — 100
0 — 100
kilometers

**GALAPAGOS IS**

**Population trend**

**Climate - Quito**

# Egypt

**Area:** 386,662 sq. miles (1,001,449 km²)
**Population:** 53,170,000
**Capital:** Cairo (pop. 6,325,000)
**Other cities:** Alexandria 2,893,000; Giza 1,671,000; Port Said 364,000
**Highest point:** Gebel Katherina 8,652 ft. (2,637 m)
**Official language:** Arabic
**Religions:** Islam, Christianity
**Currency:** Egyptian pound
**Main exports:** Petroleum, cotton
**Government:** Republic
**Per capita GNP:** U.S. $630

The densely populated areas of Egypt are along the Nile River and the Suez Canal, waterways that have dominated its ancient and modern history. The Nile valley and delta contain most of the country's farmland. The Aswan High Dam provides irrigation from the artificial Lake Nasser. On either side of the Nile are deserts: the Libyan Desert, covering about two-thirds of Egypt, and the Eastern or Arabian Desert bordering the Red Sea. The Sinai Peninsula, with a sandy plain, limestone plateau, and mountains in the south, links Africa and Asia. The climate is hot and dry. The people are mostly Arabs, Bedouins, and Nubians. Egypt's history covers 5,000 years, from the splendors of the pharaohs through periods of Roman, Arabian, Mameluke, and European influence. Independent in 1922, Egypt became a republic in 1953.

## ECONOMIC SURVEY

**Farming:** Cotton is the chief cash crop. Farmers also grow sugarcane, tomatoes, corn, potatoes, onions, wheat, rice, and fruit. Livestock include buffaloes and donkeys as working animals, cattle, goats, sheep, camels, and chickens. Crops are planted all year round with irrigation from the Nile River.
**Fishing:** Fishing, in the sea, the Nile, and the lakes, is a useful source of food.
**Mining:** Oil is the most valuable source of revenue. Other minerals include natural gas, phosphates, iron ore, and manganese.
**Industry:** Large concerns are state-run. Products include fertilizers, vehicles, cement, sugar, steel, cotton, and jute yarn.

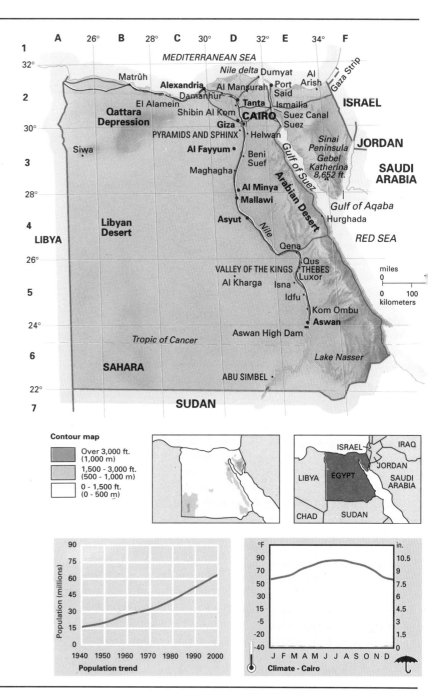

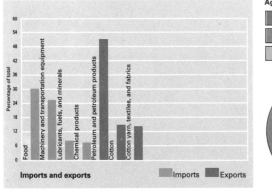

Imports and exports

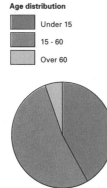

Age distribution

- Under 15
- 15 - 60
- Over 60

# El Salvador

**Area:** 8,124 sq. miles (21,041 km²)
**Population:** 5,252,000
**Capital:** San Salvador (pop. 973,000)
**Other cities:** Santa Ana 208,000; San Miguel 161,000
**Highest point:** Monte Cristo 7,933 ft. (2,418 m)
**Official language:** Spanish
**Religion:** Christianity
**Currency:** Colón
**Main exports:** Coffee, sugarcane, pharmaceuticals, textiles
**Government:** Republic
**Per capita GNP:** U.S. $1040

El Salvador is named after the feast day of the Savior (Jesus Christ). It has a Pacific coastline, with a narrow coastal plain and a mountainous interior. Two mountain ranges divide the country. There are more than 20 volcanoes. El Salvador has many small rivers but only the Lempa is navigable. Much of the natural vegetation has been removed by cultivation. Temperatures range from hot on the coast to cool in the mountains. The rainy season lasts from May to October. Most of the population is of mixed European and Native American descent. Before the Spanish conquest in 1524, the country was dominated by five Indian tribes, the most powerful of which was the Pipil. Independence from Spain came in 1821, and El Salvador became a republic in 1841. The 1980s were a period of unrest and civil strife.

## ECONOMIC SURVEY

**Farming:** About 75 percent of the land is used for agriculture. There is a mixture of small farms, large plantations, and cattle ranches. Coffee is the main crop, followed by cotton and sugar. Corn, beans, rice, fruit, and vegetables are also grown. Cattle and pigs are the chief livestock.

**Forestry:** Balsam trees yield a spicy-smelling resin that is used in medicine.

**Mining:** There are few minerals, but some silver mines are operated.

**Industry:** Manufacturing is a minor activity, but is being expanded to reduce dependence on agriculture. Factories produce chemical products, food and drinks, leather goods, and textiles.

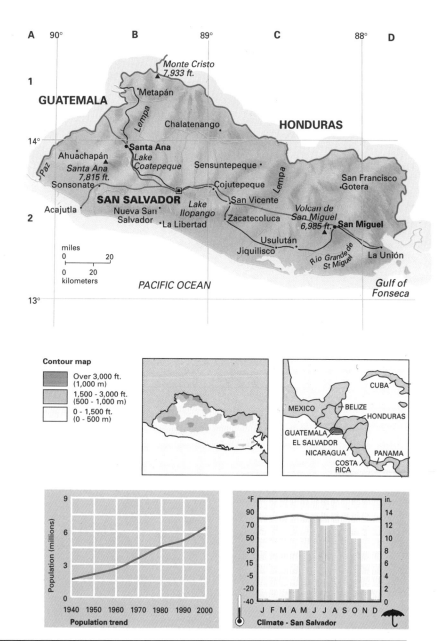

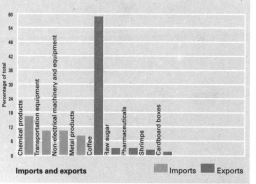

**Imports and exports**

Chemical products, Transportation equipment, Non-electrical machinery and equipment, Metal products, Coffee, Raw sugar, Pharmaceuticals, Shrimps, Cardboard boxes

Percentage of total

Imports | Exports

**Age distribution**

- Under 15
- 15 - 60
- Over 60

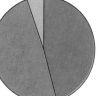

**Contour map**

- Over 3,000 ft. (1,000 m)
- 1,500 - 3,000 ft. (500 - 1,000 m)
- 0 - 1,500 ft. (0 - 500 m)

**Population trend**

Population (millions)

1940 1950 1960 1970 1980 1990 2000

**Climate - San Salvador**

J F M A M J J A S O N D

*see* CENTRAL AMERICA & THE CARIBBEAN, page 48

# Equatorial Guinea

**Area:** 10,831 sq. miles (28,051 km²)
**Population:** 351,000
**Capital:** Malabo (pop. 15,000)
**Highest point:** Mount Malabo, on Bioko Island
9,865 ft. (3,007 m)
**Official language:** Spanish
**Religions:** Christianity, various traditional
beliefs
**Currency:** Franc CFA
**Main exports:** Cocoa, timber,fuels, and
lubricants
**Government:** Single-party republic
**Per capita GNP:** U.S. $430

The republic of Equatorial Guinea is made up of Mbini on the mainland of West Africa and five offshore islands, the largest of which is Bioko (formerly Fernando Po), in the Gulf of Guinea. The capital, Malabo, is on Bioko. The islands are volcanic. Mbini and Bioko have coastal plains, with densely forested interiors. The climate is equatorial, with wet and dry seasons. The Bantu Fang form the majority of the population of the mainland. On Bioko some 60 percent are Bubis, indigenous to the island. The Portuguese explored Equatorial Guinea in the 1470s. Spain took over Bioko in 1778, and leased naval bases there to Britain. During the 19th century Spaniards settled on the mainland. Spain governed the two territories as overseas provinces from 1959. Equatorial Guinea gained its independence in 1968.

## ECONOMIC SURVEY

**Farming:** Cocoa beans are the chief cash crop, amounting to over 40 percent of exports, but some Spanish-owned commercial cocoa plantations have been abandoned. The main food crops are typical of West Africa, including bananas, cassava, sweet potatoes, and yams. Sheep and chickens are the most numerous livestock.
**Fishing:** There is fishing, but only for local consumption.
**Forestry:** Timber is exported from the rain forests of the mainland.
**Mining:** The known minerals (iron ore, lead, zinc, and others) are not mined.
**Industry:** There are very few industries. The country depends on overseas aid.

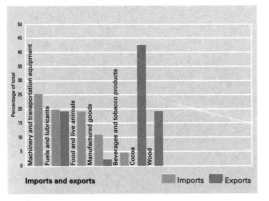

Imports and exports

Percentage of total — Machinery and transportation equipment, Fuels and lubricants, Food and live animals, Manufactured goods, Beverages and tobacco products, Cocoa, Wood

Imports / Exports

**Age distribution**

Under 15
15 - 60
Over 60

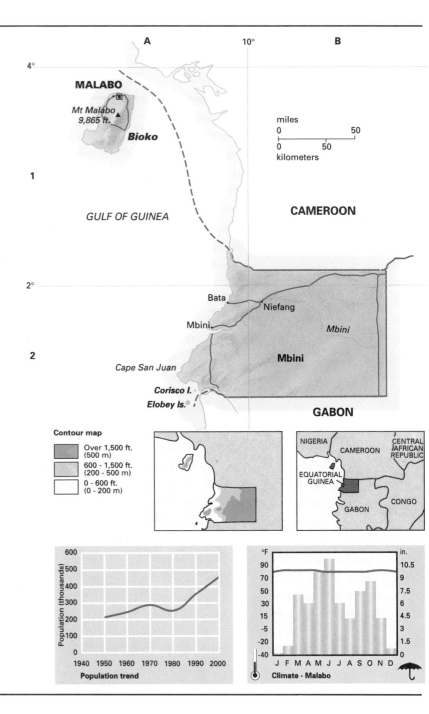

GULF OF GUINEA

MALABO
Mt Malabo 9,865 ft.
Bioko

CAMEROON

Bata
Niefang
Mbini
Mbini
Mbini
Cape San Juan
Corisco I.
Elobey Is.

GABON

miles
0        50
0        50
kilometers

**Contour map**

Over 1,500 ft. (500 m)
600 - 1,500 ft. (200 - 500 m)
0 - 600 ft. (0 - 200 m)

NIGERIA   CAMEROON   CENTRAL AFRICAN REPUBLIC
EQUATORIAL GUINEA
GABON   CONGO

Population (thousands)

1940 1950 1960 1970 1980 1990 2000
**Population trend**

°F / in.
J F M A M J J A S O N D
**Climate - Malabo**

# Eritrea

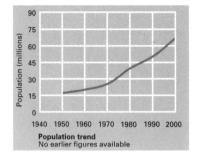

**Area:** 36,170 sq. miles (93,679 km²)
**Population:** 3,318,000 (1992 est.)
**Capital:** Asmara (pop. 500,000)
**Other cities:** n/a
**Highest point:** Mount Soira 9,885 ft. (3,013 m)
**Official language:** Tigrinya
**Religions:** Islam, Christianity
**Currency:** Birr

The region covering Eritrea and Ethiopia has two blocks of highlands, divided by the Rift Valley. There are lowlands in the east near the Red Sea coast. The main river, the Blue Nile, flows from Lake Tana in the north. The hot, dry lowlands contrast with the cooler and wetter uplands. The largest single group of people are the Oromos (Gallas). Others are the Tigreans, Somalis, and Afars. The Amhara form a traditional ruling class.

# Ethiopia

**Area:** 426,373 sq. miles (1,104,300 km²)
**Population:** 50,527,000 (1992 est.)
**Capital:** Addis Ababa (pop. 1,673,000)
**Other cities:** Dire Dawa (118,000)
**Highest point:** Ras Dashen 15,158 ft. (4,620 m)
**Official language:** Amharic
**Religions:** Ethiopian Orthodox, Islam, various traditional beliefs
**Currency:** Birr

About 100 languages are spoken in the region, most belonging to the Cushitic, Semitic, or Nilotic families. The biblical empire of Ethiopia developed about 2,000 years ago into the Aksum civilization. From 1936 to 1941 Ethiopia was occupied by Italy. In 1974 its emperor was deposed, and Ethiopia became a republic. Eritrea broke away from Ethiopia in 1993 and is now an independent country.

*The charts, graphs, and text apply to the entire area covered by Eritrea and Ethiopia.*

## ECONOMIC SURVEY

**Farming:** Most Ethiopians struggle to make a living from farming. Drought, soil erosion, and the turmoil of civil war have cut food production and led to widespread famines. Corn, barley, sorghum, wheat, beans, potatoes, and yams are grown. Coffee is the principal cash crop. Cattle, goats, sheep, camels, and chickens are reared.
**Mining:** Ethiopia has known reserves of minerals including copper, gold, and platinum, but they are not exploited.
**Industry:** Textiles are the chief factory product. Ethiopia also produces cement, shoes, processed foods, and chemicals. There is an oil refinery using imported oil.

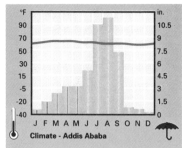

**Population trend**
No earlier figures available

**Climate - Addis Ababa**

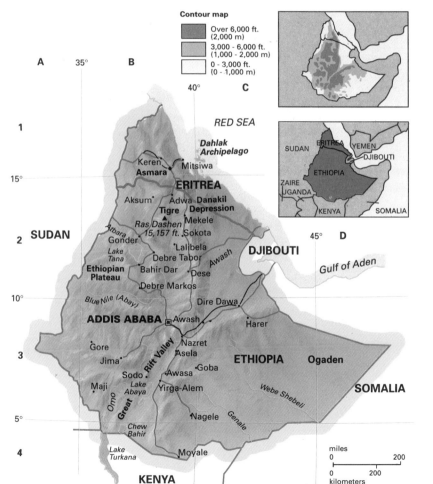

**Contour map**

Over 6,000 ft. (2,000 m)
3,000 - 6,000 ft. (1,000 - 2,000 m)
0 - 3,000 ft. (0 - 1,000 m)

*see* AFRICA, page 14

# EUROPE

**Area:** 406,743 sq. miles (10,534,600 km²), including nearly 25 percent of the former USSR, and 3 percent of Turkey
**Population:** 696,000,000
**Major cities:** Moscow (Russia) 8,967,000; Paris (France) 8,707,000; London (United Kingdom) 6,735,000; St. Petersburg (Russia) 5,020,000; Berlin (Germany) 3,301,000
**Number of independent countries:** 43
**Largest country:** Russia
**Smallest independent country:** Vatican City
**Highest mountain:** Mount Elbrus, Caucasus Mountains, 18,481 ft. (5,633 m)
**Longest river:** Volga, Russia, 2,194 miles (3,531 km)
**Largest lake:** Caspian Sea, on the Europe-Asia border, 169,381 sq. miles (438,695 km²)

Europe is the smallest continent barring Australia, and the most densely populated. It has many advantages: a friendly climate in most regions, fertile farmland, rich natural resources and few insurmountable barriers to communications. Its countries include the largest by area, Russia, and the smallest, the Vatican City. Mountain ranges in the north and south enclose a vast central plain. The coastline is irregular and long (over 37,000 miles; 60,000 km). Europe was the birthplace of Greek and Roman civilization. European ideas were spread worldwide from the late 1400s by explorers, traders, and colonizers. The Industrial Revolution began in Europe in the 1700s. Europe had the first factories with steam-driven machines, and the first steam railroads. During the 1800s millions of Europeans emigrated to the United States, Canada, and Australia. While democracy developed in some countries, new political ideas caused unrest in traditionally autocratic states such as Russia. Old rivalries and hostile alliances brought about the disaster of World War I (1914-1918). Russia collapsed into communist revolution. After the war, economic troubles weakened Europe, and the rise of Nazi tyranny in Germany precipitated World War II (1939-1945). From the ruins of war, Europe emerged with a new economic powerhouse, the European Community, and in the 1990s a new political map, with the collapse of communism in eastern Europe.

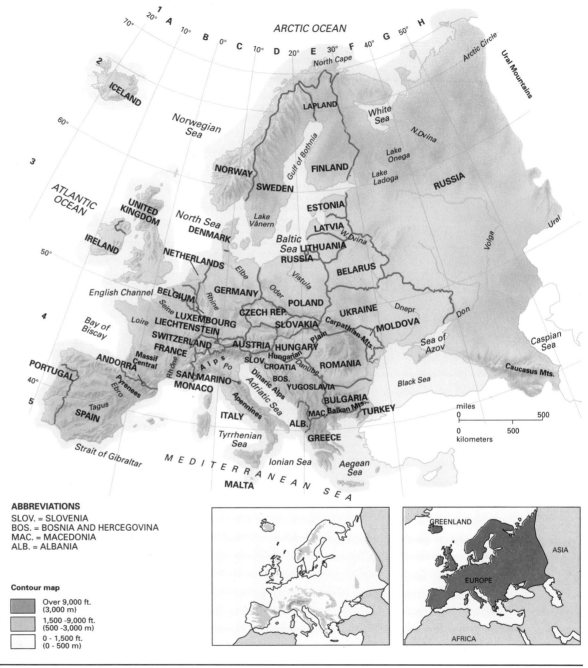

**ABBREVIATIONS**
SLOV. = SLOVENIA
BOS. = BOSNIA AND HERCEGOVINA
MAC. = MACEDONIA
ALB. = ALBANIA

**Contour map**
- Over 9,000 ft. (3,000 m)
- 1,500 -9,000 ft. (500 -3,000 m)
- 0 - 1,500 ft. (0 - 500 m)

# Finland

**Area:** 130,129 sq. miles (337,032 km²)
**Population:** 4,971,000
**Capital:** Helsinki (pop. with suburbs 987,000)
**Other cities:** Tampere 260,000; Turku 160,000;
**Highest point:** Haltiatunturi 4,357 ft. (1,328 m)
**Official languages:** Finnish, Swedish
**Religion:** Protestantism
**Currency:** Markka
**Main exports:** Paper and paper products, metal products and machinery, wood and wood products
**Government:** Constitutional republic
**Per capita GNP:** U.S. $22,060

Finland is a country sandwiched between Scandinavia and Russia. It is mostly flat, with a winding coastline. About 9 percent of Finland is covered by water. There are around 55,000 lakes that fill hollows created by glaciers during the Ice Age. The far north forms part of Lapland, home of the nomadic Lapp people, and lies within the Arctic Circle. Winters are long and severe, but the short summers are warm. Most Finns live in towns and work in industry. Agriculture is confined to the south of the country. Sweden conquered Finland in the 1200s. Russia fought Sweden for control of Finland, which came under Russian rule in 1809. It became independent in 1917. After World War II, when Finland was invaded by Soviet troops, it lost a large part of its land to the former USSR. It now has friendly relations with Russia.

## ECONOMIC SURVEY

**Farming:** Most of the farmland lies in the south of the country. Sugar beet, oats, barley, and potatoes are grown. Farmers raise cattle and pigs, and in the north reindeer are reared.
**Forestry:** Trees cover more than 70 percent of the land. Birch, pine, and spruce are logged. Wood pulp, plywood, paper and paper products are major exports.
**Mining:** Finland has useful deposits of copper, titanium, iron, and vanadium.
**Industry:** Products based on wood are the mainstay of Finland's industry. Engineering, glass, shipbuilding, textiles, and electronics are also important. Finland has hydro-electric power, but no oil, gas, or coal.

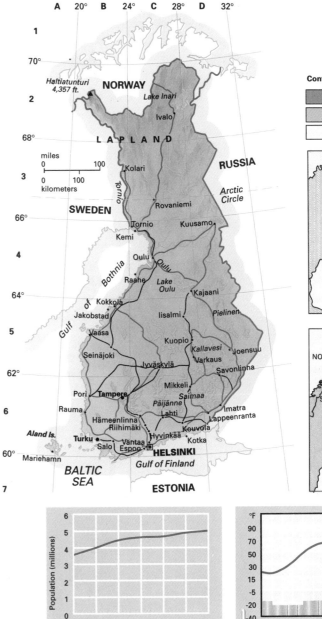

**Contour map**

- Over 3,000 ft. (1,000 m)
- 1,500 - 3,000 ft. (500 - 1,000 m)
- 0 - 1,500 ft. (0 - 500 m)

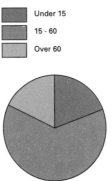

**Imports and exports**

Imports ■ Exports

**Age distribution**

■ Under 15
■ 15 - 60
■ Over 60

**Population trend**

**Climate - Helsinki**

# France

**Area:** 211,208 sq. miles (547,026 km²)
**Population:** 56,342,000
**Capital:** Paris (pop. with suburbs 8,707,000)
**Other cities:** Lyon 1,221,000; Marseilles 1,111,000; Lille 946,000
**Highest point:** Mont Blanc 15,771 ft. (4,807 m)
**Official language:** French
**Religions:** Roman Catholicism, Protestantism, Islam
**Currency:** French franc
**Main exports:** Machinery, agricultural products, chemicals, transportation equipment
**Government:** Constitutional republic
**Per capita GNP:** U.S. $17,830

France is the third largest nation in Europe, after Russia and the Ukraine. Much of the land consists of fertile plains and rolling hills. The borders are mostly mountainous; the Pyrenees in the southwest form a barrier with Spain, in the southeast the Alps separate France from Italy and Switzerland, and in the northeast are the Vosges Mountains. In central France the only high ground is the Massif Central. Paris is situated in a saucer-shaped depression enclosed by hills. The Aquitaine basin in the southwest is a low plain, partly fringed with coastal sand dunes. The climate varies from moist and cool in the north to hot and dry (in summer) in the south. Much of the land is farmland or forest. France has coastlines on the Atlantic Ocean to the west and the Mediterranean Sea to the south.

**Age distribution**
- Under 15
- 15 - 60
- Over 60

**Contour map**
- 0 - 1,500 ft. (0 - 500 m)
- 1,500 - 3,000 ft. (500 - 1,000 m)
- Over 3,000 ft. (1,000 m)

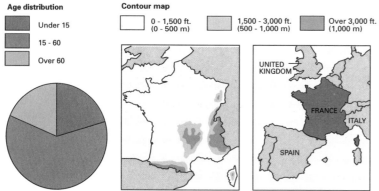

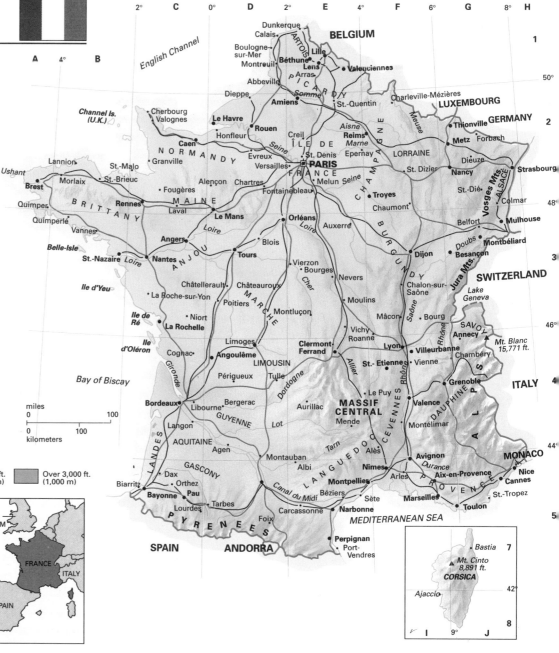

FRENCH HISTORY. In the 50s B.C. the country, then known as Gaul, was conquered by the Romans. In A.D. 486 it became an independent kingdom, and was one of Europe's leading powers throughout the Middle Ages. Kings of England claimed the French crown, and this led to the Hundred Years' War (1137-1453). The French monarchy was overthrown by the Revolution of 1789. After years of turmoil during which France was successively a republic, an empire under Napoleon Bonaparte, a monarchy, a republic again, and once more an empire, it finally settled down as a republic in 1875. France fought Germany in the Franco-Prussian War of 1870-1871, and again in World War I (1914-1918). During World War II (1939-1945) France was again invaded by German armies. Part of the country was occupied, the rest coming under the Vichy regime. After the war, France relinquished most of its overseas territories, including Indochina and Algeria. Economically, it recovered rapidly as a founder member of the European Community, this time with Germany as its main ally.

## ECONOMIC SURVEY

**Farming:** France is Europe's leading farming nation. Wheat, barley, oats, flax, sugar beet, fruit, and vegetables are grown. Livestock includes dairy cattle and sheep. France is renowned for its wines and cheeses.
**Fishing:** Catches include cod, crabs, lobsters, monkfish, scallops, oysters, mussels, and tuna.
**Mining:** Coal, iron, natural gas, and sulfur are extracted.
**Industry:** France makes machinery, vehicles, aerospace and communications equipment, chemicals, and electronic equipment. Oil refining is also important. French perfumes, silk and cotton textiles and fashion goods are world famous. France is the world's fifth ranking exporting nation. Paris, the manufacturing heart, and regional centers are served by excellent road and rail links. It relies heavily on nuclear power.

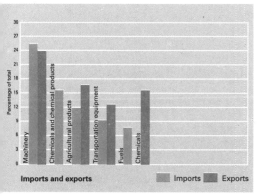

**Imports and exports**
Imports ▮ Exports

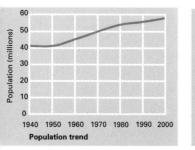

**Population trend**

**Climate - Paris**

# Monaco

**Area:** 0.7 sq. miles (1.9 km²)
**Population:** 29,000
**Capital:** Monaco
**Other towns:** Monte Carlo
**Official language:** French
**Religion:** Roman Catholicism
**Currency:** French franc
**Economy:** Trade figures included with France; tourism is a major industry
**Government:** Constitutional monarchy and principality

The principality of Monaco is one of the smallest countries in the world. It lies at the foot of the Alpes Maritimes mountains on the southeast Mediterranean coast of France. There are four districts: Monaco-Ville, the capital; La Condamine, a resort area; Monte Carlo, with its gambling casino; and Fontvieille, which is the industrial region. Its rulers since 1297 have been members of the Grimaldi family. Monaco was under Italian domination for centuries until 1793 when it was seized by France. In 1815 it was put under Sardinian protection, and from 1861 was independent under French protection. It is a constitutional monarchy, with two elected bodies — the National Council and the Communal Council. Once the playground of rich visitors, Monaco now earns most of its income from tourism and banking. Land reclaimed from the sea is being used for new building, and there are plans to develop light industries. Monaco has a harbor but no airport, the nearest main airport being at Nice in France. It is noted for its annual Grand Prix motor race around the twisting streets.

**Contour map**
☐ 0 - 1,500 ft. (0 - 500 m)

FRANCE    SWITZ.

ITALY

MONACO

**Climate - Monte Carlo**

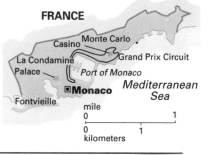

**FRANCE**
Casino   Monte Carlo
La Condamine   Grand Prix Circuit
Palace   Port of Monaco
■Monaco   Mediterranean Sea
Fontvieille
mile
0         1
0         1
kilometers

# French Guiana

**Area:** 34,749 sq. miles (90,000 km²)
**Population:** 98,000
**Capital:** Cayenne (pop. 38,000)
**Highest point:** 2,723 ft. (830 m) in the south of the country
**Official language:** French
**Religion:** Christianity
**Currency:** French franc
**Main exports:** Shrimps rice, wood, and metal products
**Government:** French Overseas Department
**Per capita GNP:** U.S. $2,130

French Guiana is the only one of the three Guianas not to achieve independence. The others are now called Guyana and Surinam. It forms part of the Guiana Highlands, but is mainly low lying because of river erosion. There is a swampy coastal plain, with mangroves. Dense, tropical, hardwood forests cover most of the interior. The climate is hot and wet. The population is mainly Creole, with Native American, black, French, Lebanese, Chinese, Brazilian, and Southeast Asian minorities. In 1503 the Spanish were the first European settlers, followed in 1643 by the French who founded Cayenne, the capital. French rule began officially in 1667. From 1852 to 1939 France used the territory as a penal colony, and Devil's Island became notorious. The country was made an overseas department of France in 1946. It is the site of the European Space Agency's rocket-launching base.

## ECONOMIC SURVEY

**Farming:** Most agriculture is at subsistence level. The farmers produce truck farm vegetables, rice and other cereals, citrus fruit, and bananas. Rice is a cash crop. Cattle, pigs, and poultry are kept.
**Forestry:** Resources are great, but remain largely untapped.
**Fishing:** U.S. and French fishing boats operate. Shrimps are exported.
**Mining:** French Guiana has few minerals, except for sand and gravel, and a small amount of gold.
**Industry:** Industrial activities include food processing, especially yogurt and other milk products, plywood and other timber products, leather goods, clothing, and beer.

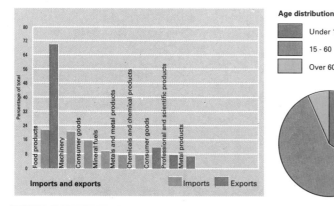

**Imports and exports**

Food products · Machinery · Consumer goods · Mineral fuels · Metals and metal products · Chemicals and chemical products · Consumer goods · Professional and scientific products · Metal products

Percentage of total

Imports · Exports

**Age distribution**

- Under 15
- 15 - 60
- Over 60

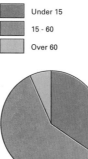

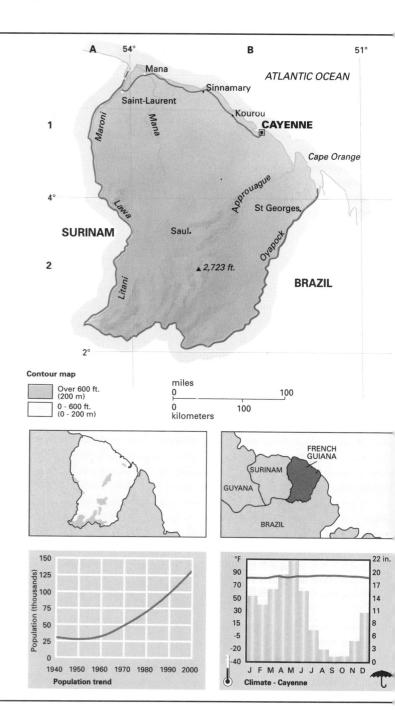

ATLANTIC OCEAN

SURINAM · BRAZIL

CAYENNE · Cape Orange · St Georges · Saul. · ▲ 2,723 ft.

Mana · Sinnamary · Saint-Laurent · Kourou

Maroni · Mana · Lawa · Litani · Approuague · Oyapock

**Contour map**

- Over 600 ft. (200 m)
- 0 - 600 ft. (0 - 200 m)

miles 0 — 100
kilometers 0 — 100

FRENCH GUIANA · SURINAM · GUYANA · BRAZIL

**Population trend**

Population (thousands)

1940 1950 1960 1970 1980 1990 2000

**Climate - Cayenne**

°F · 22 in.

J F M A M J J A S O N D

# Gabon and São Tomé and Príncipe

**GABON: Area:** 103,347 sq. miles (267,667 km²)
**Population:** 1,273,000
**Capital:** Libreville (pop. 352,000)
**Government:** Single-party republic
**Per capita GNP:** U.S. $2,770
**SÃO TOMÉ AND PRÍNCIPE: Area:** 372 sq. miles (964 km²)
**Population:** 121,000
**Capital:** São Tomé (pop. 35,000)
**Government:** Multiparty republic
**Per capita GNP:** U.S. $360

Gabon and São Tomé are two African countries linked by common trading interests. Gabon, on the mainland, has a coastal plain, behind which rise plateaus and mountains. Most of the country is drained by the Ogooué River. Rain forest covers 75 percent of the land. The people speak some 40 different languages, the biggest ethnic group being the Fang. A French colony from 1919, Gabon became independent in 1960. About 125 miles (200 kilometers) west of Gabon in the Gulf of Guinea are the islands of São Tomé and Príncipe which form a republic. The people are Creoles, of mixed African and European origins. The islands are volcanic. From 1522 they were Portuguese-ruled, and became independent in 1975.

## ECONOMIC SURVEY

**Farming:** Cocoa beans, coffee, and rice are grown for export in Gabon. Cassava is the main food crop. São Tomé's products include cocoa beans, bananas, coconuts, copra, kola nuts, and coffee.
**Fishing:** São Tomé has a busy fishing fleet.
**Forestry:** Timber is a major resource in Gabon, which has valuable hardwoods.
**Mining:** Crude petroleum and its products are Gabon's leading exports. The country has iron ore, manganese, and uranium.
**Industry:** There is little industry in São Tomé. It is developing in Gabon, based on oil.

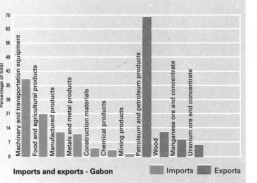

**Imports and exports - Gabon**

Percentage of total

Machinery and transportation equipment; Food and agricultural products; Manufactured products; Metals and metal products; Construction materials; Chemical products; Mining products; Petroleum and petroleum products; Wood; Manganese ore and concentrate; Uranium ore and concentrate

Imports  Exports

**Age distribution - Gabon**

Under 15
15 - 60
Over 60

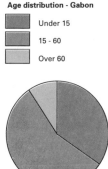

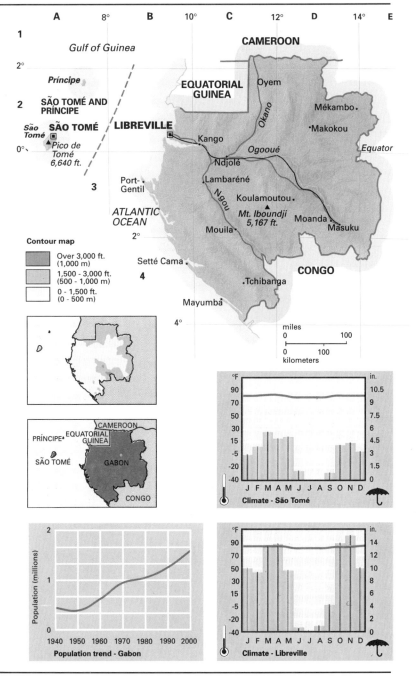

**Contour map**

Over 3,000 ft. (1,000 m)
1,500 - 3,000 ft. (500 - 1,000 m)
0 - 1,500 ft. (0 - 500 m)

miles 0 100
kilometers 0 100

**Climate - São Tomé**

°F / in.
J F M A M J J A S O N D

**Population trend - Gabon**

Population (millions)
1940 1950 1960 1970 1980 1990 2000

**Climate - Libreville**

°F / in.
J F M A M J J A S O N D

*see* AFRICA, page 14

# Germany

**Area:** 137,744 sq. miles (356,755 km²)
**Population:** 77,754,000
**Capital:** Berlin (pop. 3,301,000)
**Other cities:** Hamburg 1,594,000; Munich 1,189,000
**Highest point:** Zugspitze 9,721 ft. (2,963 m)
**Official language:** German
**Religions:** Protestantism, Roman Catholicism
**Currency:** Mark
**Main exports:** Machinery and transportation equipment, chemicals and chemical products, iron and steel, minerals, food
**Government:** Constitutional republic
**Per capita GNP:** West U.S. $20,750; East U.S. $14,420

Germany has three main land regions: the mountainous south which includes the Bavarian Alps; the hills, plateaus, and low horsts (block mountains) of the central region; and the northern plains where there are many lakes and marshes. This plains area stretches to the sandy islands and dunes on the shores of the North and Baltic seas. Major rivers of Germany are the Rhine, Danube, Oder, Weser, and Elbe. The Danube is Europe's second longest river, and rises in the Black Forest. Germany's climate is continental with moderate rainfall. The north has cooler summers and milder winters than the south. Most of the mineral wealth lies in western Germany, which contains the industrial region of the Ruhr valley, with its coalfields.

## ECONOMIC SURVEY

**Farming:** Leading crops include barley, oats, rye, potatoes, and sugar- beet. In the central uplands and the southwest grapes (for wine), hops, and tobacco are grown. The southeast has the best pasture for livestock. Farmers raise cattle, horses, pigs, poultry, and sheep.
**Fishing:** The catch includes cod, pollack, salmon, and mussels.
**Mining:** Germany has good reserves of hard coal, lignite, iron ore, potash, and other minerals.
**Industry:** Includes iron and steel, chemicals, transportation equipment and vehicles, consumer goods, precision instruments, optical goods, textiles, and electronics.

**Age distribution**
for former West Germany

- Under 15
- 15 - 60
- Over 60

**Age distribution**
for former East Germany

- Under 15
- 15 - 60
- Over 60

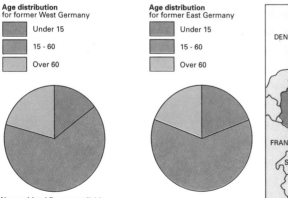

**No combined figures available**

GERMAN HISTORY. Germany was divided under the Roman Empire, with numerous Germanic tribes competing for dominance. During the Middle Ages, German dynasties supplied the rulers of the Holy Roman Empire, which was a loose federation of many small states. The Thirty Years' War (1618-1648), between Protestants and Catholics, ruined much of Germany. In the 1700s Prussia became the most powerful German state. Following Prussia's defeat of France in the war of 1870, Germany was united under Prussian leadership in 1871. Defeat in World War I (1914-1918) was followed by the disaster of Nazi rule under Adolf Hitler. The Nazis took advantage of economic problems and popular discontent following the treaty which ended World War I. They established a dictatorship, and embarked on a policy of brutal repression, persecution, and aggression. Germany's invasion of Poland led to World War II (1939-1945). After Germany's defeat, it was divided by the Allies. West Germany became a federal republic in 1949. East Germany was created by the former Soviet Union as a Communist state. West Germany thrived economically, outstripping the East. It was a founder member of the European Community, and became Europe's strongest economic power. Reunification of the two Germanies came with surprising suddenness in 1989-1990. The Communist government in the East collapsed, faced with economic stagnation and discontent among its people. The Berlin Wall, erected by the Communists in 1961, and a symbol of the Cold War, came down. The first all-German elections since the 1930s were held to choose united Germany's new government in 1990. The reunited country once more had Berlin as its capital.

**INDUSTRIAL PROFILE**
German reunification has created Europe's most powerful industrial giant. However, factories in the east are old-fashioned and inefficient, and will need much investment to bring them into line with those in the west. This has put severe economic pressure on the united country. Agriculture accounts for only 4 percent of the work force, but is still important within the German economy. More than 1.5 million immigrants or "guest workers," from Italy, Turkey, Yugoslavia, and elsewhere, work in Germany. They now compete for jobs with workers from East Germany.

**Contour map**

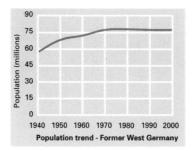

| | |
|---|---|
| ▓ | Over 3,000 ft. (1,000 m) |
| ▒ | 1,500 -3,000 ft. (500 - 1,000 m) |
| ☐ | 0 - 1,500 ft. (0 - 500 m) |

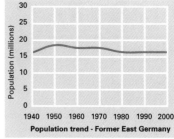

Population trend - Former West Germany

Population trend - Former East Germany

No combined figures available

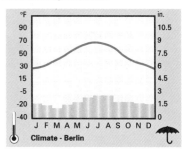

Climate - Berlin

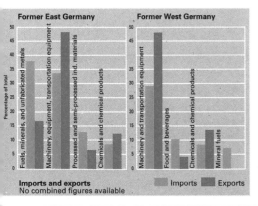

**Imports and exports**
No combined figures available

Former East Germany

Former West Germany

▨ Imports  ▧ Exports

**GERMAN LÄNDER (federal states)**

| | Länd | Area (sq. miles) | Area (km²) | Population (1987) |
|---|---|---|---|---|
| 1 | Baden-Württemberg | 13,804 | 35,751 | 9,286,000 |
| 2 | Bavaria | 27,241 | 70,553 | 10,903,000 |
| 3 | Berlin* | 341 | 883 | 3,301,000 |
| 4 | Brandenberg | 11,220 | 29,059 | 2,700,000 |
| 5 | Bremen | 156 | 404 | 660,000 |
| 6 | Hamburg | 292 | 755 | 1,593,000 |
| 7 | Hesse | 8,153 | 21,115 | 5,508,000 |
| 8 | Lower Saxony | 18,316 | 47,438 | 7,162,000 |
| 9 | Mecklenburg-West Pomerania | 9,204 | 23,838 | 2,100,000 |
| 10 | North Rhine-Westphalia | 13,154 | 34,068 | 16,712,000 |
| 11 | Rhineland -Palatinate | 7,663 | 19,848 | 3,631,000 |
| 12 | Saarland | 992 | 2,569 | 1,056,000 |
| 13 | Saxony | 7,080 | 18,337 | 5,000,000 |
| 14 | Saxony Anhalt | 7,894 | 20,445 | 3,000,000 |
| 15 | Schleswig-Holstein | 6,072 | 15,727 | 2,554,000 |
| 16 | Thuringia | 6,275 | 16,251 | 2,500,000 |

* Combined East and West Berlin

# Ghana

**Area:** 92,100 sq. miles (238,537 km²)
**Population:** 15,020,000
**Capital:** Accra (pop. 949,000)
**Other cities:** Kumasi 385,000; Sekondi-Takoradi 116,000
**Highest point:** Mount Afadjato, near Ho 2,904 ft. (885 m)
**Official language:** English
**Religions:** Christianity, traditional beliefs, Islam
**Currency:** Cedi
**Main exports:** Cocoa, gold, timber, manganese
**Government:** Military regime
**Per capita GNP:** U.S. $380

Ghana has a southern coast on the Atlantic Ocean. The country is mostly low lying and contains the artificial Lake Volta, created by damming the river Volta to generate electricity. The most fertile soils are in the hilly southwest. The only highlands are in the southeast. The climate is hot, with marked wet and dry seasons. The people are Black Africans belonging to eight major ethnic groups and speaking about 100 languages and dialects. People from northern African kingdoms settled here in the 1200s. Portuguese explorers arrived by sea in 1471, began trading in slaves, and found that the land was rich in gold. They named the region the Gold Coast. Britain governed the Gold Coast as a colony from 1875 until 1957. It then became independent as Ghana, taking in western Togo. Ghana has been a republic since 1960.

## ECONOMIC SURVEY

**Farming:** Cocoa is the chief cash crop, and the main export, although Ghana is no longer world leader in cocoa. Other crops include cassava, coconuts, palm oil and kernels, corn, yams, and other vegetables. Cattle, pigs, sheep, and goats are kept.
**Forestry:** The valuable hardwood trees, including mahogany and sapele, are being heavily exploited.
**Fishing:** Anchovies are the chief catch at sea. Inland lakes are well stocked.
**Mining:** Gold, diamonds, manganese, and bauxite are mined.
**Industry:** Aluminum smelting uses power from the Volta Dam hydroelectric scheme. Fuel oil, cement, and foodstuffs are also produced.

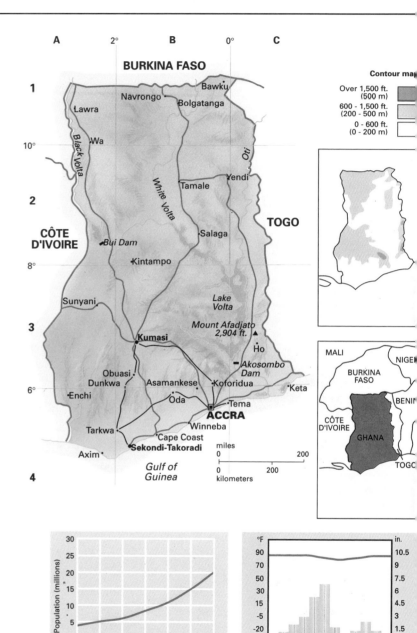

miles 0 — 200
kilometers 0 — 200

Contour map

Over 1,500 ft. (500 m)
600 - 1,500 ft. (200 - 500 m)
0 - 600 ft. (0 - 200 m)

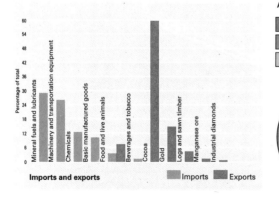

**Imports and exports**
Imports | Exports

**Age distribution**
Under 15
15 - 60
Over 60

**Population trend**

**Climate - Accra**

# Greece

**Area:** 50,944 sq. miles (131,944 km²)
**Population:** 10,141,000
**Capital:** Athens (pop. with suburbs 3,027,000)
**Other cities:** Thessaloniki 406,000
**Highest point:** Mt. Olympus 9,550 ft. (2911 m)
**Official language:** Greek
**Religion:** Greek Orthodoxy
**Currency:** Drachma
**Main exports:** Food products such as olive oil, tobacco, clothing and textiles, petroleum products
**Government:** Constitutional republic
**Per capita GNP:** U.S. $5,340

Greece occupies the southern part of the mountainous Balkan peninsula and many islands. These islands include the Cyclades, the Dodecanese or South Sporades, North Sporades, and Ionian islands. The largest island is Crete. The southern Peloponnese region of mainland Greece is linked to the north by the narrow Isthmus of Corinth. The main lowland regions are the Plain of Thessaly and the coastal plains of Macedonia and Thrace. The climate is Mediterranean, with severe winters only in the mountains. Ancient Greek civilization made an immense contribution to Western culture. Greece came under Roman rule in 146 B.C., and from A.D. 365 was under Turkish rule. It won its freedom in 1830 as a monarchy, which ended in 1974. Greece joined the European Community in 1981.

## ECONOMIC SURVEY

**Farming:** Only about one third of the land is suitable for crops. Farmers grow corn, wheat, tomatoes, sugar beet, grapes, olives, tobacco, potatoes, and citrus fruits. They rear sheep, goats, pigs, cattle, and chickens. Donkeys are still used as beasts of burden in country districts.
**Mining:** Lignite, bauxite, iron ore, lead, and zinc are mined, together with nickel, chromite, magnesite, and asbestos, and some oil is produced.
**Industry:** Greece relies heavily on tourism to earn foreign currency. Its merchant navy, the fourth largest in the world, is another important money earner. Factories turn out textiles, chemicals, clothing, shoes, and machinery.

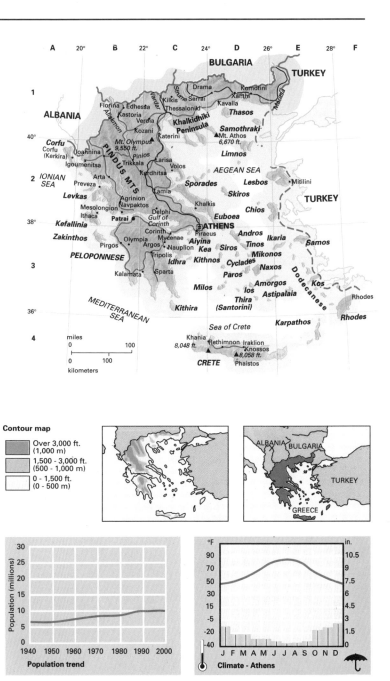

**Contour map**

- Over 3,000 ft. (1,000 m)
- 1,500 - 3,000 ft. (500 - 1,000 m)
- 0 - 1,500 ft. (0 - 500 m)

**Imports and exports**

Machinery and transportation equipment; Food, beverages, and tobacco; Crude petroleum; Chemical products; Textiles; Petroleum products; Furs

Imports · Exports

**Age distribution**

- Under 15
- 15 - 60
- Over 60

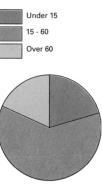

**Population trend**

**Climate - Athens**

# Greenland

**Area:** 840,004 sq. miles (2,175,600 km²)
**Population:** 56,000
**Capital:** Godthaab (Nuuk, pop. 12,000)
**Other cities:** Holsteinsborg (Sisimiut) 4,800
**Highest point:** Mount Gunnbjorn 12,139 ft. (3,700 m)
**Official languages:** Danish, Greenlandic
**Religion:** Protestantism
**Currency:** Krone
**Main exports:** Shrimps and mollusks, fish, lead
**Government:** Self-governing part of Denmark
**Per capita GNP:** See Denmark

Greenland is a self-governing region of Denmark. It is the world's largest island, and contains the world's second largest ice sheet. The ice cap covers 80 percent of the land, and the coastal areas are the only regions suitable for human settlement. The south coast has warm summers, but winters are cold. Vegetation includes grasses, shrubs, and stunted willow and birch trees. The Greenlanders are mostly people of Inuit origin. They call their island Kalatdlit-Nunat. Their main industry is fishing, but some people carry on the ancient tradition of seal hunting. Vikings founded a colony in Greenland in about A.D. 960, but it vanished in the 1400s. Greenland became a Danish colony in 1721. In 1953 Greenland became a province of Denmark rather than a colony. It was granted internal self-government in 1979.

## ECONOMIC SURVEY

**Farming:** Very little of Greenland is suitable for agriculture, but potatoes and other vegetables are grown in the southwest. In the south there is some sheep and reindeer herding. In the north people hunt seals, polar bears, and arctic hares.

**Fishing:** This is Greenland's most important economic activity. Cod forms the biggest catch. Other catches include halibut, and shrimps.

**Mining:** There is some mining for zinc, lead, and uranium but most mineral deposits are poor.

**Industry:** Fish are salted, canned, or frozen on the island, largely for export. There is a shipyard at the fishing port of Holsteinsborg.

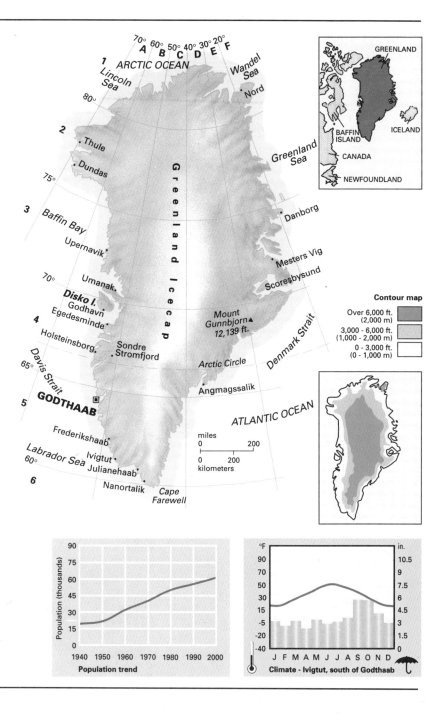

Contour map
- Over 6,000 ft. (2,000 m)
- 3,000 - 6,000 ft. (1,000 - 2,000 m)
- 0 - 3,000 ft. (0 - 1,000 m)

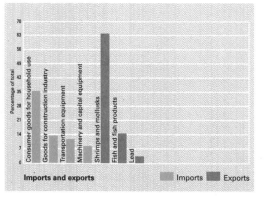

**Imports and exports**

Imports / Exports

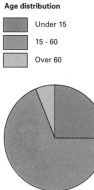

**Age distribution**
- Under 15
- 15 - 60
- Over 60

**Population trend**

**Climate - Ivigtut, south of Godthaab**

# Grenada and St. Vincent and the Grenadines

Grenada    St. Vincent

**GRENADA: Area:** 133 sq. miles (344 km²)
**Population:** 98,000
**Capital:** St. George's (pop. 7500)
**Government:** Constitutional monarchy
**Per capita GNP:** U.S. $1900
**ST. VINCENT AND THE GRENADINES:**
**Area:** 150 sq. miles (388 km²)
**Population:** 116,000
**Capital:** Kingstown (pop. 19,000)
**Government:** Constitutional monarchy
**Per capita GNP:** U.S. $1200

These two island countries are the most southerly of the Lesser Antilles. St. Vincent consists of the island of St. Vincent plus about 100 much smaller islands known as the Grenadines. Like so many Caribbean islands they are volcanic in origin, and Mount Soufrière, St. Vincent's highest point, is an active volcano. The climate is warm with tropical vegetation. Most of the people are descended from black slaves. Grenada is mountainous, forested, and very warm. Its people too are mostly blacks. St. Vincent and the Grenadines were a British colony from 1805 until independence in 1979. Grenada, French from 1674, became a British colony in 1763 and independent in 1974. U.S. forces overthrew a Marxist government there in 1983.

## ECONOMIC SURVEY

**Forestry:** Bananas, spices, and coconuts are the main cash crops on St. Vincent. The country is the world's major supplier of arrowroot (used in starch-making). Other crops include cassava, peanuts, and sweet potatoes. Grenada has a more mixed farm economy, with cocoa, spices (especially nutmeg), and bananas among its cash crops. Other fruit and cotton are also grown.
**Fishing:** Grenada's fishing fleet is being expanded.
**Industry:** In neither country has industry been developed. Food processing is the main activity. Tourism is growing.

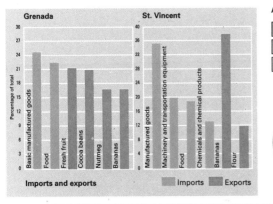

Grenada — St. Vincent
Imports and exports — Imports / Exports

**Age distribution - Grenada**
Under 15
15 - 60
Over 60

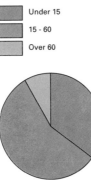

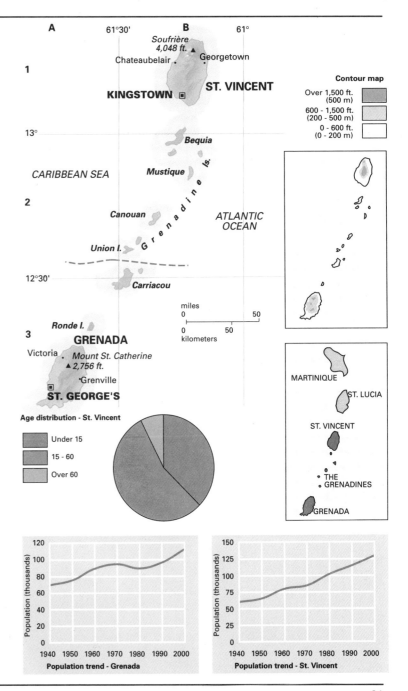

**Age distribution - St. Vincent**
Under 15
15 - 60
Over 60

Population trend - Grenada
Population trend - St. Vincent

# Guatemala

**Area:** 42,042 sq. miles (108,889 km²)
**Population:** 9,197,000
**Capital:** Guatemala City (pop. 2,000,000)
**Other cities:** Quezaltenango 246,000
**Highest point:** Volcán Tajumulco 13,845 ft. (4,220 m)
**Official language:** Spanish
**Religion:** Christianity
**Currency:** Quetzal
**Main exports:** Coffee, manufactured goods, sugar, bananas, cotton, beef, cardamom
**Government:** Multiparty republic
**Per capita GNP:** U.S. $920

Guatemala consists of a coastal plain facing the Pacific, a central highland region prone to earthquakes (having 27 volcanoes), a low forested plain in the north, and a short Caribbean coastline with mangrove swamps. The hills, where Guatemala City is situated, have a warm climate with heavy rainfall. The lowlands are hotter and even wetter. More than half the people are Mayans. The rest are of Spanish-Native American origin (known as Ladinos). A great Mayan civilization, based on the ceremonial center of Tikal, flourished until the A.D. 900s. Spain conquered the region in the 1520s. Guatemala became independent in 1821. It was part of the United Provinces of Central America (1823-1839). Its 20th-century history has been marked by political unrest and periods of military dictatorship. Civilian rule was restored in 1986.

## ECONOMIC SURVEY

**Farming:** The chief crop is coffee, grown on plantations. Bananas, cotton, sugarcane, and rubber are also grown. Guatemala is a leading source of chicle gum (from which chewing gum is made). Cardamom (a spice) is grown for the Middle Eastern market. Cattle, pigs, and sheep are reared.
**Forestry:** There are rich stands of trees such as mahogany.
**Mining:** Some oil, zinc, lead, and copper are produced.
**Industry:** There is little industry. Consumer goods such as food, drinks, and clothing are produced. Craft goods include Native American pottery and blankets. Despite attempts to start up new industries, many people lack jobs.

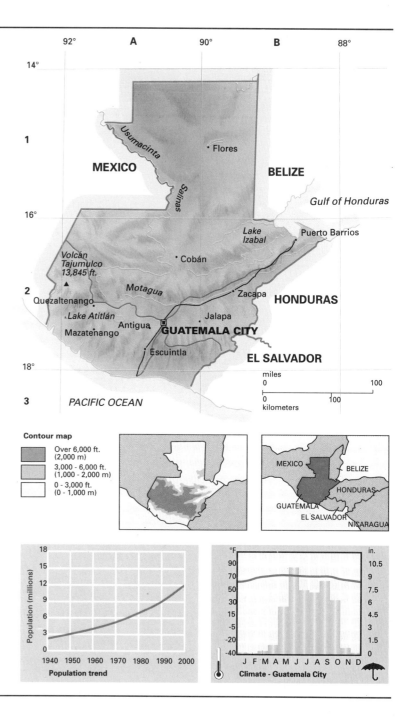

miles
0                    100

0          100
kilometers

**Contour map**

- Over 6,000 ft. (2,000 m)
- 3,000 - 6,000 ft. (1,000 - 2,000 m)
- 0 - 3,000 ft. (0 - 1,000 m)

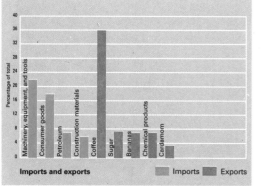

**Imports and exports**
Imports   Exports

**Age distribution**
- Under 15
- 15 - 60
- Over 60

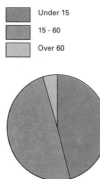

**Population trend**

**Climate - Guatemala City**

# Guinea

**Area:** 94,926 sq. miles (245,857 km²)
**Population:** 6,876,000
**Capital:** Conakry (pop. 705,000)
**Other cities:** Kankan 89,000
**Highest point:** Mount Nimba 5,800 ft. (1,768 m)
**Official language:** French
**Religions:** Islam, various traditional beliefs, Christianity
**Currency:** Guinea franc
**Main exports:** Bauxite, alumina, diamonds, coffee, hides, fruit
**Government:** Military regime
**Per capita GNP:** U.S. $430

Guinea faces the Atlantic Ocean on the west coast of Africa. Behind the coastal plain is the Fouta Djallon plateau, where the Gambia, Niger, and Sénégal rivers rise. The northeast contains the Upper Niger plains, while the southeast is mountainous, rising to Mount Nimba on the border with the Côte d'Ivoire and Liberia. The climate is tropical, with wet and dry seasons, and the vegetation is mainly savanna grassland. Most of the people of Guinea are Black Africans of the Fulani (Peul), Malinke, and Susu groups, speaking many languages. The Portuguese developed a slave trade from Guinea in the mid-1400s. Later, French traders moved in. France extended its control from 1849, despite opposition from Africans. In 1959 Guinea voted for independence from France. Sekou Touré, who died in 1984, was Guinea's first president.

## ECONOMIC SURVEY

**Farming:** About 80 percent of Guineans work on the land growing bananas, cassava, corn, groundnuts (peanuts), pineapples, plantains, rice, and sweet potatoes. Rice is the main food. Livestock are reared in the plains and the highlands.

**Minerals:** Guinea is potentially a rich country, with good reserves of minerals such as bauxite, gold, iron ore, diamonds, and uranium. Bauxite and alumina (partly processed bauxite) are the country's most valuable assets, followed by diamonds and gold.

**Industry:** Poor communications hold back development, but factories produce cigarettes and furniture, and assemble vehicles.

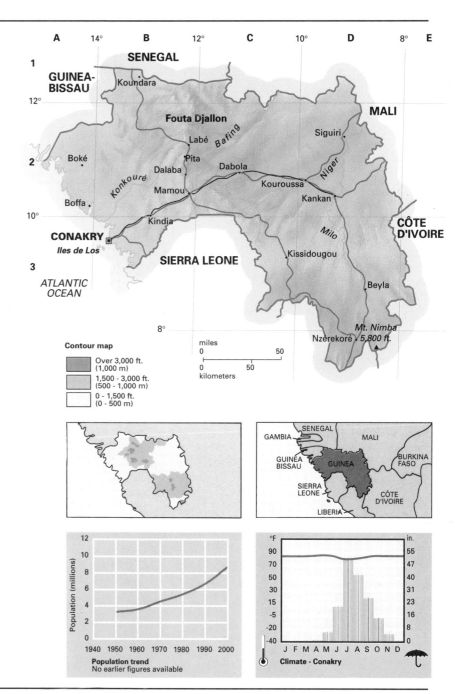

**Contour map**

- Over 3,000 ft. (1,000 m)
- 1,500 - 3,000 ft. (500 - 1,000 m)
- 0 - 1,500 ft. (0 - 500 m)

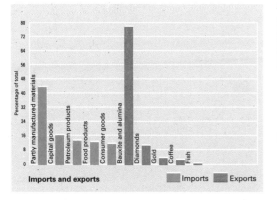

**Imports and exports**

Percentage of total

Partly manufactured materials · Capital goods · Petroleum products · Food products · Consumer goods · Bauxite and alumina · Diamonds · Gold · Coffee · Fish

Imports   Exports

**Age distribution**

- Under 15
- 15 - 60
- Over 60

**Population trend**
No earlier figures available

**Climate - Conakry**

# Guinea-Bissau

**Area:** 13,948 sq. miles (36,125 km²)
**Population:** 973,000
**Capital:** Bissau (pop. 125,000)
**Highest point:** On northeastern border, about 984 ft. (300 m)
**Official language:** Portuguese
**Religions:** Various traditional beliefs, Islam, Christianity
**Currency:** Peso
**Main exports:** Cashew nuts, fish, groundnuts (peanuts)
**Government:** Republic
**Per capita GNP:** U.S. $180

Guinea-Bissau, formerly known as Portuguese Guinea, lies between Guinea and Senegal in West Africa, with the Bijagós Islands off the coast. It is mostly low lying, with a broad coastal plain. Coastal vegetation includes rain forest and thick swamps. Inland are grassy savannas rising to higher ground. There are many rivers. The climate is tropical with wet and dry seasons. The people are more than 80 percent Black Africans, largely of the Balante, Fulani, Manjako, and Mandingo ethnic groups. Others are of mixed European and African origin. The Portuguese sighted the coast in 1447. They shipped slaves from the mainland to the Cape Verde Islands, which they ruled jointly with Portuguese Guinea from 1836 to 1879. Nationalists seeking independence began a guerrilla war in 1961, and in 1974 Guinea-Bissau became independent.

## ECONOMIC SURVEY

**Farming:** More than half of all workers are farmers, growing subsistence crops such as corn, sweet potatoes, and cassava. Beans, coconuts, palm kernels, sorghum, millet, and rice are also grown. Cashews are the principal cash crop, followed by groundnuts (peanuts) and palm kernels. Cattle, sheep, pigs, goats, and chickens are reared. The country is aiming for self-sufficiency in food. About a third of the land is forested.
**Fishing:** Shrimps and fish are exported.
**Industry:** Guinea-Bissau has few factories. Some produce palm oil products. There is some bauxite, but no other exploitable minerals have been discovered.

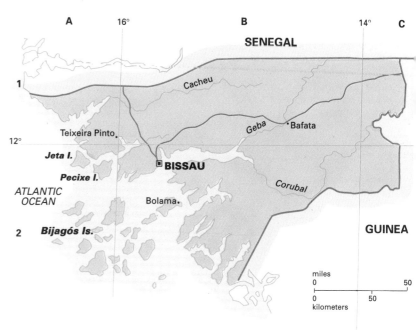

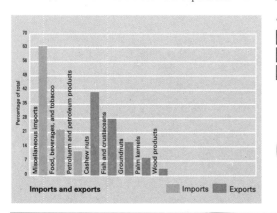

**Imports and exports** — Imports / Exports

**Age distribution**
- Under 15
- 15 - 60
- Over 60

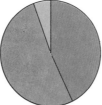

**Contour map**
- 0 - 600 ft. (0 - 200 m)

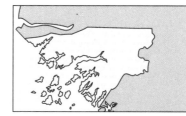

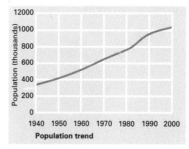

**Population trend**

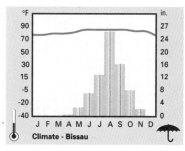

**Climate - Bissau**

# Guyana

**Area:** 83,000 sq. miles (214,969 km²)
**Population:** 754,000
**Capital:** Georgetown (pop. with suburbs 200,000)
**Other cities:** Linden 35,000
**Highest point:** Mount Roraima 9,094 ft. (2,772 m)
**Official language:** English
**Religions:** Christianity, Hinduism, Islam
**Currency:** Guyana dollar
**Main exports:** Bauxite (aluminum ore), alumina, sugarcane, rice
**Government:** Cooperative republic
**Per capita GNP:** U.S. $310

Guyana has a flat and cultivated coastal zone. Inland the ground rises through hills to the Guiana Highlands in the east and south. More than 80 percent of Guyana is covered with forest, with grassland in the higher mountains. The Essequibo is the main river. The climate is tropical. Most Guyanans live in the coastal region. About 50 percent are of Asian origin, mostly from India, about 33 percent are descendants of Black African slaves, and about 10 percent are of mixed origin. Native Americans, living mostly in the forests, make up roughly 5 percent. The region was settled by Dutch traders from about 1620. Britain captured it in 1796, and from 1814 until 1966 it formed the colony of British Guiana. In 1966 it became independent and changed its name to Guyana. The country became a republic within the Commonwealth in 1970.

## ECONOMIC SURVEY

**Farming:** Guyana is fortunate in having rich soil. Sugarcane is the most important cash crop grown. On small farms near the coast people grow rice. Other crops include citrus fruits, cocoa, coconuts, coffee, corn, and plantains. Cattle are raised on ranches.
**Forestry:** Woodlands cover 85 percent of the land. Greenheart is the country's most valuable timber tree.
**Mining:** Bauxite is the chief mineral. There are also diamond, manganese, and gold mines.
**Industry:** Most industrial activity is small-scale and is related to the processing of sugar, rice, timber, and coconuts. Clothing and pharmaceuticals are also made.

**Population trend**

**Climate - Georgetown**

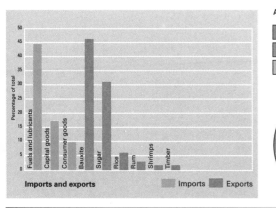

**Imports and exports**

Fuels and lubricants | Capital goods | Consumer goods | Bauxite | Sugar | Rice | Rum | Shrimps | Timber

Imports ■ Exports

**Age distribution**

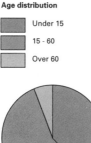

- Under 15
- 15 - 60
- Over 60

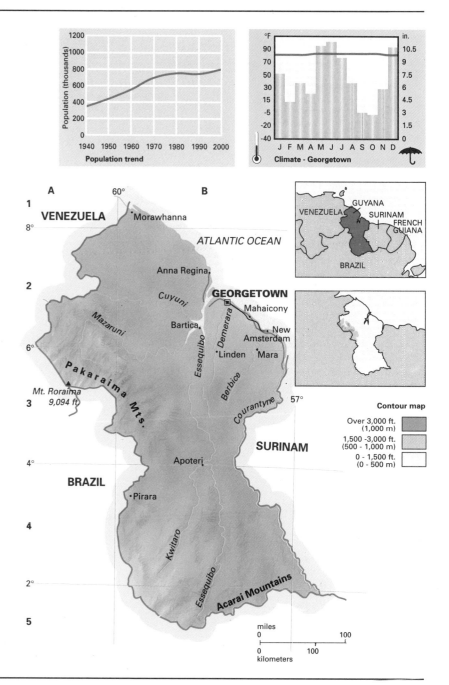

**A**     60°     **B**

1 — VENEZUELA — 8° — Morawhanna — ATLANTIC OCEAN

Anna Regina

2 — Cuyuni — GEORGETOWN — Mahaicony

Mazaruni — Bartica — New Amsterdam

6° — Essequibo — Demerara — Linden — Mara

Pakaraima Mts. — Berbice

Mt. Roraima 9,094 ft — Courantyne — 57°

3

SURINAM

4° — Apoteri

BRAZIL — Pirara

4 — Kwitaro

Essequibo — Acarai Mountains

2°

5

VENEZUELA — GUYANA — SURINAM — FRENCH GUIANA — BRAZIL

**Contour map**
- Over 3,000 ft. (1,000 m)
- 1,500 -3,000 ft. (500 - 1,000 m)
- 0 - 1,500 ft. (0 - 500 m)

miles
0      100
0    100
kilometers

*see* SOUTH AMERICA, page 159

# Haiti

**Area:** 10,714 sq. miles (27,750 km²)
**Population:** 5,590,000
**Capital:** Port-au-Prince (pop. 473,000)
**Other cities:** Cap-Haitien 72,000
**Highest point:** Mt. La Salle 8,793 ft. (2,680 m)
**Official language:** French
**Religion:** Christianity (most people practice voodoo, a blend of Christianity and traditional African beliefs)
**Currency:** Gourde
**Main exports:** Assembled goods, coffee
**Government:** Republic
**Per capita GNP:** U.S. $400

Haiti occupies the western part of the Caribbean island of Hispaniola. The interior is wooded and mountainous. Fertile plains make up roughly a fifth of the country. The climate is tropical, with the risk of hurricanes. Almost all the people of Haiti are of African slave descent. The mulattoes (people of mixed ancestry), about 5 percent of the population, form a social elite. Christopher Columbus reached Haiti in 1492 on his first voyage. The Arawak inhabitants were wiped out by ill-treatment and disease under Spanish rule. French pirates set up plantations in western Haiti, and France ruled the island from 1697 to 1804, when a revolution inspired by the earlier struggle of a black slave, Toussaint l'Ouverture, brought independence. After years of dictatorship under the Duvalier family, Haiti began moving haltingly toward democracy.

## ECONOMIC SURVEY

**Farming:** Almost all Haitians are peasant farmers. They work tiny plots, often on very steep hillsides, and most are barely self-sufficient. There are some big plantations. The most important cash crop is coffee, followed by cocoa and sugarcane. Other crops are sisal, rice, cotton, mangoes, plantains, sweet potatoes, and cassava. Cattle, pigs, horses, goats, and poultry are raised.

**Forestry:** Mahogany and other hardwood timbers are produced from the forests.

**Industry:** Small factories produce pharmaceuticals, soap, plastics, cement, fashion goods, and foodstuffs. Electronic and other components are assembled.

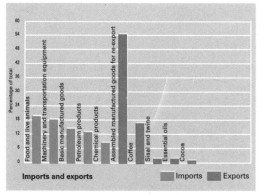

**Imports and exports**

**Age distribution**

- Under 15
- 15 - 60
- Over 60

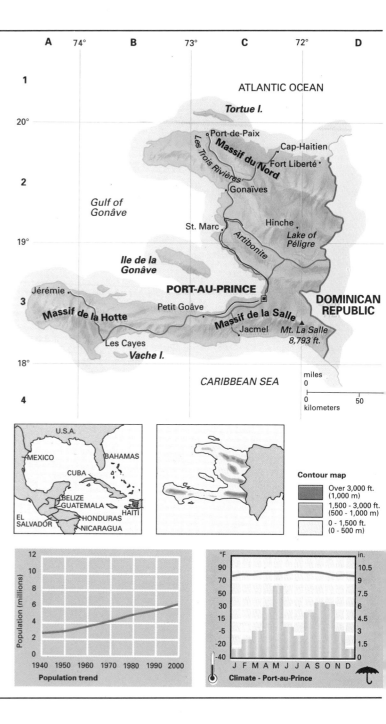

**Contour map**
- Over 3,000 ft. (1,000 m)
- 1,500 - 3,000 ft. (500 - 1,000 m)
- 0 - 1,500 ft. (0 - 500 m)

**Population trend**

**Climate - Port-au-Prince**

# Honduras

**Area:** 43,277 sq. miles (112,088 km²)
**Population:** 4,674,000
**Capital:** Tegucigalpa (pop. 605,000)
**Other cities:** San Pedro Sula 400,000;
El Progreso 105,000
**Highest point:** Cerros de Celaque 9,416 ft.
(2,870 m)
**Official language:** Spanish
**Religion:** Christianity
**Currency:** Lempira
**Main exports:** Coffee, bananas
**Government:** Republic
**Per capita GNP:** U.S. $900

Honduras has a coastline on the Caribbean Sea and an outlet to the Pacific Ocean through the Gulf of Fonseca. Behind the hot and humid Caribbean coastal plain are mountains and high plateaus, with a cooler and generally healthier climate. Forests, including oak and pine trees, cover much of the land. Most Hondurans are of mixed European and Native American origin. Honduras was part of the flourishing Mayan civilization until its sudden decline around A.D. 800. Christopher Columbus reached Honduras in 1502, and Spain ruled the region from 1525 to 1821. In 1537 Lempira (died 1539) led a brief rebellion against the Spaniards, who oppressed the native population. In 1838 Honduras became an independent republic. Its recent history has been one of military dictatorship and weak civilian governments.

## ECONOMIC SURVEY

**Farming:** The leading cash crops are coffee and bananas, grown on large plantations. The main food crop is corn. Farmers also grow beans, sugar, cotton, and tobacco. Beef and dairy cattle are reared in the upland valleys and southern grasslands.
**Forestry:** Hardwood and softwood timber is produced.
**Mining:** Lead, silver, and zinc are mined.
**Industry:** Most of the country's industrial enterprises are small, and mainly produce goods such as foods, textiles, and clothing, chemicals and light metals for local consumption. Sawmills handle the timber used in the paper, furniture, and wood-product industries. Pottery is an important craft.

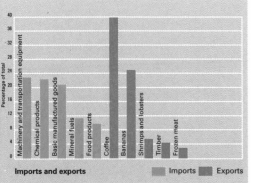

**Imports and exports**

**Age distribution**

Under 15
15 - 60
Over 60

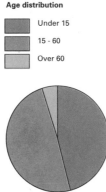

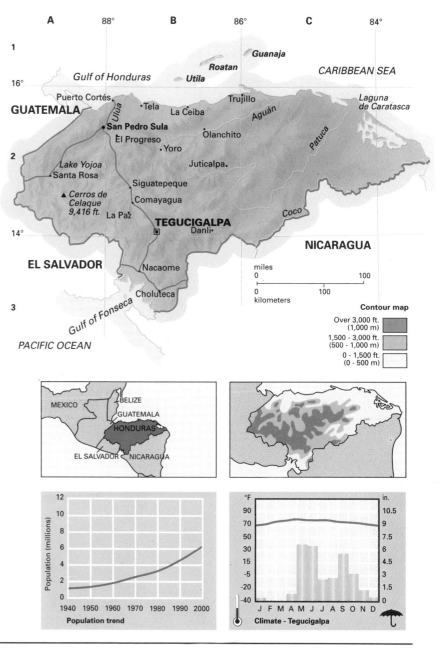

Contour map

Over 3,000 ft. (1,000 m)
1,500 - 3,000 ft. (500 - 1,000 m)
0 - 1,500 ft. (0 - 500 m)

**Population trend**

**Climate - Tegucigalpa**

# Hungary

**Area:** 35,919 sq. miles (93,030 km²)
**Population:** 10,563,000
**Capital:** Budapest (pop. 2,115,000)
**Other cities:** Debrecen 220,000
**Highest point:** Mount Kékes 3,330 ft. (1,015 m)
**Official language:** Hungarian (Magyar)
**Religions:** Roman Catholicism, Protestantism
**Currency:** Forint
**Main exports:** Machinery and transportation equipment, agricultural and food products, semi-finished products, consumer goods
**Government:** Multiparty democracy
**Per capita GNP:** U.S. $8,650

Most of Hungary is a large, flat plain, crossed by the rivers Danube and Tisza. The fertile, hilly Little Alfold in the northwest is separated from the Great Alfold by a limestone ridge known as the Bakony Forest. Lake Balaton covers 230 square miles (596 square kilometers) and is central Europe's largest lake. Winters are cold and summers are hot. The people of Hungary are mostly Magyars, speaking a language belonging to the Finno-Ugric language group. There are German, Slovak, and Romanian minorities. Magyar herding peoples settled in Hungary in the 800s. In the 1400s and 1500s the country was weakened by war against invading Turks. From 1700 Hungary came under Austrian rule. The Austro-Hungarian empire broke up in 1918. Hungary came under Communist Party rule in 1948, but moved towards democracy in the late 1980s.

## ECONOMIC SURVEY

**Farming:** About 18 percent of the work force is engaged in agriculture. Arable land, orchards, and vineyards cover more than half the country. Corn and wheat are the main crops. Other crops include sugarbeet, barley, potatoes, and sunflowers.
**Mining:** Hungary is the eighth largest producer of bauxite, the raw material of aluminum. Coal, iron ore, uranium, and other minerals are mined.
**Industry:** Hungary lacks large supplies of cheap electricity for making finished aluminum in bulk. It has to import power and many of its raw materials. Its factories produce chemicals, machinery, transportation equipment, textiles, and processed food.

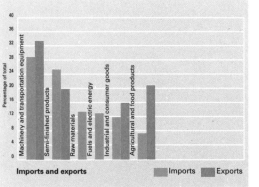

**Imports and exports**

Imports ■ Exports ■

**Age distribution**

■ Under 15
■ 15 - 60
■ Over 60

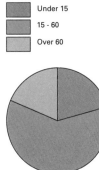

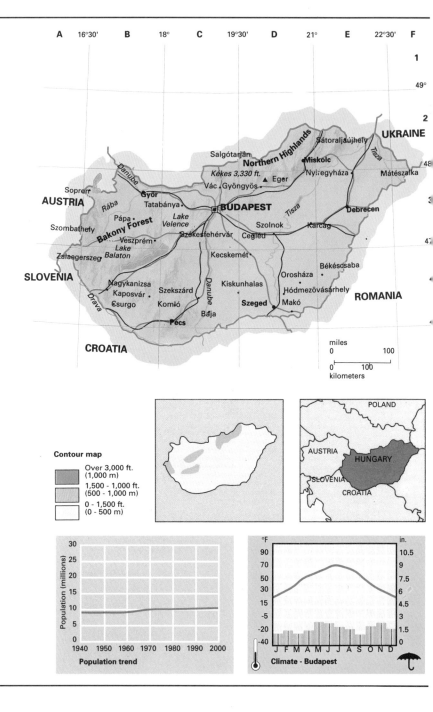

**Contour map**

■ Over 3,000 ft. (1,000 m)
■ 1,500 - 1,000 ft. (500 - 1,000 m)
■ 0 - 1,500 ft. (0 - 500 m)

**Population trend**

**Climate - Budapest**

# Iceland

**Area:** 39,769 sq. miles (103,000 km²)
**Population:** 255,000
**Capital:** Reykjavik (pop. 95,800)
**Other cities:** Kópavogur 15,500
**Highest point:** Hvannadalshnúkur 6,952 ft. (2,119 m)
**Official language:** Icelandic
**Religion:** Protestantism
**Currency:** Krona
**Main exports:** Fish, aluminum; plans began in the early 1990s to export electric power
**Government:** Constitutional republic
**Per capita GNP:** U.S. $21,240

Iceland is a small but prosperous island republic in the North Atlantic Ocean. The landscape is rugged, with large snowfields, glaciers, volcanoes, and hot springs, and a deeply indented coastline. The north of Iceland has an Arctic climate with brief summers and long, freezing cold winters. The warm ocean currents of the North Atlantic Drift bring milder weather to the south. Iceland's only large city is the capital, Reykjavik. Less than 1 percent of the land is suitable for farming, but 15 percent of the people work on the land. About 20 percent work in the main industries – fishing and processing fish products. Iceland was first colonized by Vikings from Norway in A.D. 874, and united with Norway in 1262. From 1380 it was under Danish rule, becoming self-governing in 1918 and an independent republic in 1944, during World War II.

## ECONOMIC SURVEY

**Farming:** The main crops include hay, potatoes, and turnips. Cattle and sheep are reared. Tomatoes, cucumbers, grapes, flowers, and other crops are grown in glasshouses, which are heated by water from hot springs.
**Fishing:** Capelin, cod, herring, lobsters, and shrimps are among the species caught. Fish products make up over 70 percent of Iceland's exports. Coastal waters have suffered from over-fishing.
**Industry:** There is some metalworking and furniture-making, but no heavy industry apart from an aluminum-smelting plant. Iceland has hydroelectric and geothermal energy resources, but no coal, oil, or gas.

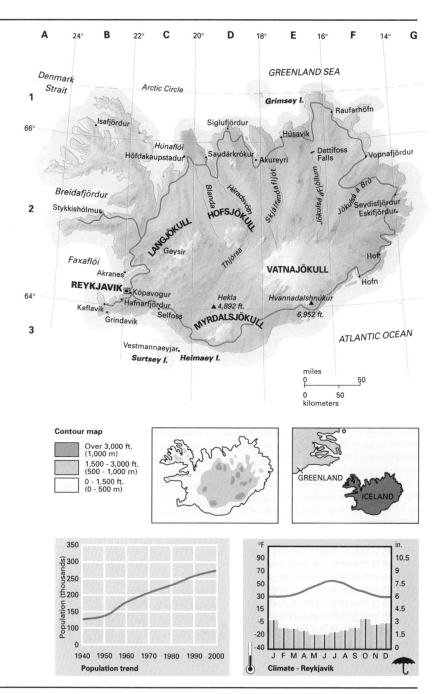

### Contour map

- Over 3,000 ft. (1,000 m)
- 1,500 - 3,000 ft. (500 - 1,000 m)
- 0 - 1,500 ft. (0 - 500 m)

GREENLAND
ICELAND

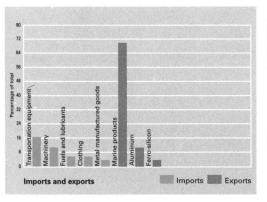

**Imports and exports**

Transportation equipment, Machinery, Fuels and lubricants, Clothing, Metal manufactured goods, Marine products, Aluminum, Ferro-silicon

Imports / Exports

### Age distribution

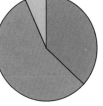

- Under 15
- 15 - 60
- Over 60

**Population trend**
1940 1950 1960 1970 1980 1990 2000

**Climate - Reykjavik**
J F M A M J J A S O N D

# India

**Area:** 1,269,346 sq. miles (3,287,590 km²)
**Population:** 853,373,000
**Capital:** New Delhi (pop. 273,000)
**Other cities:** Calcutta (pop. with suburbs)
9,166,000; Bombay 8,243,000; Delhi 4,884,000
**Highest point:** Kanchenjunga 28,208 ft. (8,598 m)
**Official language:** Hindi
**Religions:** Hinduism, Islam, Christianity,
Sikhism, Buddhism
**Currency:** Rupee
**Main exports:** Textiles, gems, machinery
**Government:** Multiparty republic
**Per capita GNP:** U.S. $350

India is the world's seventh largest country in land area, and the second largest in population. Most of India has three seasons: cool, hot, and rainy. The landscape is varied, including the Thar Desert, jungles, broad plains, and tropical lowlands. The main land regions are the Himalaya (the world's highest mountains), the northern plains, and the huge southern plateau of the Deccan. On the east and west coasts are smaller mountain ranges, the Ghats. The Brahmaputra, Ganges, and Indus river systems rise in the Himalaya mountains. The people of India belong to many different groups and religions. In the north most people are light-skinned Indo-Aryans, while in the south the people are darker Dravidians. There are 14 main languages, and over 1,000 local languages. Over 70 percent of the people live in rural areas.

## ECONOMIC SURVEY

**Farming:** India's farms are mostly small, growing food crops such as rice, wheat, millet, beans, and peas. Other crops are mangoes, nuts, sesame seeds, jute, tea, spices, and betel nuts. Seventy percent of the people work on the land.
**Forestry:** Cedar, teak, and rosewood are felled for timber.
**Fishing:** Mackerel, sardines, shark, and shrimps are caught at sea, and carp and catfish in the rivers.
**Mining:** Minerals include iron, coal, oil, mica, manganese, and diamonds.
**Industry:** Products include textiles, iron and steel, machinery, and electronic goods. Craft products include jewelry, leather, carpets, and metalwork.

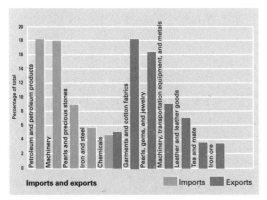

**Imports and exports**

**Age distribution**
- Under 15
- 15 - 60
- Over 60

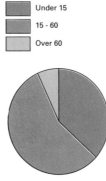

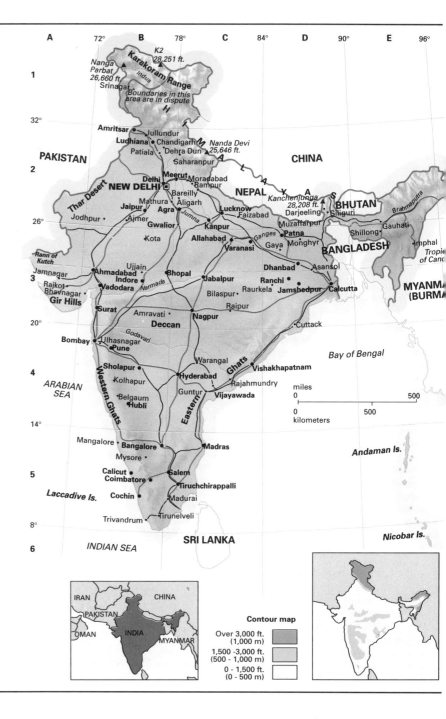

**Contour map**
- Over 3,000 ft. (1,000 m)
- 1,500 -3,000 ft. (500 - 1,000 m)
- 0 - 1,500 ft. (0 - 500 m)

**INDIAN HISTORY.** Indian history dates from the Indus Valley civilization of about 2500 B.C. Around 1500 B.C. Aryan invaders arrived from the north. Hinduism, India's main religion, dates from this time. Buddhism spread rapidly during the 200s B.C. The Mauryas, whose greatest emperor was Asoka (died 232 B.C.), and the Guptas (to about A.D. 450), made India a center of art and learning. The Mughals, who were Muslims, conquered India in the 1500s. The greatest Mughal ruler was Akbar. European trade missions, beginning when the Portuguese Vasco da Gama sailed into Calicut in 1498, led in time to rivalry between British and French trading companies. The British gained control, through wars and deals with Indian rulers. From 1858 much of India was under British government control when the powers of the East India Company were abolished. Nationalist feeling grew. India's first parliament met in 1919, but Indian leaders Mohandas Gandhi and Jawarharlal Nehru campaigned for independence, achieved in 1947. Muslims formed the separate state of Pakistan. India became a republic in 1950. The world's largest democracy, it has problems with minorities seeking self-government and an uneasy relationship with Pakistan. Urban poverty and a high birthrate are major issues.

**INDUSTRIAL PROFILE**
Although agriculture still dominates the economy and society, India has become a major industrial nation since independence in 1947. Railroads, air transportation, and nuclear power plants are state-owned, and the government is active in setting up other industrial concerns. Small industries are important. About 60 percent of the nation's electrical power is generated by coal-burning and oil-burning power plants. The rest comes mainly from hydro-electric schemes. Although main roads are good, country roads are often poor.

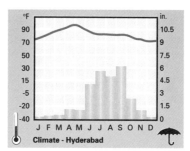
Climate - Hyderabad

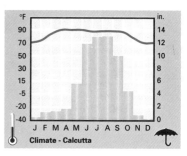
Climate - Calcutta

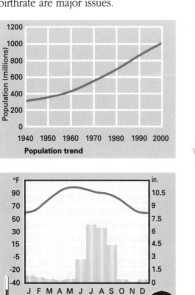

Population trend

Climate - Delhi

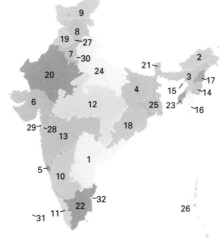

### STATES OF INDIA

| State/Capital | Area (sq. miles) | Area (km²) | Population (1981) |
|---|---|---|---|
| 1 **Andhra Pradesh** (Hyderabad) | 106,204 | 275,068 | 53,550,000 |
| 2 **Arunachal Pradesh** (Itanagar) | 32,333 | 83,743 | 632,000 |
| 3 **Assam** (Dispur) | 30,285 | 78,438 | 19,897,000 |
| 4 **Bihar** (Patna) | 67,134 | 173,877 | 69,915,000 |
| 5 **Goa** (Panaji) | 1,429 | 3,702 | 1,008,000 |
| 6 **Gujarat** (Gandhinagar) | 75,685 | 196,024 | 34,086,000 |
| 7 **Haryana** (Chandigarh) | 17,070 | 44,212 | 12,923,000 |
| 8 **Himachal Pradesh** (Shimla) | 21,495 | 55,673 | 4,281,000 |
| 9 **Jammu and Kashmir*** (Srinagar) | 39,146 | 101,387 | 5,987,000 |
| 10 **Karnataka** (Bangalore) | 74,051 | 191,791 | 37,136,000 |
| 11 **Kerala** (Trivandrum) | 15,005 | 38,863 | 25,454,000 |
| 12 **Madhya Pradesh** (Bhopal) | 171,215 | 443,446 | 52,179,000 |
| 13 **Maharashtra** (Bombay) | 118,800 | 307,690 | 62,784,000 |
| 14 **Manipur** (Imphal) | 8,621 | 22,327 | 1,421,000 |
| 15 **Meghalaya** (Shillong) | 8,660 | 22,429 | 1,336,000 |
| 16 **Mizoram** (Aizawl) | 8,139 | 21,081 | 494,000 |
| 17 **Nagaland** (Kohima) | 6,401 | 16,579 | 775,000 |
| 18 **Orissa** (Bubaneshwar) | 60,119 | 155,707 | 26,370,000 |
| 19 **Punjab** (Chandigarh) | 19,445 | 50,362 | 16,789,000 |
| 20 **Rajastan** (Jaipur) | 132,139 | 342,239 | 34,262,000 |
| 21 **Sikkim** (Gangtok) | 2,740 | 7,096 | 316,000 |
| 22 **Tamil Nadu** (Madras) | 50,216 | 130,058 | 48,408,000 |
| 23 **Tripura** (Agartala) | 4,049 | 10,486 | 2,053,000 |
| 24 **Uttar Pradesh** (Lucknow) | 113,673 | 294,411 | 110,862,000 |
| 25 **West Bengal** (Calcutta) | 34,267 | 88,752 | 54,581,000 |

\* Excludes territory occupied by China and Pakistan

### Union Territories

| | Area (sq. miles) | Area (km²) | Population (1981) |
|---|---|---|---|
| 26 **Andaman and Nicobar Islands** (Port Blair) | 3,185 | 8,249 | 189,000 |
| 27 **Chandigarh** (Chandigarh) | 44 | 114 | 451,000 |
| 28 **Dadra and Nagar Haveli** (Silvassa) | 190 | 491 | 104,000 |
| 29 **Daman and Diu** (Daman) | 43 | 112 | 79,000 |
| 30 **Delhi** (Delhi) | 573 | 1,483 | 6,220,000 |
| 31 **Lakshadweep** (Kavaratti) | 12 | 32 | 40,000 |
| 32 **Pondicherry** (Pondicherry) | 190 | 492 | 604,000 |

# Indian Ocean

**COMOROS Area:** 838 sq. miles (2,171 km²)
**Population:** 463,000
**Capital:** Moroni (pop. 21,000)
**Official languages:** Arabic, French
**Government:** Federal Islamic single-party rep.
**Per capita GNP:** U.S. $460

**MALDIVES Area:** 115 sq. miles (298 km²)
**Population:** 216,000
**Capital:** Male (pop. 46,000)
**Official language:** Divehi
**Government:** Republic
**Per capita GNP:** U.S. $420

**MAURITIUS Area:** 790 sq. miles (2,045 km²)
**Population:** 1,071,000
**Capital:** Port Louis (pop. 139,000)
**Official language:** English
**Government:** Constitutional monarchy
**Per capita GNP:** US $1950

**SEYCHELLES Area:** 108 sq. miles (280 km²)
**Population:** 68,000
**Capital:** Victoria (pop. 23,000)
**Official languages:** Creole, English, French
**Government:** Single-party republic
**Per capita GNP:** U.S. $4,170

**ECONOMIC SURVEY**
**Farming:** Many islands have poor soil. The main crop grown on Mauritius is sugarcane, with tea in the wetter uplands. On the Maldives and Seychelles coconut palms flourish. Some livestock, mainly cattle, goats, and chickens, are kept.
**Fishing:** In the Maldives the people catch bonito, tuna, and other species. Fishing is important to all the islands. Dried fish are exported.
**Industry:** Tourism is the mainstay of the Seychelles economy, and is growing on other island groups. There are few other industries though Mauritius has sugar-processing factories and local tobacco is made into cigarettes.

**Contour map (Depths)**

Over 15,000 ft. (5,000 m)
9,000 - 15,000 ft. (3,000 - 5,000 m)
0 - 9,000 ft. (0 - 3,000 m)

The third largest of the world's oceans, the Indian Ocean washes the continents of Africa, Asia, Australia, and Antarctica. Most of the ocean and its many, mainly small, rocky or coral islands have a tropical climate, free from extremes of temperature. The main winds affecting climate are the dry and wet seasonal monsoons, and westerly winds which can bring violent storms. The Indian Ocean has been an important trade route since ancient times. The island groups were first settled by people from India, Arabia, and Africa. Later the Portuguese, Dutch, and French colonized them, with Britain eventually gaining Mauritius (1810), the Seychelles (1814) and the Maldives (1887). The Maldives became independent in 1965 and Mauritius in 1968. The Seychelles gained independence in 1976.

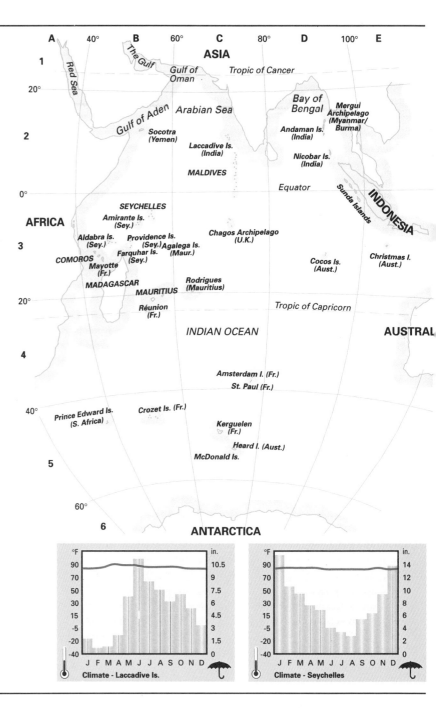

Climate - Laccadive Is.

Climate - Seychelles

# Indonesia

**Area:** 735,139 sq. miles (1,904,000 km²)
**Population:** 180,763,000
**Capital:** Jakarta (pop. 7,829,000)
**Other cities:** Surabaya 2,345,000; Medan 2,110,000; Bandung 1,463,000
**Highest point:** Puncak Jaya 16,503 ft. (5,030 m)
**Official language:** Bahasa Indonesia
**Religions:** Islam, Christianity, Hinduism, Buddhism
**Currency:** Rupiah
**Main exports:** Petroleum and natural gas
**Government:** Multiparty republic
**Per capita GNP:** U.S. $490

The republic of Indonesia is made up of more than 13,000 islands. The largest regions are Kalimantan (on Borneo), Sumatra, Irian Jaya or West Irian (part of New Guinea), Celebes, and Java. There are many mountain ranges and active volcanoes: 77 volcanoes have erupted in recent times. The climate is warm and rain falls all year round. Rain forests cover large areas. People inhabit about 6,000 of the islands, but about 60 percent of the population lives on Java. Most Indonesians are Malays and are followers of Islam. From the 700s, Hindu and Buddhist kingdoms strove to control the island trade routes. Muslims set up a kingdom in the 1500s. Soon afterward the Portuguese arrived, followed by the Dutch. Indonesia became the Dutch East Indies colony in 1799. The independent republic of Indonesia was formed in 1949.

## ECONOMIC SURVEY

**Farming:** Plantations produce sugarcane, coffee, tea, palm oil, copra, and rubber. Rice is the main food crop, and corn, cassava, spices, and vegetables are grown. Cattle, buffaloes, goats, and chickens are reared.
**Fishing:** Indonesia ranks tenth among the world's fishing nations.
**Forestry:** The forests yield valuable hardwoods such as ebony and teak.
**Mining:** Indonesia is a major oil and gas producer, and also mines tin, bauxite, coal, copper, manganese, and nickel.
**Industry:** Consumer goods such as cigarettes, cloth, and glassware are the main manufactured products. Vehicles are assembled.

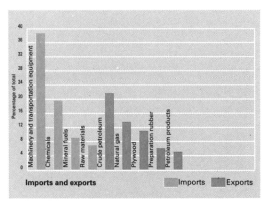

Imports and exports

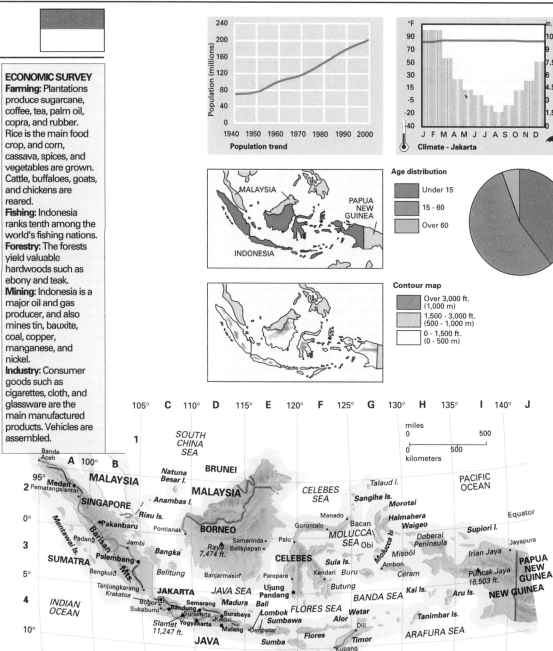

Population trend

Climate - Jakarta

Age distribution
- Under 15
- 15 - 60
- Over 60

Contour map
- Over 3,000 ft. (1,000 m)
- 1,500 - 3,000 ft. (500 - 1,000 m)
- 0 - 1,500 ft. (0 - 500 m)

see ASIA, page 22

# Iran

**Area:** 636,296 sq. miles (1,648,000 km²)
**Population:** 56,923,000
**Capital:** Tehran (pop. 6,043,000)
**Other cities:** Mashhad 1,464,000; Esfahan 987,000; Tabriz 971,000
**Highest point:** Mt Damavend 18,386 ft. (5,604 m)
**Official language:** Farsi (Persian)
**Religion:** Islam
**Currency:** Rial
**Main exports:** Petroleum and petroleum products
**Government:** Islamic republic
**Per capita GNP:** Estimated at U.S. $3,500-$6,000

## ECONOMIC SURVEY

**Farming:** About 20 percent of Iran's people work on the land. Cereals (wheat, rice, and barley), fruit, cotton, sugarcane, and tobacco are grown, as are vegetables and fruit. Sheep, goats, and cattle are kept.

**Fishing:** Sardines, shrimps, sole, and tuna are caught in the Gulf, and sturgeon (for caviar) in the Caspian Sea.

**Mining:** Iran's oil and natural gas deposits are its chief source of wealth. Iron, copper, and manganese are also extracted.

**Industry:** Factories produce fertilizers, plastics, cement, processed foods, textiles, and clothing. Iran is famous for the traditional craft industry of carpet and rug making.

Much of Iran is mountainous. Around a barren plateau, containing two deserts, the Dasht-e-Kavir and Dasht-e-Lut (Great Salt, Great Sand deserts) are mountain ranges. The highest mountains are the northern Elburz. The Zagros mountains are in the southwest, and there are other mountains in the east. The only fertile areas are near the Caspian Sea and in the mountain foothills. The climate is dry and hot, but colder in the mountains. The people are mostly Shia Muslims. About half are Persian, the rest being Kurds, Azerbaijanis, Arabs, and other minorities. Iran was the heart of the Persian Empire (550 to 330 B.C.). The country became Islamic in A.D. 641. Shahs (emperors) ruled until 1979, when the last shah was deposed in favor of an Islamic fundamentalist republic. The war with Iraq (1980-88) ended in a stalemate.

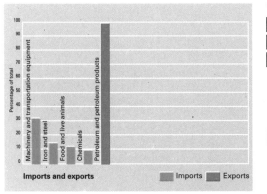

Imports and exports

Imports | Exports

**Age distribution**

Under 15
15 - 60
Over 60

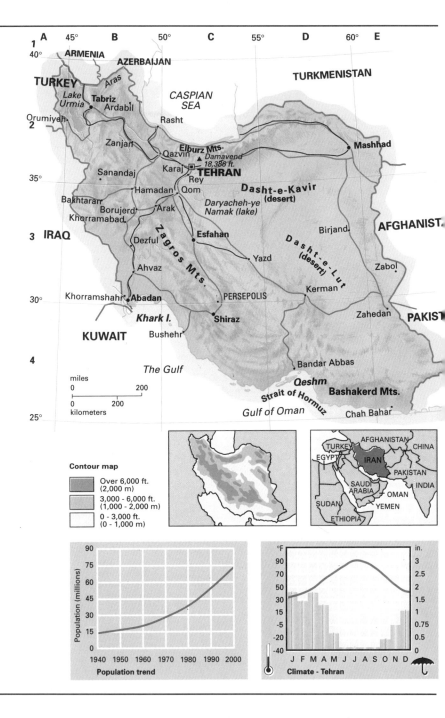

**Contour map**

Over 6,000 ft. (2,000 m)
3,000 - 6,000 ft. (1,000 - 2,000 m)
0 - 3,000 ft. (0 - 1,000 m)

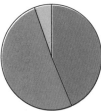

**Population trend**

**Climate - Tehran**

# Iraq

**Area:** 167,925 sq. miles (434,924 km²)
**Population:** 17,754,000
**Capital:** Baghdad (pop. 3,845,000)
**Other cities:** Basra 617,000; Mosul 571,000
**Highest point:** Zagros Mountains about 11,840 ft. (3,610 m)
**Official language:** Arabic
**Religion:** Islam
**Currency:** Dinar
**Main export:** Petroleum
**Government:** Single-party republic
**Per capita GNP:** Estimated at between U.S. $1,500 and U.S. $3,500

## ECONOMIC SURVEY

**Farming:** Irrigation is used on crops, which include dates, wheat, barley, pulses, grapes, watermelons, tomatoes, and other fruit and vegetables. Sheep and chickens are the most numerous livestock. Cattle, goats, buffalo, camels, and asses are also reared.

**Mining:** Iraq has some sulfur and gypsum deposits, but the chief mineral resource is oil.

**Industry:** A petrochemical industry is being developed as part of an extensive industrialization program. Other industries include engineering, food processing, pottery, glass, and textiles. Iraq's industry was severely disrupted by the Gulf War (1990-1) and UN sanctions.

The west and southwest of Iraq are deserts, but the north-south flow of the Tigris and Euphrates rivers waters fertile regions and creates a southern marshland. In the northeast, along the borders with Iran and Turkey, are mountains. Summers are hot and winters cool. More than half the people are Shia Muslims. In the north live Kurdish people, who are Sunni Muslims. Mesopotamia, the land between the Tigris and Euphrates, cradled the ancient civilizations of Babylon and Assyria. Iraq became Islamic in A.D. 637. From 1638 it was part of the Ottoman empire. In 1916 it came under British control, and gained its independence in 1931. Sadam Hussein, president from 1979, led Iraq into an inconclusive war with Iran (1980-8). In 1990 he invaded Kuwait, provoking a short but devastating war against United Nations forces.

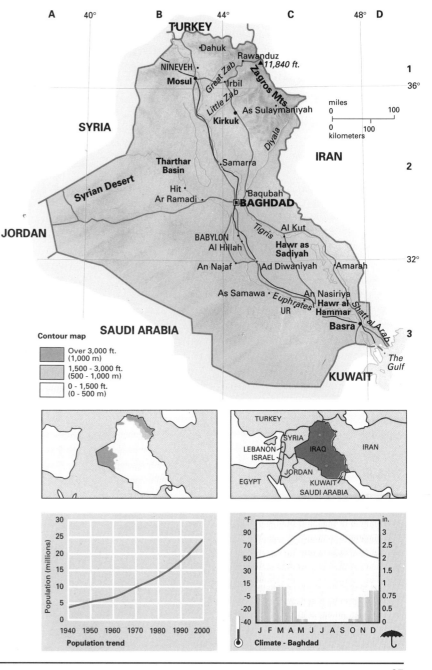

Contour map

- Over 3,000 ft. (1,000 m)
- 1,500 - 3,000 ft. (500 - 1,000 m)
- 0 - 1,500 ft. (0 - 500 m)

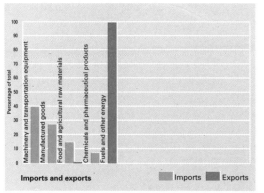

**Imports and exports**

Imports / Exports

**Age distribution**

- Under 15
- 15 - 60
- Over 60

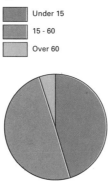

**Population trend**

**Climate - Baghdad**

# Republic of Ireland

**Area:** 27,137 sq. miles (70,284 km²)
**Population:** 3,509,000
**Capital:** Dublin (pop. with suburbs 921,000)
**Other cities:** Cork 174,000
**Highest point:** Carrauntoohill 3,414 ft. (1,041 m)
**Official languages:** English and Irish Gaelic
**Religions:** Roman Catholicism, Protestantism
**Currency:** Punt (pound)
**Main exports:** Machinery, manufactured goods, chemicals, live animals, food
**Government:** Constitutional republic
**Per capita GNP:** U.S. $8500

The Republic of Ireland covers 80 percent of the island of Ireland. It is often referred to by its Gaelic name of Eire. It is bordered in the north by Northern Ireland, which is part of the United Kingdom. The climate of the republic is mild and damp, and much of the land is farmed. Central Ireland is low lying with remnants of peat bog. The Shannon River, at 240 miles (386 km) is the longest in the British Isles. There are several lakes. Celts settled in Ireland in the early 4th century B.C. Vikings raided the country in the 800s, and formed settlements there. The rulers of England began trying to conquer Ireland in 1169, but they did not succeed until the 1500s. Ireland was made part of the United Kingdom in 1801, but the southern counties rebelled in 1916 and became a dominion in 1921. Ireland became a republic in 1949 and joined the European Community in 1973.

## ECONOMIC SURVEY

**Farming:** Ireland is rich in pastureland for cattle, sheep, and horses. Pigs are also reared. The chief crops are barley, oats, wheat, potatoes, tomatoes, and sugar beet.
**Forestry:** Ireland has lost much of its natural forest, but replanting is now going on.
**Fishing:** Inshore waters yield haddock, cod, herring, salmon, flatfish, and prawns.
**Mining:** Lead and zinc are mined. Peat and natural gas provide energy. Peat reserves are dwindling, however. There is little coal.
**Industry:** Products include machinery, chemicals, electronic equipment, textiles, glass, and plastic goods. Food products include butter, cheese, beer, and whiskey.

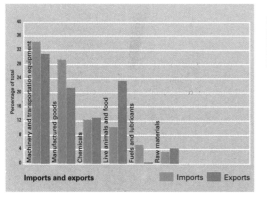

**Imports and exports** — Machinery and transportation equipment, Manufactured goods, Chemicals, Live animals and food, Fuels and lubricants, Raw materials — Imports / Exports

**Age distribution**

- Under 15
- 15 - 60
- Over 60

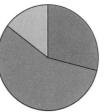

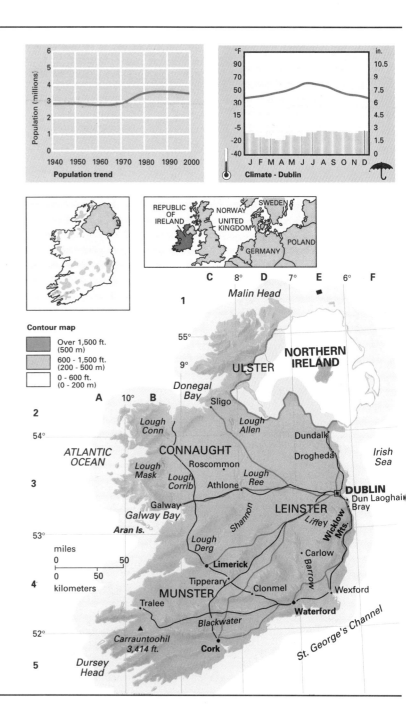

**Population trend** — 1940 1950 1960 1970 1980 1990 2000

**Climate - Dublin** — J F M A M J J A S O N D

**Contour map**

- Over 1,500 ft. (500 m)
- 600 - 1,500 ft. (200 - 500 m)
- 0 - 600 ft. (0 - 200 m)

REPUBLIC OF IRELAND — NORWAY — SWEDEN — UNITED KINGDOM — GERMANY — POLAND

# Israel

**Area:** 8,019 sq. miles (20,770 km²)
**Population:** 4,616,000
**Capital:** Jerusalem (pop. 458,000)
**Other cities:** Tel Aviv-Yafo 323,000; Haifa 225,000; Holon 135,000; Bat Yam 135,000
**Highest point:** Mount Meron 3,963 ft. (1,208 m)
**Official languages:** Hebrew, Arabic
**Religions:** Judaism, Islam, Christianity
**Currency:** Shekel
**Main exports:** Cut diamonds, machinery, chemicals, fruit
**Government:** Multiparty republic
**Per capita GNP:** U.S. $9,750

## ECONOMIC SURVEY

**Farming:** Agriculture is efficient because of extensive irrigation and cooperative farming. About 14 percent of the people work on the land, and half of these live either in kibbutzim (collectives) or are in moshavim (co-operatives). Important crops include oranges and other fruit, vegetables, cotton, and olives. Cattle and sheep are raised.
**Mining:** Israel has no coal and only a little oil and natural gas. Minerals include gypsum, zinc, and lead. Potash, salt, and magnesium come from the Dead Sea.
**Industry:** Israel produces many factory goods, including chemicals, cut diamonds, electronics, and textiles.

Israel has a low coastal plain. The Galilee highlands containing Mt. Meron are in the north. To the east are the Sea of Galilee (Lake Tiberias) and the Jordan River, and in the south is the Dead Sea. The Negev in the far south is desert. The climate is Mediterranean on the coast, with drier conditions inland and in the south. More than 80 percent of the people are Jews. The remainder are Arabs. Israel includes most of Palestine, the ancient home of the Jews. Jewish settlers began returning to Palestine, then part of the Ottoman empire, in the late 1800s. Britain ruled Palestine from 1917 until 1948, when the Republic of Israel was proclaimed as a Jewish homeland. Israel has fought four territorial wars (1948, 1956, 1967, and 1973) against its Arab neighbors. From 1967 it occupied Jordanian and Syrian territory. Israel made peace with Egypt in 1978.

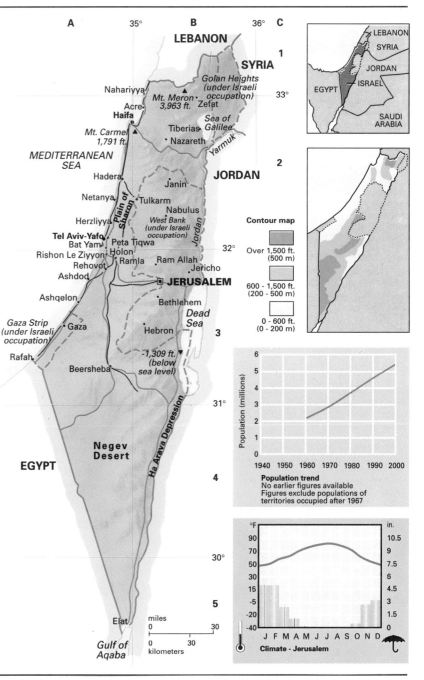

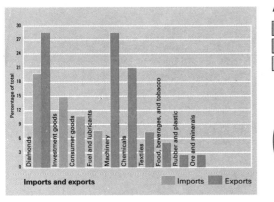

Imports and exports

Imports  Exports

Age distribution

Under 15
15 - 60
Over 60

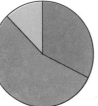

**Population trend**
No earlier figures available
Figures exclude populations of territories occupied after 1967

**Climate - Jerusalem**

Contour map
Over 1,500 ft. (500 m)
600 - 1,500 ft. (200 - 500 m)
0 - 600 ft. (0 - 200 m)

# Italy

**Area:** 116,304 sq. miles (301,225 km²)
**Population:** 57,461,000
**Capital:** Rome (pop. 2,816,000)
**Other cities:** Milan 1,464,000; Naples 1,203,000; Turin 1,012,000
**Highest point:** Mont Blanc 15,771 ft. (4,807 m)
**Official language:** Italian
**Religion:** Roman Catholicism
**Currency:** Italian lira
**Main exports:** Machinery and transportation equipment, chemicals, clothing and footwear, metals
**Government:** Constitutional republic
**Per capita GNP:** U.S. $15,150

Italy consists of a long peninsula (often likened to a long boot) projecting into the Mediterranean Sea, and the islands of Sardinia, Sicily, and Elba. The north is cool, but most of Italy has a mild climate. The Alps in the north are Italy's highest mountains. Also in the north are beautiful lakes, including Garda, Maggiore, and Como. The Apennine Mountains occupy much of peninsular Italy. Most of Italy's rivers are short. The most important are the Arno and Tiber. Rome, Italy's capital, stands on the Tiber. The North Italian Plain is drained by Italy's longest river, the Po. There are many fertile river valleys and coastal plains. In the southwest are some of Europe's most famous active volcanoes: Vesuvius near Naples; Stromboli and Vulcano in the Lipari Islands; and Etna on Sicily.

## ECONOMIC SURVEY

**Farming:** Many farms are small. Crops include barley, wheat, rice, citrus and other fruits, tomatoes, grapes for wine making, olives, sugar beet, tobacco, and vegetables. Sheep, pigs, goats, and cattle are reared.

**Fishing:** Catches in the Mediterranean, traditionally good, have been affected by pollution and shrinking stocks.

**Industry:** Italy is a major manufacturer of such goods as cars and other vehicles, machinery, office and household equipment, clothing and shoes, chemicals, and electronics. Italy is the home of pasta, and is famous for other food products such as Gorgonzola cheese and Parma ham.

**Age distribution**

- Under 15
- 15 - 60
- Over 60

**Contour map**

- 0 - 1,500 ft. (0 - 500 m)
- 1,500 - 3,000 ft. (500 - 1,000 m)
- Over 3,000 ft. (1,000 m)

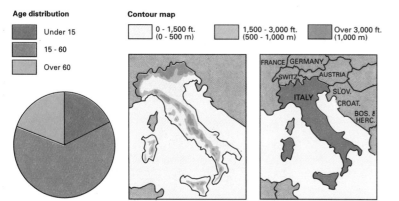

**ITALIAN HISTORY.** Italy was the birthplace of the Roman Empire, which succeeded the Etruscan and other local cultures. The Roman republic was founded in 509 B.C. The Romans ruled Italy until A.D. 476. Italy was then split into small city-states, which were often at war with one another. Rome was the seat of the papacy. During the 15th and 16th centuries the Renaissance of arts and science flourished in Italy, particularly in Venice and Florence. Italy became a battleground for foreign powers seeking to gain control. France and Spain fought over it in the 1500s. By the 1700s a large part of Italy was ruled by Austria. In the 1800s a long struggle for independence and unity of the Italian States was led by Giuseppe Garibaldi and other patriots. United in 1861 as a monarchy under the king of Sardinia, Italy had a period of fascist government under Benito Mussolini in the 1920s and 1930s. After World War II, Italy lost its African colonies. It became a democratic republic in 1946. It was a founder member of the European Community.

**INDUSTRIAL PROFILE**
Italy's economy has been transformed since the 1950s. It has become a major industrial producer. It is one of the leading members of the European Community, with a wide range of products from high-tech to quality foodstuffs. Northern Italy is wealthier than the less industrialized south. The major manufacturing region is the triangular area formed by Milan, Turin and Genoa. Hydroelectric projects supply 30 percent of the country's energy. Generally, Italy lacks minerals. Natural gas is extracted in the North Italian plain and in Sicily, but oil and coal have to be imported, as do metal ores. Manufacturing employs just under 20 percent of the work force. Tourism is a major industry, with millions of overseas visitors going to Italy each year. There is a large film industry.

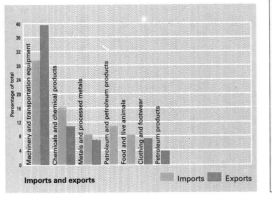

**Imports and exports** — Imports, Exports

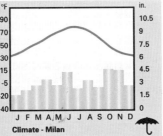
**Population trend** — 1940 1950 1960 1970 1980 1990 2000

**Climate - Milan**

# San Marino

**Area:** 24 sq. miles (61 km²)
**Population:** 23,000
**Capital:** San Marino
**Highest point:** Mount Titano 2,477 ft. (755 m)
**Official language:** Italian
**Religion:** Roman Catholicism
**Currency:** Italian lira
**Main exports:** ceramics, chemicals, textiles, wheat, wine, wood (trade figures included with Italy)
**Government:** Constitutional republic
**Per capita GNP:** U.S. $8,590

**Contour map**

0 - 500 m
(0 - 1500 ft)

# Vatican City

**Area:** 109 acres (44 ha)
**Population:** about 1,000
**Official language:** Italian
**Currency:** Italian lira
**Government:** Vatican City is the governing center of the Roman Catholic Church; the Pope is its absolute ruler.

**Climate - Vatican City (Rome)**

**ROME**

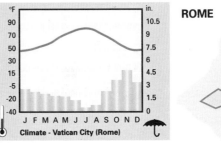

# Jamaica and the Cayman Islands

**JAMAICA: Area:** 4,244 sq. miles (10,991 km²)
**Population:** 2,396,000
**Capital:** Kingston (pop. with suburbs 525,000)
**Highest point:** Blue Mountain Peak 7,402 ft. (2,256 m)
**Official language:** English
**Currency:** Jamaican dollar
**Government:** Constitutional monarchy
**Per capita GNP:** U.S. $1,260
**CAYMANS: Area:** 100 sq. miles (259 km²)
**Population:** 25,000

Jamaica is a country of spectacular mountain scenery. The coastal lowlands have a tropical climate, but receive less rainfall than the Blue Mountains. The Cayman Islands lie about 200 miles (320 km) northwest of Jamaica and enjoy a tropical maritime climate. Many islanders are descendants of African slaves, and there are minorities of Asians, Afro-Asians, and whites. Jamaica was discovered by Christopher Columbus in 1494. Spain ruled the island until 1655, when the English captured it, and ruled it and the Caymans as a colony. Jamaica was a center of piracy and of slavery, until slavery was abolished in the 1830s. Jamaican independence came in 1962, but the Caymans preferred to be a separate British dependency.

## ECONOMIC SURVEY

**Farming:** Sugarcane is the chief crop and sugar is Jamaica's leading farm export. Bananas, allspice, cocoa, citrus fruits, coconuts, and yams are also grown.
**Mining:** Jamaica is one of the world's leading producers of bauxite (aluminum ore). Gypsum is mined for making plaster.
**Industry:** Alumina, extracted from the bauxite ore, is processed. Factories produce building materials, clothing, molasses and rum, paints, and chemicals. Jamaica is a popular center for tourism. Low taxes attract businesses to the Cayman Islands.

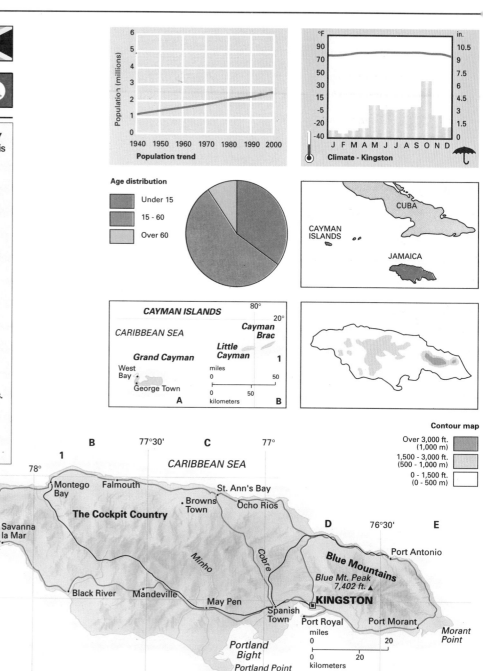

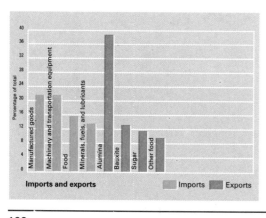

# Japan

**Area:** 145,834 sq. miles (377,708 km²)
**Population:** 123,700,000
**Capital:** Tokyo (pop. with suburbs 11,719,000)
**Other cities:** Yokohama 3,151,000; Osaka 2,645,000; Nagoya 2,148,000
**Highest point:** Mount Fuji 12,388 ft. (3,776 m)
**Official language:** Japanese
**Religions:** Shintoism, Buddhism
**Currency:** Yen
**Main exports:** Vehicles and machinery, metals and metal products, chemicals, textiles
**Government:** Constitutional monarchy
**Per capita GNP:** U.S. $23,730

Japan is an island country. Its four main islands are Honshu, Hokkaido, Kyushu, and Shikoku. There are about 3,000 smaller islands, including the Ryukyu chain. The islands are mountainous. Japan has 165 volcanoes, of which 54 are active. Earthquakes are frequent. The Kanto Plain on Honshu is Japan's biggest lowland region. The country's rivers are short and fast flowing. There are many lakes and hot springs. Most Japanese are descendants of people from mainland Asia. The imperial monarchy dates from 660 B.C. For hundreds of years Japan was isolated from the rest of the world. Modernization, following Western contact, began in the 1800s. After defeat in World War II (1939-1945) Japan adopted a democratic constitution. Its rapid recovery made it one of the world's leading industrial powers, exporting a wide range of products.

## ECONOMIC SURVEY

**Farming:** Japanese farmers produce much of the nation's food, despite the shortage of farmland. About half the usable land is given over to rice. Fruit and vegetables are grown, and dairy production is increasing.

**Fishing:** Japan has the world's biggest fishing industry, with more than 400,000 vessels.

**Mining:** Japan has only a small quantity of minerals, and has to import most raw materials and fuel.

**Industry:** Japan is a leading producer of iron and steel and chemicals. Japanese manufactured goods include watches, cameras, electronic products, cars, machinery, ships, ceramics, plastics, silk, and other textiles.

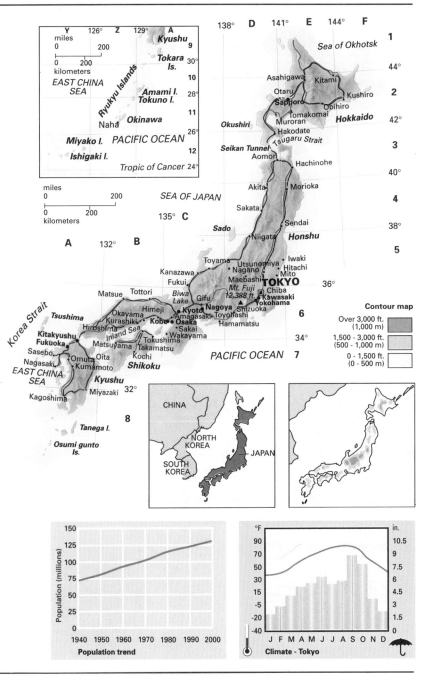

Contour map

Over 3,000 ft. (1,000 m)
1,500 - 3,000 ft. (500 - 1,000 m)
0 - 1,500 ft. (0 - 500 m)

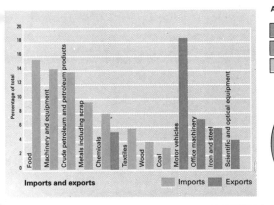

**Imports and exports**

Imports   Exports

(y-axis) Percentage of total

Food | Machinery and equipment | Crude petroleum and petroleum products | Metals including scrap | Chemicals | Textiles | Wood | Coal | Motor vehicles | Office machinery | Iron and steel | Scientific and optical equipment

**Age distribution**

Under 15
15 - 60
Over 60

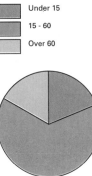

Population (millions)

1940 1950 1960 1970 1980 1990 2000

**Population trend**

°F / in.

J F M A M J J A S O N D

**Climate - Tokyo**

*see* ASIA, page 22

# Jordan

**Area:** 37,738 sq. miles (97,740 km²), including the Israeli-occupied West Bank
**Population:** 3,173,000 (excluding West Bank)
**Capital:** Amman (pop. 900,000)
**Other cities:** Az-Zarqa 306,000; Irbid 122,000
**Highest point:** Jebel Ram 5,755 ft. (1,754 m)
**Official language:** Arabic
**Religion:** Islam
**Currency:** Dinar
**Main exports:** Phosphates and other chemicals, fertilizers
**Government:** Constitutional monarchy
**Per capita GNP:** U.S. $1,730

## ECONOMIC SURVEY

**Farming:** Only about 5 percent of the land, around the valley of the Jordan River, is usable, more than 80 percent of the country being desert. Farms must rely on irrigation. Farmers grow crops of tomatoes, citrus fruits, vegetables, olives, wheat, and barley. Sheep, goats, and some cattle and horses are kept. Near the desert, nomads herd camels and other animals.
**Mining:** The chief minerals are potash, natural gas, and phosphates.
**Industry:** Factories process the potash and phosphates into fertilizers. Others produce chemicals, cement, textiles, and items such as processed foods, detergents, leather goods, and batteries.

The Hashemite Kingdom of Jordan lies to the east of Israel. Jordanian territory on the west bank of the Jordan River was occupied by Israel in 1967. Here fertile uplands overlook the rift valley, containing the river and the Dead Sea. Jordan's only outlet to the Red Sea is the Gulf of Aqaba. The east consists mainly of barren uplands, and about 87 percent of Jordan is desert. Only in the cooler highlands is rainfall adequate for cultivation. Most Jordanians are Arabs, and the population includes Bedouin nomads. Many Palestinian refugees have moved to Jordan from Israeli-occupied territory. Historically, the region was part of successive empires. It passed from Turkish to British control after World War I. The country was called Transjordan until 1949, when it changed its name, three years after becoming completely independent in 1946.

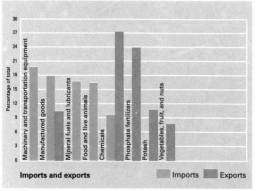

**Imports and exports**
Imports Exports

### Age distribution

Under 15
15 - 60
Over 60

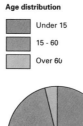

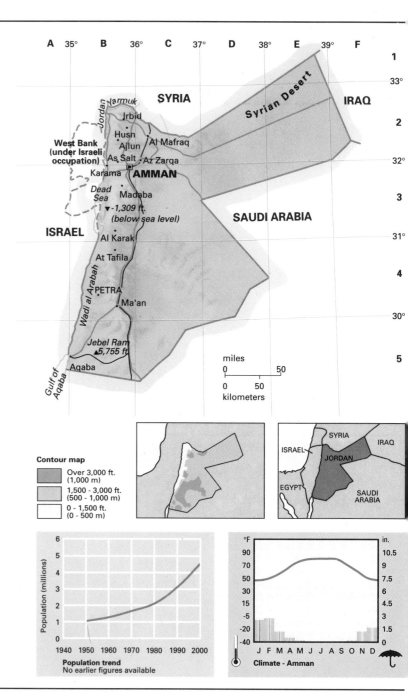

**Contour map**
Over 3,000 ft. (1,000 m)
1,500 - 3,000 ft. (500 - 1,000 m)
0 - 1,500 ft. (0 - 500 m)

**Population trend**
No earlier figures available

**Climate - Amman**

# Kenya

**Area:** 224,961 sq. miles (582,646 km²)
**Population:** 24,872,000
**Capital:** Nairobi (pop. 1,429,000)
**Other cities:** Mombasa 426,000; Kisumu 153,000; Nakuru 93,000
**Highest point:** Mount Kenya 17,060 ft. (5,200 m)
**Official languages:** Swahili, English
**Religions:** Christianity, traditional beliefs, Islam
**Currency:** Kenya shilling
**Main exports:** Coffee, tea, petroleum products, vegetables
**Government:** Single-party republic
**Per capita GNP:** U.S. $380

## ECONOMIC SURVEY

**Farming:** About one worker in every five farms the land. The variety of soil and climate makes for an equal variety of crops, such as barley, wheat, cotton, and coconuts. The main cash crops are tea, coffee, vegetables, and fruit. Other food crops include corn, cassava, sweet potatoes, plantains, beans, sorghum, and millet. Cattle are reared, along with goats and sheep.
**Fishing:** Freshwater fish account for almost all the catch.
**Minerals:** The mineral deposits are chiefly limestone, soda ash, salt, and fluorite.
**Industry:** Factories manufacture petroleum products, cement, food, drinks, and paint. Tourism is important.

Kenya has a narrow coastal plain. Behind it is a region of thorn scrub, rising to a large savanna-covered plateau broken by volcanic mountains, including Mount Kenya. The Great Rift Valley runs through the country. It contains lakes Nakuru, Naivasha, and Turkana. In the southeast, part of Lake Victoria lies within Kenya. The climate is hot and humid on the coast and cooler on the plateau. Much of Kenya has unreliable rainfall. The highlands are forested. Kenya is noted for its wildlife reserves. Most Kenyans are Black Africans belonging to about 40 language groups. The population also includes Europeans and Asians. The protectorate of British East Africa was formed in 1895. From it the colony of Kenya was created in 1920. After a violent terrorist campaign in the 1950s, Kenya became independent in 1963.

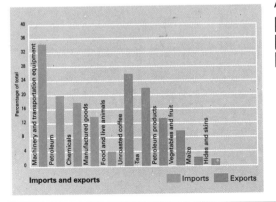

**Imports and exports**

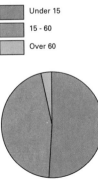

**Age distribution**

Under 15

15 - 60

Over 60

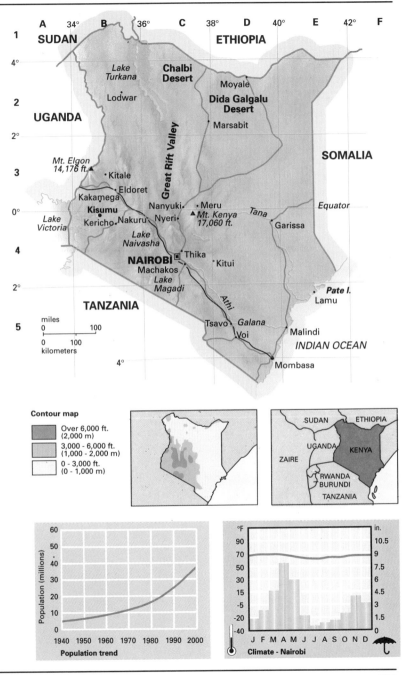

**Contour map**

Over 6,000 ft. (2,000 m)

3,000 - 6,000 ft. (1,000 - 2,000 m)

0 - 3,000 ft. (0 - 1,000 m)

**Population trend**

**Climate - Nairobi**

# Kuwait

**Area:** 6,880 sq. miles (17,818 km²)
**Population:** 2,143,000
**Capital:** Kuwait (pop. 44,000)
**Other cities:** As Salimiyah 153,000; Hawalli 145,000
**Highest point:** As Shaqaya 928 ft. (283 m)
**Official language:** Arabic
**Religion:** Islam
**Currency:** Dinar
**Main exports:** Petroleum and petroleum products
**Government:** Monarchy (emir is head of state)
**Per capita GNP:** U.S. $16,380

Kuwait is a small oil-rich emirate at the northern end of the Persian Gulf. It is a low-lying desert country, with erratic rainfall. Summers are hot, with temperatures above 90°F. Winters are cooler, averaging about 57°F. Over 90 percent of the Kuwaitis are Muslims, mostly Sunnis. Kuwaitis make up 40 percent of the population, other Arabs and Asians forming most of the remainder. In 1889 the ruler of Kuwait accepted British protection. After Kuwait became independent in 1914, Britain still controlled its foreign policy. Full independence was achieved in 1961. Iraq claimed Kuwait, and in 1990 its forces invaded the country, precipitating an international crisis. Kuwait was liberated by United Nations forces in January 1991, but suffered severe damage to its economy, most of its hundreds of oil wells having been set on fire by the Iraqis.

## ECONOMIC SURVEY

**Farming:** Water is scarce, despite the exploitation of underground sources and the distillation of seawater. Some fruit and vegetables, including pumpkins, cucumbers and tomatoes, are grown. Hydroponic cultivation of crops in sand fed with water and plant foods is encouraged. Sheep, goats, camels, some cattle, and chickens are raised.

**Industry:** Kuwait's oil and natural gas reserves are the basis of its economy. Petrochemical plants have been set up to produce petroleum by-products such as plastics. Japan is Kuwait's major oil customer. Production was severely hit as a result of the Gulf War (1990-1) and the firing of the oil wells.

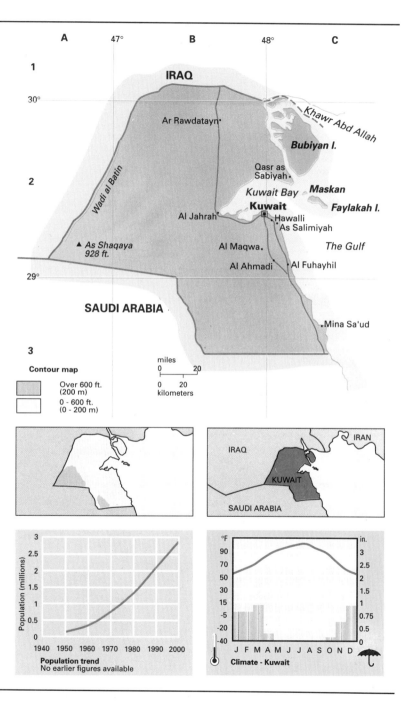

Contour map

Over 600 ft. (200 m)

0 - 600 ft. (0 - 200 m)

**Population trend**
No earlier figures available

**Climate - Kuwait**

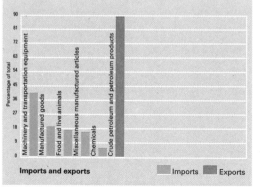

**Imports and exports**

Imports   Exports

**Age distribution**

Under 15

15 - 60

Over 60

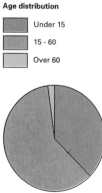

# Laos

**Area:** 91,429 sq. miles (236,800 km²)
**Population:** 4,024,000
**Capital:** Vientiane (pop. 377,000)
**Other cities:** Savannakhet 53,000
**Highest point:** Mount Bia 9,252 ft. (2,820 m)
**Official language:** Lao
**Religions:** Buddhism, various tribal religions
**Currency:** Kip
**Main exports:** Electricity, timber, coffee, tin
**Government:** People's republic
**Per capita GNP:** U.S. $170

Laos is a country of mountains and dense forests. Most people live in the fertile lowlands near the Mekong River and its tributaries. The Annamite Mountains form a natural frontier with Vietnam. Monsoon winds bring heavy rains from May to September. The Lao-Lum or Valley Lao, a people of Thai origin, form a dominant majority. Other groups are Lao-Theung tribes in the uplands and Lao-Soung agriculturalists. Small princely states existed from the A.D. 800s, later unifying to form a kingdom with part of what is now northern Thailand. France controlled Laos as part of Indochina from 1893. Laos became independent in 1954. Its governments were unstable and subject to external pressure, especially during the Vietnam War (1957-1975). In 1975 the king of Laos was deposed. A communist state under Vietnamese influence was set up.

## ECONOMIC SURVEY

**Farming:** Laos is a farming nation, though most farms are small and use old-fashioned methods. Rice is the most important crop. Farmers also grow coffee, corn, cotton, tobacco, and vegetables. Chickens, buffaloes, and pigs are the most numerous farm animals.
**Forestry:** Much of the land is forested, producing teak and other valuable woods.
**Mining:** Laos has mineral reserves including gypsum, rock salt, and tin.
**Industry:** The country has few factories. Pottery and silverwork are produced in small workshops. Most trade is with China, the United States, and Thailand. Hydro-electric power is exported to Thailand.

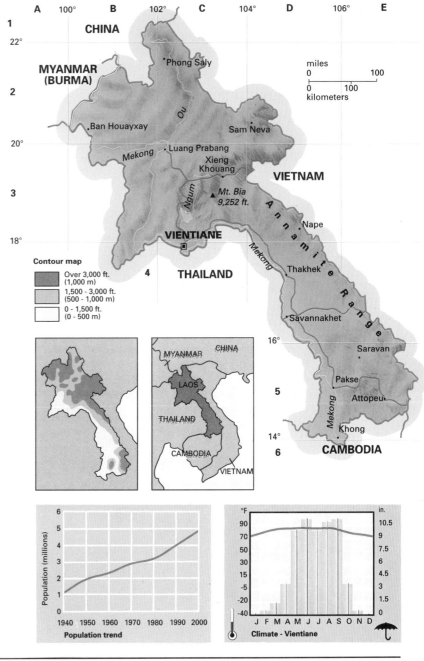

**Contour map**

- Over 3,000 ft. (1,000 m)
- 1,500 - 3,000 ft. (500 - 1,000 m)
- 0 - 1,500 ft. (0 - 500 m)

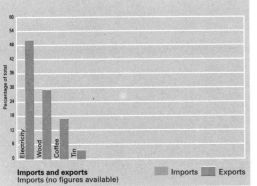

**Imports and exports**
Imports (no figures available)

Imports   Exports

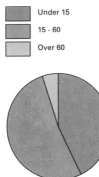

**Age distribution**

- Under 15
- 15 - 60
- Over 60

**Population trend**

**Climate - Vientiane**

*see* ASIA, page 22  **105**

# Lebanon

**Area:** 4,015 sq. miles (10,400 km²)
**Population:** 2,965,000
**Capital:** Beirut (pop. 200,000)
**Other cities:** Tripoli 500,000; Zahlah 200,000
**Highest point:** Qurnat as Sawda, in the Lebanon range 10,125 ft. (3,086 m)
**Official language:** Arabic
**Religions:** Islam, Christianity
**Currency:** Lebanese pound
**Main exports:** Jewelry, clothing
**Government:** Multiparty republic
**Per capita GNP:** Estimated at between U.S. $1,500 and U.S. $3,500

## ECONOMIC SURVEY

**Farming:** Important farm products include oranges, lemons, limes, grapes, apples, tomatoes, potatoes, vegetables, wheat, and sugar beet. Goats, sheep, cattle, and chickens are raised. Most of the forests where the cedars of Lebanon grew have been cut down.
**Industry:** Lebanon's economy, based on banking and other service industries, has been ruined by years of civil war. Many factories have been destroyed. Those that remain produce processed foods, cement, chemicals, textiles, and furniture. Trading with other countries continues. Tourism was an important money-earner before the civil war which began in the mid-1970s.

At the eastern end of the Mediterranean, Lebanon is sandwiched between Syria and Israel. Behind the narrow coastal plain are the Lebanon Mountains. An interior plateau contains the fertile Bekaa valley and the Litani River. The climate is Mediterranean. Most of the people are Arabs. About 60 percent are Muslims, and the rest are Christians. In the 2000s B.C. Lebanon was the home of the Phoenicians, a sea-trading people. It was later ruled by Egyptians, Babylonians, Persians, Greeks, Romans, Arabs, and Turks. Lebanon was ruled by France from 1918 to 1946, when it became an independent republic. Tensions caused by the Israel-Palestine problem and divisions between Muslims and Christians led to civil war in 1975. Israel and Syria intervened, but war continued. A new government (1991) brought hope of stability.

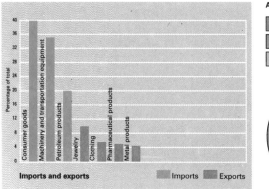

**Imports and exports**

Imports   Exports

**Age distribution**

Under 15

15 - 60

Over 60

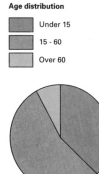

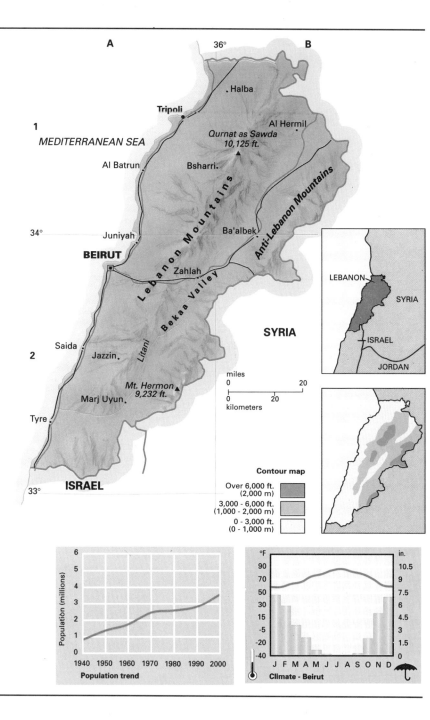

**Contour map**

Over 6,000 ft. (2,000 m)

3,000 - 6,000 ft. (1,000 - 2,000 m)

0 - 3,000 ft. (0 - 1,000 m)

**Population trend**

**Climate - Beirut**

# Lesotho

**Area:** 11,720 sq. miles (30,355 km²)
**Population:** 1,760,000
**Capital:** Maseru (pop. 109,000)
**Highest point:** Thabana-Ntlenyana 11,424 ft. (3,482 m)
**Official languages:** Sesotho, English
**Religions:** Christianity, various traditional religions
**Currency:** Loti
**Main exports:** Diamonds, food and live animals, manufactured goods
**Government:** Monarchy, with military council
**Per capita GNP:** U.S. $470

This mountainous country is landlocked and entirely surrounded by South Africa. It includes the Drakensberg range in the east and the Maloti range in the center. The only lowlands are in the west. The Orange River rises in northeast Lesotho. The summers are moist and warm, winters cold and dry. The people are mostly Basuto, who speak a Bantu language called Sesotho. Most of them live in the lowlands and the Orange River valley. Tribal wars and invasions swept through southern Africa in the 1700s and 1800s. In the 1820s Moshoeshoe, a Basuto chief, established a fortified kingdom near the site of present-day Maseru. Through a treaty with Moshoeshoe, Britain established a protectorate in 1868. Called Basutoland, it was a colony until 1966 when it became independent as Lesotho. Moshoeshoe's dynasty still reigns.

## ECONOMIC SURVEY

**Farming:** Livestock herding is the main activity. Cattle, goats, and sheep are reared. Wool is an important export. The chief food crops are wheat, corn, sorghum, barley, oats, beans, and other vegetables. Soil fertility has been seriously damaged by over-grazing and over-cultivation, and some food has to be imported.
**Mining:** Commercial diamond mining was halted in the 1980s, but individual digging continues. Oil prospecting has begun.
**Industry:** Food processing, textiles, household and leather goods, metal products, chemicals, and tiles are the main industries. Many men work in South Africa, sending cash home.

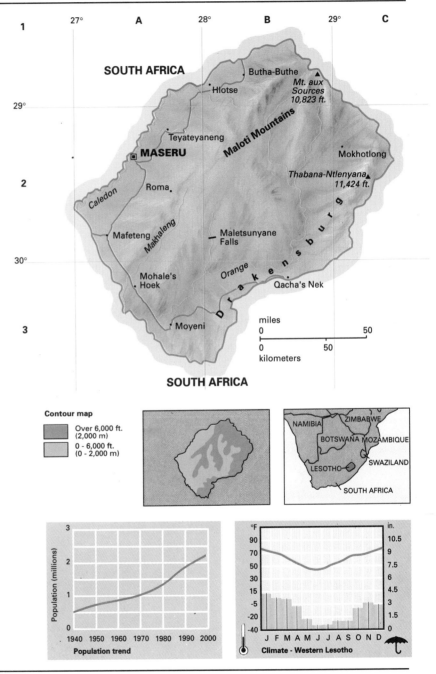

miles
0 — 50
0 — 50
kilometers

**Contour map**

- Over 6,000 ft. (2,000 m)
- 0 - 6,000 ft. (0 - 2,000 m)

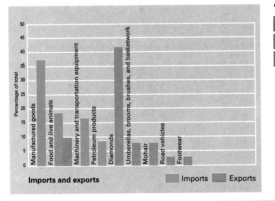

**Imports and exports**

Imports   Exports

**Age distribution**

- Under 15
- 15 - 60
- Over 60

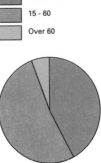

**Population trend**

**Climate - Western Lesotho**

# Liberia

**Area:** 43,000 sq. miles (111,369 km²)
**Population:** 2,591,000
**Capital:** Monrovia (pop. 425,000)
**Other cities:** Buchanan 24,000
**Highest point:** Mount Nimba 5,800 ft. (1,768 m)
**Official language:** English
**Religions:** Christianity, Islam, various traditional beliefs
**Currency:** Liberian dollar
**Main exports:** Iron ore, rubber, timber, uncut diamonds
**Government:** Republic
**Per capita GNP:** U.S. $440

Liberia is Africa's oldest republic, though not its oldest sovereign state. Situated on the southwestern coast of West Africa, the country has a coastal plain with mangrove swamps and savannas, behind which rise forested plateaus and grassy highlands. The climate is very warm with heavy rainfall in the wet season. There are 16 main language groups. The dominant social group, the Americo-Liberians, are descended from former Black American slaves. In 1822 the American Colonization Society founded Monrovia (named after U.S. President James Monroe and now Liberia's capital) as a settlement for freed slaves. In 1847 Liberia became an independent republic. U.S. aid during World War II led to the development of the harbor and roads. In 1980 a military coup deposed the Americo-Liberian regime. Civil war broke out in 1990.

## ECONOMIC SURVEY

**Farming:** Most of the Liberians are farmers. They grow rice and cassava for their own needs. Cash crops include coffee, bananas, citrus fruits, and cocoa beans.
**Forestry:** Rubber is the chief woodland product. The forests also yield mahogany, African walnut, and other hardwoods.
**Shipping:** Liberia has one of the world's largest merchant fleets. Ships owned by other nations are Liberian-registered for tax benefits. Liberia derives a large income from registration fees.
**Mining:** Iron ore is the chief mineral. Other minerals include diamonds, gold, lead, manganese, zinc, and bauxite.
**Industry:** Civil war has hit what little industry there is.

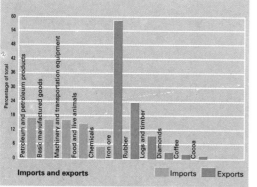

Imports and exports

**Age distribution**

- Under 15
- 15 - 60
- Over 60

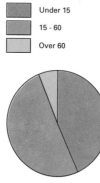

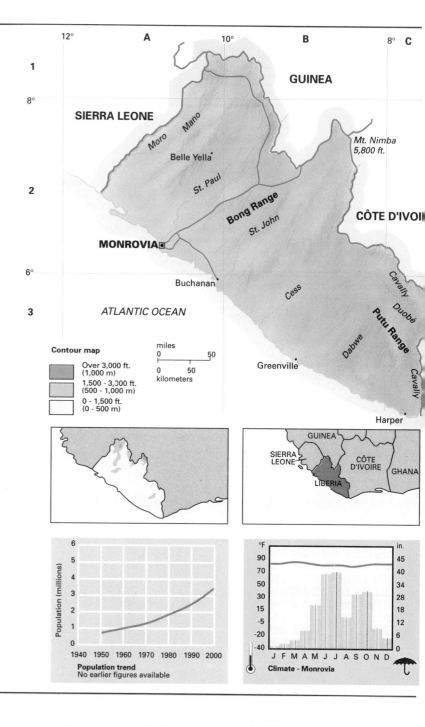

### Contour map

- Over 3,000 ft. (1,000 m)
- 1,500 - 3,000 ft. (500 - 1,000 m)
- 0 - 1,500 ft. (0 - 500 m)

miles
0 — 50
0 — 50
kilometers

ATLANTIC OCEAN

**Population trend**
No earlier figures available

**Climate - Monrovia**

# Libya

**Area:** 679,362 sq. miles (1,759,540 km²)
**Population:** 4,206,000
**Capital:** Tripoli (pop. 591,000)
**Other cities:** Benghazi 446,000; Misratah 285,000; Sabhah 113,000
**Highest point:** Bette Peak 7,500 ft. (2,286 m)
**Official language:** Arabic
**Religion:** Islam
**Currency:** Dinar
**Main exports:** Petroleum
**Government:** Socialist jamahiriya (state of the masses)
**Per capita GNP:** U.S. $5,410

Oil-rich Libya is a mainly desert country with a coastline on the Mediterranean Sea. The land rises toward the south. Most people live on the northeast (Cyrenaican) and northwest (Tripolitanian) coastal plains, where the rainfall is moderate despite high temperatures. Most Libyans are of Arab or Berber origin. Phoenicians, Greeks, and Romans all influenced the early history of Libya. Muslim Arab domination began in the A.D. 600s. In the 1500s Ottoman Turks controlled the region, although Libyan rulers had almost unlimited power. In 1912 Italy took control of Libya, but lost the colony after it was defeated in World War II. Libya became independent first as a monarchy (1951) and then as a centrally controlled republic (1963). The radical and pro-revolutionary Colonel Muammar Gadaffi has led the country since 1969.

## ECONOMIC SURVEY

**Farming:** Only about 8 percent of the land can be farmed. Fruit (dates, olives, grapes, peaches, and oranges) and vegetables are grown near the coast, where oases are famous for fertility. Irrigation schemes involve the Great Man-Made River project to pump water from inland wells to the coastal region. Livestock grazing (mostly sheep) is the main activity.
**Fishing:** Tuna is the leading catch.
**Mining:** Libya's wealth comes from oil, by far the most valuable source of revenue.
**Industry:** Funded by oil revenue, many ambitious projects have been started for the local manufacture of building materials, processed foods, and clothing.

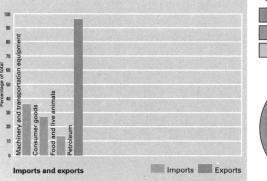

**Imports and exports**
Imports — Exports

### Age distribution
- Under 15
- 15 - 60
- Over 60

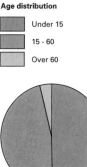

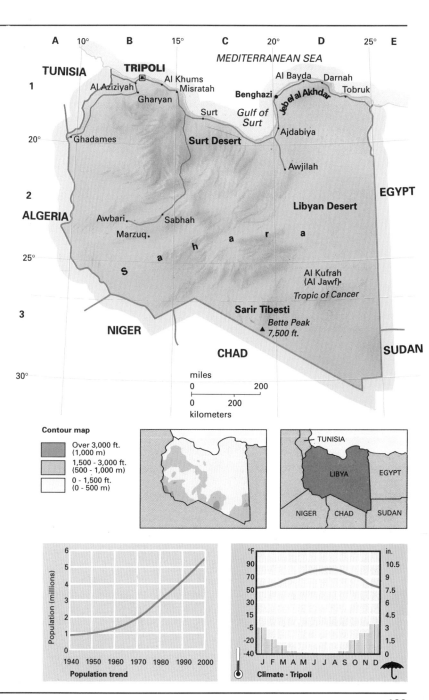

**Contour map**
- Over 3,000 ft. (1,000 m)
- 1,500 - 3,000 ft. (500 - 1,000 m)
- 0 - 1,500 ft. (0 - 500 m)

**Population trend**

**Climate - Tripoli**

*see* AFRICA, page 14

# Liechtenstein

**Area**: 61 sq. miles (157 km²)
**Population**: 29,000
**Capital**: Vaduz (pop. 4900)
**Highest point**: Grauspitz 8,527 ft. (2,599 m)
**Official language**: German
**Religion**: Roman Catholicism
**Currency**: Swiss franc
**Main exports**: Machinery and transportation equipment, metal products, chemical products
**Government**: Constitutional monarchy
**Per capita GNP**: U.S. $16,500

The principality of Liechtenstein lies between Austria and Switzerland. It is linked with Switzerland in a customs union, and uses Swiss currency. Switzerland also controls its postal and telephone services. The north of the country is lowland, and includes the river plain of the Rhine. There are mountains in the south. The country has a comparatively mild climate which is very similar to that of Switzerland. In the Middle Ages it consisted of two small states, Vaduz and Schellenberg, within the Holy Roman (German) empire. The modern principality was founded in 1719 when an Austrian prince, Johann-Adam Liechtenstein, bought both states. From 1815 Liechtenstein was part of the German Confederation, but it became independent in 1866. It is a constitutional monarchy, ruled by princes of the House of Liechtenstein, descended from Prince Johann-Adam. The country has remained neutral in the 20th century and does not have an army.

## ECONOMIC SURVEY

**Farming:** Only about 10 percent of the work force is engaged in agriculture. Farmers grow cereals, fruits, grapes for wine, and vegetables. Cattle are reared. The mountain slopes are clothed with pine forests.

**Industry:** Since the 1950s Liechtenstein has changed from a mainly farming country to an industrial one. It makes machinery and transportation equipment, while its light industries produce ceramics, textiles, and precision instruments. Low taxes encourage foreign firms to set up bases in the principality. Tourism and the sale of postage stamps help to boost the country's revenues. Hydro-electric power is sold to Switzerland.

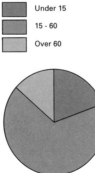

**Imports and exports**

Age distribution
- Under 15
- 15 - 60
- Over 60

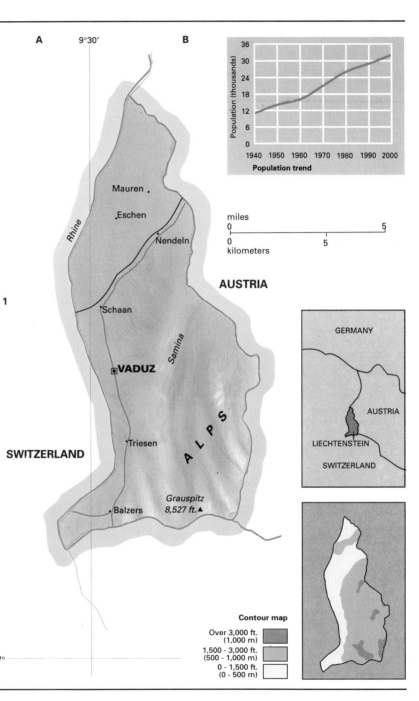

**Population trend**

miles 0 — 5
kilometers 0 — 5

AUSTRIA

SWITZERLAND

GERMANY

AUSTRIA

LIECHTENSTEIN

SWITZERLAND

**Contour map**
- Over 3,000 ft. (1,000 m)
- 1,500 - 3,000 ft. (500 - 1,000 m)
- 0 - 1,500 ft. (0 - 500 m)

# Luxembourg

**Area:** 998 sq. miles (2,586 km²)
**Population:** 377,000
**Capital:** Luxembourg (pop. 77,000)
**Other cities:** Esch-sur-Alzette 24,000
**Highest point:** Buurgplatz 1,854 ft. (565 m)
**Official languages:** French, German, Letzeburgesch (a form of German)
**Religions:** Roman Catholicism, Protestantism
**Currency:** Luxembourg franc
**Main exports:** Steel, metal products, machinery and transportation equipment, plastics
**Government:** Constitutional monarchy
**Per capita GNP:** U.S. $24,860

The Grand Duchy of Luxembourg is a small state bordered by Belgium, France, and Germany. The Ardennes region in the north is hilly. In the south there are fertile lowlands. The mild, moist climate is suitable for farming. Luxembourg's picturesque scenery is popular with tourists. Most people live in the south of the country. Luxembourg became a Grand Duchy in 1354. Until 1795 first Spain, and then Austria, ruled it. Luxembourg was annexed by France, but in 1815 it became part of the Netherlands. Much of the Grand Duchy became part of Belgium in 1831. The remainder became self-governing as Luxembourg in 1839. In 1867 the neutrality of Luxembourg was guaranteed. In 1948 Belgium, the Netherlands, and Luxembourg formed the Benelux customs union. Luxembourg was a founder member of the European Community in 1957.

## ECONOMIC SURVEY

**Farming:** The south with its fertile plains is the chief agricultural region. Barley, wheat, oats, and potatoes are grown, and some wine is made. Cattle and pigs are reared.

**Industry:** Having no coal or oil reserves, Luxembourg depends on imported energy supplies. It has iron ore deposits, is a leading European steel producer, and exports iron and steel. Luxembourg has developed many newer industries such as electronics and computers, chemicals, plastics, and car components. The country is a major financial center. Many foreign banks are based there, as are the European Court of Justice and the European Coal and Steel Community.

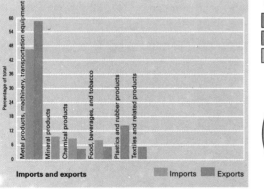

**Imports and exports**

Imports  Exports

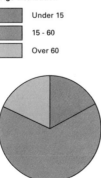

**Age distribution**

Under 15
15 - 60
Over 60

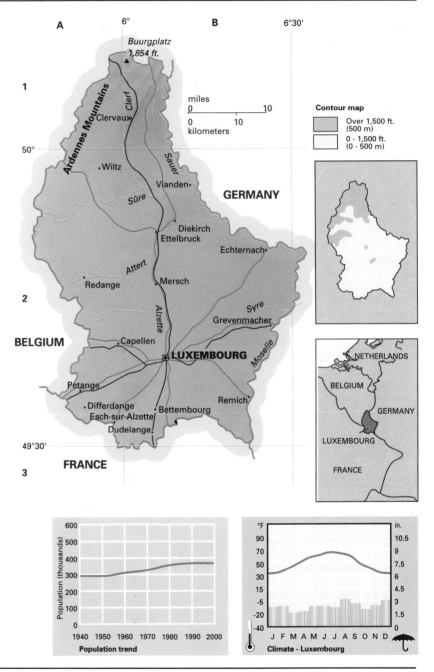

**Contour map**

Over 1,500 ft. (500 m)
0 - 1,500 ft. (0 - 500 m)

**Population trend**

**Climate - Luxembourg**

# Madagascar

**Area:** 226,658 sq. miles (587,041 km²)
**Population:** 11,980,000
**Capital:** Antananarivo (pop. 703,000)
**Other cities:** Fianarantsoa 111,000; Mahajanga 111,000
**Highest point:** Maromokotro 9,436 ft. (2,876 m)
**Official languages:** Malagasy, French
**Religions:** Christianity, various traditional beliefs
**Currency:** Malagasy franc
**Main exports:** Coffee, vanilla, sugar, cloves
**Government:** Republic
**Per capita GNP:** U.S. $230

This island country is separated from the African mainland by the Mozambique Channel. More than two thirds of Madagascar is a high plateau, with volcanic peaks such as the Tsaratanana Massif rising above it. In the east is a narrow coastal plain, and there are broader lowlands in the west. The forested east coast is hot and humid. The grassy and savanna-covered plateau is cool with abundant rainfall. The southwestern lowlands are semi-desert. The wildlife includes unique birds and mammals, such as lemurs. The people are of Indonesian and African origin. They speak Malagasy, which is based on the language of the Merina, the largest ethnic group. Portuguese sailors discovered Madagascar in 1500. France made it a protectorate in 1885. Independence was achieved in 1960. It was called the Malagasy Republic until 1975.

## ECONOMIC SURVEY

**Farming:** About 80 percent of the people are farmers. They grow rice, cassava, sugar-cane, sweet potatoes, bananas, corn, mangoes, and coconuts. Coffee is the most valuable cash crop. The island also produces vanilla and cloves, and sisal. Cattle, reared in the the western lowlands, are the most important livestock.
**Forestry:** Forests (much reduced in some parts of the island) yield valuable timbers, gums, and resins.
**Mining:** Some chromite, graphite, salt, mica, and gold are produced.
**Industry:** There are few factories. They process sugar and other farm products. Communications are inadequate.

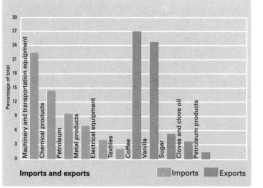

**Imports and exports**

**Age distribution**
- Under 15
- 15 - 60
- Over 60

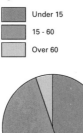

Imports  Exports

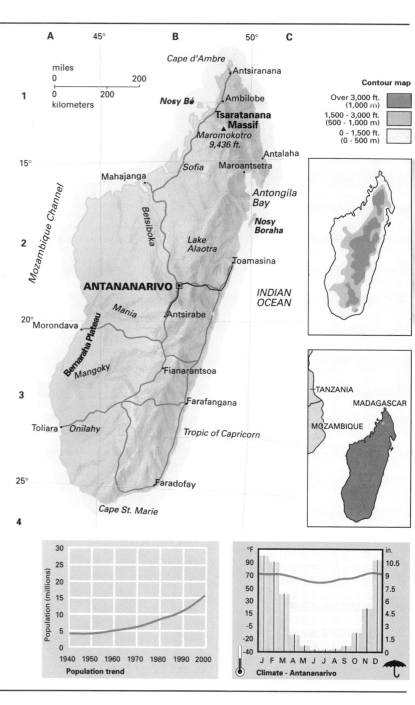

**Population trend**

**Climate - Antananarivo**

# Malawi

**Area:** 45,747 sq. miles (118,484 km²)
**Population:** 8,831,000
**Capital:** Lilongwe (pop. 220,000)
**Other cities:** Blantyre 403,000
**Highest point:** Sapitwa 9,842 ft. (3,000 m)
**Official languages:** Chichewa, English
**Religions:** Christianity, various traditional beliefs, Islam
**Currency:** Kwacha
**Main exports:** Tobacco, sugar, tea, groundnuts (peanuts)
**Government:** Single-party republic
**Per capita GNP:** U.S. $180

The landlocked republic of Malawi in southern Africa includes part of Lake Nyasa (Lake Malawi) in the Great Rift Valley. The Shire River flows from the lake into the Zambezi River in Mozambique. There are highlands west of Lake Nyasa (Lake Malawi). They are wet and cool, whereas the lowlands are hot and humid. Forests and savanna cover much of the country. The volcanic soil is fertile. Besides Chichewa, the people speak several Bantu languages, including Nyanja, Yao, and Tumbuka. Bantu kingdoms arose in the region about 2,000 years ago. In the 1800s the area was ravaged by tribal wars and slave-trading. British missionaries and traders moved in, and in 1891 a British protectorate, known as Nyasaland from 1907, was set up. The country became independent in 1964 and took the name Malawi. It has been a republic since 1966.

## ECONOMIC SURVEY

**Farming:** Malawi is predominantly a nation of farmers. Most small farmers grow subsistence crops, such as sorghum, corn, millet, beans, and other vegetables, and pumpkins. Tobacco (the most valuable cash crop) and tea are grown on large farms. Sugarcane, groundnuts (peanuts) and rice are also exported.
**Fishing:** Lake Nyasa (Lake Malawi) supports a commercial fishery.
**Mining:** Malawi lacks minerals apart from small amounts of limestone, marble, and coal. There are deposits of bauxite.
**Industry:** Malawi's industries produce building materials, cement, cotton goods, and processed foods.

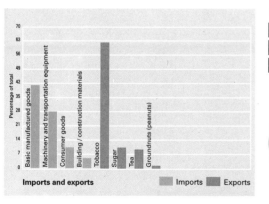

**Imports and exports**

Imports | Exports

**Age distribution**

- Under 15
- 15 - 60
- Over 60

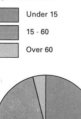

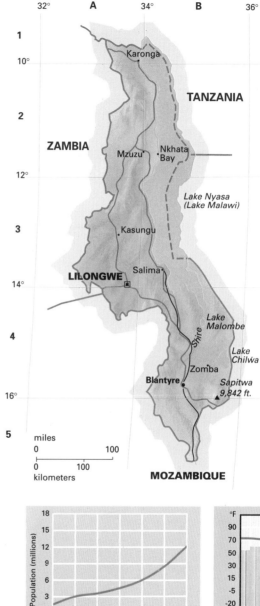

**Contour map**

- Over 3,000 ft. (1,000 m)
- 1,500 - 3,000 ft. (500 - 1,000 m)
- 0 -1,500 ft. (0 - 500 m)

miles
0          100
0      100
kilometers

**Population trend**

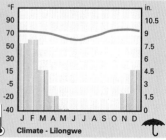

**Climate - Lilongwe**

# Malaysia

**Area:** 127,317 sq. miles (329,749 km$^2$)
**Population:** 17,886,000
**Capital:** Kuala Lumpur (pop. 1,103,000)
**Other cities:** Ipoh 301,000
**Highest point:** Mount Kinabalu 13,432 ft. (4,094 m)
**Official language:** Bahasa Malaysia
**Religions:** Islam, Buddhism
**Currency:** Malaysian dollar
**Main exports:** Manufactured goods, petroleum, palm oil, rubber, timber, tin
**Government:** Federal constitutional monarchy
**Per capita GNP:** U.S. $2,130

Malaysia has two main land areas: the southern Malay peninsula and northern Borneo (Sabah and Sarawak). Much of the land is mountainous and forested. The chief lowlands are in the Malay peninsula. The climate is tropical, with heavy monsoon rains. The people are Malays (about 50 percent of the population), Chinese (about 35 percent) and Indians (about 10 percent). Minority ethnic groups include the Dyaks of Sabah and Sarawak. Most Malays are Muslims. The Chinese follow Buddhism and Confucianism, and the Indians are mainly Hindus. In the Middle Ages important trading kingdoms arose in Malaya, notably Melaka. European contact began in the 1500s. Britain gained control of Malaya in the 1800s. On September 16, 1963 the independent Federation of Malaysia was formed. Singapore was part of it, but left in 1965.

## ECONOMIC SURVEY

**Farming:** Rubber and palm oil, from large plantations, are among Malaysia's most important products. Farmers grow rice, coconuts, peppers, vegetables, and fruit. Cattle, pigs, goats, and buffaloes are reared.
**Forestry:** The country's hardwood forests are being exploited for timber.
**Fishing:** Offshore fishing is important.
**Mining:** Malaysia has large reserves of minerals. It leads the world in tin production. It also has petroleum, gold, copper, bauxite, iron ore, and titanium ore.
**Industry:** The chief products of Malaysia's factories are electronic goods, vehicles, textiles, clothing, and foodstuffs.

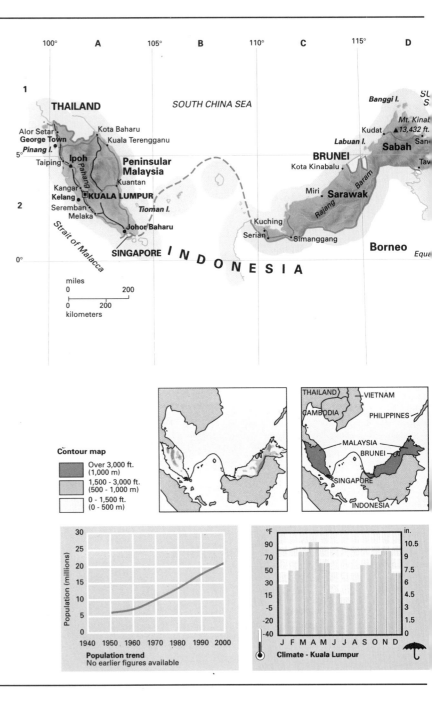

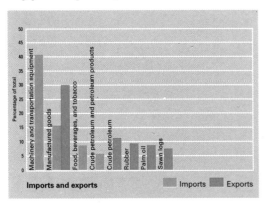

**Imports and exports**

Imports | Exports

**Age distribution**

Under 15
15 - 60
Over 60

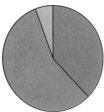

**Contour map**

Over 3,000 ft. (1,000 m)
1,500 - 3,000 ft. (500 - 1,000 m)
0 - 1,500 ft. (0 - 500 m)

**Population trend**
No earlier figures available

**Climate - Kuala Lumpur**

# Mali

**Area:** 478,767 sq. miles (1,240,000 km²)
**Population:** 8,047,000
**Capital:** Bamako (pop. 646,000)
**Other cities:** Ségou 89,000
**Highest point:** Hombori Tondo 3,789 ft.
(1,155 m)
**Official language:** French
**Religions:** Islam, various traditional beliefs
**Currency:** Franc CFA
**Main exports:** Cotton, live animals, groundnuts
(peanuts)
**Government:** Single-party republic
**Per capita GNP:** U.S. $260

Mali is landlocked and mostly flat. The Sahara Desert covers the northern half of the country. There are uplands in the northeast and south. The Niger River flows in an arc through southern Mali, creating an interior delta. The river valley provides the only arable farmland. Rainfall in the south is adequate, and the climate throughout the country is warm. Some of the people are of Arab and Berber origin, such as the Tuaregs, and some are of mixed origin, such as the Fulani (Peul), but more than 80 percent belong to Black African ethnic groups. The presence of prehistoric settlements is known from rock paintings. From A.D. 300 to the 1500s the Mali empire controlled caravan routes across the region. From 1591 Mali was under Moorish influence. In 1880 France made the area a protectorate. Mali achieved independence in 1960.

## ECONOMIC SURVEY

**Farming:** Most people are rural farmers, growing subsistence crops of corn, cassava, millet, sorghum, rice, and yams. Cotton is the main cash crop. In the Sahel, the drought-prone region south of the Sahara, and the southern grasslands cattle, sheep, goats, camels, horses, and donkeys are grazed by nomads. There is little forest. Live animals and groundnuts (peanuts) are exported.
**Fishing:** Fish are caught in the rivers and salted for export.
**Mining:** Mali's limited mineral resources include marble, limestone, iron ore, and salt.
**Industry:** Factories produce cotton fibers and process animal products such as meat and skins.

**Age distribution**

- Under 15
- 15 - 60
- Over 60

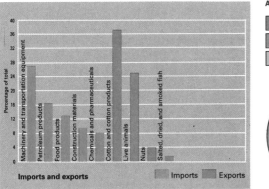

Imports and exports — Imports / Exports

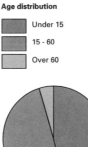

**Population trend**

**Climate - Bamako**

**Contour map**

- Over 1,500 ft. (500 m)
- 0 - 1,500 ft. (0 - 500 m)

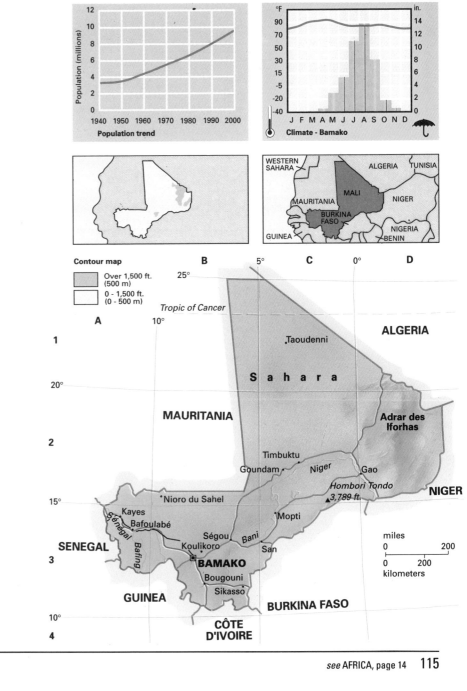

# Malta

**Area:** 122 sq. miles (316 km²)
**Population:** 351,000
**Capital:** Valletta (pop. 9,000)
**Other towns:** Birkirkara 20,000
**Highest point:** 829 ft. (253 m)
**Official languages:** Maltese, English
**Religion:** Roman Catholicism
**Currency:** Maltese lira
**Main exports:** Manufactured goods, machinery, transportation equipment; tourism is a major source of foreign income
**Government:** Constitutional republic
**Per capita GNP:** U.S. $5,820

Malta is a republic in the Mediterranean, south of Sicily. It consists of the islands of Malta, Gozo, Comino, and two smaller islets. The island of Malta has a rocky coastline, with deep bays and inlets. Malta has warm summers and mild winters. Much of the native vegetation, which because of the shortage of water was never luxurious, has been destroyed by development. The smaller island of Gozo is greener and has more farmland. Malta has few minerals, and tourism is the main source of income. Most Maltese are of Arab, Italian, and English descent. Malta was fought over for centuries because of its strategic importance. It was a British colony from 1814 until it became independent in 1964. Its courage in withstanding a long siege in World War II earned the island the British valor award, the George Cross.

## ECONOMIC SURVEY

**Farming:** Malta and Gozo have poor soil, but farmers grow crops of wheat, barley, potatoes, onions, and other vegetables in small terraced fields. Grapes, honey, figs, and other fruits are produced. Small numbers of goats, sheep, cattle, and pigs are kept, and chickens are reared. However, the islands do not produce enough food to feed the population.
**Industry:** Most of the work force is engaged in industry, including tourism. The Maltese produce plastics, metal goods, textiles, engineering, and craft goods using imported materials. Electronics, including making semiconductors, is a growth industry. The former British naval dockyard is now a ship repair yard.

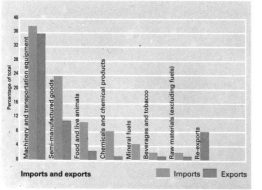

**Imports and exports**

Machinery and transportation equipment; Semi-manufactured goods; Food and live animals; Chemicals and chemical products; Mineral fuels; Beverages and tobacco; Raw materials (excluding fuels); Re-exports

Percentage of total

**Age distribution**

Under 15
15 - 60
Over 60

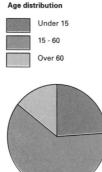
Imports | Exports

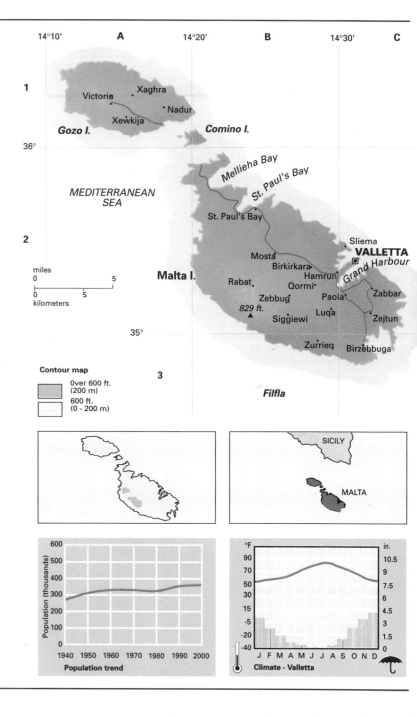

**Contour map**

Over 600 ft. (200 m)
600 ft. (0 - 200 m)

**Population trend**

**Climate - Valletta**

# Mauritania

**Area:** 397,956 sq. miles (1,030,700 km²)
**Population:** 1,999,000
**Capital:** Nouakchott (pop. 600,000)
**Other cities:** Kaédi 32,000
**Highest point:** Kediet Hill 3,002 ft. (915 m)
**Official languages:** Arabic, French
**Religion:** Islam
**Currency:** Ouguiya
**Main exports:** Fish, iron ore
**Government:** Military regime
**Per capita GNP:** U.S. $490

The Islamic Republic of Mauritania in northwest Africa is largely in the barren Sahara region. Low plateaus, which are desert except for scattered oases, cover most of the country. In the southwest are plains and grasslands watered by the Sénégal River. Average temperatures are high. More than 60 percent of the people are of Arab and Berber origins. The rest are Black Africans. Mauritania was dominated from the A.D. 300s to the 1500s by two great African empires: Ghana` and Mali. Kumbi Saleh, the capital of Ancient Ghana, was in southeastern Mauritania. Later the region came under Arab domination, with European contact increasing from the 1600s. Mauritania became a protectorate of France in 1903 and a French colony in 1920. The country was granted independence in 1960. For a time it claimed to share Spain's old colony of Western Sahara with Morocco.

## ECONOMIC SURVEY

**Farming:** Mauritania's internal economy is based on agriculture and herding. Most people are farmers. The south is the best crop-growing area. The main farm crops include sorghum, millet, dates, corn, beans, sweet potatoes, peanuts, and rice. Sheep, cattle, and goats are kept. Nomads wander with their animals on the savannas.
**Fishing:** The coastal waters are rich in fish and shellfish, and fish-canning factories have been set up. Fish is an important export.
**Mining:** There are rich deposits of iron ore in the northwest of the country, and copper is mined.
**Industry:** There is little manufacturing, but factories process meat, milk, and hides.

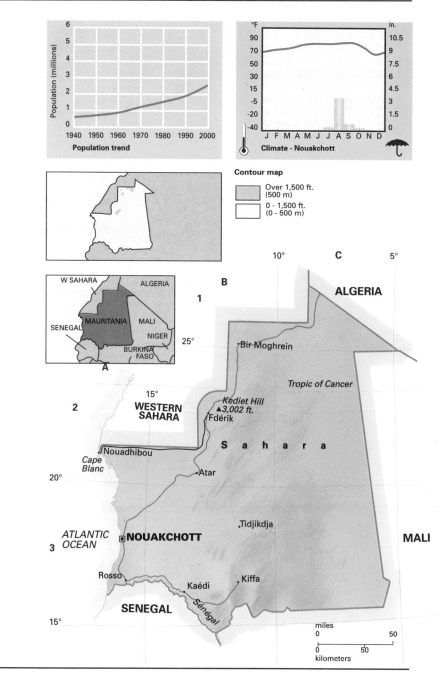

**Population trend**

**Climate - Nouakchott**

**Contour map**

Over 1,500 ft. (500 m)

0 - 1,500 ft. (0 - 500 m)

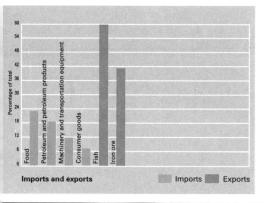

**Imports and exports**

Imports  Exports

**Age distribution**

Under 15

15 - 60

Over 60

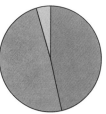

# Mexico

**Area:** 761,605 sq. miles (1,972,547 km²)
**Population:** 85,784,000
**Capital:** Mexico City (pop. with suburbs 18,748,000)
**Other cities:** Guadalajara 2,245,000
**Highest point:** Citlaltépetl 18,865 ft. (5,750 m)
**Official language:** Spanish
**Religion:** Christianity
**Currency:** Peso
**Main exports:** Petroleum and petroleum products, cars and trucks, fertilizers, minerals
**Government:** Federal republic
**Per capita GNP:** U.S. $1,990

Mexico is largely mountainous, with high plateaus and volcanoes. The chief mountain ranges are the Sierra Madre Occidental and Sierra Madre Oriental. Baja (Lower) California is a long peninsula. There are three main climatic zones, by altitude: the tropical *tierra caliente*, the mild *tierra templada*, and the colder *tierra friada*. The northwest is dry. The population is a mixture of people of Native American and European origin. They speak Spanish, and most are Catholics. Hunter-gatherers inhabited Mexico more than 22,000 years ago. Between A.D. 100 and 1500 the Olmec, Toltec, Mayan, and Aztec civilizations flourished. Spaniards under Hernán Cortés conquered the Aztecs in 1521. Spain ruled Mexico until 1821, and the Mexican republic was founded in 1824. The country has had many revolutions, the last in 1920.

## ECONOMIC SURVEY

**Farming:** Corn is the principal food crop. Other important crops are bananas, beans, coffee, cotton, oranges, sorghum, sugarcane, and wheat. Tropical fruits and vegetables, such as chilli peppers, are grown as cash crops. Livestock includes cattle, pigs, sheep, poultry, horses, and mules.
**Fishing:** Sardines, anchovies, shrimps, and tuna are caught.
**Mining:** Silver, gold, copper, and oil are the main minerals.
**Industry:** Petroleum products lead the field, followed by vehicles, steel, machinery, chemicals, and fertilizers. Craft goods such as silverware, jewelry, and baskets are sold to the six million annual tourists.

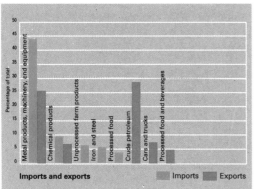

**Imports and exports**

**Age distribution**

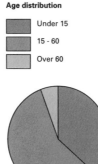

- Under 15
- 15 - 60
- Over 60

Imports    Exports

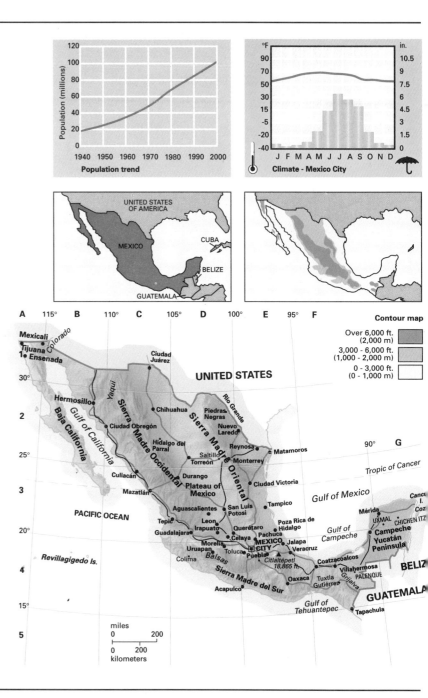

Population trend

Climate - Mexico City

Contour map

Over 6,000 ft. (2,000 m)
3,000 - 6,000 ft. (1,000 - 2,000 m)
0 - 3,000 ft. (0 - 1,000 m)

# Mongolia

**Area:** 604,250 sq. miles (1,565,000 km²)
**Population:** 2,150,000
**Capital:** Ulan Bator (pop. 500,000)
**Other cities:** Darhan 80,000
**Highest point:** Najramdal Uul 14,314 ft.
(4,363 m)
**Official language:** Mongolian
**Religion:** Buddhism
**Currency:** Tugrik
**Main exports:** Coal, metals, farm products
including livestock, wool, and meat
**Government:** Multiparty republic
**Per capita GNP:** U.S. $1,820

The landlocked republic of Mongolia lies between China and Russia in northern Asia. A featureless plateau covers much of Mongolia, with rugged mountains in the west. The Gobi Desert stretches over much of the southeast, covering a third of the country. One of the main rivers is the Selenga. Most of the population are Mongols, with Chinese, Kazakh, and Russian minorities. Most of them were formerly nomadic herders who now live on state-managed farms. A few Mongols still follow their traditional wandering life, living in collapsible tents called gers or yurts. The powerful Mongol empire created in the 1200s by Genghis Khan was later absorbed by Manchuria and China. A Mongolian Buddhist kingdom was set up in 1912. It became an independent communist republic in 1924.

## ECONOMIC SURVEY

**Farming:** Production of wheat and other crops is increasing as the economy shifts away from traditional herding. The nomadic people reared sheep, goats, horses, cattle, and camels. State or collective farms now own 80 percent of livestock. In the early 1990s there was some movement toward a market economy.
**Mining:** Mineral deposits include coal, copper, gold, iron ore, molybdenum, oil, and tin, but production levels are low.
**Industry:** Mongolia is developing its industry. Manufactured products include bricks, cement, foods, wool, and woolen goods (such as sheepskin coats), furniture, glass, and pottery.

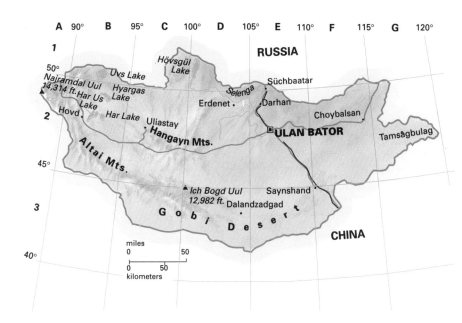

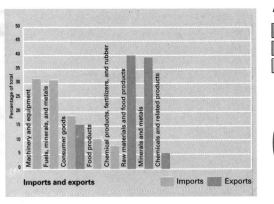

**Imports and exports**
Imports ▮ Exports ▮

**Age distribution**

▮ Under 15
▮ 15 - 60
▮ Over 60

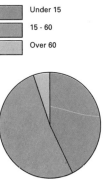

**Contour map**
▮ Over 6,000 ft. (2,000 m)
▮ 3,000 - 6,000 ft. (1,000 - 2,000 m)
▯ 0 - 3,000 ft. (0 - 1,000 m)

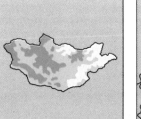

**Population trend**

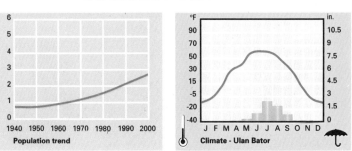

**Climate - Ulan Bator**

# Morocco

**Area:** 177, 117 sq. miles (458,730 km²)
**Population:** 25,228,000
**Capital:** Rabat (pop. 519,000)
**Other cities:** Casablanca 2,139,000; Fez 448,000; Marrakesh 440,000
**Highest point:** Jebel Toubkal 13,665 ft. (4,165 m)
**Official language:** Arabic
**Religion:** Islam
**Currency:** Dirham
**Main exports:** Phosphates and phosphate products, clothing, fish, fruit, vegetables
**Government:** Constitutional monarchy
**Per capita GNP:** U.S. $900

## ECONOMIC SURVEY

**Farming:** The chief crops include wheat, barley, corn, sugar-beet, citrus fruits, potatoes, tomatoes, beans, and olives. Large farms produce more than 80 percent of the crops. Sheep, cattle, and goats are the main livestock.
**Fishing:** Sardines, mackerel, tuna, and anchovies are caught, for export or for use in animal feed and fertilizers.
**Mining:** Morocco has 65 percent of the world's phosphates. It also has useful deposits of cobalt, lead, salt, coal, oil, and natural gas.
**Industry:** Factories make carpets, clothing, foods, chemicals, and petroleum products. Tourism is now an increasingly important industry.

The Atlas Mountains cross Morocco from southwest to northeast in three ranges: the Anti Atlas, Grand Atlas, and the Middle Atlas. Coastal lowlands watered from shallow rivers rise inland to a plateau. South and east of the Atlas Mountains is the Sahara, a barren region of rock and sand. Northern Morocco has a Mediterranean climate; the south is cooler. Most people are Arabs, with about 30 percent Berbers and a few Europeans. An Arab-Berber Kingdom of Morocco was created in the late 700s. The Alawi dynasty has reigned since the 1600s. France and Spain divided and controlled Morocco from 1912 until its independence in 1956. In the 1970s Morocco claimed at first part, then all, of Western Sahara (area 102,710 sq. miles, pop. 180,000). Western Saharan nationalists fought for independence, but a truce was agreed in 1990, pending a referendum.

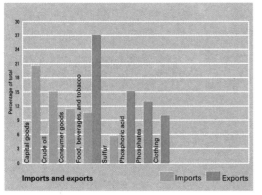
Imports and exports

Age distribution — Under 15 / 15 - 60 / Over 60

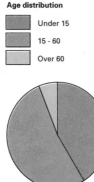

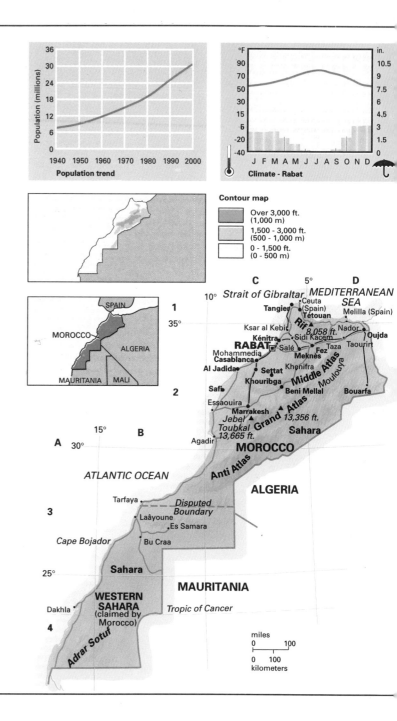

# Mozambique

**Area:** 309,496 sq. miles (801,590 km²)
**Population:** 15,696,000
**Capital:** Maputo (pop. 1,070,000)
**Other cities:** Beira 292,000; Nampula 197,000
**Highest point:** Mount Binga 7,972 ft. (2,430 m)
**Official language:** Portuguese
**Religions:** Various traditional beliefs, Christianity, Islam
**Currency:** Metical
**Main exports:** Shrimps, cashew nuts, cotton, sugar, copra
**Government:** Republic
**Per capita GNP:** U.S. $80

Roughly half of Mozambique is a flat plain, with swampy and sandy stretches, which extends inland from the coastal region. The land rises inland, and the upland plateaus and hills are mostly covered with grassland and forest. Mozambique shares Lake Nyasa (Lake Malawi) with Malawi and Tanzania. The Cabora Bassa Dam on the Zambezi River has created an artificial lake. Rivers flow east into the Indian Ocean; the river basin soils are fertile. The climate is tropical in the north, but cooler in the south. The people belong to 12 major Bantu-speaking groups. Mozambique was Portuguese-ruled from the 1500s. A guerrilla war from 1964 to 1974 brought independence under a Marxist government in 1975. Mozambique was involved in border fighting with Rhodesia (Zimbabwe) in the late 1970s, and a crippling civil war raged in the 1980s.

## ECONOMIC SURVEY

Mozambique is one of the world's poorest countries, and needs overseas aid.
**Farming:** Cashews are a major cash crop, together with cotton, sugarcane, and copra. Other crops include coconuts, corn, bananas, rice, and cassava. Cattle are the most numerous livestock. Farming methods are simple.
**Fishing:** Indian Ocean fisheries supply shrimps and lobsters.
**Mining:** Coal is mined, though production is unreliable. Other products include sea salt, hydraulic lime, bauxite (aluminum ore), and copper.
**Industry:** Food processing and oil refining are the leading industries. Neighboring states pay for rail and port access.

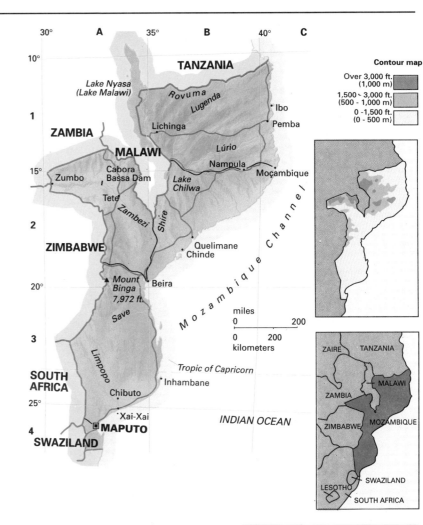

**Contour map**

Over 3,000 ft. (1,000 m)
1,500 - 3,000 ft. (500 - 1,000 m)
0 -1,500 ft. (0 - 500 m)

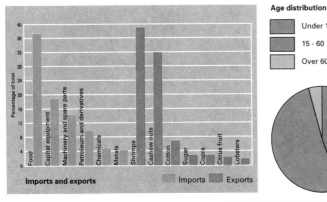

**Age distribution**

Under 15
15 - 60
Over 60

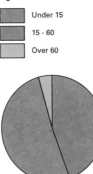

Imports and exports    Imports    Exports

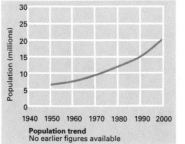

**Population trend**
No earlier figures available

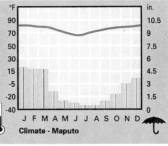

**Climate - Maputo**

# Myanmar

**Area:** 261,218 sq. miles (676,552 km²)
**Population:** 41,675,000
**Capital:** Rangoon (Yangon, pop. 2,459,000)
**Other cities:** Mandalay 533,000; Bassein 380,000; Henzada 321,000
**Highest point:** Hkakabo Razi 19,295 ft. (5,881 m)
**Official language:** Burmese
**Religions:** Buddhism, Christianity, Islam
**Currency:** Kyat Main
**Exports:** Teak, rice
**Government:** Military regime
**Per capita GNP:** Under U.S. $500

The Union of Myanmar, known as Burma before 1989, is a republic in Southeast Asia. Much of the country is mountainous. The most fertile areas are the southern valleys of the Irrawaddy and Sittang rivers. The delta of the Irrawaddy is one of the world's great rice-growing areas. The climate is mainly tropical, with heavy monsoon rains from May to September. The people are mostly Burmese. Minorities, including the Karen, Sha, Naga, and other hill peoples, have resisted central government in an attempt to preserve their cultures and establish local self-government. Internal opposition has impeded the economy. A Burmese kingdom existed in the A.D. 1000s. The country was annexed by Britain in the 1800s, but became independent in 1948. From the 1960s the country had few foreign contacts. Pro-democracy movements challenged the socialist rulers in the 1980s.

## ECONOMIC SURVEY

**Farming:** More than 60 percent of workers are farmers. Rice is the chief crop. Other crops include vegetables, fruit, sesame seeds, sugarcane, peanuts, corn, millet, jute, and rubber.
**Forestry:** Woodlands cover half the country. Myanmar's forests are noted for their teak wood.
**Fishing:** Catches are made in rivers and coastal waters, and fish are also farmed.
**Mining:** Minerals include zinc, lead, tungsten and precious stones. But mining is not well developed.
**Industry:** Small factories produce cement, glass, fertilizers, and sugar. Burma has oil and natural gas reserves, but relies mostly on hydroelectric plants for its power.

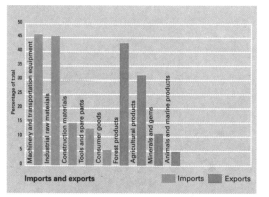

**Imports and exports**

Imports    Exports

**Age distribution**

Under 15
15 - 60
Over 60

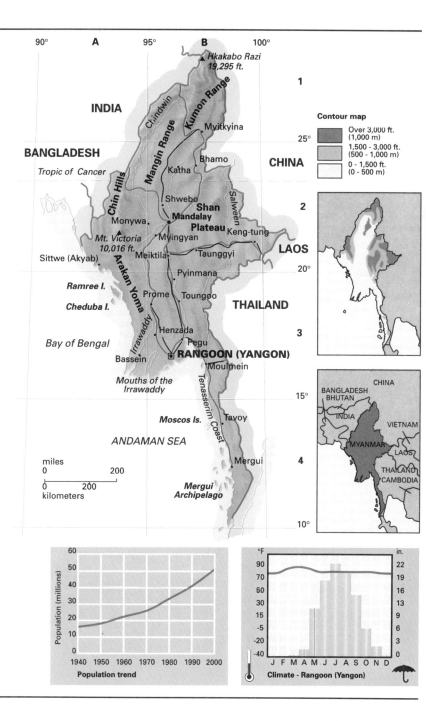

**Contour map**

Over 3,000 ft. (1,000 m)
1,500 - 3,000 ft. (500 - 1,000 m)
0 - 1,500 ft. (0 - 500 m)

Population trend

Climate - Rangoon (Yangon)

# Namibia

**Area:** 318,261 sq. miles (824,292 km²)
**Population:** 1,302,000
**Capital:** Windhoek (pop. 114,000)
**Other cities:** Swakopmund 15,500; Rundu 15,000; Rehoboth 15,000
**Highest point:** Brandberg 8,550 ft. (2,606 m)
**Official languages:** Afrikaans, English
**Religion:** Christianity
**Currency:** Rand
**Main exports:** Diamonds and other minerals, cattle and farm products
**Government:** Multiparty republic
**Per capita GNP:** U.S. $1,300

Namibia, formerly known as South West Africa, is a largely dry and infertile country. Behind the coastal plain and the Namib Desert is a central plateau some 4,000 ft. (1,200 m) above sea level. In the east is the Kalahari, a desert with some vegetation. The north has a tropical climate, the south is subtropical and dry. The Namib Desert is almost rainless. The people include Bantu-speaking Africans, who make up the majority, Europeans (12 percent), people of mixed origin (6 percent) and Khoi-San (Hottentots and Bushmen). German settlers began colonizing the coast in the 1860s, and Germany annexed 'Süd-West Afrika' in 1884. South Africa occupied the territory after World War I, under a League of Nations mandate. Prolonged United Nations attempts to win South African withdrawal and Namibia's independence succeeded in 1990.

## ECONOMIC SURVEY

**Farming:** Most farmers grow subsistence crops of corn, millet, root crops, and vegetables, but some food has to be imported. Cattle, sheep, and goats are reared, and animal products including hides and fleeces – especially karakul (persian lamb) pelts – are exported.
**Fishing:** Over-fishing has reduced Atlantic catches. Anchovies, pilchards, and mackerel are caught.
**Mining:** Minerals account for 80 percent of all exports. Most important are gem quality diamonds, together with zinc, lead, copper, uranium, gold, and silver.
**Industry:** There are small chemical and metal industries, and fish is canned.

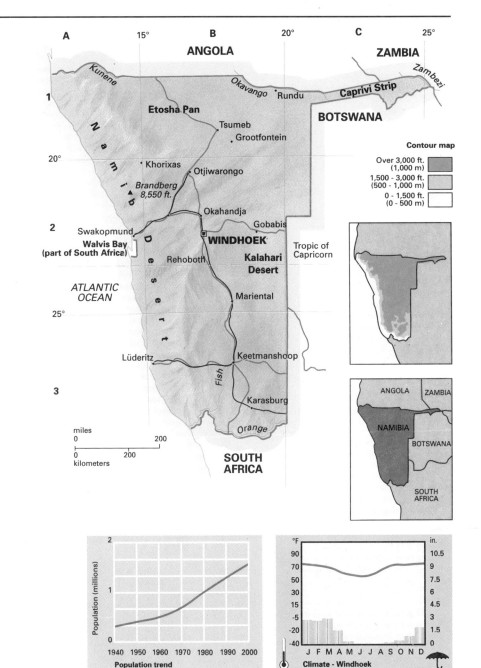

**Contour map**

- Over 3,000 ft. (1,000 m)
- 1,500 - 3,000 ft. (500 - 1,000 m)
- 0 - 1,500 ft. (0 - 500 m)

miles 0 — 200
kilometers 0 — 200

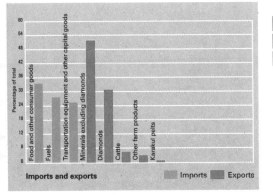

**Imports and exports**

Food and other consumer goods; Fuels; Transportation equipment and other capital goods; Minerals excluding diamonds; Diamonds; Cattle; Other farm products; Karakul pelts

Imports / Exports

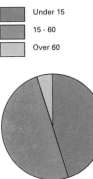

**Age distribution**

- Under 15
- 15 - 60
- Over 60

**Population trend**

Population (millions)
1940 1950 1960 1970 1980 1990 2000

**Climate - Windhoek**

°F / in.
J F M A M J J A S O N D

*see* AFRICA, page 14

# Nepal

**Area:** 54,362 sq. miles (140,797 km²)
**Population:** 18,910,000
**Capital:** Kathmandu (pop. 235,000)
**Other cities:** Biratnagar 94,000
**Highest point:** Mount Everest 29,028 ft.
(8,848 m)
**Official language:** Nepali
**Religions:** Hinduism, Buddhism
**Currency:** Rupee
**Main exports:** Manufactured goods, food
products, livestock, jute, timber
**Government:** Constitutional monarchy
**Per capita GNP:** U.S. $170

The Himalayan kingdom of Nepal is a land of
mountains with a flat, fertile river plain, the Tarai. The
country has some of the world's highest mountains,
including Mount Everest on the border with China. The
mountains have a harsh climate, and are inhabited only
by herders of sheep and yaks. The lower valleys, south
of the Himalayas, are forested. The Tarai has a tropical
climate, with jungles and swamps. Many people of
Nepal resemble those of northern India. Others are of
Tibetan origin. Most live in villages. The Sherpas are
renowned for their mountaineering feats. The Gurkhas
are famed as soldiers, serving with the British army.
Nepal's history as a unified state dates from the 1700s.
The Rana family controlled the government until the
1950s, since when Nepal has been a monarchy with
limited democracy.

## ECONOMIC SURVEY

**Farming:** Most of the
Nepalese work on the
land. Crops include
rice, corn, millet,
wheat, sugarcane,
jute, and medicinal
herbs. The best
farmland is in the
Tarai, where cattle and
water buffalo are
raised. Sheep and
yaks are the only
livestock able to
withstand the climate
in the mountains.
**Forestry:** The main
product is the heavy
brown timber of the
sal trees, used for
building work.
**Industry:** Nepal is
developing an
industrial economy.
There are jute and
sugar mills, chemical
works and small
factories making
shoes and cigarettes.
Foreign aid is devoted
to road building and
hydroelectric
development.

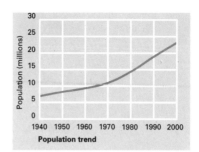

**Population trend**

**Climate - Kathmandu**

**Contour map**

Over 9,000 ft.
(3,000 m)
3,000 - 9,000 ft.
(1,000 - 3,000 m)
0 - 3,000 ft.
(0 - 1,000 m)

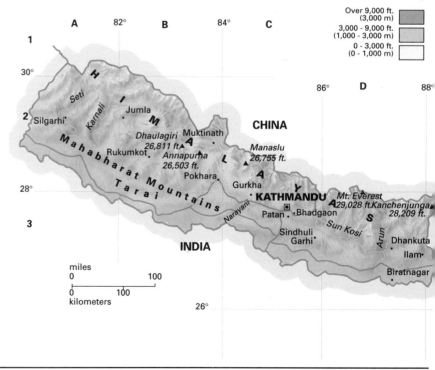

**Age distribution**

Under 15
15 - 60
Over 60

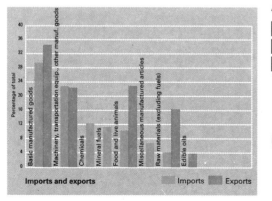

**Imports and exports**

Imports    Exports

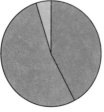

# Netherlands

**Area:** 15,770 sq. miles (40,844 km²)
**Population:** 14,927,000
**Capital:** Amsterdam (pop. 1,038,000)
**Other cities:** Rotterdam 1,040,000
**Highest point:** Vaalser Berg 1,053 ft. (321 m)
**Official language:** Dutch
**Religions:** Roman Catholicism, Protestantism
**Currency:** Guilder
**Main exports:** Machinery and transportation equipment, food, drink, and tobacco, chemicals, fuels, metals and metal products, textiles
**Government:** Constitutional monarchy
**Per capita GNP:** U.S. $16,010

## ECONOMIC SURVEY

**Farming:** Nearly 70 percent of the land is farmed, but only five out of every 100 people work on farms. Butter, cheese, and eggs are produced, as are potatoes, sugar-beet, and wheat. Flowers and bulbs are grown in glasshouses.
**Fishing:** There are fishing ports along the coast of the IJsselmeer and Zeeland. Herring is the chief catch.
**Industry:** There is little mining, but natural gas and oil are extracted offshore. Rotterdam is Europe's leading container port. Manufactured goods include electrical products, vehicles, textiles, china, pottery, and processed foods and drinks. Amsterdam is a center of the diamond-cutting trade.

About 40 percent of the Netherlands is below sea level at high tide. The North Sea is held back by dikes enclosing reclaimed land called polders. These polders make up a quarter of the total land area. The coastline is marshy and sandy. The chief rivers are the Rhine and Maas (Meuse). The country has a mild climate. Agriculture includes dairying and flower- and bulb-growing. Population density is one of the highest in the world, at 900 people per square mile. More than 75 percent of the Dutch people live in towns. The Netherlands were successively under the rule of the dukes of Burgundy and the Habsburg rulers of the German empire and Spain. The Dutch won independence in wars lasting from 1568 to 1648, and built a large maritime empire. The Netherlands became a member of the European Community in 1957.

**Population trend**

**Climate - Vlissingen**

miles 0 — 50
kilometers 0 — 50

**Age distribution**
- Under 15
- 15 - 60
- Over 60

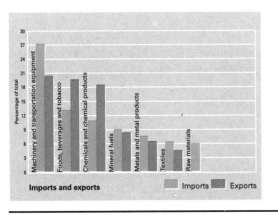

**Imports and exports**
Imports / Exports

(y-axis: Percentage of total)

Categories: Machinery and transportation equipment; Foods, beverages and tobacco; Chemicals and chemical products; Mineral fuels; Metals and metal products; Textiles; Raw materials

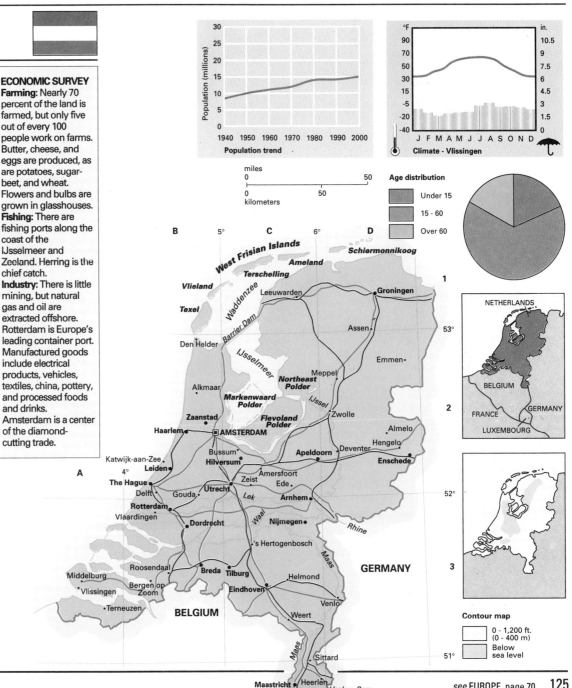

**Contour map**
- 0 - 1,200 ft. (0 - 400 m)
- Below sea level

see EUROPE, page 70

# New Zealand

**Area:** 103,736 sq. miles (268,676 km²)
**Population:** 3,390,000
**Capital:** Wellington (pop. with suburbs 325,000)
**Other cities:** Auckland 851,000; Christchurch 301,000
**Highest point:** Mount Cook 12,349 ft. (3,764 m)
**Official language:** English
**Religion:** Christianity
**Currency:** New Zealand dollar
**Main exports:** Dairy products (butter and cheese), lamb, wool, fish
**Government:** Constitutional monarchy
**Per capita GNP:** U.S. $11,800

New Zealand is made up of North Island and South Island, together with Stewart Island, the Chatham islands and some smaller islands. Most people live on North Island, which has fertile plains, a volcanic central plateau and mountains in the east. Lake Taupo is the crater of an extinct volcano. Active volcanoes include Ngauruhoe and Tongariro, and there are hot springs around Rotorua. On South Island, the mountains reappear as the Southern Alps. The island has glaciers and a coastline indented by fjords. The Canterbury Plains and the Otago Plateau are fertile lowlands. New Zealand's climate is temperate. Maoris settled in New Zealand from the 1300s, and now make up 9 percent of the population. British settlement began in the 1800s. New Zealand was a British colony from 1841 and became independent in 1907.

## ECONOMIC SURVEY

**Farming:** Wool and sheep meat are major products. There are about 20 sheep for every human. New Zealand's butter and cheese are world-famous. Cereals, fruit, and vegetables are grown.
**Forestry:** Nearly a quarter of the land is forested. Timber is harvested to make paper and pulp.
**Fishing:** The sea is rich in barracuda, red cod, and lobsters.
**Mining:** Minerals are few, but include coal and iron sands.
**Industry:** Electricity comes from volcanic steam (geothermal) and hydro-electric sources. Aluminum, iron, and steel are processed. Factories produce processed foods, machinery, metal and timber products.

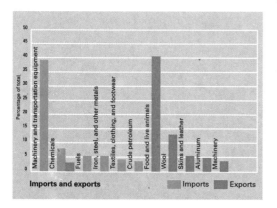

**Imports and exports**

Imports ▪ Exports

**Age distribution chart**

▪ Under 15
▪ 15 - 60
▪ Over 60

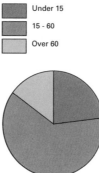

Population trend

Climate - Wellington

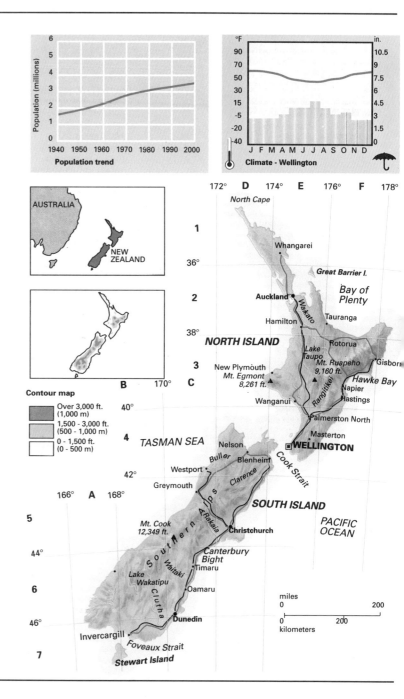

**Contour map**

Over 3,000 ft. (1,000 m)
1,500 - 3,000 ft. (500 - 1,000 m)
0 - 1,500 ft. (0 - 500 m)

# Nicaragua

**Area:** 50,193 sq. miles (130,000 km²)
**Population:** 3,871,000
**Capital:** Managua (pop. 682,000)
**Other cities:** León 101,000
**Highest point:** 8,000 ft. (2,438 m) in Cordillera Isabella
**Official language:** Spanish
**Religion:** Christianity
**Currency:** Córdoba
**Main exports:** Coffee, cotton, sugar, bananas, beef, gold
**Government:** Republic
**Per capita GNP:** U.S. $830

Nicaragua is bounded to the north by Honduras and to the south by Costa Rica. Forested plains border the Caribbean Sea. In the center is a highland region with active volcanoes. The Pacific coastlands contain the huge lakes of Managua and Nicaragua. The climate is hot and humid. Most people are of mixed European and Native American origin. There is a tiny minority of pure Native Americans. The language is Spanish. Spain conquered Nicaragua in the 1500s. The country gained its independence in 1821. From 1823 to 1838 it was part of the United Provinces of Central America. The Somoza family ruled as dictators from 1937 to 1979. The victorious Sandinistas (named after a former leader, General Augusto Sandino) formed a government, but were opposed in civil war by U.S.-backed Contras. Free elections were held in 1990.

## ECONOMIC SURVEY

**Farming:** Agriculture is the chief economic activity. The volcanic soil of the Pacific region is the main farming zone. Cotton and coffee are the principal export crops. Other cash crops include sugarcane, bananas, rice, and sesame. Corn, beans, and rice are the most important food crops. Beef cattle and pigs are reared.
**Forestry:** About half the land area is forested. The trees include mahogany, cedar, and rosewood.
**Mining:** There is some mining of gold, silver, and copper.
**Industry:** Local industries include textile production, sugar refining, brewing, and food processing. Chemical and oil products are manufactured.

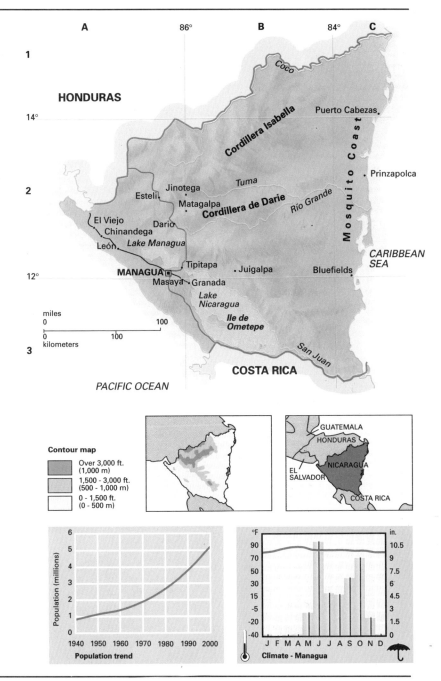

**Contour map**
- Over 3,000 ft. (1,000 m)
- 1,500 - 3,000 ft. (500 - 1,000 m)
- 0 - 1,500 ft. (0 - 500 m)

**Population trend**

**Climate - Managua**

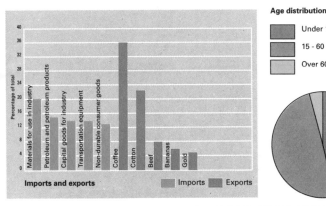

**Imports and exports**

Imports / Exports

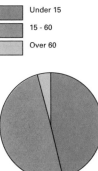

**Age distribution**
- Under 15
- 15 - 60
- Over 60

*see* CENTRAL AMERICA & THE CARIBBEAN, page 48

# Niger

**Area:** 489,191 sq. miles (1,267,000 km²)
**Population:** 7,779,000
**Capital:** Niamey (pop. 399,000)
**Other cities:** Zinder 83,000
**Highest point:** Mount Gréboun 6,562 ft. (2,000 m)
**Official language:** French; Hausa is the language used by traders
**Religions:** Islam, various traditional beliefs
**Currency:** Franc CFA
**Main exports:** Uranium, animals, vegetables
**Government:** Republic
**Per capita GNP:** U.S. $290

Niger is a landlocked country of West Africa. It is largely desert in the north. In that region are the high peaks of the Aïr Mountains, where there is some pasture land. A grassy plain with a few trees extends toward the south. The only river is the Niger in the southwest. In the southeast there is access to Lake Chad. The people are almost all Black Africans. They belong to several groups, including Hausa, Djerma-Songhai, Kanuri, and Fulani (Peul). The Hausa make up about half the population. A few Tuareg nomads roam the northern desert region. In medieval times the Tuareg controlled local trade routes. In the 1400s and 1500s the powerful Songhai empire ruled most of Niger. Europeans arrived in the 1800s. Niger was part of the colony of French West Africa from 1922. It became independent in 1960.

## ECONOMIC SURVEY

**Farming:** Most people are small farmers or herders. Nomads tend cattle, camels, goats, and sheep. Severe droughts in the 1980s reduced the herds. Cash crops include groundnuts (peanuts), cotton, gum arabic, and cowpeas. Food crops include millet, rice, sorghum, cassava, sugarcane, and onions. Chickens are kept. In the desert region, dates are grown in oases.

**Mining:** Niger's main mineral resource is uranium. It also has deposits of iron ore, phosphate, tin, tungsten, natron, and salt. There is open-pit coal mining.

**Industry:** Niger is a poor country with few industries apart from construction and those making textiles and leather goods.

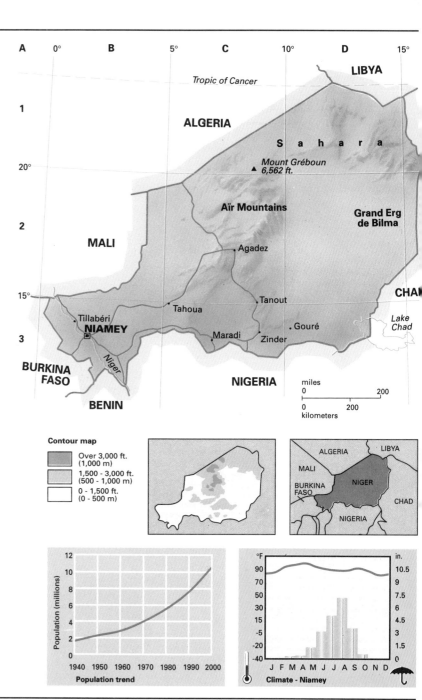

**Contour map**

- Over 3,000 ft. (1,000 m)
- 1,500 - 3,000 ft. (500 - 1,000 m)
- 0 - 1,500 ft. (0 - 500 m)

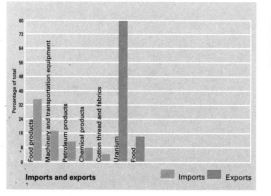

Imports and exports

Imports   Exports

**Age distribution**

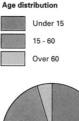

- Under 15
- 15 - 60
- Over 60

**Population trend**

**Climate - Niamey**

# Nigeria

**Area:** 356,669 sq. miles (923,768 km²)
**Population:** 119,812,000
**Capital:** Lagos (pop. 1,274,000); Abuja (capital designate)
**Other cities:** Ibadan 1,201,000; Ogbomosho 613,000; Kano 566,000
**Highest point:** Dimlang 6,699 ft. (2,042 m)
**Official language:** English
**Religions:** Islam, Christianity, traditional beliefs
**Currency:** Naira
**Main exports:** Petroleum, cocoa, rubber
**Government:** Republic
**Per capita GNP:** U.S. $250

## ECONOMIC SURVEY

**Farming:** Nigeria's cash crops include palm nuts, groundnuts (peanuts), and rubber. Food crops include beans, cassava, corn, millet, sorghum, rice, and yams. Cattle rearing is important in the northern grasslands.
**Forestry:** Timber, including sapele, mahogany, iroko, obechwe, and ebony is being felled too fast to ensure forest survival.
**Fishing:** Shrimps and fish are caught.
**Minerals:** Nigeria is a major oil producing country. Other minerals are coal, columbite, iron ore, tin, lead, and zinc.
**Industry:** Factories produce foodstuffs, chemicals, textiles, rubber and plastic, and paper. The construction industry is large.

Nigeria is Africa's most populous nation. Most of the country is drained by the Niger and Benue rivers. North of the rivers are the grassy plains of Hausaland and high plateaus. The Sokoto plains are in the northwest. The Chad Basin, swampy in the wet season but otherwise dry, is in the northeast. A broad coastal plain extends to the swampy Niger delta. The climate is equatorial. About 250 languages and dialects are spoken. The largest ethnic groups are the Muslim Hausa and Fulani (Peul), the Ibo and Yoruba. Southern Nigeria was a slaving center from the 1400s. Britain extended its control in the 1800s. Nigeria was a British colony from 1914. It became independent in 1960 and a republic in 1973. A ruinous civil war (1967-70) ended an attempted secession of the Eastern Region, under the name of Biafra.

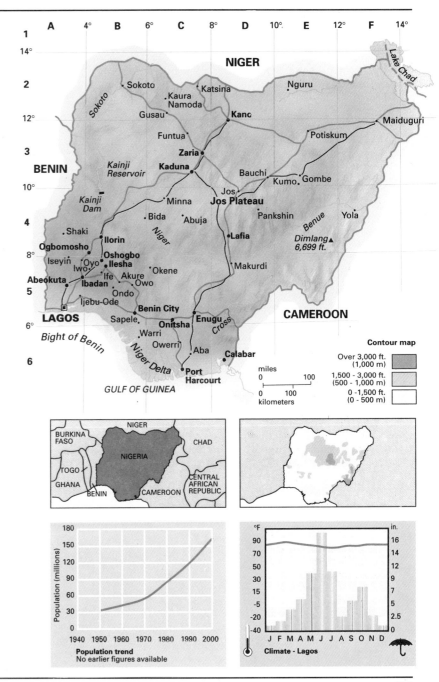

Contour map
- Over 3,000 ft. (1,000 m)
- 1,500 - 3,000 ft. (500 - 1,000 m)
- 0 -1,500 ft. (0 - 500 m)

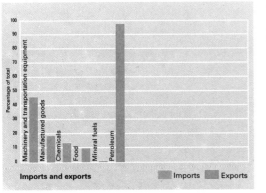

**Imports and exports**

Imports · Exports

**Age distribution**
- Under 15
- 15 - 60
- Over 60

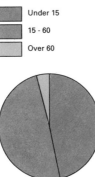

**Population trend**
No earlier figures available

**Climate - Lagos**

# NORTH AMERICA

**Area:** 9,072,243 sq. miles (23,497,000 km²)
**Population:** 363,000,000
**Major cities:** Mexico City 18,748,000; New York City (U.S.A.) 7,346,000; Toronto (Canada) 3,427,000; Los Angeles (U.S.A.) 3,402,000; Chicago (U.S.A.) 2,994,000
**Number of independent countries:** 3 (the 20 countries of Central America and the Caribbean are sometimes included)
**Largest country:** Canada
**Smallest independent country:** Mexico
**Highest mountain:** Mount McKinley (Alaska) 20,320 ft. (6,194 m)
**Longest river:** Mississippi 2,348 miles (3,779 km)
**Largest lake:** Lake Superior 31,700 sq. miles (82,103 km²)

North America is the third largest continent. It extends from Greenland, northern Canada, and Alaska in the cold north to the sub-tropics of the southern United States and Mexico. South of Mexico are the countries of Central America. The people of Mexico and Central America speak Spanish. (For more about Central America see page 48). In most of the rest of North America people speak English, though there are large language minorities, including Spanish-speakers and, in Canada, French-speakers. The landscape of North America includes snow-covered polar regions, high mountain ranges, flat grasslands or prairies, and thick forests. North America has some of the world's longest rivers and the largest freshwater lake, Superior. It has some of the world's great cities, with the tallest skyscrapers. The continent's economy and culture is dominated by the United States of America, which has by far the biggest population of the continent. The United States has grown rapidly since the mid-1800s. The Native Americans and the Inuit, whose ancestors came from Asia probably before the last Ice Age, were dispossessed by Europeans who began settling in North America in the 1500s. Many North Americans have European ancestors. Others are descendants of Black African slaves. Recent immigrants have come from Central America and Asia. Greenland is the world's largest island. It is a province of Denmark, in Europe. Most of the island is uninhabited.

**Contour map**

Over 6,000 ft. (2,000 m)
3,000 - 6,000 ft. (1,000 - 2,000 m)
0 - 3,000 ft. (0 - 1,000 m)

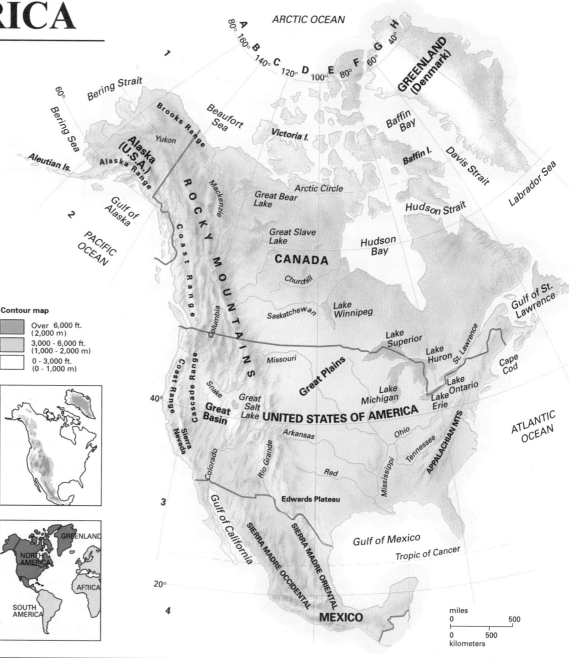

# North Korea

**Area:** 46,540 sq. miles (120,538 km²)
**Population:** 22,937,000
**Capital:** Pyongyang (pop. 2,639,000)
**Other cities:** Chongjin 754,000; Nampo 691,000; Hamhung 525,000
**Highest point:** Mount Paektu 9,003 ft. (2,744 m)
**Official language:** Korean
**Religions:** Traditional beliefs, Ch'ondogyo
**Currency:** Won
**Main exports:** Minerals (copper, iron ore, lead, tungsten, zinc), machinery, rice
**Government:** Single-party republic
**Per capita GNP:** U.S. $910

## ECONOMIC SURVEY

**Farming:** Less than a fifth of the land in North Korea is suitable for farming, but four out of ten North Koreans work on the land. Main crops include rice, vegetables, wheat, corn, soya beans, and pulses. Pigs and cattle are the most numerous livestock. Farms are state-run, with 300 families on each farm.
**Mining:** North Korea's rich deposits of minerals include iron ore, phosphate, coal, copper, sulfur, and zinc.
**Industry:** North Korea produces chemicals, iron and steel, machinery, and textiles. There is no private industry. The country was, before partition, the most industrialized part of Korea.

North Korea occupies the northern part of the Korean peninsula, which stretches southward toward Japan from China. North Korea is mainly mountainous, and most of its people live in the eastern coastal plains. The northwestern plain is the principal farming area. The Yalu River forms the border with China, and is North Korea's longest river. Korea was formerly known as Choson. It was occupied by Japan in 1910. After World War II it was partitioned, and North Korea became a communist state. Under its dictatorial ruler, Kim Il Sung, North Korea was governed by a rigid regime, concentrating on industrial and military development. The Korean War (1950-53) began when Northern troops invaded South Korea. The United Nations supported South Korea, and China backed North Korea. The war ended with victory for neither side. North Korea retreated into isolation, with the dictatorial rule of Kim Il Sung seemingly unaffected by changes in the communist world outside. The government enforced a collective farm system and embarked on a program of heavy industry and millitary development. Tension and suspicion between the two Koreas remained high in the years following the Korean War. By the early 1990s there were signs of a slow thaw, with tentative diplomatic contacts betweeen North Korea and South Korea and between North Korea and Japan.

**No reliable data for North Korea's import and export trade are available.**

### Age distribution

- Under 15
- 15 - 60
- Over 60

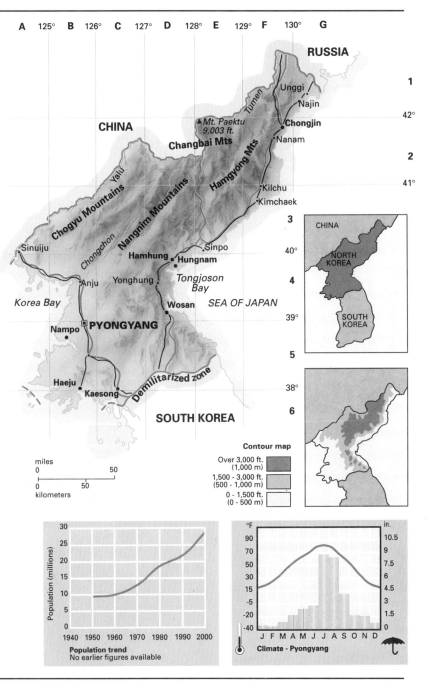

**Contour map**
- Over 3,000 ft. (1,000 m)
- 1,500 - 3,000 ft. (500 - 1,000 m)
- 0 - 1,500 ft. (0 - 500 m)

miles 0 — 50
kilometers 0 — 50

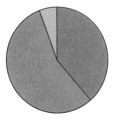

**Population trend**
No earlier figures available

**Climate - Pyongyang**

# Norway

**Area:** 125,182 sq. miles (324,219 km$^2$)
**Population:** 4,245,000
**Capital:** Oslo (pop. 456,000)
**Other cities:** Bergen 211,000; Trondheim 137,000
**Highest point:** Galdhøppigen 8,100 ft. (2,469 m)
**Official language:** Norwegian
**Religion:** Protestantism
**Currency:** Krone
**Main exports:** Petroleum and natural gas, metals, machinery, and transportation equipment
**Government:** Constitutional monarchy
**Per capita GNP:** U.S. $21,850

## ECONOMIC SURVEY

**Farming:** Less than 3 percent of the land is cultivated. Barley and potatoes are grown, and cattle and pigs are kept.
**Forestry:** Timber is logged for making wood pulp and paper.
**Fishing:** The fleet is based in the fjords and on the many islands. The catch includes herring, cod, capelin, whiting, and shrimps.
**Mining:** Oil and natural gas account for a third of Norway's exports. There are huge oil reserves in the North Sea.
**Industry:** Norway has electro-metallurgical, electro-chemical and paper industries. Engineering includes shipbuilding and oil-rig construction. The country has one of the world's largest merchant fleets.

Norway forms the western part of Scandinavia, in northern Europe. It has a long and irregular coastline, with many islands and fjords — deep sea inlets. Much of the land is mountainous, and about a quarter of it is covered with coniferous forest. The climate is relatively mild, due to the warming influence of the North Atlantic Drift. The Vikings controlled Norway in the 800s. Norway became a Christian kingdom in the early 1000s. From 1380 to 1814 the country was part of Denmark. In the peace settlements at the end of the Napoleonic Wars, Denmark ceded Norway to Sweden. An attempt to become independent failed after a few months, and union with Sweden lasted until 1905. Having decided not to join the European Community in 1971, Norway and other countries have now forged closer links with the EC.

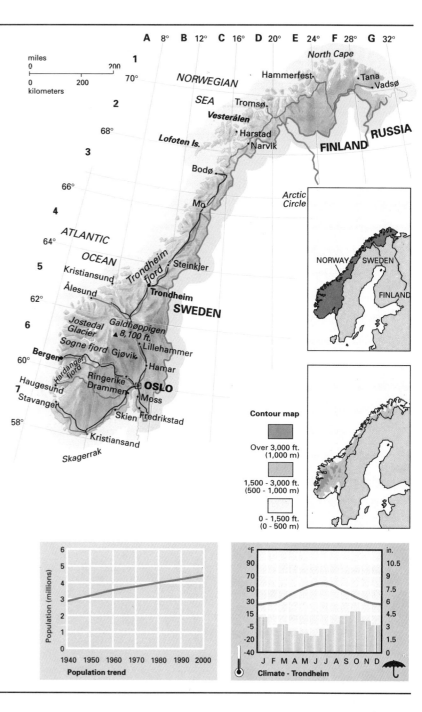

Contour map

Over 3,000 ft. (1,000 m)

1,500 - 3,000 ft. (500 - 1,000 m)

0 - 1,500 ft. (0 - 500 m)

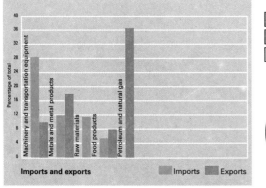

**Imports and exports**

Imports  Exports

**Age distribution**

Under 15

15 - 60

Over 60

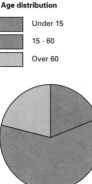

**Population trend**

**Climate - Trondheim**

# OCEANIA

**Area:** 3,285,730 sq. miles (8,510,000 km²)
**Population:** 26,500,000
**Major cities:** Sydney (Australia) 3,531,000; Melbourne (Australia) 2,965,000; Brisbane (Australia) 1,215,000; Perth (Australia) 1,083,000
**Number of independent countries:** 11
**Largest country:** Australia
**Smallest independent country:** Nauru
**Highest mountain:** Mount Wilhelm (Papua New Guinea) 14,793 ft. (4,509 m)
**Longest river:** Murray (Australia) is the longest permanently flowing river, 1,609 miles (2,589 km); its tributary, the Darling, mostly dry in winter, is 1,702 miles (2,739 km) long
**Largest lake:** Lake Eyre (Australia) 3,700 sq. miles (9,583 km²)

Oceania is the name given to the many countries in the Pacific Ocean. By far the greatest land mass in Oceania is Australia — a continent in its own right — much of which is empty desert. Next in size come Papua New Guinea and New Zealand. Scattered across the ocean are about 30,000 islands. Some are high and volcanic, others are low coral atolls. The islands form three main groups: Melanesia, Micronesia, and Polynesia. Melanesia is in the western Pacific, south of the equator. This group includes the Bismarck Archipelago, the Solomons, Vanuatu, Fiji, New Caledonia, and the Loyalty Islands. Micronesia is north of Melanesia. The islands of Micronesia include Guam, and the Mariana Islands, Caroline, Marshall, Gilbert, Phoenix, and Line islands. The Gilbert Islands form part of the Republic of Kiribati. The Ellice Islands form part of Tuvalu. Polynesia includes the Society Islands (the most important of which is Tahiti), the Marquesas, Samoa, the Wallis and Futuna Islands, Tonga, the Cook Islands, Niue, and the Tokelau Islands. Few islands are rich in natural resources. The people are mostly descendants of migrants from Asia who settled thousands of years ago, or of more recent settlers from Europe. European exploration began in the 1500s and was followed by colonization of Australia and New Zealand by Britain, and of the the Pacific Islands by Britain, France, the United States, and Spain. Most of Oceania is now independent.

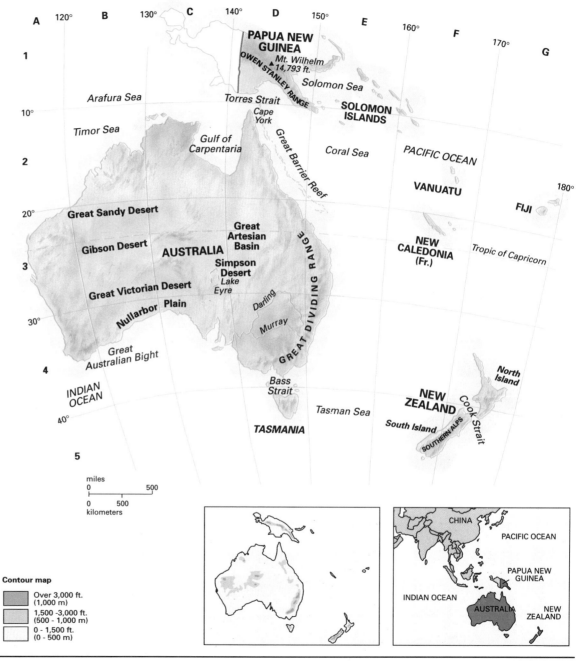

**Contour map**

- Over 3,000 ft. (1,000 m)
- 1,500 -3,000 ft. (500 - 1,000 m)
- 0 - 1,500 ft. (0 - 500 m)

# Oman

**Area:** 82,030 sq. miles (212,457 km²)
**Population:** 1,468,000
**Capital:** Muscat (pop. 85,000)
**Other cities:** Nizwa 10,000; Salalah 10,000
**Highest point:** Jabal Ash Sham 9,957 ft. (3,035 m)
**Official language:** Arabic
**Religion:** Islam
**Currency:** Rial
**Main exports:** Petroleum
**Government:** Monarchy with consultative council
**Per capita GNP:** U.S. $5,220

The sultanate of Oman is on the southeastern coast of the Arabian peninsula. The northern coastal region is fertile, and there is another fertile region along the southwest coast. Inland is a barren upland that merges into a dry plateau. Little rain falls, and temperatures are high all year round. Arabs make up 90 percent of Oman's population. The country is strictly Muslim. Formerly known as Muscat and Oman, Oman has since ancient times been an important trade center, famed for frankincense. Oman's influence extended to East Africa, notably Zanzibar. Britain established a special relationship with Oman in the late 1800s, supporting the sultans. Slavery was practiced until the 1960s. A revolt in 1970 brought to power Sultan Qaboos, who began modernizing the country. However, Oman remains an absolute monarchy.

## ECONOMIC SURVEY

**Farming:** Oman has two small areas of fertile land, while most of the rest of the country is rocky and dry. About a quarter of the people work on the land. The main crops grown are bananas, dates, pomegranates, limes and other fruit, tobacco, vegetables, and wheat. Goats, sheep, cattle, and chickens are kept. Fishermen catch sardines and other fish in the Gulf and the Arabian Sea.
**Industry:** Oman depends on its oil revenues. Development of the oil industry was encouraged by Sultan Qaboos bin Said during the 1970s. Many Omanis work in the oil industry, in associated businesses or in construction.

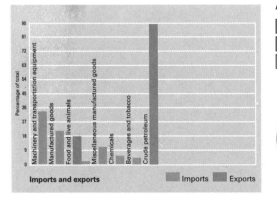

**Imports and exports**

Imports | Exports

**Age distribution**

Under 15
15 - 60
Over 60

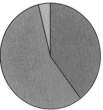

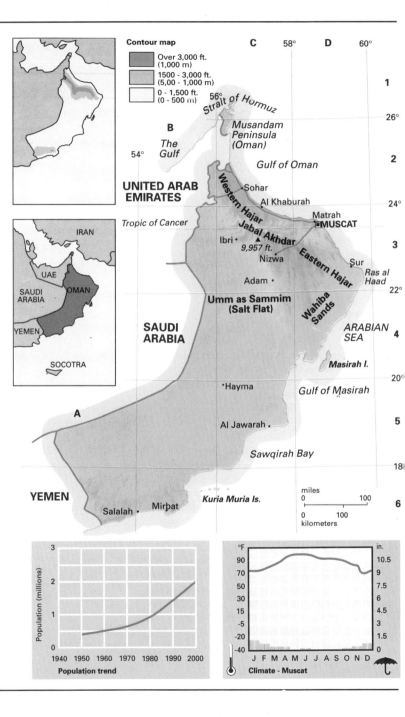

**Contour map**

- Over 3,000 ft. (1,000 m)
- 1500 - 3,000 ft. (5,00 - 1,000 m)
- 0 - 1,500 ft. (0 - 500 m)

**Population trend**

**Climate - Muscat**

# Pacific Islands

**FIJI Area:** 7,056 sq. miles (18,274 km²)
**Population:** 741,000
**Capital:** Suva (pop. 70,000)
**Highest point:** Mount Tomanivi 4,341 ft.
(1,323 m)
**Official language:** English
**Religions:** Christianity, Hinduism, Islam
**Currency:** Fiji dollar
**Main exports:** Sugar, gold, fish, timber,
coconut products

**KIRIBATI Area:** 281 sq. miles (728 km²)
**Population:** 71,000
**Capital:** Bairiki, on Tarawa (pop. 23,000)
**Highest point:** The summit of Banaba Island
265 ft. (81 m)
**Official language:** English
**Religion:** Christianity
**Currency:** Australian dollar
**Main exports:** Copra (from coconuts), fish and
fish products

**MARSHALL ISLANDS Area:** 70 sq. miles
(181.5 km²)
**Population:** 50,000
**Capital:** Majuro
**Official languages:** Marshallese, English
**Religion:** Christianity
**Currency:** U.S. dollar
**Main exports:** Coconut oil, live animals, fish

**MICRONESIA, FEDERATED STATES OF**
**Area:** 271 sq. miles (701 km²)
**Population:** 114,000
**Capital:** Palikir
**Official language:** English
**Religion:** Christianity
**Currency:** U.S. dollar
**Main exports:** Copra, manufactured goods

**NAURU Area:** 8 sq. miles (21 km²)
**Population:** 9,000
**Capital:** Yaren
**Highest point:** 229 ft. (70 m)
**Official language:** Nauruan
**Religion:** Christianity
**Currency:** Australian dollar
**Main exports:** Phosphates (the only important
resource)

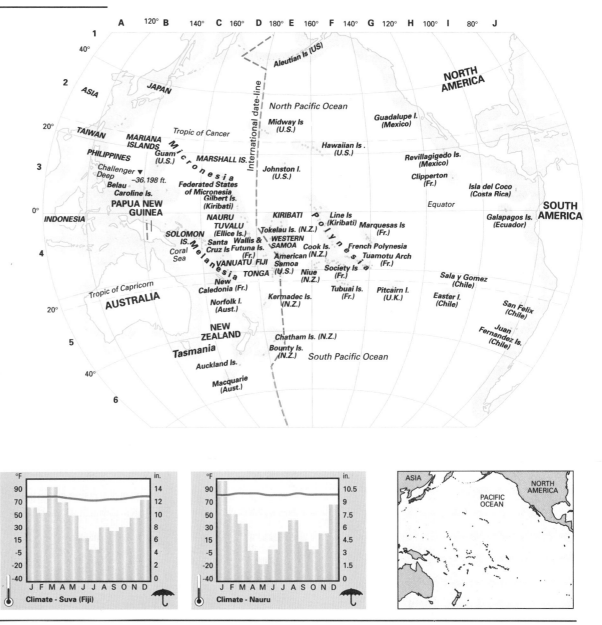

Climate - Suva (Fiji)

Climate - Nauru

**SOLOMON ISLANDS Area:** 10,983 sq. miles (28,446 km²)
**Population:** 329,000
**Capital:** Honiara (pop. 30,000)
**Official language:** English
**Religion:** Christianity
**Currency:** Solmon Islands dollar
**Main exports:** Fish, wood products, copra, cocoa

**TONGA Area:** 270 sq. miles (699 km²)
**Population:** 102,000
**Capital:** Nuku'alofa (pop. 21,000)
**Official languages:** Tongan, English
**Religion:** Christianity
**Currency:** Pa'anga
**Main exports:** Coconut products, bananas, vanilla

**TUVALU Area:** 10 sq. miles (26 km²)
**Population:** 9,000
**Capital:** Fongafale, on Funafuti, (pop. 2,800)
**Official languages:** Tuvaluan, English
**Religion:** Christianity
**Currency:** Australian dollar
**Main exports:** Copra

**VANUATU Area:** 5,700 sq. miles (14,763 km²)
**Population:** 159,000
**Capital:** Vila (pop. 15,000)
**Official languages:** Bislama, English, French
**Religions:** Christianity, traditional beliefs
**Currency:** Vatu
**Main exports:** Copra, meat, cocoa, timber

**WESTERN SAMOA Area:** 1,097 sq. miles (2,842 km²)
**Population:** 195,000
**Capital:** Apia (pop. 33,000)
**Official languages:** Samoan, English
**Religion:** Christianity
**Currency:** Tala
**Main exports:** Coconut and copra, taro, cocoa

## ECONOMIC SURVEY

**Farming:** Many islands have good soils. Most islanders grow their own food. Copra is the main product, and bananas, sugar, cocoa, and coffee are other leading cash crops.
**Fishing:** The islanders have traditionally lived from the sea, by fishing and trading. Most of the fishing is carried on from canoes, but some islands have modern powered vessels. There are local fish canning industries.
**Mining:** Minerals include phosphates (Nauru), nickel, chrome, manganese and other ores (New Caledonia), gold (Fiji and Solomons), and bauxite (Solomons).
**Industry:** Mills and factories produce coconut oil, soap, and sugar. The Solomons and Western Samoa produce timber. Tourism is an important and growing business.

**FIJI: Age distribution**

Under 15
15 - 60
Over 60

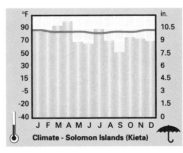

## The Pacific Ocean

The Pacific Ocean is the largest and deepest ocean in the world, covering a third of the Earth's surface. Its deepest point is in the Mariana Trench, over 36,100 feet (11,000 meters) down. It has thousands of islands. Some are the tops of volcanic mountains. Others are coral reefs, many resting on the peaks of submarine mountains. Some of the islands have rugged mountains, many of them have active volcanoes. Others are coral reefs and atolls only a few feet above sea level. The central and southern Pacific are the areas with the most islands. There are few islands in the east and north of the great ocean.

## The Pacific Islands

The Pacific island states are small, isolated, and mostly dependent on agriculture, minerals, and tourism. Almost all enjoy tropical climates. The people, like the islands, fall into three groups: Melanesians, Micronesians, and Polynesians. Their ancestors "island-hopped" from Asia thousands of years ago. Settlers may also have reached some islands (Easter Island, for instance) by boat from the Americas. The first European to sail into the Pacific was Ferdinand Magellan in the early 1500s. Exploration by Europeans continued with the voyages of James Cook and others in the 1700s. Missionaries, traders, and administrators followed the explorers. Some territories such as American Samoa are governed as dependencies. Independent states include island groups such as Fiji and the Solomon Islands, and tiny islands such as Nauru. The Hawaiian Islands form one of the states of the United States. English is the most widely used non-native language in the Pacific. French is used in French Polynesia. In Melanesia many people speak pidgin, a mixture of English and local words. The main religion is Christianity.

**SOLOMON ISLANDS: Age distribution**

Under 15
15 - 60
Over 60

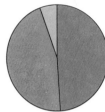

**TONGA: Age distribution**

Under 15
15 - 60
Over 60

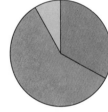

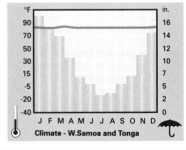

Climate - Solomon Islands (Kieta)

Climate - W.Samoa and Tonga

# Pakistan

**Area:** 307,374 sq. miles (796,095 km²)
**Population:** 122,666,000
**Capital:** Islamabad (pop. 204,000)
**Other cities:** Karachi 5,208,000; Lahore 2,953,000
**Highest point:** K2 28,250 ft. (8,611 m)
**Official language:** Urdu
**Religion:** Islam
**Currency:** Rupee
**Main exports:** Cotton and cotton goods, rice, leather, carpets
**Government:** Islamic republic
**Per capita GNP:** U.S. $370

The republic of Pakistan is mountainous in the north, where the Hindu Kush and Himalaya ranges rise. Central and southern Pakistan contain fertile plains watered by the Indus River and its tributaries. In the southwest is the dry Baluchistan plateau and in the southeast is the Thar desert. The north has cold winters and the most rainfall. The Pakistanis are descended from many peoples who invaded the region over the centuries. Languages spoken include Punjabi, Sindhi, Pashto, and Baluchi. Most people live in rural villages. A great civilization flourished in the Indus valley from 2500 B.C. until 1700 B.C. Islam was introduced in the A.D. 700s. Pakistan was part of the British Indian empire until 1947, when it became a separate Muslim state. In 1971 East Pakistan broke away and became the republic of Bangladesh.

## ECONOMIC SURVEY

**Farming:** The proportion of people working on the land is falling, but farming is still a major activity. The chief crops are rice, cotton, sugar-cane, wheat, and corn. Goats, sheep, cattle, buffalo, camels, and chickens are reared.
**Fishing:** Catches in the Arabian Sea include herring, mackerel, and sardines.
**Mining:** Mineral resources include natural gas, gypsum, rock salt, and limestone.
**Industry:** Hydro-electric power supplies industries producing cement, textiles – notably cotton goods and jute – fertilizers, steel, engineering products such as bicycles, and electrical goods including transformers.

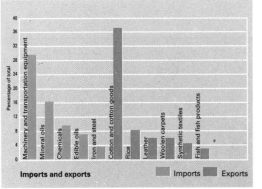

**Imports and exports**

Imports  Exports

**Age distribution**

Under 15

15 - 60

Over 60

**Population trend**

**Climate - Islamabad**

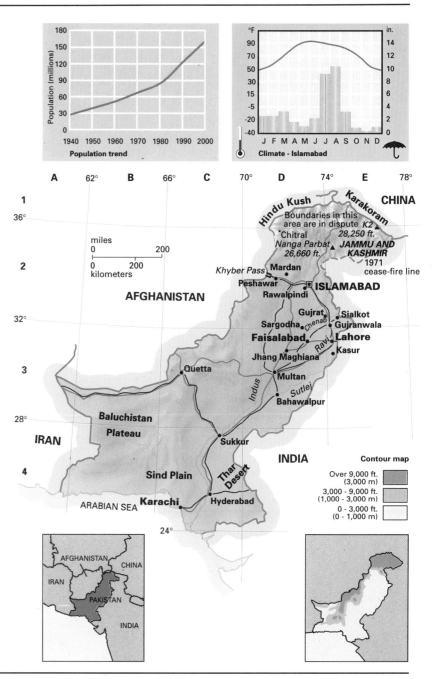

Contour map

Over 9,000 ft. (3,000 m)
3,000 - 9,000 ft. (1,000 - 3,000 m)
0 - 3,000 ft. (0 - 1,000 m)

*see* ASIA, page 22 137

# Panama

**Area:** 29,762 sq. miles (77,082 km²)
**Population:** 2,418,000
**Capital:** Panama City (pop. 435,000)
**Other cities:** San Miguelito (suburb of Panama City (253,000)
**Highest point:** Volcán Barú 11,401 ft. (3,475 m)
**Official language:** Spanish
**Religion:** Christianity
**Currency:** Balboa
**Main exports:** Bananas, shrimps, coffee, sugar, textiles
**Government:** Republic
**Per capita GNP:** U.S. $1,780

The republic of Panama occupies the narrow isthmus between North and South America. It contains the Panama Canal, which links the Pacific and Atlantic oceans. The interior is mountainous, and the best farmland is in the lowlands along the Pacific coast. East of the canal lie swamps and forests. About 800 islands off the Pacific coast form part of Panama's territory. The climate is tropical. Most of the people are of mixed white and Native American origin. Spanish colonizers in the early 1500s exploited the Native Americans and imported black slaves. In 1821 Panama declared its independence from Spain in union with Colombia; it became fully independent in 1903. The Panama Canal opened in 1914. The United States controlled the Canal Zone, a strip either side of the canal, until 1979, and controls the canal until 1999.

## ECONOMIC SURVEY

**Farming:** Most farmers work only small plots of land. They grow subsistence crops such as rice, corn, and beans. Cash crops (bananas, cocoa, coffee, and sugar) are grown on large plantations. Cattle, pigs, and poultry are reared.
**Forestry:** Panama's forests include many valuable mahogany trees.
**Fishing:** Coastal fishing is potentially rich. Shrimps are the leading catch.
**Mining:** Panama has copper reserves which are not developed.
**Industry:** There is little manufacturing, but local industries produce foodstuffs, clothing, and building materials. The Panama Canal provides income.

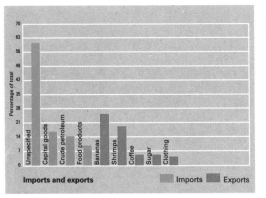

Imports and exports

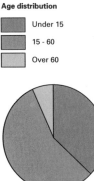

**Age distribution**
- Under 15
- 15 - 60
- Over 60

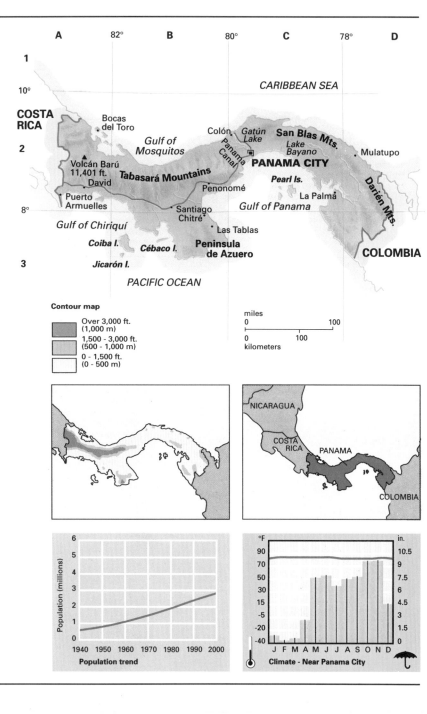

Contour map

| | |
|---|---|
| | Over 3,000 ft. (1,000 m) |
| | 1,500 - 3,000 ft. (500 - 1,000 m) |
| | 0 - 1,500 ft. (0 - 500 m) |

Population trend

Climate - Near Panama City

# Papua New Guinea

**Area:** 178,260 sq. miles (461,691 km²)
**Population:** 3,671,000
**Capital:** Port Moresby (pop. 152,000)
**Other cities:** Lae 80,000
**Highest point:** Mount Wilhelm 14,793 ft. (4,509 m)
**Official language:** English (but the people speak more than 700 languages)
**Religions:** Christianity, traditional beliefs
**Currency:** Kina
**Main exports:** Copper, coffee, timber
**Government:** Constitutional monarchy
**Per capita GNP:** U.S. $900

Papua New Guinea consists of eastern New Guinea, and a chain of tropical islands including the Bismarck Archipelago and Bougainville in the Solomon Islands. Eastern New Guinea is mountainous and forested, with broad swampy river valleys. There are 40 active volcanoes in the north. The climate is hot and humid, though cooler in the uplands. Most people are Melanesians, with Chinese, European, and Polyesian minorities. Some tribes in remote regions have had little if any contact with the outside world, and until recently many had a Stone Age civilization. New Guinea was first explored by European seamen in the 1500s. In the 1800s, Germany annexed the northeast and Britain the southeast. Australia governed Papua, the British part, from 1906 and the rest from 1920. In 1975 Papua New Guinea became independent.

## ECONOMIC SURVEY

**Farming:** The economy is based on agriculture. Most people live in villages and grow their own food. The chief food crops are sweet potatoes, yams, cassava, and taro. Pigs are the most valued livestock, but farmers also keep cattle, goats, and chickens. Coffee, cocoa beans, and palm oil are important cash crops.
**Fishing:** Around the coasts people catch fish from canoes and there is some commercial fishing.
**Mining:** There are copper mines on Bougainville and in New Guinea. The country also produces gold and silver.
**Industry:** There are few factories. Development is hindered by poor road links.

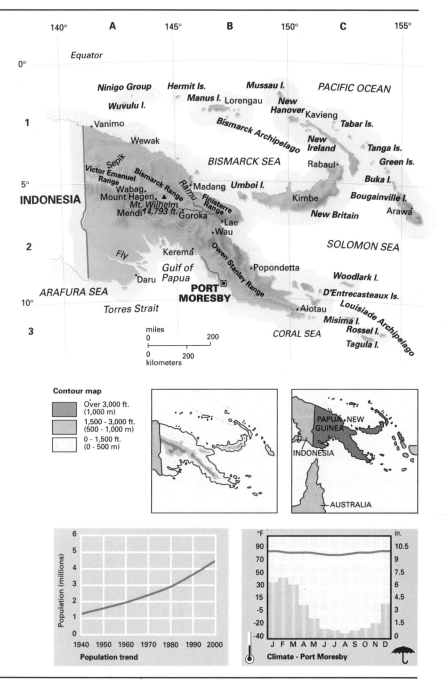

### Contour map

| | |
|---|---|
| Over 3,000 ft. (1,000 m) | |
| 1,500 - 3,000 ft. (500 - 1,000 m) | |
| 0 - 1,500 ft. (0 - 500 m) | |

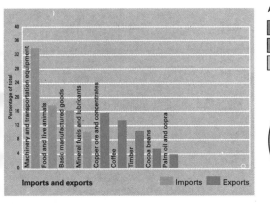

Imports and exports

### Age distribution

- Under 15
- 15 - 60
- Over 60

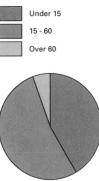

Population trend

Climate - Port Moresby

*see* OCEANIA, page 133  **139**

# Paraguay

**Area:** 157,048 sq. miles (406,752 km²)
**Population:** 4,277,000
**Capital:** Asunción (pop. 568,000)
**Other cities:** San Lorenzo (near Asunción) 124,000; Puerto Presidente Stroessner 50,000
**Highest point:** Near Villarrica 2,231 ft. (680 m)
**Official language:** Spanish
**Religion:** Christianity
**Currency:** Guarani
**Main exports:** Cotton, soya beans, meat, coffee, timber
**Government:** Republic
**Per capita GNP:** U.S. $1,030

Paraguay, like its neighbor Bolivia, is landlocked. The Paraguay River divides it into two regions. To the west is the Gran Chaco, a flat wilderness of grassland, scrub, and marsh. To the east are rolling hills, thick forests, and areas with fertile soil. The climate is subtropical. About 75 percent of the people are of mixed Native American and European origin, 21 percent are of European origin, and 3 percent are pure Native Americans. More than 95 percent of Paraguayans live east of the Paraguay River. They speak either Spanish or Guarani, an ancient language. Spanish explorers and Jesuit priests arrived in the 1500s. Paraguay freed itself from Spanish rule in 1818. But war with Argentina, Brazil, and Uruguay (1865-70) ruined the country. Its recent history included dictatorship under Alfredo Stroessner from 1954 until a coup in 1989.

## ECONOMIC SURVEY

**Farming:** Cattle are herded on large ranches in the grasslands. Sheep, horses, and pigs are also kept. In the east, farmers grow cassava, cotton, rice, soya beans, corn, and sugarcane. A traditional drink, yerba maté, is made from holly leaves.

**Forestry:** Valuable forest trees include cedar and quebracho (a source of tannin). Palm and other trees yield oils.

**Industry:** Hydro-electric power from the Acaray and Paraná rivers provides potentially enough energy for Paraguay to sell some to Brazil and Argentina. Industries include the processing of timber, meat, grains, and oils. There are small textile and cigarette factories.

**Contour map**
- Over 1,500 ft. (500 m)
- 600 - 1,500 ft. (200 - 500 m)
- 0 - 600 ft. (0 - 200 m)

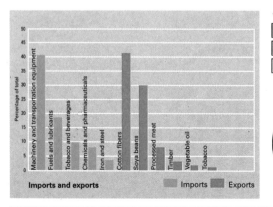

Imports and exports

Imports  Exports

**Age distribution**
- Under 15
- 15 - 60
- Over 60

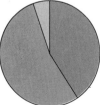

Population trend

Climate - Asunción

# Peru

**Area:** 496,225 sq. miles (1,285,216 km²)
**Population:** 22,332,000
**Capital:** Lima (pop. 5,494,000)
**Other cities:** Arequipa 592,000; Callao 560,000; Trujillo 240,000
**Highest point:** Huascarán 22,205 ft. (6,768 m)
**Official languages:** Spanish, Quechua
**Religion:** Christianity
**Currency:** Sol
**Main exports:** Copper, petroleum and petroleum products, lead, zinc
**Government:** Multiparty republic
**Per capita GNP:** U.S. $1,090

## ECONOMIC SURVEY

**Farming:** Coffee, cotton, and sugarcane are the main cash crops. Domestic food crops include beans, bananas, corn, rice, and potatoes. Sheep and chickens are the main livestock.
**Fishing:** Peru is a major fishing nation. Sardines, anchovetas, and tuna are caught within the large territorial limit which Peru claims.
**Mining:** Peru is a leading producer of silver, copper, lead, and zinc. It also mines iron ore and gold and has working oil wells. Guano (bird droppings) is collected from offshore islands for making fertilizer.
**Industry:** Chemicals, processed food, especially fish, textiles, petroleum-based products, and metals are manufactured.

Peru has a narrow and dry coastal plain, behind which rise the Andes Mountains. The mountains contain the headwaters of the Amazon River, notably the Marañon and Ucayali. Lake Titicaca is the world's highest navigable lake. Eastern Peru is in the low Amazon basin, and has a tropical climate. The highlands are cooler and drier. The coastal plain is cloudy but dry, influenced by the cold Humboldt, or Peru current which flows north and is rich in fish. The people are a mixture of pure Native Americans (roughly half the population) and those of American-European origin. Peruvian civilization goes back some 10,000 years. The Incas created an empire from 1438, but they were conquered by the Spaniards in the 1500s. Spanish rule was ended by José de San Martín and Simón Bolívar, and Peru was declared independent in 1821.

**Population trend**

**Climate - Lima**

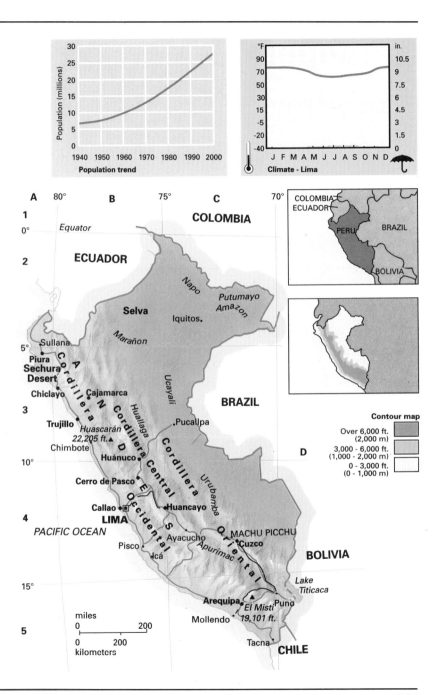

**Contour map**

Over 6,000 ft. (2,000 m)
3,000 - 6,000 ft. (1,000 - 2,000 m)
0 - 3,000 ft. (0 - 1,000 m)

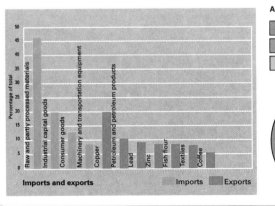

**Imports and exports**

Imports Exports

**Age distribution**

Under 15
15 - 60
Over 60

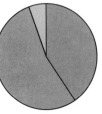

# Philippines

**Area:** 115,831 sq. miles (300,000 km²)
**Population:** 61,483,000
**Capital:** Manila (pop. with suburbs 5,926,000)
**Other cities:** Davao 610,000
**Highest point:** Mount Apo 9,692 ft. (2,954 m)
**Official languages:** Filipino, English
**Religions:** Christianity, Aglipayan (Independent Church), Islam
**Currency:** Peso
**Main exports:** Electronics, clothing, farm products, wood
**Government:** Multiparty republic
**Per capita GNP:** U.S. $700

The Philippines is a republic made up of more than 7000 islands. The largest, Luzon and Mindanao, together make up two-thirds of the land area. The larger islands are volcanic and mountainous. Many small islands are coral outcrops. The climate is tropical, with monsoon rains. The plains are hot and humid, the uplands are cooler and wetter. The people, known as Filipinos, are related to the Malays. There are also Chinese, Americans, Europeans, Indians, and Japanese, as well as Negritos, a native mountain people. The Philippines is Asia's only predominantly Christian country. Spain ruled the Philippines from 1565 to 1898, when the islands were ceded to the United States. An independent republic was founded in 1946. Ferdinand Marcos, president from 1965, was overthrown in 1986 and a new constitution was voted in.

## ECONOMIC SURVEY

**Farming:** Many Filipinos work in farming or forestry. Main crops are rice, maize, cassava, sweet potatoes, bananas, sugarcane, and coconuts. Pigs, buffaloes, goats, cattle, and chickens are reared.
**Forestry:** Valuable forest trees include Philippine mahogany, pine, and kapok.
**Fishing:** Filipino fishermen catch tuna, mackerel, and many other fishes.
**Mining:** The leading mineral is copper. There are deposits of gold, chromite, coal, iron ore, limestone, manganese, nickel, and silver.
**Industry:** The chief manufactured goods include electrical products, clothing, shoes, furniture, and foodstuffs.

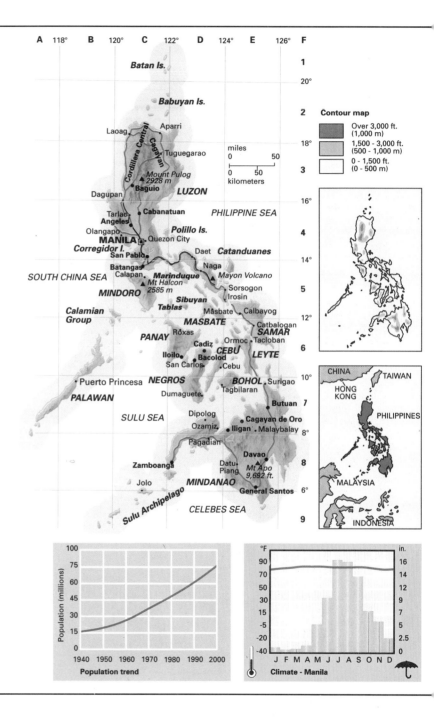

**Contour map**

- Over 3,000 ft. (1,000 m)
- 1,500 - 3,000 ft. (500 - 1,000 m)
- 0 - 1,500 ft. (0 - 500 m)

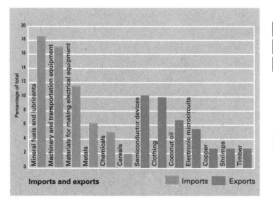

**Imports and exports** — Imports / Exports

**Age distribution**
- Under 15
- 15 - 60
- Over 60

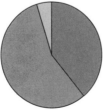

**Population trend**

**Climate - Manila**

# Poland

**Area:** 120,725 sq. miles² (312,677 km)
**Population:** 38,064,000
**Capital:** Warsaw (pop. 1,649,000)
**Other cities:** Łódź 849,000; Krakow 716,000; Wroclaw 637,000; Poznań 575,000
**Highest point:** Rysy Peak 8,199 ft. (2,499 m)
**Official language:** Polish
**Religion:** Roman Catholicism
**Currency:** Zloty
**Main exports:** Machinery and transportation equipment, chemicals, fuel and power, textiles
**Government:** Multiparty republic
**Per capita GNP:** U.S. $7,200

The republic of Poland in eastern Europe is a mostly flat country. Much of it is a large plain, the north of which is either infertile or forested. The central lowlands, where Warsaw, Poznań, and Lodź are situated, are better farmland. In the south the land rises towards the Sudeten and Carpathian mountain ranges. Poland's western border with Germany is formed by the Oder and Neisse rivers. Its other major river is the Vistula. Summers become warmer from north to south. Poland was a kingdom in the 1100s, but its frontiers have changed frequently. In 1795 it was swallowed up by Russia, Prussia, and Austria. Poland reemerged in 1918, but was overrun by Germany in 1939 and again divided. Recreated with new frontiers in 1945 under Communist Party rule, Poland reestablished democratic government in the late 1980s.

## ECONOMIC SURVEY

**Farming:** Farmland covers 60 percent of Poland. Most farms are small and are privately owned . Cereals, sugarbeet, and potatoes are grown. Cattle, pigs, sheep, and poultry are reared. Much of the soil is poor, and methods are old-fashioned by western European standards.
**Fishing:** Polish vessels catch fish in the Baltic and North seas, and the North Atlantic Ocean. Cod, hake, and herring are the leading catches.
**Mining:** Poland is the world's fifth largest producer of coal. It has reserves of copper, lead, zinc, nickel, and other minerals.
**Industry:** Factories produce iron and steel, ships, chemicals, machinery, and textiles.

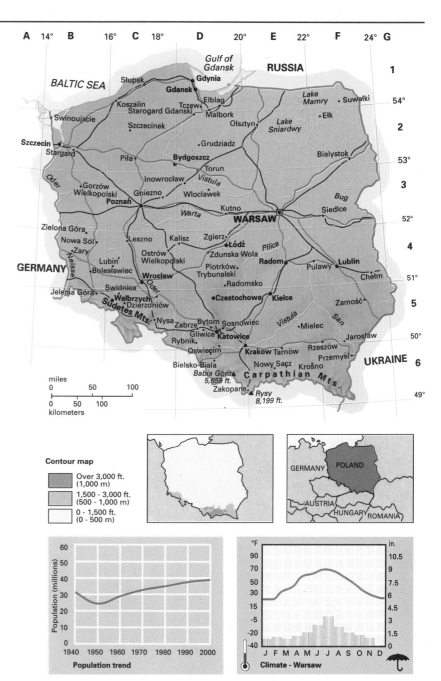

**Age distribution**

- Under 15
- 15 - 60
- Over 60

**Contour map**

- Over 3,000 ft. (1,000 m)
- 1,500 - 3,000 ft. (500 - 1,000 m)
- 0 - 1,500 ft. (0 - 500 m)

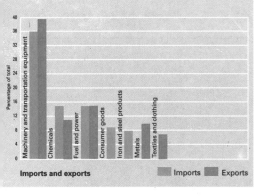

**Imports and exports** — Imports / Exports

**Population trend**

**Climate - Warsaw**

# Portugal

**Area:** 35,553 sq. miles (92,082 km²)
**Population:** 10,434,000
**Capital:** Lisbon (pop. 830,000)
**Other cities:** Oporto 350,000
**Highest point:** Estrela 6,532 ft. (1,991 m)
**Official language:** Portuguese
**Religion:** Roman Catholicism
**Currency:** Escudo
**Main exports:** Clothing and textiles, machinery and transportation equipment, footwear, wood pulp, paper and paper products, cork
**Government:** Constitutional republic
**Per capita GNP:** U.S. $4,260

Portugal is Spain's neighbor on the Iberian peninsula of southwestern Europe. The Atlantic islands of Madeira and the Azores (see Atlantic Ocean) are part of Portugal. The southern mainland is low lying. The north is more mountainous. Portugal has hot, dry summers and mild, moist winters. Although most people still live in rural villages, the main cities are growing in size. Lisbon is the chief political, economic, and cultural center. Spain recognized Portugal as an independent kingdom in 1385. From the 1400s Portugal led European maritime trade and exploration in Asia and Africa, and built up an overseas empire which has now virtually gone. Portugal became a republic in 1910. Democratic government was restored in 1971 after nearly 40 years of dictatorship. Portugal joined the European Community in 1986.

## ECONOMIC SURVEY

**Farming:** Cereals, including rice and wheat, are the main crops. The vineyards of the mainland and Madeira produce wines. Other crops include almonds, limes, olives, and oranges. Sheep, pigs, and cattle are kept.
**Forestry:** Woodland covers one third of Portugal, which leads the world in cork production.
**Fishing:** Cod and sardines are the chief species caught.
**Mining:** Portugal has valuable deposits of coal, copper, and tungsten ore.
**Industry:** Machinery is a major export. Other products are ships, processed food, shoes, textiles, leather, and goods made from cork. Tourism is a major source of income.

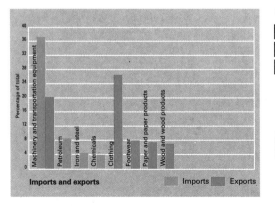

**Imports and exports**

**Age distribution**
- Under 15
- 15 - 60
- Over 60

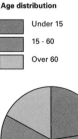

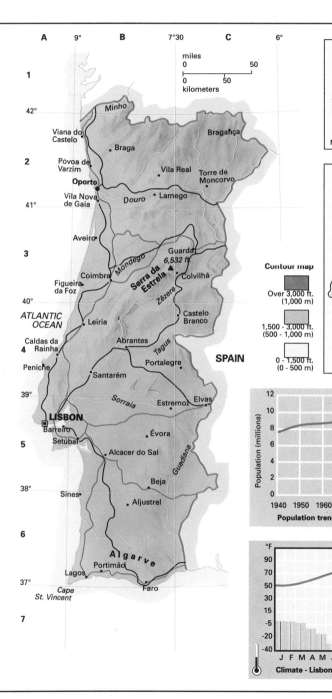

miles 0 — 50
kilometers 0 — 50

**Contour map**
- Over 3,000 ft. (1,000 m)
- 1,500 - 3,000 ft. (500 - 1,000 m)
- 0 - 1,500 ft. (0 - 500 m)

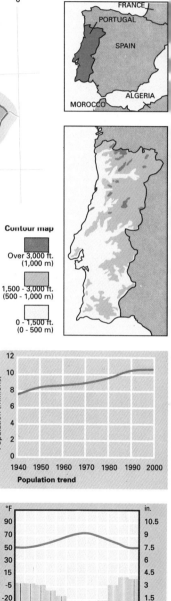

**Population trend**

**Climate - Lisbon**

# Puerto Rico and the Virgin Islands

**PUERTO RICO: Area:** 3,435 sq. miles (8,897 km²)
**Population:** 3,316,000
**Capital:** San Juan (pop. 431,000)
**Government:** U.S. Commonwealth
**VIRGIN ISLANDS (U.K.): Area:** 59 sq. miles (153 km²)
**Population:** 13,000
**Capital:** Road Town (pop. 4,000)
**Government:** British dependency
**VIRGIN ISLANDS (U.S.): Area:** 132 sq. miles (342 km²)
**Population:** 108,000
**Capital:** Charlotte Amalie (pop. 12,000)
**Government:** Self-governing U.S. territory

Puerto Rico has a mountainous interior, a northern plateau, and coastal plains. The people are mostly of Spanish and African descent. Arawak Native Americans lived there when Spaniards colonized it in 1508. In 1898 it passed to the United States. It has internal self-government. The Virgin Islands lie about 40 miles (65 km) east of Puerto Rico. The U.S.-governed islands include St. Croix, St. John, St. Thomas and some 50 islets and cays. The U.S. bought the islands from Denmark in 1917. The British Virgin Islands (a colony since 1666) consist of Tortola, Anegada, Virgin Gorda, Jost Van Dyke, and 36 islets.

## ECONOMIC SURVEY

*Puerto Rico* **Farming:** Milk, poultry, and eggs are the country's leading farm products. Cattle are reared for beef. Crops include sugarcane, coffee, tobacco, bananas, pineapples, and other fruit.
**Fishing:** Lobsters are the most important catch.
**Industry:** Products include chemicals, electrical machinery, foodstuffs, clothing, leather goods, and plastics. Tourism is important.
*The Virgin Islands:* There is little agriculture. The islands' economy is based on tourism, and the associated construction and service industries.

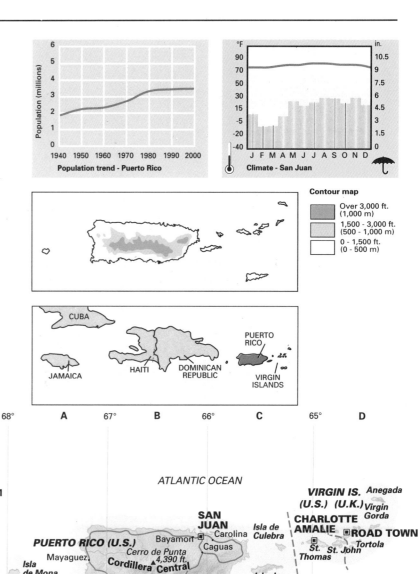

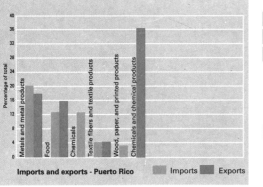

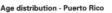

**Imports and exports - Puerto Rico**   Imports   Exports

**Age distribution - Puerto Rico**
Under 15
15 - 60
Over 60

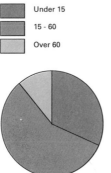

# Qatar

**Area:** 4,247 sq. miles (11,000 km²)
**Population:** 444,000
**Capital:** Doha (pop. 217,000)
**Other cities:** Umm Said 40,000
**Highest point:** 338 ft. (103 m)
**Official language:** Arabic
**Religion:** Islam
**Currency:** Riyal
**Main exports:** Crude petroleum, fertilizers
**Government:** Constitutional monarchy (the head of state is an emir)
**Per capita GNP:** U.S. $9,920

This Arabian state occupies the Qatar peninsula, projecting north into the Persian Gulf. The peninsula is some 124 miles (200 km) long. Like other Gulf states, Qatar has a hot, dry climate and most of the land is desert. Temperatures in summer (July-August) reach over 100° F in some places. There is some rainfall in winter. Natural vegetation is restricted to desert species, and there is little wildlife. The people, known as Qataris, are Muslim Arabs, and include desert nomads. The majority of the population is non-Qatari, mainly from other parts of southwest Asia, India, and Pakistan. Qatar was Turkish-ruled before coming under British protection in 1916. It became independent in 1971. The ruler, an emir, appoints government ministers, and there is no elected parliament. Large oil revenues have financed a comprehensive welfare system and free education.

## ECONOMIC SURVEY

**Farming:** Most of Qatar is desert, so agriculture is limited. Irrigation, using water drawn from underground wells, has increased cultivation. Fruit including dates, and vegetables, as well as some cereals, are grown. Livestock includes goats, sheep, camels, and cattle.
**Fishing:** There is a government-owned fishing fleet.
**Mining:** Oil provides 95 percent of the national income. There is some mining of limestone, salt, and gypsum.
**Industry:** Fertilizers, cement, and petrochemical products are manufactured. Industry is being encouraged, to reduce the country's dependence on oil.

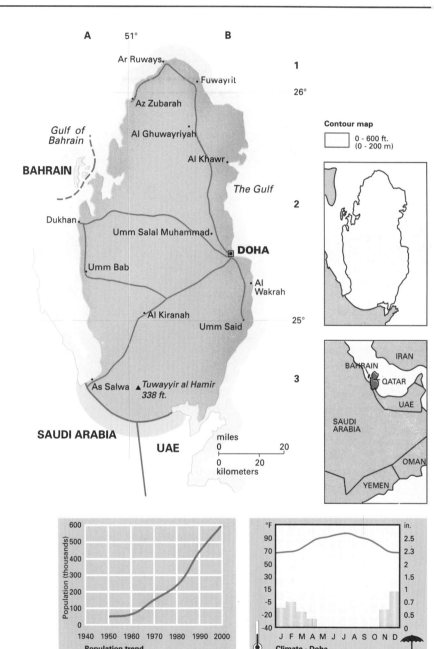

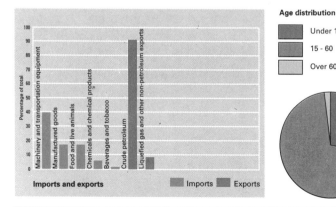

Imports and exports

Age distribution
- Under 15
- 15 - 60
- Over 60

Population trend
No earlier figures available

Climate - Doha

# Romania

**Area:** 91,699 sq. miles (237,500 km²)
**Population:** 23,278,000
**Capital:** Bucharest (pop. 2,298,000)
**Other cities:** Braşov 347,000; Constanţa
323,000; Laşi 310,000; Timişoara 309,000
**Highest point:** Mount Negoiu 8,360 ft. (2,548 m)
**Official language:** Romanian
**Religions:** Eastern Orthodoxy, Roman
Catholicism
**Currency:** Leu
**Main exports:** Machinery, petroleum products
**Government:** Multiparty republic
**Per capita GNP:** U.S. $6,400

Romania has a marshy plain where the delta of the Danube River opens onto the Black Sea. There are more plains in the far west and south, but the country is dominated by the mountain ranges of the Carpathians and Transylvanian Alps, which enclose the central region of Transylvania. Romania has hot, dry summers and cold winters. The country's origins lie in the ancient state of Dacia, part of the Roman empire. The Romanian language is based on Latin, with many Slav words, and symbolizes the cultural independence of Romania from its neighbors. Romania was created in 1861 from the union of Moldavia and Wallachia, formerly Turkish-ruled provinces. Romania fought on Germany's side in World War II. In 1946 a communist republic was set up. Nicolae Ceauşescu, dictator from 1967, was overthrown in 1989.

## ECONOMIC SURVEY

**Farming:** Main crops are corn, wheat, potatoes, sugarbeet, and vegetables. Sheep and pigs are the most numerous livestock. Cattle, horses, and poultry are also kept. Farms include large state farms and smaller collectives. About a quarter of the land is forested.

**Mining:** Romania mines iron ore, bauxite, lead, and zinc, and also has silver and gold. Oil and natural gas reserves are of declining importance.

**Industry:** Most of Romania's industry has developed since World War II. It produces heavy machinery, transportation equipment, food, timber, and clothing. Trade with the West has grown steadily.

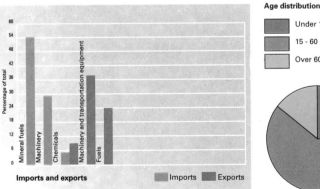

**Imports and exports**

**Age distribution**
- Under 15
- 15 - 60
- Over 60

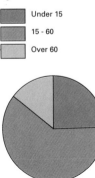

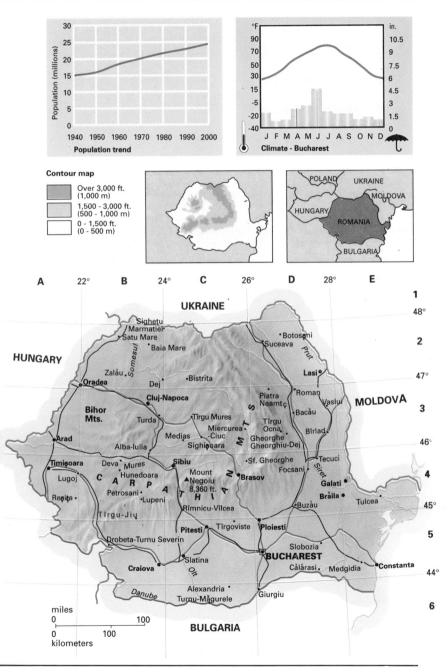

**Population trend**

**Climate - Bucharest**

**Contour map**
- Over 3,000 ft. (1,000 m)
- 1,500 - 3,000 ft. (500 - 1,000 m)
- 0 - 1,500 ft. (0 - 500 m)

# Russia and its neighbors

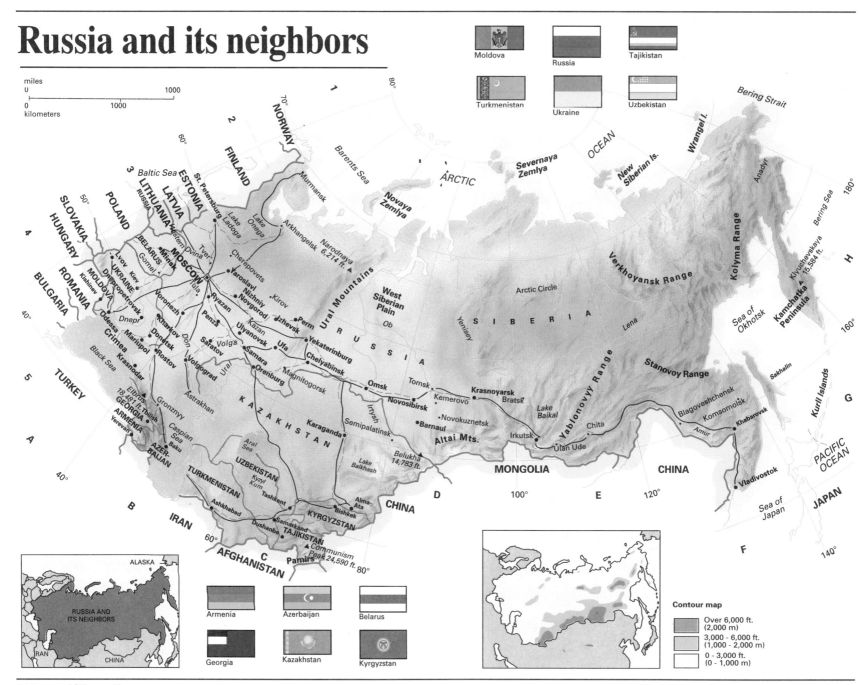

miles
0
0          1000
kilometers
1000

Moldova

Russia

Tajikistan

Turkmenistan

Ukraine

Uzbekistan

80°

Bering Strait

1

70°

NORWAY

60°

FINLAND

Barents Sea

OCEAN

ARCTIC

Severnaya Zemlya

New Siberian Is.

Wrangel I.

Anadyr

180°

H

2

Baltic Sea

ESTONIA

St. Petersburg

Lake Ladoga

Lake Onega

Murmansk

Arkhangelsk

Novaya Zemlya

Kolyma Range

Bering Sea

Klyuchevskaya 15,584 ft.

3

50°

SLOVAKIA

HUNGARY

POLAND

LITHUANIA

LATVIA

RUSSIA

Western Dvina

Cherepovets

Narodnaya 6,214 ft.

Verkhoyansk Range

160°

Kamchatka Peninsula

4

40°

BULGARIA

ROMANIA

BELARUS

Lvov

Gomel

Minsk

Kiev

MOSCOW

Tver

Yaroslavl

Kirov

Ural Mountains

West Siberian Plain

SIBERIA

Lena

Arctic Circle

Sea of Okhotsk

G

ARMENIA

MOLDOVA

Kishinev

UKRAINE

Dnepropetrovsk

Dnepr

Voronezh

Nizhniy Novgorod

Izhevsk

Perm

Ob

Yenisey

RUSSIA

5

40°

TURKEY

Black Sea

Crimea

Krasnodar

Odessa

Mariupol

Donetsk

Rostov

Kharkov

Don

Saratov

Volga

Penza

Ryazan

Kazan

Ulyanovsk

Ufa

Yekaterinburg

Chelyabinsk

Orenburg

Samara

Magnitogorsk

Volgograd

Ural

Astrakhan

Elbrus 18,481 ft. Tbilisi

Groznny

GEORGIA

AZERBAIJAN

Caspian Sea

Baku

Yerevan

KAZAKHSTAN

Aral Sea

Lake Balkhash

Omsk

Irtysh

Tomsk

Novosibirsk

Kemerovo

Krasnoyarsk

Bratsk

Lake Baikal

Yablonovyy Range

Stanovoy Range

Blagoveshchensk

Komsomolsk

Khabarovsk

Amur

Sakhalin

Kuril Islands

Sea of Japan

PACIFIC OCEAN

F

JAPAN

A

B

Karaganda

Semipalatinsk

Barnaul

Novokuznetsk

Altai Mts.

Belukha 14,783 ft.

Irkutsk

Ulan Ude

Chita

MONGOLIA

100°

CHINA

120°

Vladivostok

140°

IRAN

TURKMENISTAN

Kyzyl Kum

UZBEKISTAN

Tashkent

Ashkhabad

Samarkand

Dushanbe

TAJIKISTAN

Communism Peak 24,590 ft.

Pamirs

80°

Alma-Ata

Bishkek

KYRGYZSTAN

CHINA

C

AFGHANISTAN

60°

ALASKA

RUSSIA AND ITS NEIGHBORS

IRAN

CHINA

Armenia

Azerbaijan

Belarus

Georgia

Kazakhstan

Kyrgyzstan

**Contour map**

Over 6,000 ft. (2,000 m)

3,000 - 6,000 ft. (1,000 - 2,000 m)

0 - 3,000 ft. (0 - 1,000 m)

 *see* ASIA, page 22
*see* EUROPE, page 70

**BELARUS Area:** 80,155 sq. miles (207,600 km²)
**Population:** 10,321,000 (1992)
**Capital:** Minsk (pop. 1,633,000)
**Official language:** Belorussian
**Currency:** Ruble

**GEORGIA Area:** 26,911 sq. miles (69,700 km²)
**Population:** 5,482,000 (1992)
**Capital:** Tbilisi (pop. 1,283,000)
**Official language:** Georgian
**Currency:** Ruble

**KAZAKHSTAN Area:** 1,049,159 sq. miles (2,717,300 km²)
**Population:** 17,008,000 (1992)
**Capital:** Almaty (Alma-Ata, pop. 1,156,000)
**Official language:** Kazakh
**Currency:** Ruble.

**RUSSIA Area:** 6,592,850 sq. miles (17,075,400 km²)
**Population:** 149,469,000 (1992)
**Capital:** Moscow (pop. 8,801,500)
**Official language:** Russian
**Currency:** Ruble

**ARMENIA Area:** 11,506 sq. miles (29,800 km²)
**Population:** 3,426,000 (1992)
**Capital:** Yerevan (pop. 1,283,000)
**Official language:** Armenian
**Currency:** Ruble

**AZERBAIJAN Area:** 33,436 sq. miles (86,600 km²)
**Population:** 7,237,000 (1992)
**Capital:** Baku (pop. 1,080,000)
**Official language:** Azerbaijani
**Currency:** Manat (ruble still in use)

**KYRGYZSTAN Area:** 76,641 sq. miles (198,500 km²)
**Population:** 4,533,000 (1992)
**Capital:** Bishkek (pop. 631,000)
**Official language:** Kyrgyz
**Currency:** Som

**MOLDOVA Area:** 13,012 sq. miles (33,700 km²)
**Population:** 4,394,000 (1992)
**Capital:** Kishinev (pop. 753,000)
**Official language:** Romanian
**Currency:** Ruble

**TAJIKISTAN Area:** 55,251 sq. miles (143,100 km²)
**Population:** 5,568,000 (1992)
**Capital:** Dushanbe (pop. 582,000)
**Official language:** Tajik
**Currency:** Ruble

## ECONOMIC SURVEY

**Farming:** The republics have varied agricultural products. The region is a world leader in producing apples, barley, coniferous wood, milk, sheep and goat meat, oats, rye, wheat, sugarbeet, and potatoes. Most farm land is still state-owned, but workers keep private plots.

**Mining:** There is vast mineral wealth, with the world's leading production in asbestos, coal, steel, iron ore, oil, lead, manganese, mercury, nickel, potash, and silver production.

**Industry:** A series of five-year plans expanded the old USSR's industry until it was second only to the U.S.A. in production. However, it lagged in providing sufficient consumer goods for its people. The republics are developing their own industries.

**Age distribution**

Under 15

15 - 60

Over 60

**TURKMENISTAN Area:** 188,456 sq. miles (488,100 km²)
**Population:** 3,859,000 (1992)
**Capital:** Ashgabat (Ashkhabad, pop. 8,801,500)
**Official language:** Turkmen
**Currency:** Ruble

**UKRAINE Area:** 233,090 sq. miles (603,700 km²)
**Population:** 52,135,000 (1992)
**Capital:** Kiev (pop. 2,643,000)
**Official language:** Ukrainian
**Currency:** Karbovanets'

**UZBEKISTAN Area:** 172,742 sq. miles (447,400 km²)
**Population:** 21,363,000 (1992)
**Capital:** Toshkent (Tashkent, pop. 2,120,000)
**Official language:** Uzebek
**Currency:** Ruble

This entry covers the 12 countries that, apart from the three Baltic states (which have their own entry), formerly made up the Union of Soviet Socialist Republics. The region spans both Europe and Asia. Russia, the world's largest nation, is the dominant and most populous country.

In 1991 the then leader, Mikhail Gorbachev, survived an abortive coup, but his role as head of state no longer existed. The old USSR was dead. Major republics such as Ukraine voted for independence. Forging new links within a commonwealth of independent states, the republics set up their own governments and military and economic systems.

*The charts, graphs, and text apply to the area as a whole.*

## INDUSTRIAL PROFILE

The main industrial regions are in Russia and Ukraine. Siberia (Russian Republic) has vast reserves of raw materials and bountiful supplies of energy. Under the old Soviet system, the failings of a central administration hindered economic development. State-run agriculture failed to produce the goods. This resulted in food shortages in the stores and a flourishing black market. The change to free enterprise is causing considerable problems in most of the republics.

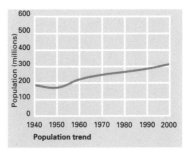

**Population trend**

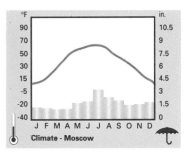

**Climate - Moscow**

# Rwanda

**Area:** 10,169 sq. miles (26,338 km²)
**Population:** 7,232,000
**Capital:** Kigali (pop. 157,000)
**Other cities:** Butare 22,000
**Highest point:** Mount Karisimbi 14,787 ft. (4,507 m)
**Official languages:** Kinyarwanda, French
**Religions:** Christianity, various traditional beliefs, Islam
**Currency:** Rwanda franc
**Main exports:** Coffee, tea
**Government:** Single-party republic
**Per capita GNP:** U.S. $310

Rwanda and its neighbor Burundi shared their history until recent times. Rwanda is a mountainous country. In the west the Rift Valley contains Lake Kivu, part of which is Rwandan territory. The highlands descend in a series of plateaus to the Kagera River. The northwest is volcanic. The climate is relatively cool, with two wet seasons and most rainfall in the west. The population includes Hutu (more than 90 percent), Tutsi (about 9 percent) and Twa or pygmies (about 1 percent). Many Tutsi, whose traditional hierarchy was destroyed by Hutu violence, are refugees in Burundi. The region was a Tutsi-dominated kingdom until German colonization in the 1890s. After World War I, Belgium took responsibility for the trust territory of Ruanda-Urundi until 1962, when it became two independent nations: Rwanda and Burundi.

## ECONOMIC SURVEY

**Farming:** Most farms produce only enough to feed their owners. Bananas, beans, cassava, sorghum, and sweet potatoes are the chief food crops. Coffee and tea are the country's two main cash crops. The fine grade arabica coffee is grown on the higher ground, the coarser robusta on lower slopes. Cattle (including the traditionally prized Ankole breed), goats, sheep, and pigs are reared.
**Mining:** Cassiterite (tin ore), wolframite (tungsten ore) and natural gas from the Lake Kivu area are the main minerals.
**Industry:** Rwanda has small but modern plants for food processing, construction, and brewing.

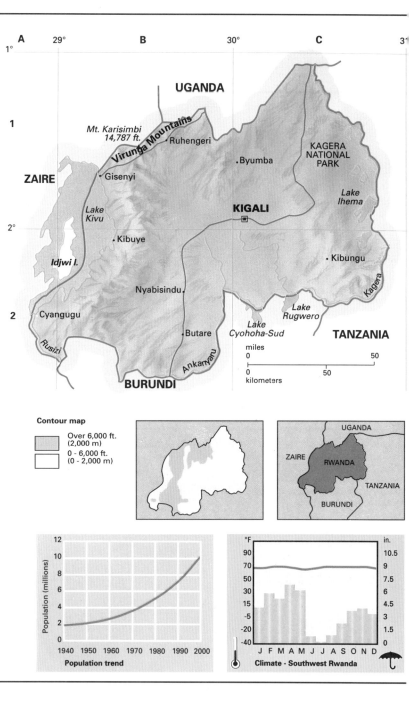

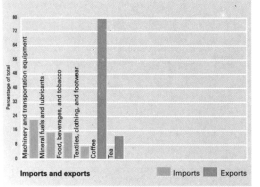

**Imports and exports** — Imports, Exports

**Age distribution**
- Under 15
- 15 - 60
- Over 60

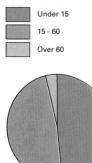

# St. Lucia and Barbados

**ST. LUCIA: Area:** 238 sq. miles (616 km²)
**Population:** 153,000
**Capital:** Castries (pop. 53,000)
**Government:** Constitutional monarchy
**Per capita GNP:** U.S. $1,810
**BARBADOS: Area:** 166 sq. miles (431 km²)
**Population:** 256,000
**Capital:** Bridgetown (pop. 7,500)
**Government:** Constitutional monarchy
**Per capita GNP:** U.S. $6,370

These islands in the West Indies form the southern part of the Antilles chain. St. Lucia is volcanic in origin. It is mountainous and thickly forested, with a tropical climate. Barbados, the most easterly island in the West Indies, is flat with a mild climate. It is devastated by hurricanes from time to time. The coral rock of which it is formed makes good agricultural land. The islands' people are mostly descended from African slaves. Others are of mixed African and European origin. Discovered by Christopher Columbus and later European voyagers from the 1490s onward, the islands were colonized by European planters. Barbados was British from 1628 to 1966, when it became independent. St. Lucia was British from 1814 until it gained its independence in 1979.

## ECONOMIC SURVEY

**Farming:** There is limited farmland on St. Lucia, and most farmers grow food just for themselves. Bananas and coconuts are cash crops. More than 80 percent of the land in Barbados is suitable for agriculture, and sugarcane is the leading cash crop. Farmers also grow corn and vegetables.

**Industry:** Barbados has the bigger range of industries, such as chemicals, clothes, electronics, and sugar processing (for molasses and rum). Edible oils and margarine are also made. Factories in St. Lucia make textiles. Tourism is growing on both islands.

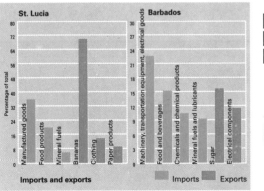

**Imports and exports**

St. Lucia
Barbados

Imports
Exports

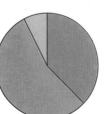

Age distribution - St. Lucia

Under 15
15 - 60
Over 60

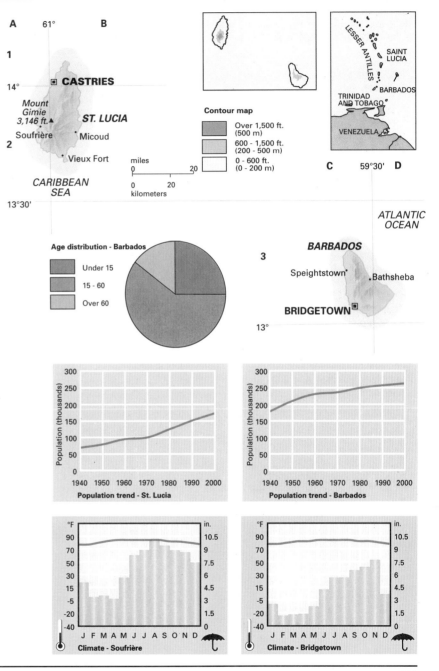

# Saudi Arabia

**Area:** 830,000 sq. miles (2,149,690 km²)
**Population:** 14,131,000
**Capital:** Riyadh (pop. 1,308,000)
**Other cities:** Jiddah 1,500,000; Mecca 550,000; Al Taif 204,000; Medina 198,000
**Highest point:** Peak near Abha in the Asir region 10,279 ft. (3,133 m)
**Official language:** Arabic
**Religion:** Islam
**Currency:** Riyal
**Main export:** Petroleum
**Government:** Monarchy
**Per capita GNP:** U.S. $6,230

The kingdom of Saudi Arabia occupies most of the Arabian peninsula. There is a narrow coastal Red Sea plain, and inland is a highland zone including the Hejaz in the north and the Asir Mountains in the south. To the east are plateaus sloping gently toward lowlands near the Gulf coast; these plateaus cover 90 percent of the country and include the deserts of An Nafud and the Rub al Khali. The lowlands are hot, and rainfall is low to almost nonexistent, but the highlands are cooler. Most Saudis are Muslim Arabs. Mecca, the birthplace of Muhammad, and Medina are the two holiest places of Islam. The region was part of the Ottoman empire from 1517 to 1916, when the Arabs revolted. Abd Al-Aziz Ibn Saud was the first king of modern Saudi Arabia (unified in 1932) and he founded the dynasty which rules the oil-rich kingdom.

## ECONOMIC SURVEY

**Farming:** Most of Saudi Arabia is desert, but thanks to irrigation projects and government aid, farming is developing steadily. About 25 percent of workers are on the land. They grow crops of wheat, dates, melons, tomatoes, barley, and other vegetables and fruits. Poultry and dairy cattle are reared, alongside sheep, goats, camels, and asses. Even so, Saudi Arabia imports most of its food.
**Mining:** Saudi Arabia's economy is based on oil, which accounts for 94 percent of exports. Other minerals include coal, iron, and gold.
**Industry:** Modern heavy industrial complexes produce petrochemicals, fertilizers, and steel.

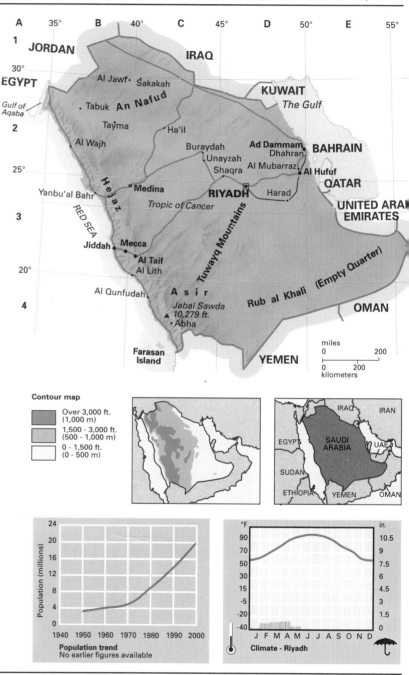

**Contour map**

- Over 3,000 ft. (1,000 m)
- 1,500 - 3,000 ft. (500 - 1,000 m)
- 0 - 1,500 ft. (0 - 500 m)

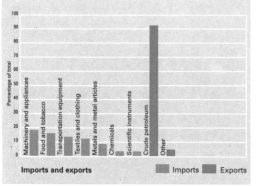

**Imports and exports** — Imports / Exports

**Age distribution**

- Under 15
- 15 - 60
- Over 60

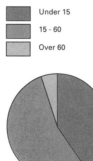

**Population trend**
No earlier figures available

**Climate - Riyadh**

# Senegal and Gambia

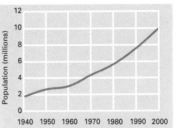

**SENEGAL: Area:** 75,750 sq. miles (196,192 km²)
**Population:** 7,618,000
**Capital:** Dakar (pop. 1,382,000)
**Government:** Multiparty republic
**Per capita GNP:** U.S. $650
**GAMBIA: Area:** 4,361 sq. miles (11,295 km²)
**Population:** 860,000
**Capital:** Banjul (pop. 44,000)
**Government:** Multiparty republic
**Per capita GNP:** U.S. $230

Gambia is the smallest nation in mainland Africa. It consists of a narrow strip of land bordering the Gambia River, and is entirely enclosed by Senegal except for a short Atlantic coast. There are swamps in low-lying areas, savannas in the uplands, and forests beside the rivers. Senegal is drained by the Sénégal, Gambia, and Casamance rivers. The coast has a pleasant climate, less hot than the interior. The north is very dry but the south has more rain. The people are Black Africans, belonging to the Wolof, Fulani (Peul), Serer, Toucouleur, Lebon, and other groups. Gambia was a British colony from 1888, becoming independent in 1965 and a republic in 1970. Senegal was a French colony from 1887 until independence in 1960. The two nations cooperate closely in the Senegambia Confederation.

## ECONOMIC SURVEY

**Farming:** Senegal's chief crops are sugar, peanuts, millet and sorghum, corn, beans, cotton, and rice. Rice is the staple food of the people. Gambia's crops are similar, but its economy is dominated by peanuts (groundnuts).
**Fishing:** Senegal exports shellfish and canned and fresh fish, especially tuna.
**Mining:** Senegal has phosphate mines, and deposits of ilmenite, zircon, and rutile.
**Industry:** Senegal's capital, Dakar, has ship-repairing facilities and factories making cement, petroleum products, and peanut oil. Gambia's tourism is growing.

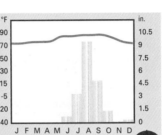

Population trend - Senegal

Population trend - Gambia

Climate - Dakar

Climate - Banjul

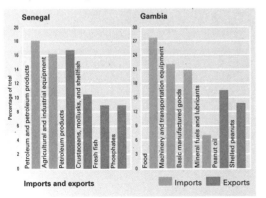

Senegal

Gambia

**Imports and exports**

Imports    Exports

**Age distribution - Senegal**

Under 15

15 - 60

Over 60

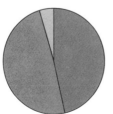

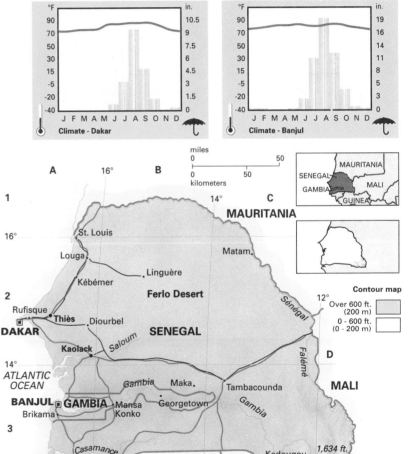

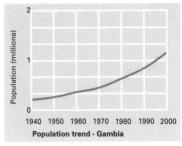

**Contour map**

Over 600 ft. (200 m)

0 - 600 ft. (0 - 200 m)

1,634 ft. ▲

# Sierra Leone

**Area:** 27,699 sq. miles (71,740 km²)
**Population:** 4,033,000
**Capital:** Freetown (pop. 470,000)
**Highest point:** Loma Mansa 6,390 ft. (1,948 m)
**Official language:** English
**Religions:** Various traditional beliefs, Islam, Christianity
**Currency:** Leone
**Main exports:** Rutile, diamonds, bauxite, cocoa, gold
**Government:** Single-party republic
**Per capita GNP:** U.S. $200

Sierra Leone is made up of interior plateaus and mountains, and a broad coastal plain. Swamps cover much of the coastal region. In more than half of Sierra Leone the soil is largely sand or gravel, supporting only grasses. The climate is tropical, with heavy rainfall in the wet season. Most of the people are Black Africans of the Temne and Mende groups. A small number, known as Creoles, are the descendants of freed slaves. Most of these people are Christians. Although English is the official language, most people speak local languages. Some Portuguese explorers sighted the coast of Sierra Leone in 1460. From the 1500s European slave traders operated in the area. In 1786 a settlement for freed slaves from the Americas was begun by a British philanthropist, Granville Sharp. Sierra Leone became a British colony in 1808. It gained independence in 1961, becoming a republic in 1971.

## ECONOMIC SURVEY

**Farming:** Rice is grown for food. Other crops include corn, cassava, vegetables, and mangoes for local consumption. Cash crops include palm kernels, cocoa beans, coffee, kola, and ginger. In the north cattle are reared. Pigs and chickens are also kept. Piassava, a fiber used for making brooms, is an important product.
**Forestry:** The industry is government-run and produces timber for construction and furniture.
**Mining:** Bauxite, chromite, rutile (titanium ore), iron ore, and diamonds are mined.
**Industry:** Diamond cutting is a leading industry. Factories process palm oil and rice, and make nails, shoes, and cigarettes.

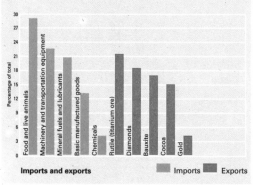

**Imports and exports**

Food and live animals; Machinery and transportation equipment; Mineral fuels and lubricants; Basic manufactured goods; Chemicals; Rutile (titanium ore); Diamonds; Bauxite; Cocoa; Gold

Imports | Exports

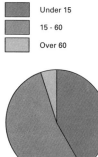

**Age distribution**

Under 15
15 - 60
Over 60

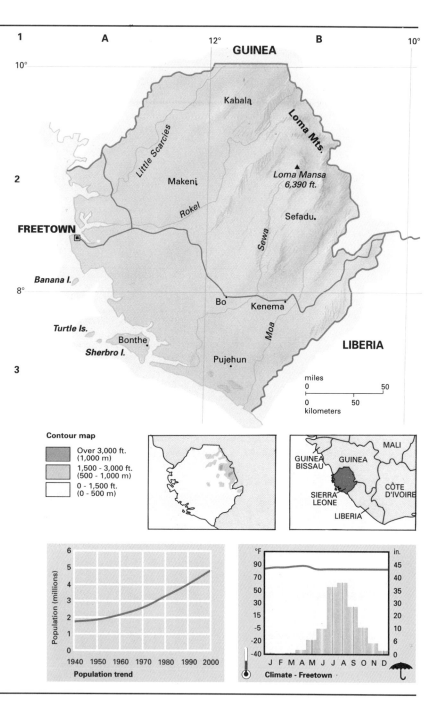

**Contour map**

Over 3,000 ft. (1,000 m)
1,500 - 3,000 ft. (500 - 1,000 m)
0 - 1,500 ft. (0 - 500 m)

**Population trend**

**Climate - Freetown**

# Singapore

**Area:** 224 sq. miles (581 km²)
**Population:** 2,702,000
**Capital:** Singapore City
**Highest point:** Timah Hill 581 ft. (177 m)
**Official languages:** Chinese, English, Malay, Tamil
**Religions:** Buddhism, Christianity, Islam, Taoism, Hinduism
**Currency:** Singapore dollar
**Main exports:** Telecommunications apparatus, office machines, petroleum products, clothing
**Government:** Multiparty republic
**Per capita GNP:** U.S. $10,450

Despite its small size, the republic of Singapore is one of the most prosperous nations in Asia. The low-lying island of Singapore is separated from the southern tip of the Malay peninsula by the Johor Strait. There are 55 smaller islands. The climate is warm and moist. Little remains of the original vegetation, as high-density housing and industrial development cover much of the island. The people are mostly Chinese (76 percent), Malays (15 percent) and Indians (7 percent). Once a small fishing village amid swampy jungle, Singapore was founded as a British trading base in 1819 by Sir Stamford Raffles. In 1826 it became part of the Straits Settlements. During World War II it was captured by the Japanese. Singapore gained internal self-government in 1959. It was part of Malaysia from 1963 to 1965, when it became a separate republic.

## ECONOMIC SURVEY

**Farming:** There is little agriculture. Small farms produce eggs, poultry, pork, vegetables, and fruit. Orchids are grown and there are also fish farms. Water is piped from the Malaysian mainland.

**Industry:** With few resources, Singapore's wealth comes from trade through its port, which is the busiest in Southeast Asia, its oil refineries and manufacturing. Leading products are office machines, transportation and telecommunications equipment, petroleum products, and clothing. Other products include ships, chemicals, electronics, foods, and timber products. Singapore is an important banking and finance centre.

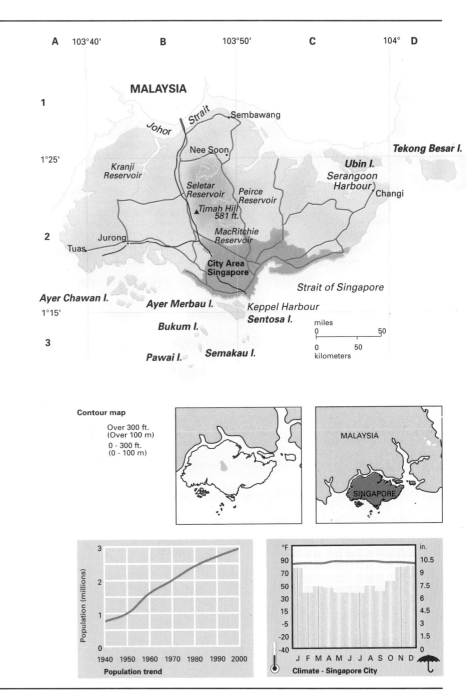

**Contour map**

Over 300 ft.
(Over 100 m)
0 - 300 ft.
(0 - 100 m)

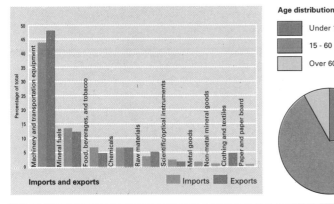

**Imports and exports**

Imports   Exports

**Age distribution**

Under 15
15 - 60
Over 60

**Population trend**

**Climate - Singapore City**

# Somalia

**Area:** 246,201 sq. miles (637,657 km²)
**Population:** 7,555,000
**Capital:** Mogadishu (pop. 500,000)
**Other cities:** Hargeisa 70,000; Borama 65,000; Kismayu 60,000
**Highest point:** Surud Ad 7,900 ft. (2,408 m)
**Official languages:** Somali, Arabic
**Religion:** Islam
**Currency:** Somali shilling
**Main exports:** Live animals, bananas, animal hides, fish
**Government:** Republic
**Per capita GNP:** U.S. $170

## ECONOMIC SURVEY

**Farming:** The main activity is herding camels, cattle, goats, and sheep. Live animals are exported. There are banana plantations (started during the Italian colonial period) and bananas form the chief cash crop. Other crops include citrus fruits, sugarcane, and cotton. Corn, sorghum, rice, beans, dates, and groundnuts (peanuts) are grown.
**Fishing:** The main Somali fishing fleets are based on the northern coast.
**Mining:** Salt is the only mineral yet exploited, but there are deposits of coal, iron ore, and gypsum.
**Industry:** Small factories process hides and skins, and manufacture paper products, plastics, chemicals, and drinks.

Forming the seaward edge of the Horn of Africa, Somalia, also called the Somali Republic, faces the Gulf of Aden in the north and the Indian Ocean in the east. Behind the narrow northern coastal plain are the Ogo Highlands. In the south are plateaus and plains, and the only rivers that flow all year, the Shebele and the Juba (Giuba), which provide water for farming. The south has the most rainfall. Temperatures are high all year round. The main vegetation is semi-desert scrub and savanna. Most Somali people belong to a group known as the Samaal (herders). Others are Sabs (farmers). Historically, Somalia was an important trading center. By the 1880s Britain controlled the north as British Somaliland, while by 1905 Italy ruled the south as Italian Somaliland. In 1960 the two united as an independent republic.

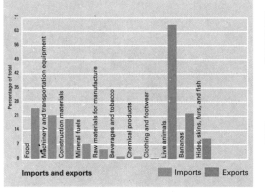

**Imports and exports** — Imports, Exports

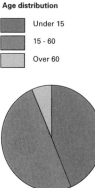

**Age distribution**
Under 15
15 - 60
Over 60

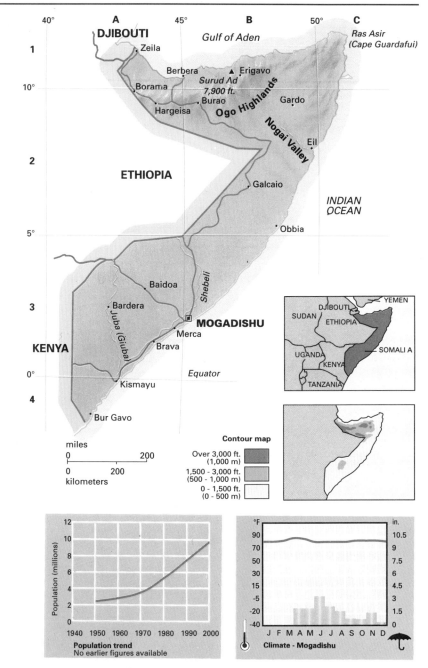

miles
0 — 200
0 — 200
kilometers

**Contour map**
Over 3,000 ft. (1,000 m)
1,500 - 3,000 ft. (500 - 1,000 m)
0 - 1,500 ft. (0 - 500 m)

**Population trend**
No earlier figures available

**Climate - Mogadishu**

# South Africa

**Area:** 471,445 sq. miles (1,221,037 km²)
**Population:** 37,466,000
**Capitals:** Pretoria, administrative (pop. 823,000); Cape Town, legislative (1,912,000)
**Other cities:** Johannesburg 1,609,000; Durban 928,000
**Highest point:** Injasuti 11,348 ft. (3,459 m)
**Official languages:** Afrikaans, English
**Religions:** Christianity, Hinduism, Islam
**Currency:** Rand
**Main exports:** Gold, metals, precious stones
**Government:** Multiparty republic
**Per capita GNP:** U.S. $2,460

The interior of South Africa is a saucer-shaped plateau with an uptilted rim, the Great Escarpment, which rises to the high Drakensberg range. On the plateau are the High Veld, Middle Veld, and Transvaal Basin, where the vegetation is grassland with scattered trees. Around Johannesburg is the mineral-rich Witwatersrand region. The Orange and Limpopo rivers drain much of the plateau, from which the land drops in steps to the sea. Between the Cape Mountains and the Great Escarpment are the Little Karroo and Great Karroo tablelands. Most of South Africa has a subtropical climate and low rainfall, especially in the Namib and Kalahari deserts. The people of South Africa include whites of Dutch (Boer) and British origin, Asians, Coloreds (people of mixed origin), and Black Africans, who form the majority.

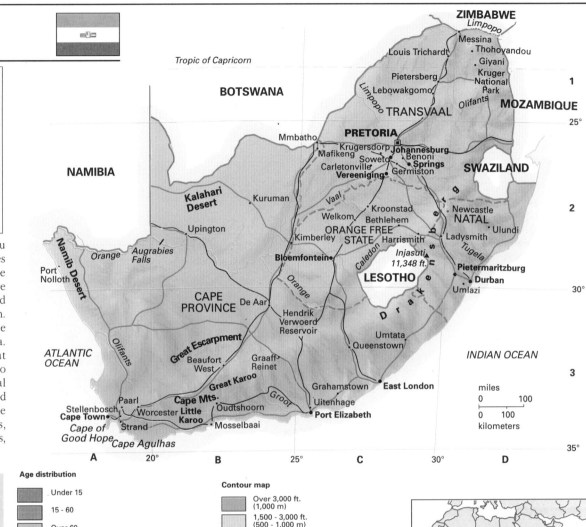

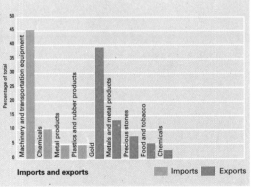

Imports and exports

Imports | Exports

Age distribution

Under 15
15 - 60
Over 60

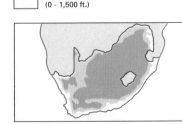

Contour map

Over 3,000 ft. (1,000 m)
1,500 - 3,000 ft. (500 - 1,000 m)
0 - 500 m (0 - 1,500 ft.)

**SOUTH AFRICAN HISTORY.** Southern Africa was home to hominids (humanlike beings) more than 2 million years ago. In the past 2,000 years successive migrations took place. First came the San (Bushmen) and the Khoi (Hottentots), then Bantu-speaking tribes. Dutch settlers arrived at the Cape in 1652, and slowly spread inland. Cape Colony became British in 1814. The Dutch farmers or Boers resented British rule and set up free states in the interior. But British military power subdued both the Boers and black groups such as the Zulus. The self-governing Union of South Africa (1910) became independent in 1931. The National Party instituted the policy of apartheid (separation of races) in 1948. Blacks had no share in government. South Africa became a republic in 1961. The South African government set up four "independent" black-ruled homelands. They are Bophuthatswana, Ciskei, Transkei, and Venda. Their independence was not recognized by the United Nations and people living in them have asserted their desire for eventual reincorporation within South Africa. In addition, six areas are designated as self-governing black states. South Africa's apparently rigid apartheid system, and its consequent international isolation, began to crumble in the 1990s, following the election in 1989 of reformist President F.W. De Klerk. In 1990 African National Congress leader Nelson Mandela was freed from prison after 27 years. The government, the ANC, and the Zulu Inkatha Freedom Party talked of partnership, although violence in the black townships and right-wing white hostility threatened this new found optimism. Apartheid was abolished in public places. Also abolished were the Land Acts reserving most land for the white minority. A Convention for a Democratic South Africa (CODESA) began drawing up a new constitution to introduce multi-racial democracy. Despite its many problems, South Africa is Africa's economic and industrial giant.

**ECONOMIC SURVEY**
**Farming:** Cattle, sheep, goats, and pigs are raised. Wool is a major export. Other products are fruit, tobacco, and wines. The chief food crops are corn, sorghum, wheat, oats, barley, and sugarcane.
**Forestry:** South Africa's forests supply the national needs, including softwoods and hardwoods.
**Fishing:** The fleet has over 4,000 vessels. Catches include anchovy and hake.
**Mining:** The country is a major producer of gold, coal, copper, chromite, diamonds, iron ore, manganese, platinum, and uranium.
**Industry:** South Africa is Africa's most highly industrialized country. Trade sanctions because of apartheid spurred development of self-sufficient local industries, especially in the armaments, electronics, and chemicals fields. Machinery, iron and steel, vehicles, and processed foods are produced.

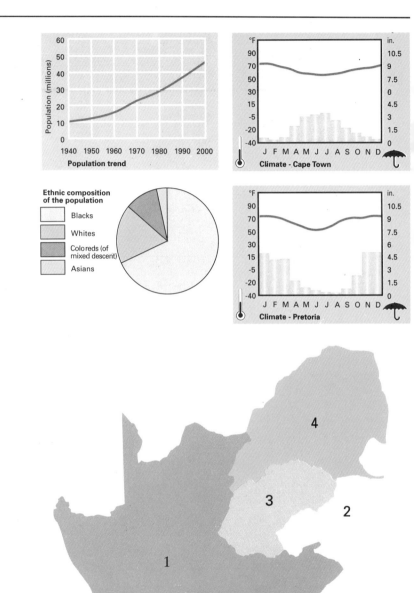

**Population trend**

**Climate - Cape Town**

**Climate - Pretoria**

**Ethnic composition of the population**
- Blacks
- Whites
- Coloreds (of mixed descent)
- Asians

**SOUTH AFRICAN PROVINCES**

| Province and capital | Area (sq. miles) | Area (km²) | Population (1985) |
|---|---|---|---|
| 1  **Cape Province** (Cape Town) | 247,638 | 641,379 | 5,041,000 |
| 2  **Natal** (Pietermaritzburg) | 35,272 | 91,355 | 5,892,000 |
| 3  **Orange Free State** (Bloemfontein) | 49,418 | 127,993 | 1,958,000 |
| 4  **Transvaal** (Pretoria) | 101,351 | 262,499 | 10,494,000 |

* Figures do not include the four "independent" homelands of Bophuthatswana, Ciskei, Transkei, and Venda, which had a combined population of about 6,724,000 in 1986.

# SOUTH AMERICA

**Area:** 6,879,183 sq. miles (17,817,000 km²)
**Population:** 298,200,000
**Major cities:** São Paulo (Brazil) 16,832,000; Rio de Janeiro (Brazil) 11,141,000; Buenos Aires (Argentina) 9,968,000; Lima (Peru) 5,494,000; Santiago (Chile) 4,858,000
**Number of independent countries:** 12
**Largest country:** Brazil
**Smallest independent country:** Surinam
**Highest mountain:** Aconcagua (in Argentina) 22,831 ft. (6,959 m)
**Longest river:** Amazon 4,007 miles (6,448 km)
**Largest lake:** Lake Maracaibo 5,217 sq. miles (13,511 km²)

**Contour map**

- Over 6,000 ft. (2,000 m)
- 3,000 - 6,000 ft. (1,000 - 2,000 m)
- 0 - 3,000 ft. (0 - 1,000 m)

The fourth largest continent, South America forms the major part of Latin America, so-called because its people speak languages — Spanish and Portuguese — derived from Latin. It has widely varying climates and landscapes, including the world's largest tropical rain forest, in the Amazon River basin, and the high Andes Mountains. The central plains include grasslands known as Llanos in the north and Pampa in the south. Much of the continent is thinly populated, since about 75 percent of South Americans live in cities. The continent is rich in natural resources. In parts of Amazonia unrestricted development has caused environmental damage. South America's Native Americans now form a threatened minority. Europeans (mostly Spanish at first) began settling in the 1500s, conquering the Incas of Peru, and importing black slaves from Africa. Spanish control weakened, and the present republics gained their freedom in the 1800s. Early attempts at federation failed, and few South American nations have enjoyed democratic stability for long periods. Many South American governments have been dictatorial. They have failed to come to grips with severe social and economic problems, such as extremes of poverty, unemployment, fast-rising birth rates, and illiteracy. Narcotics-based crime and terrorism are problems in some countries. However, the continent's natural resources offer hope for the future. Brazil is the largest and economically most powerful country in South America, and is likely to become the continent's 21st-century superstate.

# South Korea

**Area:** 30,025 sq. miles (98,484 km$^2$)
**Population:** 42,791,000
**Capital:** Seoul (pop. 10,513,000)
**Other cities:** Pusan 3,754,000; Taegu 2,206,000; Inchon 1,388,000
**Highest point:** Mount Halla 6,398 ft. (1,950 m)
**Official language:** Korean
**Religions:** Buddhism, Christianity
**Currency:** Won
**Main exports:** Cars, textiles and clothing, ships, shoes, steel, fish
**Government:** Multiparty republic
**Per capita GNP:** U.S. $4,400

South Korea is slightly smaller than North Korea, but has nearly twice as many people. Much of the Central Mountains region is forested. The southern plain is an important farming area covering the southern coastal region. South Korea's longest river is the Naktong. South Korea also has Korea's largest offshore island, Cheju. The climate resembles that of North Korea, with the east coast being milder than other parts of the country. During the Middle Ages Korea was occupied by the Mongols, and in 1627 it was conquered by China. Japan took over Korea in 1910, ruling it harshly. When Japan was defeated in 1945, Korea was divided. A democratic form of government was set up in the south. Since the inconclusive Korean War (1950-53) North and South Korea have remained mutually suspicious and hostile.

## ECONOMIC SURVEY

**Farming:** Rice is the main crop, followed by vegetables, apples, oranges, barley, and soya beans. Pigs, cattle, and chickens are reared.
**Fishing:** South Korea's fishing fleet ranks ninth in the world, and the catch includes pollack and oysters.
**Mining:** South Korea's mineral deposits include coal, zinc, silver, and tungsten.
**Industry:** The economy is growing rapidly. The food, shoe, and garment industries employ most workers. Heavy industry includes chemicals, fertilizers, iron and steel, machinery, and shipbuilding. Cars, paper and paper products, domestic appliances, television sets, and computers are also produced.

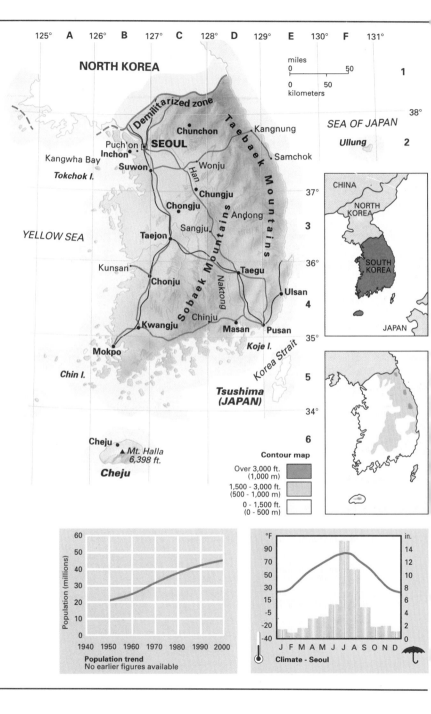

Contour map

Over 3,000 ft. (1,000 m)
1,500 - 3,000 ft. (500 - 1,000 m)
0 - 1,500 ft. (0 - 500 m)

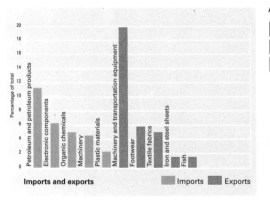

**Imports and exports**

Imports   Exports

**Age distribution**

Under 15
15 - 60
Over 60

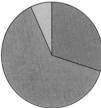

**Population trend**
No earlier figures available

**Climate - Seoul**

# Spain

**Area:** 194,897 sq. miles (504,782 km²), including Canary Islands 2,808 sq. miles (7,273 km²)
**Population:** 39,322,000
**Capital:** Madrid (pop. 3,124,000)
**Other cities:** Barcelona 1,694,000; Valencia 739,000; Seville 668,000
**Highest point:** Pico de Teide (Canary Islands) 12,162 ft. (3,707 m)
**Official language:** Spanish
**Religion:** Roman Catholicism
**Currency:** Peseta (Spain)
**Main exports:** Transportation equipment, especially cars, agricultural products, chemicals
**Government:** Constitutional monarchy
**Per capita GNP:** U.S. $9,150

The kingdom of Spain occupies the largest part of the Iberian Peninsula. Most of the country is a meseta, or plateau, broken by mountain ranges. The highest peaks rise in the Pyrenees in the north and the Sierra Nevada in the south. The coastal plains of Alicante and Valencia are the most fertile farming regions. The Balearic Islands (notably Majorca, Minorca, and Ibiza) form a province in the Mediterranean Sea. The volcanic Canary Islands form two provinces in the Atlantic Ocean off southern Morocco: Las Palmas de Gran Canaria and Santa Cruz de Tenerife. Northern coastal Spain is mild and wet in winter and cool in summer. The interior has colder winters and less rain, and the south is hot in summer. Tourism is important.

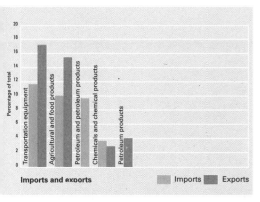

**Imports and exports**

Imports    Exports

**Age distribution**

- Under 15
- 15 - 60
- Over 60

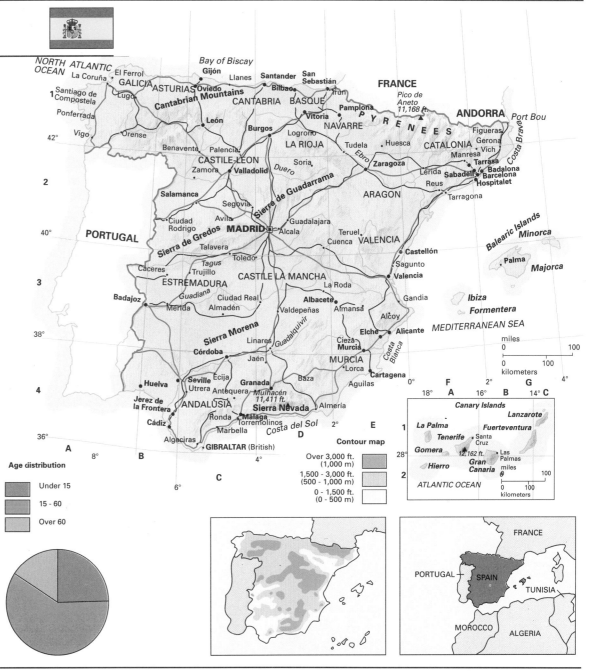

**Contour map**

- Over 3,000 ft. (1,000 m)
- 1,500 - 3,000 ft. (500 - 1,000 m)
- 0 - 1,500 ft. (0 - 500 m)

**SPANISH HISTORY.** Most Spanish people speak Castilian, but minorities speak Basque, Catalan, and Galician. The reason for these differences is that Spain was once several independent kingdoms. Spain was originally settled by the Iberians, Basques, and Celts. Rome conquered the country around 2000 B.C. Moors from North Africa invaded in 711 and controlled much of southern Spain until they were driven out in the 1400s. In 1479 Isabella of Castile married Ferdinand of Aragon, leading to union of their countries. A leading Roman Catholic power in Europe, Spain built up a huge overseas empire, notably in America, but lost most of it by the early 1800s. Spain was neutral in World War I. From 1923 to 1930 General Miguel Primo de Rivera was prime minister and virtual dictator. King Alfonso XIII left Spain in 1931 and a republic was set up. Civil war raged from 1936 to 1939. The war's victors, the Nationalists, were led by General Francisco Franco. He ruled as dictator from 1939 to 1975. Spain was neutral during World War II. Not until after Franco's death did Spain return to democracy, as a constitutional monarchy with Juan Carlos (grandson of King Alfonso) as king. Spain joined the European Community in 1986. The government has given greater self-government to regional peoples, such as the Basques and Catalans.

**ECONOMIC SURVEY**
**Farming:** Even though 75 percent of the Spanish people now live in urban areas, agriculture is important, with farms producing cereals, citrus fruit, olives, vegetables, and rice. Sherry and other wines are important products.
**Fishing:** Catches include anchovies, cod, hake, mussels, squid, and tuna.
**Mining:** Spain has reserves of coal, iron ore, copper, lead, mercury, and zinc.
**Industry:** Spain's manufactures include textiles, chemicals, machinery, and vehicles. Tourism is a major income earner.

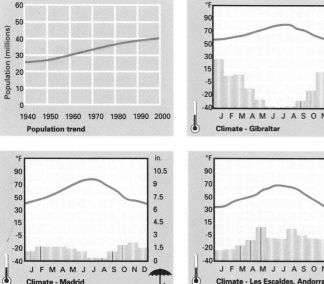

**Population trend**

**Climate - Gibraltar**

**Climate - Madrid**

**Climate - Les Escaldes, Andorra**

# Gibraltar

**Area:** 2 sq. miles (6 km$^2$)
**Population:** 30,000
**Capital:** Gibraltar
**Official language:** English
**Religion:** Roman Catholicism
**Currency:** English pound
**Economy:** Tourism is a major industry
**Government:** British dependency

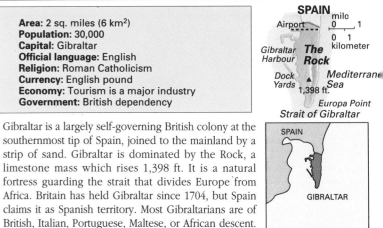

Gibraltar is a largely self-governing British colony at the southernmost tip of Spain, joined to the mainland by a strip of sand. Gibraltar is dominated by the Rock, a limestone mass which rises 1,398 ft. It is a natural fortress guarding the strait that divides Europe from Africa. Britain has held Gibraltar since 1704, but Spain claims it as Spanish territory. Most Gibraltarians are of British, Italian, Portuguese, Maltese, or African descent. Gibraltar was once an important military and naval base, but now relies mostly on tourism.

# Andorra

**Area:** 175 sq. miles (435 km$^2$)
**Population:** 51,000
**Capital:** Andorra la Vella (pop. 16,000)
**Other towns:** Les Escaldes 16,000
**Official language:** Catalan
**Religion:** Roman Catholicism
**Currency:** French franc and Spanish peseta
**Main exports:** Furniture, handicrafts, tobacco products
**Government:** Principality
**Per capita GNP:** U.S. $9,000

Andorra is a tiny, mountainous co-principality in the Pyrenees mountains between France and Spain. There are two heads of state: the Spanish Bishop of Urgel and the French President. The effective government is a 28-member elected General Council. The Andorrans herd sheep and goats, and grow tobacco. Tourism provides most of the state's income. Andorra's minimal tax and customs regulations attract millions of shoppers and winter sports enthusiasts.

# Sri Lanka

**Area:** 25,332 sq. miles (65,610 km²)
**Population:** 17,108,000
**Capital:** Colombo (pop. 683,000)
**Other cities:** Dehiwela-Mount Lavinia 191,000; Moratuwa 143,000
**Highest point:** Pidurutalagala 8,261 ft. (2,518 m)
**Official languages:** Sinhalese, Tamil
**Religions:** Buddhism, Hinduism, Islam, Christianity
**Currency:** Rupee
**Main exports:** Textiles, tea, rubber, coconuts
**Government:** Multiparty republic
**Per capita GNP:** U.S. $430

An island in the Indian Ocean, Sri Lanka was called Ceylon until 1972. The land is mostly low lying, with central highlands. Much of the southwest is covered by rain forest. The climate is tropical, with high temperatures and moderate to high rainfall. Most people are Sinhalese, who are mainly Buddhists. The next largest group is the Tamils, who are descendants of people from southern India and are mostly Hindus. Smaller ethnic groups include Moors, Burghers, Malays, and Veddas. Most Sri Lankans live in rural villages. The Sinhalese arrived on the island about 2,400 years ago, and were followed by the Tamils. Europeans began trading from the 1500s. Ceylon was a British colony from 1802 until 1948, when it became independent. Rivalry between the ruling Sinhalese and the Tamils led to terrorism and civil war in the 1980s.

## ECONOMIC SURVEY

**Farming:** About 45 per cent of the work force is employed in agriculture. The chief products are tea, rice, rubber and coconuts. Cattle, buffaloes, sheep, goats and poultry are raised.
**Fishing:** Sri Lanka's 30,000 vessels catch about 17,000 tons of fish a year.
**Mining:** Minerals include gemstones such as sapphires and rubies, and graphite.
**Industry:** Factories produce foods, drinks including tea, clothing, ceramics, paper, tiles, fertilizers, leather goods, plastics and chemicals. Salt is produced by the evaporation of sea water. About a third of the work force is employed in service industries. Tourism has been disrupted by civil war.

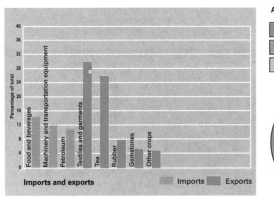

**Imports and exports**

**Age distribution**

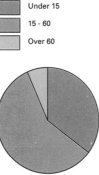

Under 15
15 - 60
Over 60

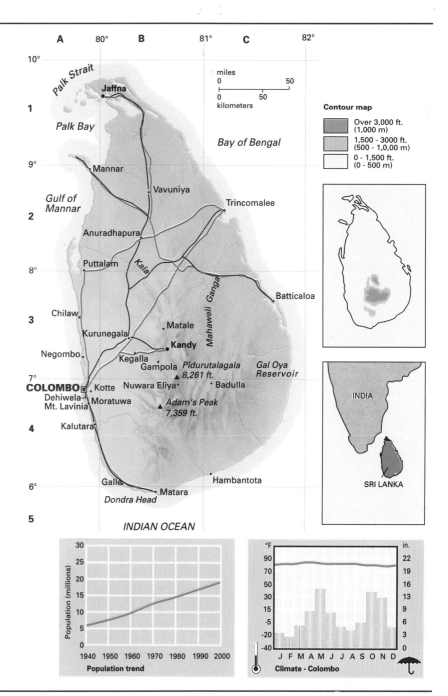

**Contour map**

Over 3,000 ft. (1,000 m)
1,500 - 3000 ft. (500 - 1,0,00 m)
0 - 1,500 ft. (0 - 500 m)

INDIA
SRI LANKA

**Population trend**

**Climate - Colombo**

# Sudan

**Area:** 967,500 sq. miles (2,505,813 km²)
**Population:** 28,311,000
**Capital:** Khartoum (pop. 476,000)
**Other cities:** Omdurman 526,000; Khartoum North 341,000; Port Sudan 207,000
**Highest point:** Kinyeti 10,456 ft. (3,187 m)
**Official language:** Arabic
**Religions:** Islam, traditional beliefs, Christianity
**Currency:** Sudanese pound
**Main exports:** Cotton, gum arabic, sesame seeds, sheep
**Government:** Military regime
**Per capita GNP:** U.S. $420

## ECONOMIC SURVEY

**Farming:** Farming is carried out along the Nile River and on irrigated land owned by the government. Cotton is the main currency earner. Gum arabic and sesame seeds are also cash crops. Food crops include sorghum, millet, wheat, yams, and cassava. Livestock herding (cattle, sheep, goats, and camels) is important.

**Mining:** There are deposits of gold, graphite, sulfur, chromium, and many other minerals, though few are exploited. There is oil in southwestern Sudan.

**Industry:** Factories produce sugar, flour, plastics, yarn, and textiles. Drought, famine, and civil war have hampered development.

Sudan, Africa's largest country in area, is mostly flat. It includes much of the upper Nile River basin. Highlands border the Red Sea plains in the northeast. The Darfur highlands are in the west. Average annual temperature is high. There is virtually no rainfall in the north. In the south, rain is usually plentiful, but Sudan has had several drought years recently. Much of the land is desert, but large areas of sudd (swampland) occur in the Nile region. In the north most Sudanese are Arabs or light-skinned Hamites. In the south of the country most people are Black Africans. Ancient Sudan was under Egyptian influence. Later, northern rulers raided the south for slaves. Egypt took over Sudan in the 1830s, and ruled it jointly with Britain from 1889. The country became independent in 1956. Civil war has raged since the early 1980s.

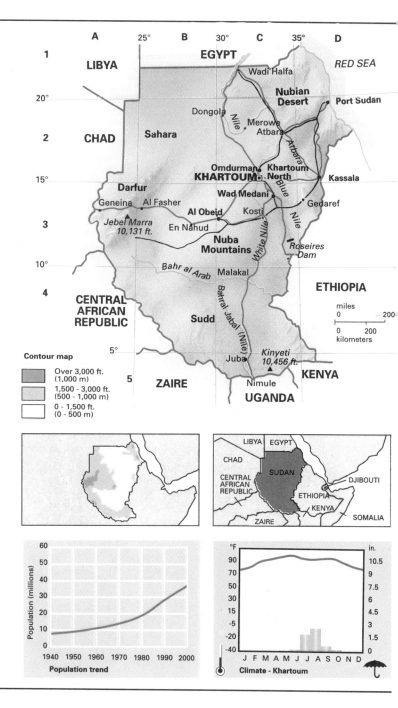

**Contour map**

Over 3,000 ft. (1,000 m)
1,500 - 3,000 ft. (500 - 1,000 m)
0 - 1,500 ft. (0 - 500 m)

**Age distribution**

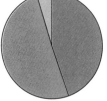

Under 15
15 - 60
Over 60

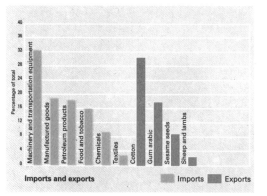

Imports and exports

Imports   Exports

Population trend

Climate - Khartoum

# Surinam

**Area:** 63,037 sq. miles (163,265 km²)
**Population:** 411,000
**Capital:** Paramaribo (pop. with suburbs 192,000)
**Highest point:** Juliana Top 4,200 ft. (1,280 m)
**Official languages:** Dutch.
**Religions:** Christianity, Hinduism, Islam
**Currency:** Surinam guilder
**Main exports:** Alumina, bauxite and aluminum, shrimps, rice
**Government:** Multiparty republic
**Per capita GNP:** U.S. $3,020

This republic in northeastern South America was formerly called Dutch Guiana. A wide, marshy coastal plain gives way inland to savanna-covered hills, rising to forested highlands. The Marowijne River separates Surinam from French Guiana in the east, and the Corantijn River forms the boundary with Guyana in the west. The climate is tropical, with very heavy rainfall particularly in coastal regions. Flooding is frequent. The people are mainly of Creole, Asian Indian, and Chinese origin, with a small Native American minority. Many people have emigrated to the Netherlands. Beside the official language, Surinamers speak a local dialect, Spanish, English, Hindi, Javanese, and Chinese. Having been founded as a colony by the English in 1650, Surinam became a Dutch colony in 1667 by treaty with Britain. It remained Dutch (except for brief periods of British control during the Napoleonic Wars) until it gained independence in 1975.

## ECONOMIC SURVEY

**Farming:** Rice is the leading cash crop. It is grown on about 75 percent of the usable farmland, in the flat plain which borders the ocean. Sugar-cane, citrus fruit, coconuts, and palm oil are also produced.
**Forestry:** Woodlands yield good supplies of hardwood.
**Fishing:** Shrimps are an important catch.
**Mining:** Bauxite is the most important mineral. Much is exported raw, but some is processed into alumina and aluminum.
**Industry:** There is little manufacturing. Apart from the bauxite-processing plants, Surinam has sugar-mills and rice-mills, shrimp-freezing factories, and food and timber processing industries.

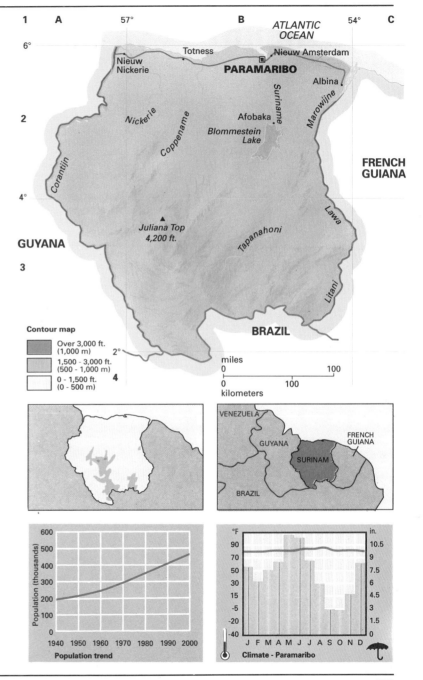

### Contour map

| | |
|---|---|
| ■ | Over 3,000 ft. (1,000 m) |
| ▨ | 1,500 - 3,000 ft. (500 - 1,000 m) |
| □ | 0 - 1,500 ft. (0 - 500 m) |

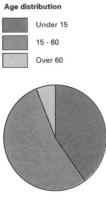

**Imports and exports**

**Age distribution**
- Under 15
- 15 - 60
- Over 60

**Population trend**

**Climate - Paramaribo**

*see* SOUTH AMERICA, page 159  165

# Swaziland

**Area:** 6,704 sq. miles (17,363 km²)
**Population:** 770,000
**Capital:** Mbabane (pop. 38,000)
**Highest point:** Mount Emlembe, on the northwest frontier, 6,109 ft. (1,862 m)
**Official languages:** English and Swazi
**Religions:** Christianity, various traditional beliefs
**Currency:** Lilangeni
**Main exports:** Sugar, wood and wood products, minerals and fuels
**Government:** Monarchy
**Per capita GNP:** U.S. $900

A small country of diverse landscapes, Swaziland has pine forests and mountains on its western border. East of the mountains are rolling grasslands, and this is the most densely populated region. Farther east is a low plain with scrub and grassland. On the eastern border are the Lebombo Mountains. The three main rivers that water Swaziland are the Komati, Usutu, and Ingwavuma. The climate is pleasant, with good rainfall. The people are mostly Swazis, who speak a Bantu language called Swazi. There are also people of European and mixed origins. By tradition, Swaziland was founded as a kingdom in the 1700s. British and Boers from South Africa arrived in the region in the 1830s seeking gold and farmland. Boer control ended in 1902. Britain ruled Swaziland until 1968, when the country became independent.

## ECONOMIC SURVEY

**Farming:** The most important cash crop is sugarcane. Other cash crops include pineapples, citrus fruits, cotton, rice, and tobacco. Swazi farmers also grow corn, millet, sorghum, potatoes, sweet potatoes, and beans. Cattle are reared for meat and hides.
**Forestry:** Large plantations of pine and eucalyptus produce timber.
**Mining:** Asbestos, iron ore, diamonds, coal, gold, tin, barium ore, and kaolin are mined.
**Industry:** Factories produce foodstuffs (such as canned fruit), fertilizers, furniture, wood and paper products, chemicals, metal goods, and textiles. Swaziland has a customs union with South Africa.

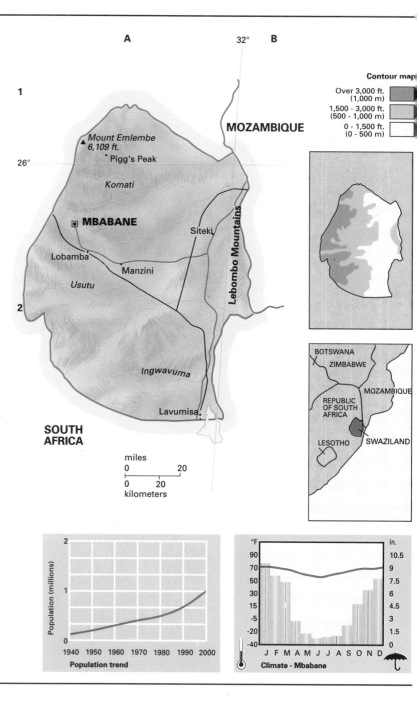

**Contour map**
Over 3,000 ft. (1,000 m)
1,500 - 3,000 ft. (500 - 1,000 m)
0 - 1,500 ft. (0 - 500 m)

miles
0    20
0    20
kilometers

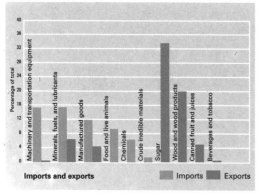

Imports and exports
Imports  Exports

**Age distribution**
Under 15
15 - 60
Over 60

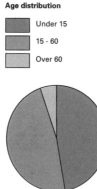

Population trend

Climate - Mbabane

# Sweden

**Area:** 173,732 sq. miles (449,964 km²)
**Population:** 8,523,000
**Capital:** Stockholm (pop. 669,000)
**Other cities:** Göteborg 431,000; Malmö 232,000
**Highest point:** Kebnekaise 6,926 ft. (2,111 m)
**Official language:** Swedish
**Religion:** Protestantism
**Currency:** Krona
**Main exports:** Machinery and transportation equipment, electrical machinery, paper products, wood, chemicals, iron and steel
**Government:** Constitutional monarchy
**Per capita GNP:** U.S. $21,170

Sweden is a land of coniferous forests, glaciated valleys, lakes, and mountains. It includes Europe's third largest lake, Lake Vänern, 2,157 sq. miles (5,585 sq. km). The far north forms part of Lapland, where the Lapp people live. This region lies within the Arctic Circle. Sweden's major cities are in the center and south of the country, which has a milder climate. In its early days Sweden was inhabited by the piratical Vikings. The country's conversion to Christianity in about 1000 ended the piracy. Sweden was united with Norway and Denmark in 1397, but broke away in 1523. Under rulers such as Gustavus Adolphus (died 1632), it was the leading power in the Baltic region until the early 1700s. Sweden has been at peace since the early 1800s. Through social and economic reform it has developed one of the highest standards of living in the world.

## ECONOMIC SURVEY

**Farming:** Farmers produce cereals particularly barley, oats and wheat, potatoes, sugar beet and cattle fodder. They grow fruit, and rear cattle and pigs.
**Forestry:** Forests cover 57 percent of the country and provide timber and wood products.
**Fishing:** Herring is the main fish catch.
**Industry:** Sweden has rich mineral resources, especially of iron ore. It also has copper, gold, lead, and uranium. Steel and steel products are made, together with vehicles, machinery, and transportation equipment, chemicals, and food and drink products. Hydro-electric and nuclear power stations produce most of Sweden's energy.

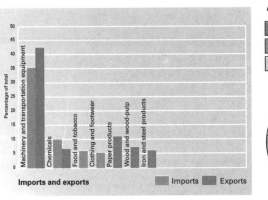

**Imports and exports**

**Age distribution**
- Under 15
- 15 - 60
- Over 60

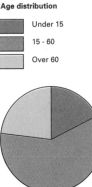

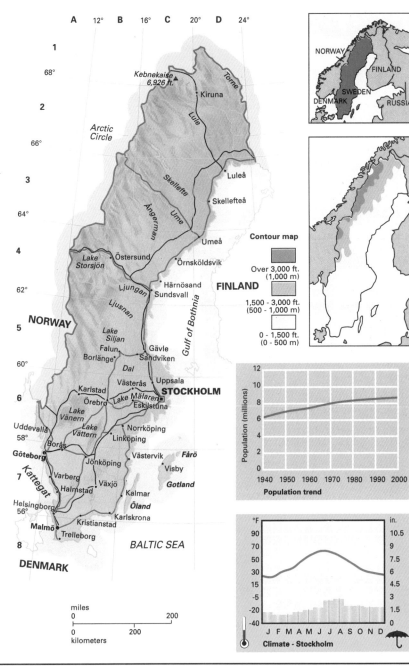

**Contour map**
- Over 3,000 ft. (1,000 m)
- 1,500 - 3,000 ft. (500 - 1,000 m)
- 0 - 1,500 ft. (0 - 500 m)

**Population trend**

**Climate - Stockholm**

miles
0        200
0        200
kilometers

# Switzerland

**Area:** 15,943 sq. miles (41,293 km²)
**Population:** 6,724,000
**Capital:** Bern (pop. with suburbs 299,000)
**Other cities:** Zürich 839,000; Geneva 389,000
**Highest point:** Dufourspitze of Monte Rosa 15,197 ft. (4,632 m)
**Official languages:** German, French, Italian
**Religions:** Roman Catholicism, Protestantism
**Currency:** Swiss franc
**Main exports:** Machinery, pharmaceuticals, precious metals and jewelry, watches
**Government:** Constitutional federal republic
**Per capita GNP:** U.S. $30,270

Switzerland has no sea coasts and is surrounded by mountains, which for hundreds of years hampered communications with the outside world. The spectacular Alps to the south and the Jura Mountains to the north cover 65 percent of the land. Most of the people live on the central plateau, the Mittelland. There are many lakes, ranging from Lake Geneva (Lac Léman) in the southwest to Lake Constance (Bodensee) in the northeast. The Rhine and Rhône rivers rise in Switzerland. The climate is temperate on the plateau, but cold with snow in winter in the mountains. Switzerland was formed in the 1200s and 1300s by a league of cantons (provinces) and won independence from Austrian rule after several wars. It has remained neutral since 1815. Today, Switzerland is a federation of 20 full cantons and 6 half cantons.

## ECONOMIC SURVEY

**Farming:** Dairying is the main activity. Cereals, potatoes, sugar beet, and fruits are grown, and some wine is produced. Farmers drive their herds of cattle, sheep, and goats to the high mountain pastures for the summer and back to the valleys for the winter.

**Industry:** Switzerland is renowned for its precision-engineering products such as clocks, watches, and optical instruments. Factories also make glassware, machinery, textiles, and processed foods such as chocolate and dairy products. More than 11 million tourists visit the country every year, many of them for winter sports. The country is a center of international banking and finance.

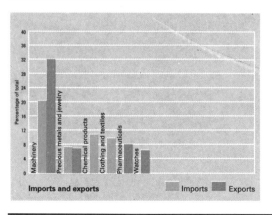

**Imports and exports** — Imports, Exports

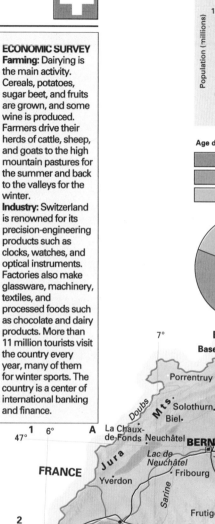

**Population trend**

**Climate - Zürich**

**Age distribution**
- Under 15
- 15 - 60
- Over 60

**Contour map**
- Over 6,000 ft. (2,000 m)
- 3,000 - 6,000 ft. (1,000 - 2,000 m)
- 0 - 3,000 ft. (0 - 1,000 m)

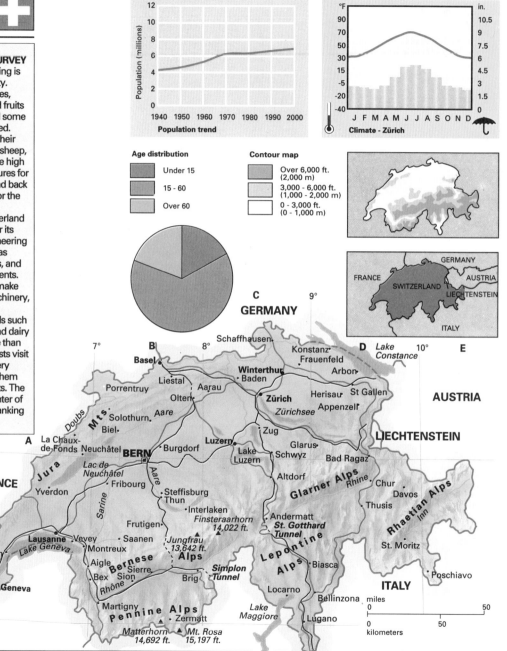

# Syria

**Area:** 71,498 sq. miles (185,180 km$^2$)
**Population:** 12,113,000
**Capital:** Damascus (pop. 1,361,000)
**Other cities:** Aleppo 1,308,000; Homs 464,000; Latakia 234,000
**Highest point:** Mount Hermon 9,232 ft. (2,814 m)
**Official language:** Arabic
**Religions:** Islam (90 percent), Christianity
**Currency:** Syrian pound
**Main exports:** Petroleum and petroleum products, chemicals, textiles
**Government:** Multiparty republic
**Per capita GNP:** U.S. $1,020

Syria has a coastal plain, behind which is a low mountain range, the Jabal an Nusayriyah. The waters of the Orontes and Euphrates rivers irrigate otherwise arid land. The Anti-Lebanon range in the southwest contains Syria's highest mountains. In the east, the land slopes down to hot desert. Rainfall is highest near the coast, with 60 percent of the country having very little rain. Most of the people are Arabs, with minority groups of Kurds, Druzes, Turkmens, and Palestinians. Syria's history is ancient, and includes rule by the Assyrians, Egyptians, Seleucids, Romans, Arabs, Turks, and French. It became independent in 1946. Briefly united with Egypt in the United Arab Republic (1958-1961), Syria has been a leader of Arab opposition to Israel, and from the mid 1970s was deeply involved in the politics of war-torn Lebanon.

## ECONOMIC SURVEY

**Farming:** Syria is still a mainly agricultural country, although large parts of it are desert. Crops include cotton, wheat, barley, olives, lentils, millet, and sugar beet. There are as many sheep as people, and goats and cattle are also kept.
**Mining:** The country has some oil, natural gas, and phosphates. It also produces cement, sand and gravel, and building stone.
**Industry:** Developing rapidly, Syrian industry is basically light rather than heavy. Factory products include foodstuffs, chemicals, soap, textiles (especially cotton goods), footwear, pottery, glass, and copper and brass goods. Tourism is a growing currency earner.

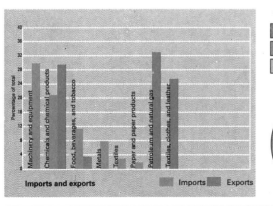

**Imports and exports**

Imports | Exports

**Age distribution**

- Under 15
- 15 - 60
- Over 60

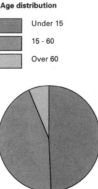

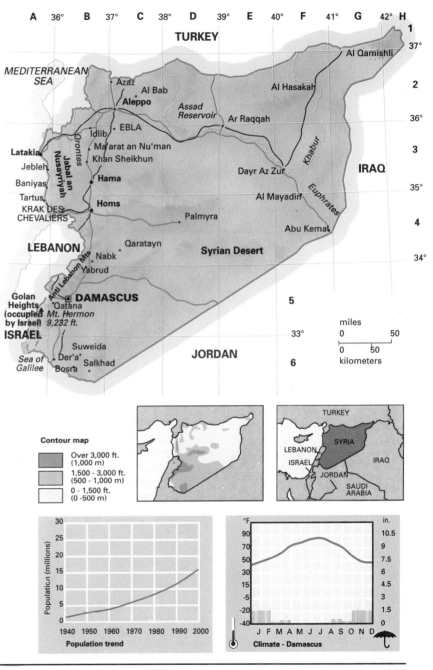

**Contour map**

- Over 3,000 ft. (1,000 m)
- 1,500 - 3,000 ft. (500 - 1,000 m)
- 0 - 1,500 ft. (0 -500 m)

**Population trend**

**Climate - Damascus**

*see* ASIA, page 22

# Taiwan

**Area:** 13,900 sq. miles (36,000 km²)
**Population:** 20,262,000
**Capital:** Taipei (pop. 2,680,000)
**Other cities:** Kaohsiung 1,343,000; Taichung 730,376; Tainan 667,622
**Highest point:** Yu Shan 13,113 ft. (3,997 m)
**Official language:** Chinese
**Religions:** Taoism, Buddhism, Christianity
**Currency:** New Taiwan dollar
**Main exports:** Electronic products, clothing and textiles, plastic articles
**Government:** Multiparty republic
**Per capita GNP:** U.S. $6,020

## ECONOMIC SURVEY

**Farming:** Farmers grow rice and vegetables on terraced hillside fields. Sugarcane, sweet potatoes, and tea are other leading crops. Pigs, chickens, and ducks are reared.
**Fishing:** Shrimps and tuna are caught at sea, and carp are reared on fish farms.
**Forestry:** Taiwan's major natural resource is its forests, which yield oak, cedar, and other hardwoods.
**Mining:** Taiwan has some coal but few minerals in quantity.
**Industry:** Wood products including furniture, paper, and plywood are among the most important products. Taiwan's factories produce textiles, clothing, plastic goods, toys, electronic and electrical products.

Taiwan, formerly called Formosa, is an island republic off the southeastern coast of China. It is mostly mountainous and forested. Swiftly flowing rivers cut through gorges. In the west, there are rolling hills and lowland. The climate is subtropical: hot and humid in summer, and mild in winter. Summer monsoons bring rain, and typhoons are common. The people are Chinese, mostly descendants of people who came from the mainland. There is a minority population of non-Chinese aboriginals. Taiwan became part of China in the 1680s. Japan ruled it from 1895 to 1945, when China regained it. The communists under Mao Zedong seized power in mainland China in 1949, and the nationalists under Chiang Kai-shek retreated to Taiwan and set up a government there. Taiwan held China's seat in the United Nations until 1971.

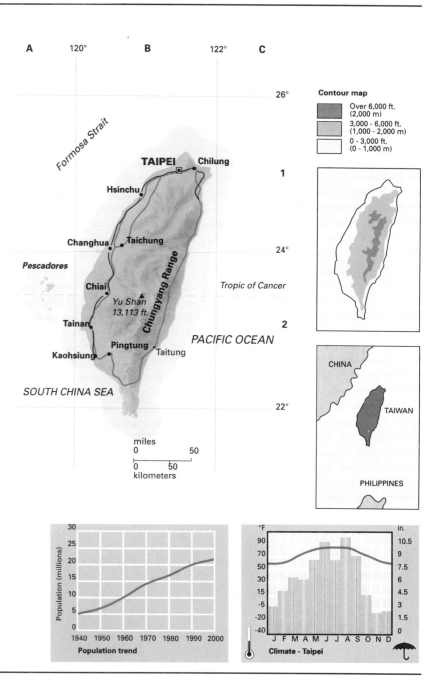

**Contour map**

Over 6,000 ft. (2,000 m)
3,000 - 6,000 ft. (1,000 - 2,000 m)
0 - 3,000 ft. (0 - 1,000 m)

miles 0 50
kilometers 0 50

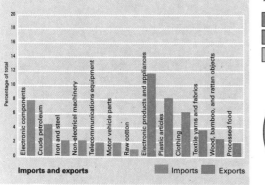

**Imports and exports**
Imports   Exports

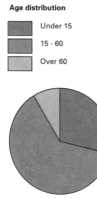

**Age distribution**
Under 15
15 - 60
Over 60

**Population trend**

**Climate - Taipei**

# Tanzania

| |
|---|
| **Area:** 364,900 sq. miles (945,087 km²) |
| **Population:** 24,403,000 |
| **Capital:** Dodoma (pop. 46,000) |
| **Other cities:** Dar-es-Salaam 1,100,000; Mwanza 252,000 |
| **Highest point:** Mt. Kilimanjaro 19,340 ft. (5,895 m) |
| **Official languages:** Swahili, English |
| **Religions:** Christianity, Islam, various traditional beliefs |
| **Currency:** Tanzanian shilling |
| **Main exports:** Coffee, cotton |
| **Government:** Single-party republic |
| **Per capita GNP:** U.S. $120 |

Tanzania consists of mainland Tanganyika in East Africa, and the islands of Zanzibar and Pemba. Most of Tanganyika forms a high plateau broken by arms of the Great Rift Valley. The western arm encloses lakes Nyasa (Malawi) and Tanganyika. There are small salt lakes in the eastern arm. Lake Victoria is in the northwest. In the north and south are mountains, including Africa's highest peak, Mount Kilimanjaro. Savanna vegetation is the most common. The climate is hot and humid, with cooler temperatures in the higher altitudes. There are more than 100 tribal groups. Most of the people speak Bantu languages. Britain ruled Tanganyika (formerly a German colony) from 1919 until independence in 1961. Zanzibar was a British protectorate from 1890. It became independent in 1963, joining with Tanganyika in 1964 to form Tanzania.

## ECONOMIC SURVEY

**Farming:** Most of the people are farmers, growing coffee and cotton (the main cash crops), cashew nuts, and sisal. Zanzibar is a leading producer of cloves. Other crops include bananas, plantains, cassava, corn, rice, sugarcane, coconuts, sweet potatoes, and millet. Cattle, goats, sheep, and chickens are reared.

**Fishing:** Catches include tuna and sardines for export.

**Mining:** Diamonds are the most important mineral; others include copper, lead, gold, and phosphate.

**Industry:** Textiles, petroleum and chemical products, food and drink, and paper products are the principal outputs. Tourists visit the game preserves.

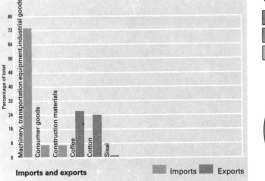

**Imports and exports**

Imports  Exports

**Age distribution**

■ Under 15
■ 15 - 60
■ Over 60

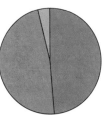

**Population trend**
No earlier figures available

**Climate - Dodoma**

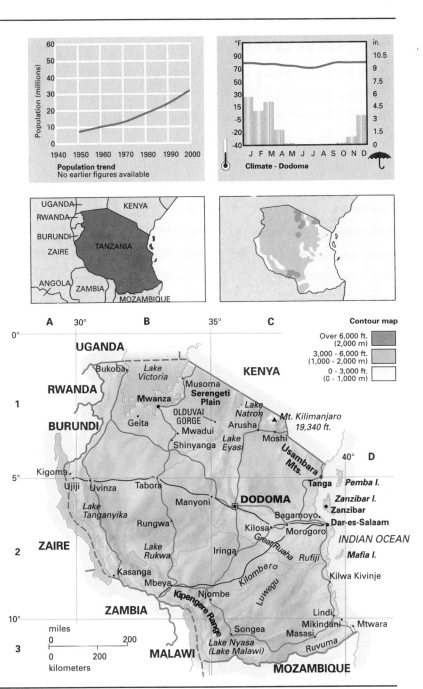

**Contour map**

■ Over 6,000 ft. (2,000 m)
■ 3,000 - 6,000 ft. (1,000 - 2,000 m)
□ 0 - 3,000 ft. (0 - 1,000 m)

# Thailand

**Area:** 198,457 sq. miles (514,000 km²)
**Population:** 56,147,000
**Capital:** Bangkok (pop. with suburbs 5,609,000)
**Other cities:** Chiang Mai 150,000
**Highest point:** Inthanon Mountain 8,514 ft. (2,595 m)
**Official language:** Thai
**Religions:** Buddhism, Islam
**Currency:** Baht
**Main exports:** Textiles and clothing, rice, rubber, tapioca, teak
**Government:** Monarchy; military rule
**Per capita GNP:** U.S. $1,170

This southeast Asian kingdom was known as Siam until 1939. The fertile Chao Phraya river basin is bordered by mountains in the east, west, and north. Northeast Thailand is an infertile plateau, drained by the Mekong River. The country has a tropical climate and most areas have plentiful rainfall. The monsoon brings heavy rains in the second half of the year. Most Thais are descendants of migrants from China who arrived between A.D. 200 and 1100. There are also people of Burmese, Vietnamese, and Malay origin, and a sizeable Chinese community. Tribal groups such as the Karen, Mao, Khmu, and Yao peoples live in remote mountain regions. The Thai kingdom was set up in the 1300s. It came under Western influence from the 1600s. In 1932 the king gave up his absolute authority, and he became a constitutional monarch.

## ECONOMIC SURVEY

**Farming:** Over half the Thai people work on the land. Sugarcane, cassava (for tapioca), and rice are the main crops. Cotton, corn, pineapples, rubber, and tobacco are also produced. Livestock includes buffaloes, cattle, pigs, and chickens.
**Fishing:** Anchovies, mackerel, crabs, and shrimps are among the main catches, and fish are farmed.
**Forestry:** About 60 percent of Thailand is forested. Teak, bamboo, and rattan are produced.
**Mining:** Thailand is a leader in tin mining, and also has bauxite, iron ore, lead, manganese, and precious stones.
**Industry:** Cement, tinplate, and motorcycles are manufactured.

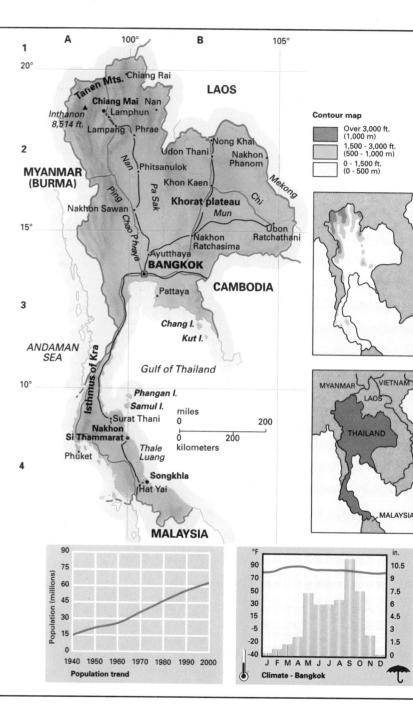

Contour map
- Over 3,000 ft. (1,000 m)
- 1,500 - 3,000 ft. (500 - 1,000 m)
- 0 - 1,500 ft. (0 - 500 m)

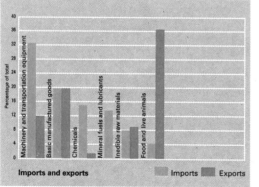

**Imports and exports**

Imports  Exports

**Age distribution**
- Under 15
- 15 - 60
- Over 60

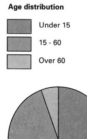

**Population trend**

**Climate - Bangkok**

# Togo

**Area:** 21,925 sq. miles (56,785 km²)
**Population:** 3,764,000
**Capital:** Lomé (pop. 366,000)
**Other cities:** Sokodé 48,000
**Highest point:** Bauman Peak, near Kpalimé, 3,235 ft. (986 m)
**Official language:** French
**Religions:** Traditional beliefs, Christianity, Islam
**Currency:** Franc CFA
**Main exports:** Phosphate fertilizers, cotton, coffee, cocoa
**Government:** Single-party republic
**Per capita GNP:** U.S. $390

This West African republic is a long, narrow country between Ghana and Benin. It is bounded by the Togo Hills in the west, and the Mono River flows through the east. The central mountains separate a low northern plateau from fertile southern plains. The climate is hot, and in the dry season is influenced by dry winds from the Sahara. Rainfall increases from the coast inland. Vegetation is mostly scrub, with patches of forest. The people are Black Africans belonging to some 30 main ethnic groups. Briefly under Danish control, Togo became a German protectorate in 1884. After World War I it was divided between Britain and France. In 1957 western Togo (British Togoland) joined Ghana. French Togo became independent in 1960. After spells of military government, and rivalry between north and south, a single-party government was established.

## ECONOMIC SURVEY

**Farming:** Food crops include corn, rice, cassava, yams, plantains, and millet. The main cash crops are coffee and cocoa beans, followed by tea, spices, palm oil and kernels, copra, groundnuts (peanuts), and cotton. Sheep and goats are the most numerous livestock.
**Fishing:** Togo has only a small coastline, but its fishermen contribute to the food supply.
**Mining:** Togo is rich in phosphates, and fertilizer is the largest product. Togo also has bauxite, limestone, iron ore, marble, and salt.
**Industry:** The small industrial sector is growing, and now includes oil refining, cement-making, light engineering, and food processing.

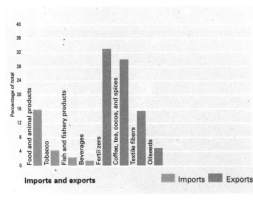
**Imports and exports**

**Age distribution** — Under 15, 15 - 60, Over 60

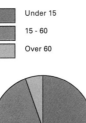

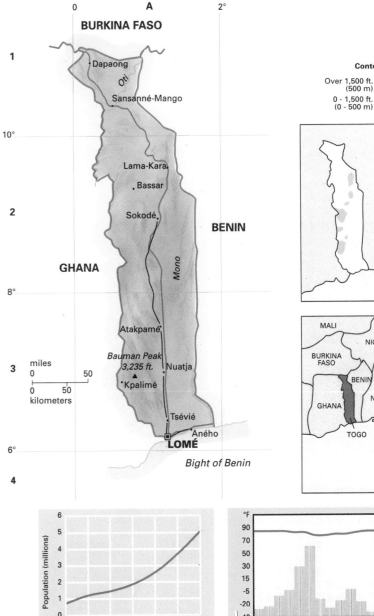

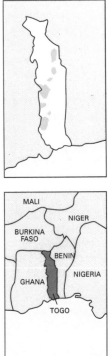

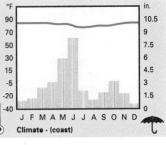

**Population trend**

**Climate - (coast)**

# Trinidad and Tobago

**Area:** 1,981 sq. miles (5,130 km²)
**Population:** 1,321,000
**Capital:** Port-of-Spain (pop. 58,000)
**Other cities:** San Fernando 33,000
**Official language:** English
**Religions:** Christianity, Hinduism, Islam
**Currency:** Trinidad and Tobago dollar
**Main exports:** Petroleum and petroleum products, chemicals
**Government:** Multiparty republic
**Per capita GNP:** U.S. $1,360

The republic of Trinidad and Tobago consists of two islands lying close to South America. Trinidad is much the larger island, comprising 94 percent of the total area. Tobago lies about 18.6 miles (30 km) to the northeast. Both islands are hilly and wooded, and have a tropical climate. The soil of Trinidad is very fertile. Many people are descendants of African slaves, but more than a third of the population is of Indian or other Asian origin. The native inhabitants of the islands were Arawaks and Caribs. Christopher Columbus named Trinidad (Spanish for 'the Trinity') in 1498, but few Spanish settlers went there. In 1797 Britain captured the island. It remained a British colony until 1962 when it became independent.

## ECONOMIC SURVEY

**Farming:** Sugar is the chief crop, followed by coconuts. Farmers also grow oranges, grapefruit, rice, corn, cocoa, coffee, and bananas. Pigs are the most numerous livestock.

**Mining:** Trinidad is the world's main source of natural asphalt. The country also produces natural gas and oil.

**Industry:** Two refineries process Trinidad's own crude oil and imported crude oil as well. There is a modern iron- and steel-making plant. Other factories produce molasses and rum from sugar, ammonia, fertilizers, cement, televisions, and vehicles. Tourism is important.

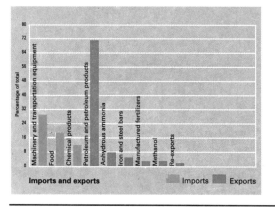

**Imports and exports** — Imports / Exports

**Age distribution**
- Under 15
- 15 - 60
- Over 60

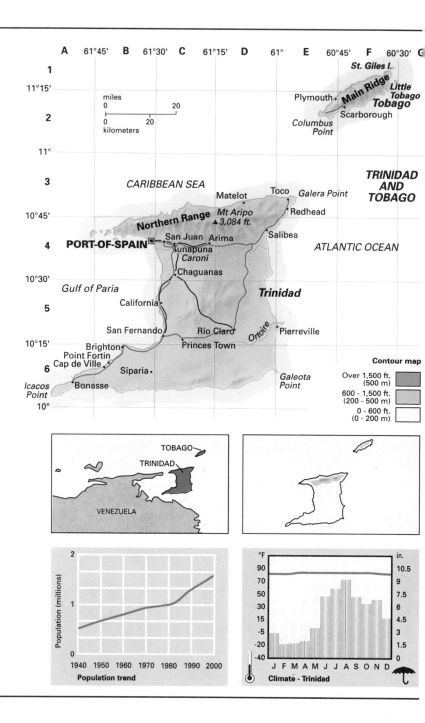

**Contour map**
- Over 1,500 ft. (500 m)
- 600 - 1,500 ft. (200 - 500 m)
- 0 - 600 ft. (0 - 200 m)

**Population trend**

**Climate - Trinidad**

# Tunisia

**Area:** 63,170 sq. miles (163,610 km$^2$)
**Population:** 8,182,000
**Capital:** Tunis (pop. 774,000)
**Other cities:** Sfax 232,000; Bizerte 94,000; Gabès 92,000
**Highest point:** Mount Chambi 5,066 ft. (1,544 m)
**Official language:** Arabic
**Religion:** Islam
**Currency:** Dinar
**Main exports:** Clothing, hosiery, petroleum products, phosphoric acid
**Government:** Multiparty republic
**Per capita GNP:** U.S. $1,260

This North African country includes an extension of the Atlas Mountains in the north, surrounded by plains. A depression with salt lakes, called the Chott Jerid, lies in the center. To the south are plateaus within the Sahara. Rainfall becomes less from north to south, and most people live near the coast. Oases in the southern desert are, however, famous for their dates. The population is mostly Arab and Berber. The Arab conquest of Tunisia took place in A.D. 647. The country came under Ottoman Turkish rule in 1537, and was a French protectorate from the 1880s. French influence on the culture and architecture, as in other French-ruled North African colonies, has remained significant. Tunisia became independent in 1956, declaring a republic in 1957 under President Habib Bourguiba, who had led the independence movement.

## ECONOMIC SURVEY

**Farming:** Tunisia's farmers grow barley, wheat, corn, oats, and sorghum for food; and citrus fruit, olives, dates, and grapes (for wine) as cash crops. Dates are grown at oases in the south of the country. Large numbers of cattle, sheep, and goats are grazed on the central plateaus.
**Mining:** Phosphate (used for fertilizer and for making phosphorus) is important. Petroleum is exported. There are also deposits of iron, lead, zinc, and salt, and offshore gas.
**Industries:** There are few large factories. Products include clothing, chemicals, cement, vehicles, and television sets. Tourism has developed along the coast.

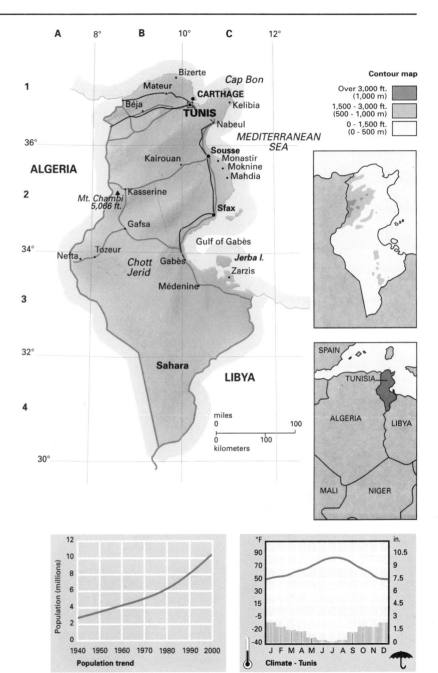

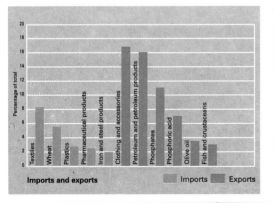

Imports and exports — Imports, Exports

**Age distribution**
Under 15
15 - 60
Over 60

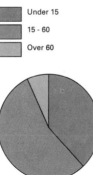

**Population trend**

**Climate - Tunis**

# Turkey

**Area:** 301,382 sq. miles (780,576 km²)
**Population:** 56,941,000
**Capital:** Ankara (pop. 2,252,000)
**Other cities:** Istanbul 5,495,000; Izmir 1,490,000; Adana 776,000
**Highest point:** Mount Ararat 17,011 ft. (5,165 m)
**Official language:** Turkish
**Religion:** Islam
**Currency:** Lira
**Main exports:** Textiles, iron and steel, agricultural products, food, chemicals
**Government:** Multiparty republic
**Per capita GNP:** U.S. $1,360

Turkey lies partly in Europe, but mostly in Asia. European Turkey is west of three waterways — the Dardanelles, the Sea of Marmara and the Bosporus — which link the Mediterranean, and Black seas. Its coastal lowlands are fertile. Asian Turkey (Anatolia) has a central, dry plateau with a more extreme climate. Several of the mountain ranges have peaks topping 13,000 ft. (4,000 m). Most people speak Turkish, but there is a small Kurdish minority. Constantinople (modern Istanbul) was the capital of the Eastern Roman and Byzantine empires. It was captured by the Ottoman Turks in 1453. For hundreds of years the Ottoman empire dominated the Balkans, southwest Asia, and North Africa, but it declined during the 1700s and 1800s. It was ruled by sultans until 1918. Turkey became a republic in 1923.

## ECONOMIC SURVEY

**Farming:** About 35 percent of Turkey is cultivated, and almost half the labor force works on the land. The main crops include barley, wheat, cotton, grapes, fruit, nuts, raisins, sugar beet, and potatoes. Sheep and goats are the main animals kept. There is some fishing.

**Mining:** Turkey produces coal and lignite, some oil, chrome and iron ore, and copper. Oil is also produced.

**Industry:** One Turkish worker in every six is in manufacturing or construction. The industrial output includes iron and steel, petroleum and chemical products, food products, paper, cement, textiles, and machinery. Germany is Turkey's main trading partner.

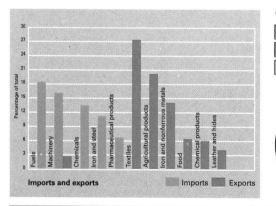

**Imports and exports** — Imports / Exports

**Age distribution**
- Under 15
- 15 - 60
- Over 60

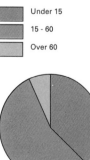

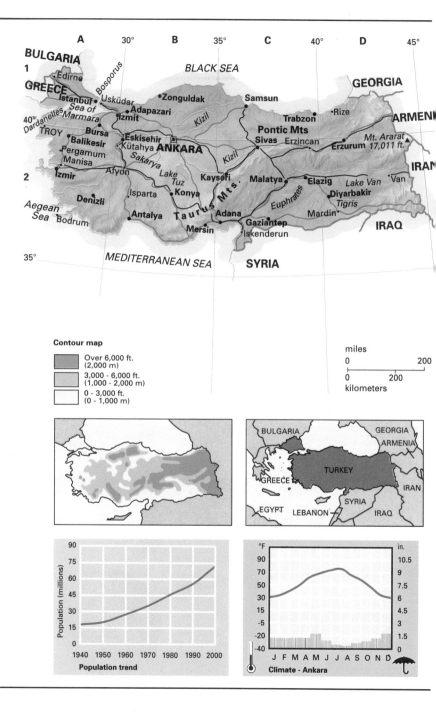

**Contour map**
- Over 6,000 ft. (2,000 m)
- 3,000 - 6,000 ft. (1,000 - 2,000 m)
- 0 - 3,000 ft. (0 - 1,000 m)

**Population trend**

**Climate - Ankara**

# Uganda

**Area:** 91,134 sq. miles (236,036 km²)
**Population:** 16,928,000
**Capital:** Kampala (pop. 458,000)
**Highest point:** Margherita Peak in the Ruwenzori Range 16,761 ft. (5,109 m)
**Official languages:** Swahili, English
**Religions:** Christianity, Islam
**Currency:** Uganda shilling
**Main export:** Coffee
**Government:** Republic
**Per capita GNP:** U.S. $250

Most of Uganda, a landlocked country in East Africa, is made up of a plateau some 4,000 feet (1,200 metres) above sea level. Part of Africa's largest lake, Victoria, lies in the southeast. The marshy Lake Kyoga is in the center. Lakes Edward and Albert (also called Mobutu Sese Seko) lie in the Rift Valley in the west. The climate is tropical, with the altitude and cool breezes moderating temperatures. In the north of the country most of the land is covered with savanna, but there is desert in the northeast. The people are almost all Black Africans. The largest tribal group is the Buganda. Two thirds of the people speak Bantu languages. Some Nilotic languages are also spoken. Uganda was a British protectorate from 1894. In 1962 it became independent. The dictator Idi Amin ruled from 1971 until 1979. His regime, and the unrest following his overthrow, severely impeded Uganda's political and economic development.

## ECONOMIC SURVEY

**Farming:** The chief crops are cassava, bananas, plantains, corn, millet, sweet potatoes, beans, and groundnuts (peanuts). The main export crop is coffee, Uganda's principal source of income, but tea, cotton, and sugarcane are also grown as cash crops. Cattle, sheep, and goats are reared.
**Fishing:** There is an active fishing industry based on lakes Victoria, Kyoga, and Edward.
**Mining:** Only copper is mined on a large scale, though other minerals such as tin and tungsten exist in commercial amounts.
**Industry:** The Owen Falls hydroelectric plant provides power for copper smelting. There are some small industrial projects.

**Population trend**

**Climate - Kampala**

**Contour map**

| | |
|---|---|
| Over 6,000 ft. (2,000 m) | |
| 1,000 - 2,000 m (3,000 - 6,000 ft. | |
| 0 - 3,000 ft. (0 - 1,000 m) | |

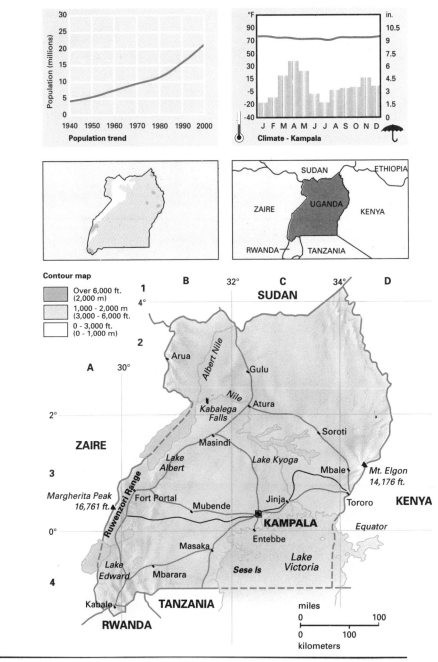

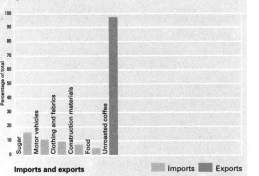

**Imports and exports**

Sugar · Motor vehicles · Clothing and fabrics · Construction materials · Food · Unroasted coffee

Imports   Exports

**Age distribution**
Under 15
15 - 60
Over 60

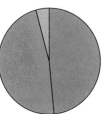

# United Arab Emirates

**Area:** 32,278 sq. miles (83,600 km$^2$)
**Population:** 1,881,000
**Capital:** Abu Dhabi (pop. 243,000)
**Other cities:** Dubai 266,000
**Highest point:** Jabal Yibir 5,010 ft. (1,527 m)
**Official language:** Arabic
**Religion:** Islam
**Currency:** Dirham
**Main export:** Petroleum
**Government:** Monarchy; union of emirates
**Per capita GNP:** U.S. $18,430

## ECONOMIC SURVEY

**Farming:** Little of the land in the United Arab Emirates is suitable for crops. Oasis cultivation, irrigation, and glasshouses make it possible to produce dates, fruits such as lemons and pumpkins, and vegetables. Goats, sheep, camels, some cattle, and chickens are reared.

**Fishing:** Fish, shrimps, and other shellfish are caught in the Gulf. Pearl fishing is also carried out there.

**Industry:** Oil, first drilled for in the 1950s, now makes up 90 percent of the UAE's foreign trade. Crude oil is shipped out and the UAE has its own refineries.

Seven emirates, formerly known as the Trucial States, make up the federation of the United Arab Emirates. These are Abu Dhabi, Dubai, Ash Shariqah, Ajman, Umm al Qaywayn, Ras al Khaymah, and Al Fujayrah. It is a desert region, with little vegetation or fertile land. The climate is hot and dry. The population is about 70 percent Arab, the rest being mainly Indians, Pakistanis, and Iranians. The area was important as a regional trade center from pre-Roman times. The emirates fought many wars, until Britain compelled them to sign truces. They were bound by treaty to Britain from 1820 until 1971, when Britain withdrew its forces from the Gulf. The emirates then merged and a federation was set up. Each state retains its own sheik.

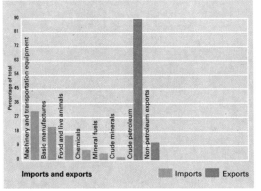

**Imports and exports**

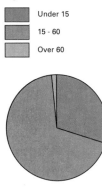

**Age distribution**
- Under 15
- 15 - 60
- Over 60

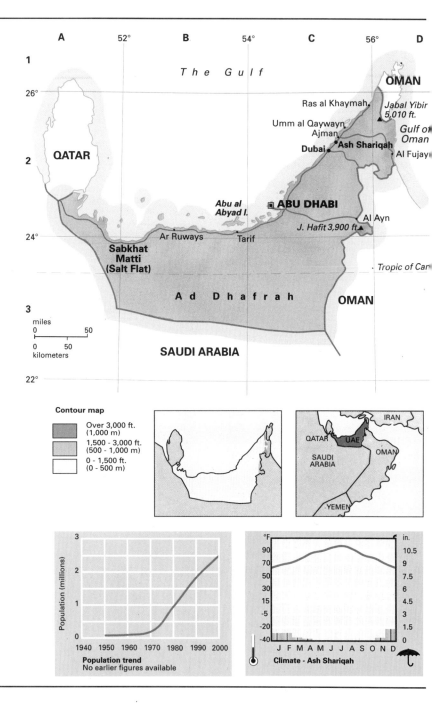

**Contour map**
- Over 3,000 ft. (1,000 m)
- 1,500 - 3,000 ft. (500 - 1,000 m)
- 0 - 1,500 ft. (0 - 500 m)

**Population trend**
No earlier figures available

**Climate - Ash Shariqah**

# United Kingdom

**Area:** 94,247 sq. miles (244,100 km²)
**Population:** 57,376,000
**Capital:** London (pop. 6,735,000)
**Other cities:** Birmingham 994,000; Leeds 710,000; Glasgow 703,000
**Highest point:** Ben Nevis 4,406 ft. (1,343 m)
**Official language:** English
**Religions:** Protestantism, Roman Catholicism
**Currency:** Pound
**Main exports:** Machinery, chemicals, petroleum, road vehicles
**Government:** Constitutional monarchy
**Per capita GNP:** U.S. $14,570

The United Kingdom of Great Britain and Northern Ireland occupies most of the islands of the British Isles group. It has four main parts: England, Wales, and Scotland, which form the island of Great Britain, and Northern Ireland. The Channel Islands and the Isle of Man belong to the British crown, but are not part of the United Kingdom. The highest uplands are in the north and west, in Wales and the Scottish Highlands. The greatest density of population is in the south. The climate is temperate and vegetation varied. A series of unions, in which England was the dominant partner, created the United Kingdom. Wales was the first annexation, in the 1300s. Acts of union in 1707 and 1800 brought first Scotland, then Ireland into parliamentary union with England. In 1922 southern Ireland broke away to become the Republic of Ireland.

## INDUSTRIAL PROFILE
The United Kingdom no longer enjoys its once-powerful position as a major manufacturing nation. The mass-employment heavy industries (coal, steel, shipbuilding, and textiles) have declined. Traditional industrial regions such as northern England and south Wales have suffered economic decay while newer industries (such as electronics, foods, financial services) developed in the south and west. Membership of the European Community, and in the 1980s privatization of many state-run industries, have reshaped the U.K.'s industrial base. But low productivity and investment hamper its competitiveness.

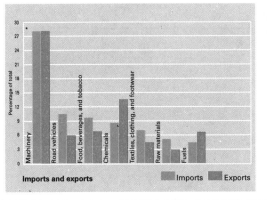

**Imports and exports**

**Age distribution**

- Under 15
- 15 - 60
- Over 60

Imports  Exports

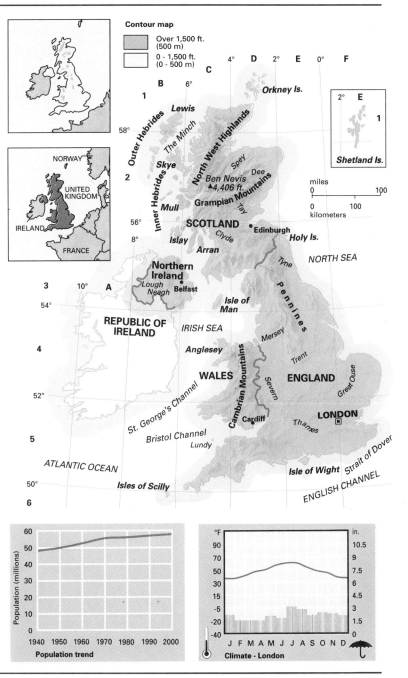

**Contour map**

- Over 1,500 ft. (500 m)
- 0 - 1,500 ft. (0 - 500 m)

miles 0 — 100
kilometers 0 — 100

**Population trend**

**Climate - London**

# England and Wales

**ENGLAND Area:** 50,363 sq. miles (130,439 km²)
**Population:** 47,536,000
**Capital:** London (pop. 6,735,000)
**Other cities:** Birmingham 994,000
**Highest point:** Scafell Pike 3,212 ft. (979 m)
**Official language:** English
**Religions:** Protestantism, Roman Catholicism, Judaism, Islam
**Currency:** Pound
**Main exports:** Chemicals, machinery, petroleum, transportation equipment
**Government:** Part of the United Kingdom, a constitutional monarchy

**WALES Area:** 8,018 sq. miles (20,768 km²)
**Population:** 2,857,000
**Capital:** Cardiff (pop. 284,000)
**Other cities:** Swansea 187,000
**Highest point:** Snowdon 3,561 ft. (1,085 m)
**Official languages:** Welsh, English
**Religion:** Protestantism
**Currency:** Pound
**Main exports:** Manufactures, including electronics and machinery, food, fuels and other minerals
**Government:** Part of the United Kingdom, a constitutional monarchy

## INDUSTRIAL PROFILE

England's old industrial heart (the north and Midlands) has seen the decline of once dominant heavy industries. Engineering, textiles, and vehicle-building all face problems. New industries, such as electronics, food processing, and services, have arisen chiefly in the south and east, close to European markets. London is the center of government and of the financial services industry. The Welsh coal-mining industry is almost dead, and being replaced by light industry. Tourism is encouraged, as are foreign-owned enterprises (such as Japanese car plants). In the 1980s state-run utilities (gas, water, electricity) were privatized.

England is the largest part of the United Kingdom of Great Britain and Northern Ireland. Northern England contains the Cumbrian Mountains in the Lake District and the Pennines. Either side of the Pennines are major industrial regions. The central or Midlands area of England is a mixture of farmland and industry. The east is mostly flat farmland. The southeast, around London, is the most urbanized part. Wales, Cymru in Welsh, has a mountainous and thinly populated central region. Its main industrial centers are in the north and south. The country was invaded by Romans (A.D. 43), Anglo-Saxons (A.D. 500s onward), and Normans (1066). By the late Middle Ages England was the most powerful British kingdom and had annexed Wales.

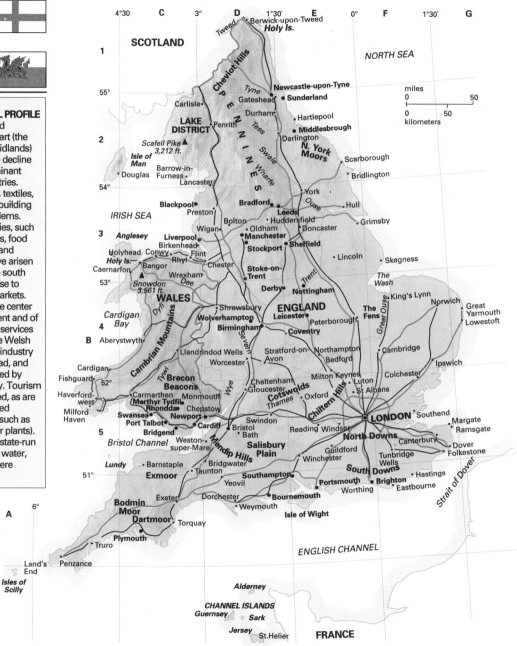

# Scotland and N. Ireland

**SCOTLAND Area:** 30,414 sq. miles (78,772 km²)
**Population:** 5,094,000
**Capital:** Edinburgh (pop. 433,000)
**Other cities:** Glasgow 703,000; Aberdeen 215,000; Dundee 178,000
**Highest point:** Ben Nevis 4,406 ft. (1,343 m)
**Official language:** English
**Religions:** Protestantism, Roman Catholicism
**Currency:** Pound
**Main exports:** Petroleum, machinery and electronic equipment, textiles, whisky
**Government:** Part of the United Kingdom, a constitutional monarchy

**N.IRELAND Area:** 5,452 sq. miles (14,121 km²)
**Population:** 1,578,000
**Capital:** Belfast (pop. 300,000)
**Other cities:** Londonderry 99,000
**Highest point:** Slieve Donard in the Mourne Mountains 2,796 ft. (852 m)
**Official language:** English
**Religions:** Protestantism, Roman Catholicism
**Currency:** Pound
**Main exports:** Clothing and textiles, clothing machinery, food products
**Government:** Part of the United Kingdom, a constitutional monarchy

**INDUSTRIAL PROFILE**
In the 1960s reserves of natural gas and petroleum were discovered off the east coast of Scotland. Oil and gas are now piped to the mainland, and the Shetland and Orkney islands. Coal is mined in the central Lowlands, and other minerals include limestone, clay, and silica. Manufacturing industries include chemicals, electronic equipment, machinery, textiles and whisky. Service industries in Northern Ireland employ three-fourths of the workforce. The textile industry uses imported raw materials. Shipbuilding, aircraft manufacture, chemicals, computers, and processed food are other important industries.

Scotland is the most northerly part of Great Britain. Two-thirds of the land, the Highlands, is mountainous with a chain of lochs (lakes). Most Scots live in the central Lowlands. Northern Ireland is mostly rolling farmland, with hills along the coast. Lough Neagh is the United Kingdom's biggest lake. Scotland was an independent kingdom until united with England under King James VI of Scotland (James I of England) in 1603. In 1707 the Act of Union combined the two nations' parliaments. Northern Ireland consists of six of the nine counties of the ancient Irish province of Ulster, settled by Protestants from England and Scotland in the 1600s. When the rest of Ireland became independent in 1921, the six counties of Northern Ireland chose to stay under British rule as part of the United Kingdom.

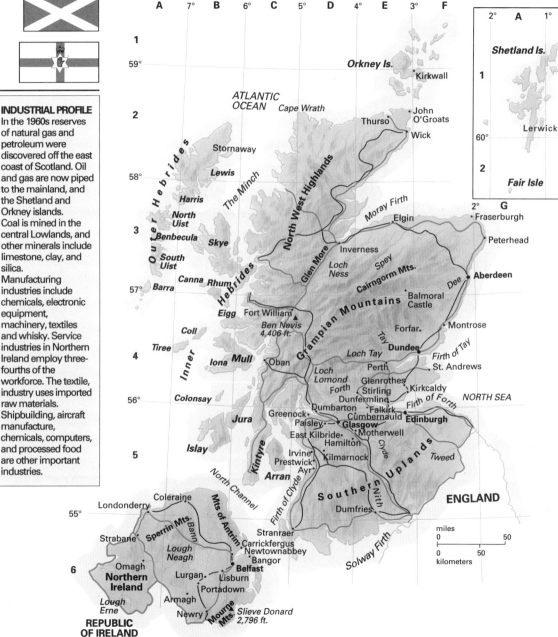

# U.S.A.

## Alaska (inset)
170° 160° 150° 140° 130°
A B C D
Bering Strait
ARCTIC OCEAN
Barrow • Prudhoe Bay
Brooks Range
ALASKA
Arctic Circle
St. Lawrence I. • Yukon • Fairbanks
CANADA
Bering Sea
Kuskokwim
Mt. McKinley 20,320 ft.
Anchorage
Nunivak I.
Seward
Gulf of Alaska
Juneau
Aleutian Is. • Alaska Peninsula
Alexander Archipelago
NORTH PACIFIC OCEAN
miles 0 500
kilometers

## North America (inset)
ALASKA
CANADA
USA
ATLANTIC OCEAN
MEXICO
PACIFIC OCEAN
BRAZIL

## Main map
CANADA

WASHINGTON — Seattle, Olympia, Spokane, Mt. Rainier, Mt. St. Helens, Columbia
Portland, Salem
OREGON — Boise
Cascade Mts, Coast Range
MONTANA — Great Falls, Helena, Billings, Missouri, Yellowstone
IDAHO, Snake
ROCKY MOUNTAINS
Great Plains
NORTH DAKOTA — Bismarck
SOUTH DAKOTA — Pierre, Rapid City
WYOMING — Casper, Cheyenne
NEVADA
Great Salt Lake
NEBRASKA — Omaha, Lincoln, Platte
UTAH — Salt Lake City
Reno, Carson City, Great Basin
Sierra Nevada, Mt. Whitney 14,495 ft.
Death Valley -282 ft.
Las Vegas
Colorado Plateau
COLORADO — Denver, Colorado Springs, Pueblo, Mt. Elbert 14,432 ft.
KANSAS — Topeka, Wichita
MINNESOTA — Duluth, Minneapolis, St. Paul
Lake Superior
WISCONSIN — Madison, Milwaukee
IOWA — Sioux City, Sioux Falls, Des Moines, Davenport
MICHIGAN — Lansing, Detroit, Grand Rapids
Lake Michigan, Lake Huron, Lake Erie, Lake Ontario
Chicago, Gary
ILLINOIS — Springfield
INDIANA — Indianapolis
OHIO — Columbus, Toledo, Cleveland, Cincinnati
Mississippi
MISSOURI — Kansas City, Jefferson City, St. Louis, Springfield
Sacramento, Oakland, San Francisco, San Jose
CALIFORNIA
PACIFIC OCEAN
Mojave Desert
Los Angeles, San Diego
Sonora Desert
ARIZONA — Phoenix, Tucson
Grand Canyon
NEW MEXICO — Santa Fe, Albuquerque
El Paso
Rio Grande
OKLAHOMA — Oklahoma City, Tulsa, Fort Smith
Amarillo, Canadian, Red, Arkansas
TEXAS — Abilene, Dallas, Forth Worth, Austin, San Antonio, Houston, Corpus Christi, Brazos
MEXICO
Gulf of Mexico
ARKANSAS — Little Rock, Ouachita Mts
Memphis
TENNESSEE — Nashville, Chattanooga
KENTUCKY — Louisville, Frankfort, Evansville
Ohio
WEST VIRGINIA — Charleston
VIRGINIA — Richmond, Norfolk
WASHINGTON D.C.
MARYLAND — Baltimore, Annapolis, Dover
DEL.
N.J. — Trenton, Newark
PENNSYLVANIA — Pittsburgh, Harrisburg, Philadelphia
NEW YORK — Buffalo, Niagara Falls, Syracuse, Albany, New York City
Lake St. Lawrence
VERMONT — Montpelier
NEW HAMP. — Concord
MAINE — Bangor, Augusta, Portland
MASS. — Boston
CONN. — Hartford
R.I. — Providence
MONTANA... St. Lawrence
NORTH ATLANTIC OCEAN
NORTH CAROLINA — Raleigh, Charlotte
SOUTH CAROLINA — Columbia, Charleston
GEORGIA — Atlanta, Columbus, Savannah
ALABAMA — Birmingham, Montgomery, Mobile
MISSISSIPPI — Jackson
LOUISIANA — Shreveport, Monroe, Baton Rouge, New Orleans
Tennessee, Mississippi
FLORIDA — Jacksonville, Tallahassee, Orlando, Saint Petersburg, Tampa, Cape Canaveral, Fort Lauderdale, Miami, Lake Okeechobee, Everglades, Florida Keys
APPALACHIAN MTS.

miles 0 500
kilometers 0 500

## Hawaii (inset)
A 160° B 155° C
Kauai
Niihau
Pearl Harbor • Oahu
Honolulu
NORTH PACIFIC OCEAN
Molokai
Lanai • Maui • Wailuku
HAWAII
Kahoolawe
Mauna Kea 13,796 ft.
Hilo
Hawaii
Mauna Loa 13,678 ft.
miles 0 100
kilometers 0 100

NEW HAMP. = NEW HAMPSHIRE      R.I. = RHODE ISLAND
MASS. = MASSACHUSETTS          N.J. = NEW JERSEY
CONN. = CONNECTICUT            DEL. = DELAWARE

**Area:** 3,618,787 sq. miles (9,372,614 km²)
**Population:** 250,941,000
**Capital:** Washington,D.C. (pop. 615,000)
**Other cities:** New York City 7,346,000; Los Angeles 3,402,000; Chicago 2,994,000
**Highest point:** Mt. McKinley 20,320 ft. (6,194 m)
**Official language:** English
**Religions:** Christianity, Judaism, Islam
**Currency:** U.S. dollar
**Main exports:** Aircraft, cars, chemicals, coal, machinery, corn, soybeans, wheat
**Government:** Federal republic
**Per capita GNP:** U.S. $21,100

Forty-eight of the 50 states of the United States lie in North America, between Canada and Mexico. Two are isolated: Alaska in the far northwest, and Hawaii in the Pacific Ocean some 2,400 miles (3,870 km) southwest of San Francisco. In the east and west are long mountain ranges: the Appalachians in the east, the Coast Range, Sierra Nevada, and Rocky Mountains in the west. The Rocky Mountains form the largest mountain system in North America. Many great rivers, including the Colorado, Missouri and Rio Grande, begin in the Rockies. In the north are the five Great Lakes. The central region, of vast plateaus and great plains, is drained by the Mississippi River system. Outstanding natural features include the Grand Canyon, carved by the Colorado River, Niagara Falls, and the San Andreas Fault in California. North America's highest peak is Mt. McKinley, Alaska. The climate is mostly temperate, but ranges from arctic in Alaska to desert in the southwest and subtropical in the southeast.

## ECONOMIC SURVEY

**Farming:** The U.S.A.'s large farms make it the world's leading food producer. Major farm products are beef, dairy foods, pigs, chickens, turkeys, cereals including corn and wheat, soybeans, cotton, tobacco, fruit, and vegetables.

**Forestry:** Timber is produced, plus pulp for paper making.

**Fishing:** Three fishing grounds, the Atlantic, the Gulf of Mexico, and the Pacific, yield 4 million tons of fish a year.

**Mining:** Petroleum, natural gas, coal (of which the country is the world's second largest producer), copper, gold, iron ore, silver, and uranium are mined.

**Industry:** Products include machinery, cars, aircraft, electronic goods, chemicals, and foods. Service industries are important.

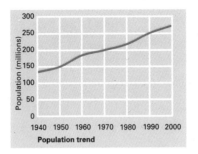
**Population trend**

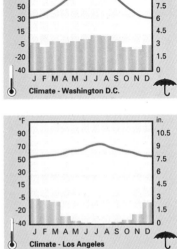
Climate - Washington D.C.

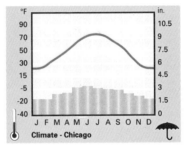
Climate - Chicago

Climate - Los Angeles

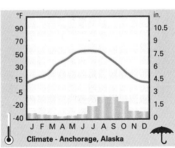
Climate - Anchorage, Alaska

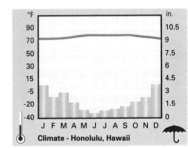
Climate - Honolulu, Hawaii

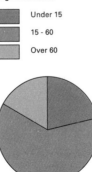

**Imports and exports**  Imports  Exports

**Age distribution**

- Under 15
- 15 - 60
- Over 60

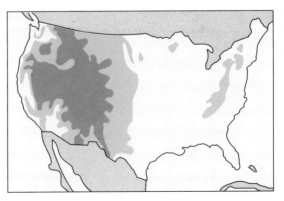

**Contour map**

- Over 6,000 ft. (2,000 m)
- 3,000 - 6,000 ft. (1,000 - 2,000 m)
- 0 - 1,500 ft. (0 - 500 m)

UNITED STATES HISTORY. Native Americans migrating from Asia reached America more than 30,000 years ago and perhaps much earlier. Norse voyagers arrived around A.D. 1,000 but their settlers died out. European rediscovery came in the 1490s, with the voyages of Columbus and Cabot. Spaniards, French, Dutch, and English traded and colonized in the east and south. The United States was founded in 1776 by 13 British colonies which rebelled and declared their independence. The new country became a federal republic and spread rapidly westward. The Civil War (1861-1865) freed the black slaves in the southern states. Industrialized and innovative, the United States by the 1900s rivaled Europe. After World War II (1939-1945) the United States became the world's supreme superpower.

The American people include descendants of migrants from every part of the world. Native Americans, originally from Asia, now make up less than one percent of the population. The Inuit (Eskimos) and Hawaiians are other small minorities. More than 80 percent of the people are whites, many with ancestors in Europe. The largest minority group are blacks, most of whose ancestors were taken to America from Africa as slaves from the 1600s to the 1800s. Hispanics include people from Latin America, Mexico, Puerto Rico, and Cuba. Asian immigrants to the United States include Chinese, Japanese, Vietnamese, Koreans, Filipinos, Indians, and Pakistanis. All immigrant groups maintain some cultural traditions from their past and give the United States a diverse cultural texture.

**INDUSTRIAL PROFILE**
With a huge home market and vast resources, the U.S. has the world's most powerful economy. Its gross national product (the annual value of all goods and services) far exceeds that of any other country. It has major financial and commodity markets in New York and Chicago. There is a vast transportation and communications network. Road transportation is more important than rail. The U.S. economy is based on free enterprise. Industrial methods are generally efficient and in factories automation is widespread. In certain fields, such as civil aviation, U.S. manufacturers dominate the world market. However, since the 1960s the value of imported goods has exceeded the value of U.S. exports.

Alaska

Hawaiian Islands

**STATES OF THE UNITED STATES (with capitals)**

| | | Area (sq. miles) | Area (km²) | Population (1989) |
|---|---|---|---|---|
| 1 | **Alabama** (Montgomery) | 51,705 | 133,915 | 4,150,000 |
| 2 | **Alaska** (Juneau) | 591,004 | 1,530,693 | 565,000 |
| 3 | **Arizona** (Phoenix) | 114,000 | 295,259 | 3,649,000 |
| 4 | **Arkansas** (Little Rock) | 53,187 | 137,754 | 2,414,000 |
| 5 | **California** (Sacramento) | 158,076 | 411,047 | 28,067,000 |
| 6 | **Colorado** (Denver) | 104,091 | 269,594 | 3,393,000 |
| 7 | **Connecticut** (Hartford) | 5,018 | 12,997 | 3,257,000 |
| 8 | **Delaware** (Dover) | 2,044 | 5,294 | 658,000 |
| 9 | **Florida** (Tallahassee) | 58,664 | 151,939 | 12,535,000 |
| 10 | **Georgia** (Atlanta) | 58,910 | 152,576 | 6,524,000 |
| 11 | **Hawaii** (Honolulu) | 6,471 | 16,760 | 1,121,000 |
| 12 | **Idaho** (Boise) | 83,564 | 216,430 | 1,013,000 |
| 13 | **Illinois** (Springfield) | 57,871 | 149,885 | 11,599,000 |
| 14 | **Indiana** (Indianapolis) | 36,413 | 94,309 | 5,542,000 |
| 15 | **Iowa** (Des Moines) | 56,275 | 145,752 | 2,870,000 |
| 16 | **Kansas** (Topeka) | 82,277 | 213,096 | 2,485,000 |
| 17 | **Kentucky** (Frankfort) | 40,409 | 104,659 | 3,742,000 |
| 18 | **Louisiana** (Baton Rouge) | 47,752 | 123,677 | 4,510,000 |
| 19 | **Maine** (Augusta) | 33,265 | 86,156 | 1,203,000 |
| 20 | **Maryland** (Annapolis) | 10,460 | 27,091 | 4,655,000 |
| 21 | **Massachusetts** (Boston) | 8,284 | 21,455 | 5,863,000 |
| 22 | **Michigan** (Lansing) | 97,102 | 251,493 | 9,266,000 |
| 23 | **Minnesota** (St. Paul) | 86,614 | 224,329 | 4,298,000 |
| 24 | **Mississippi** (Jackson) | 47,689 | 123,514 | 2,680,000 |
| 25 | **Missouri** (Jefferson City) | 69,697 | 180,514 | 5,163,000 |
| 26 | **Montana** (Helena) | 147,046 | 380,847 | 808,000 |
| 27 | **Nebraska** (Lincoln) | 77,355 | 200,349 | 1,590,000 |
| 28 | **Nevada** (Carson City) | 110,561 | 286,352 | 1,049,000 |
| 29 | **New Hampshire** (Concord) | 9,279 | 24,032 | 1,116,000 |
| 30 | **New Jersey** (Trenton) | 7,787 | 20,168 | 7,827,000 |
| 31 | **New Mexico** (Santa Fe) | 121,593 | 314,924 | 1,595,000 |
| 32 | **New York** (Albany) | 52,735 | 136,583 | 17,761,000 |
| 33 | **North Carolina** (Raleigh) | 52,669 | 136,412 | 6,602,000 |
| 34 | **North Dakota** (Bismarck) | 70,702 | 183,117 | 664,000 |
| 35 | **Ohio** (Columbus) | 44,787 | 115,998 | 10,787,000 |
| 36 | **Oklahoma** (Oklahoma City) | 69,956 | 181,185 | 3,285,000 |
| 37 | **Oregon** (Salem) | 97,073 | 251,418 | 2,750,000 |
| 38 | **Pennsylvania** (Harrisburg) | 46,043 | 119,251 | 11,844,000 |
| 39 | **Rhode Island** (Providence) | 1,212 | 3,139 | 996,000 |
| 40 | **South Carolina** (Columbia) | 31,113 | 80,582 | 3,507,000 |
| 41 | **South Dakota** (Pierre) | 77,116 | 199,730 | 708,000 |
| 42 | **Tennessee** (Nashville) | 42,144 | 109,152 | 4,933,000 |
| 43 | **Texas** (Austin) | 266,807 | 691,027 | 17,451,000 |
| 44 | **Utah** (Salt Lake City) | 84,899 | 219,887 | 1,750,000 |
| 45 | **Vermont** (Montpelier) | 9,614 | 24,900 | 557,000 |
| 46 | **Virginia** (Richmond) | 40,767 | 105,586 | 6,068,000 |
| 47 | **Washington** (Olympia) | 68,139 | 176,479 | 4,612,000 |
| 48 | **West Virginia** (Charleston) | 24,231 | 62,758 | 1,871,000 |
| 49 | **Wisconsin** (Madison) | 66,215 | 171,496 | 4,803,000 |
| 50 | **Wyoming** (Cheyenne) | 97,809 | 253,324 | 503,000 |

Washington D.C. covers an area of 69 sq. miles (179 km2)

# Uruguay

**Area:** 68,037 sq. miles (176,215 km²)
**Population:** 3,033,000
**Capital:** Montevideo (pop. 1,246,000)
**Other cities:** Salto 81,000; Paysandú 75,000
**Highest point:** Mirador Nacional 1,644 ft. (513 m)
**Official language:** Spanish
**Religion:** Christianity
**Currency:** New Uruguayan peso
**Main exports:** Textiles and textile products, live animals, hides and skins, vegetable products
**Government:** Republic
**Per capita GNP:** U.S. $2,620

Uruguay has a coastline on the Atlantic Ocean with fine beaches. The coastal plains are where most of the people live. Inland are rolling grasslands covering about 80 percent of the country. The land is generally less than 1,640 feet (500 meters) above sea level. The estuary of the Plata River forms part of the southern border with Argentina. The biggest river in the interior is the Negro River, a tributary of the Uruguay River. The climate of Uruguay is mild and humid. More than 90 percent of the people are of European origin. Most of the rest are of mixed European and Native American descent. Portugal and Spain were rivals for the control of Uruguay in the 17th and 18th centuries. Spain had won by 1777 but gave up the region in 1814. Portugal reasserted control briefly until, with British aid, Uruguay won independence in 1828.

## ECONOMIC SURVEY

**Farming:** Livestock ranching is the chief activity. More than 30 million cattle and sheep graze over huge areas. Animals, meat, and hides make up a third of all Uruguay's exports. On fertile soils close to the Uruguay and Plata rivers, farmers grow corn, potatoes, sugar beet, wheat, oranges, grapes, and linseed. Rice is grown in the east.

**Fishing:** Hake and anchovies are caught.

**Industry:** Uruguay lacks mineral resources and has few industries. Meat and food processing, including sugar refining, are important. Textiles are the leading export. Most textile mills are small. Other plants produce plywood, tires, and glass.

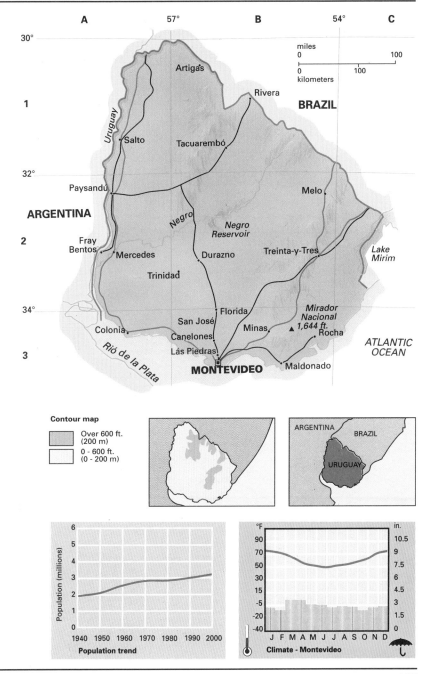

### Contour map

Over 600 ft. (200 m)

0 - 600 ft. (0 - 200 m)

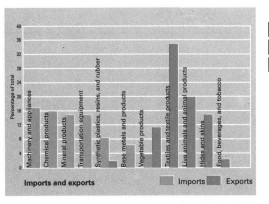

**Imports and exports**

Machinery and appliances · Chemical products · Mineral products · Transportation equipment · Synthetic plastics, resins, and rubber · Base metals and products · Vegetable products · Textiles and textile products · Live animals and animal products · Hides and skins · Food, beverages, and tobacco

Percentage of total

Imports · Exports

### Age distribution

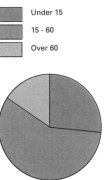

Under 15

15 - 60

Over 60

**Population trend**

Population (millions)

1940 1950 1960 1970 1980 1990 2000

**Climate - Montevideo**

J F M A M J J A S O N D

# Venezuela

**Area:** 352,145 sq. miles (912,050 km²)
**Population:** 19,735,000
**Capital:** Caracas (pop. 1,276,000)
**Other cities:** Maracaibo 1,179,000; Valencia 922,000
**Highest point:** Pico Bolívar 16,427 ft. (5,007 m)
**Official language:** Spanish
**Religion:** Christianity
**Currency:** Bolívar
**Main exports:** Petroleum and petroleum products, iron ore
**Government:** Multiparty federal republic
**Per capita GNP:** U.S. $2,450

This country in northern South America has, in Lake Maracaibo, a freshwater lake open to the sea which contains the continent's largest known oil deposits. The lake is surrounded by lowlands, overlooking which are highlands forming an extension of the Andes. The central grassy plains are drained by the Orinoco River. In the Guiana Highlands to the southeast are the Angel Falls, the world's highest waterfall (3,212 ft., 979 m). Most people are mestizos (of mixed origin), the rest are blacks, whites, and Native Americans. Spain ruled Venezuela from the 1500s until 1821 when it united with the republic of Gran Colombia. Since 1830 it has been an independent republic. Neighboring Aruba (population 60,000) and the Netherlands Antilles (population 193,000) are both self-governing parts of the Netherlands.

## ECONOMIC SURVEY

**Farming:** Coffee is the leading cash crop. Other important crops include cocoa (cacao beans), sugar, corn, rice, wheat, tobacco, cotton, beans, and sisal. Millions of cattle and horses are reared on ranches. In the forests, plants such as vanilla and balata (used for gum) are collected.
**Mining:** Venezuela is a leading oil producer. Most of the oil comes from around Maracaibo. The country also has reserves of bauxite, iron ore, nickel, diamonds, gold, and phosphates.
**Industry:** Refineries process steel and aluminum, and factories produce petrochemicals, ammonia, fertilizers, machinery, cement, and vehicles.

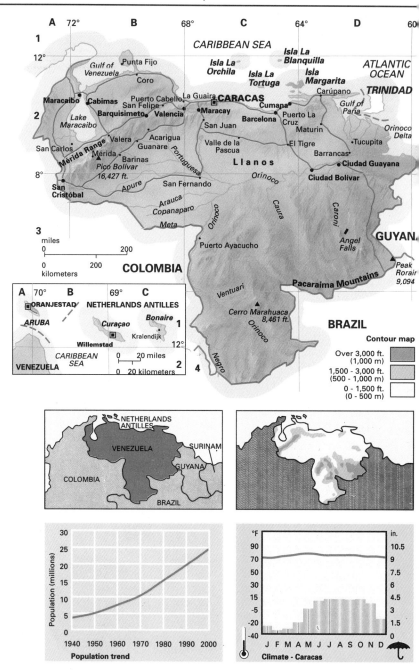

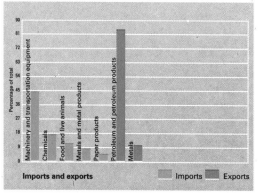

Imports and exports — Imports / Exports

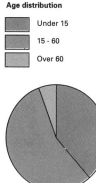

**Age distribution**
- Under 15
- 15 - 60
- Over 60

Population trend

Climate - Caracas

# Vietnam

**Area:** 127,242 sq. miles (329,556 km²)
**Population:** 66,111,000
**Capital:** Hanoi (pop. 3,100,000)
**Other cities:** Ho Chi Minh City (Saigon) 3,900,000; Haiphong 1,191,000
**Highest point:** Fan Si Pan 10,312 ft. (3,143 m)
**Official language:** Vietnamese
**Religions:** Taoism, Buddhism, Christianity
**Currency:** Dong
**Main exports:** Coal, farm produce, livestock, marine products
**Government:** Single-party socialist republic
**Per capita GNP:** Under U.S. $500

Vietnam has a long coastline, from the Gulf of Tonkin to the southern waters of the South China Sea. In the north are highlands, and more mountains to the west border Cambodia and Laos. The Red River delta stretches from the northern highlands to the Gulf of Tonkin. The coastal lowlands and the Mekong River delta are more densely populated than the forested mountains. Temperatures are high all year round, with generally abundant rainfall. The people are mostly Vietnamese, with some Khmers and tribal groups such as the Montagnards. Vietnam was once part of ancient Chinese and Khmer empires. It was under French control from 1883 until 1954, when it was split into North Vietnam (communist) and South Vietnam (U.S.-backed). In 1976, after the Vietnam War between North and South, it was reunited under communist rule.

## ECONOMIC SURVEY

**Farming:** The Red and Mekong river deltas are major farming areas. Rice is the main crop. Other crops include sugarcane, cassava, corn, coconuts, jute, peanuts, soybeans, sweet potatoes, tea, and rubber. Poultry, pigs, and cattle are raised.

**Fishing:** Many kinds of fish are caught off the coasts, also lobsters and other shellfish.

**Mining:** The country has coal reserves. Some phosphates, salt, and chromite are mined, but Vietnam lacks other minerals.

**Industry:** There is a small iron and steel industry, and Vietnam produces farm machinery, bicycles, cement, fertilizers, and textiles. Foreign investment is being encouraged.

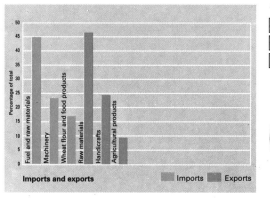

Imports and exports — Imports, Exports

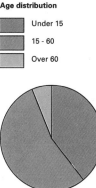

Age distribution — Under 15, 15 - 60, Over 60

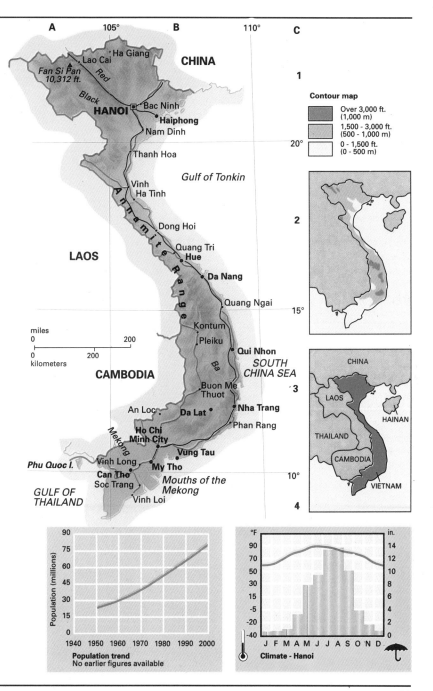

Contour map
Over 3,000 ft. (1,000 m)
1,500 - 3,000 ft. (500 - 1,000 m)
0 - 1,500 ft. (0 - 500 m)

Population trend
No earlier figures available

Climate - Hanoi

# Yemen

**Area:** 203,850 sq. miles (527,968 km²)
**Population:** 11,528,000
**Capital:** Sana (pop. 427,000)
**Other cities:** Aden 318,000
**Highest point:** Hadur Shu'ayb 12,336 ft. (3,760 m)
**Official language:** Arabic
**Religion:** Islam
**Currency:** Yemeni dinar; Riyal
**Main exports:** Food and live animals, petroleum products, coffee
**Government:** Republic
**Per capita GNP:** U.S. $640

Yemen lies at the southern tip of Arabia. Its territory includes the island of Socotra in the Gulf of Aden. Narrow coastal plains, generally dry and barren, give way inland to mountains rising to 10,000 feet in places and pierced by wadis (valleys). The highland valleys, notably the Hadhramaut, have moderate rainfall. With mild summers and cool winters, western Yemen has the best climate in Arabia. The east is drier, with high temperatures. Most of the Yemeni people are Arabs. Ancient Yemen was the kingdom of Sheba. Muslim since the A.D. 600s, most of Yemen was Turkish-controlled until 1918. Aden was a British colony from 1839 to 1967. Two states, the People's Democratic Republic (South Yemen) and the Yemen Arab Republic (North Yemen) emerged, but united to form the Yemeni Republic in 1990.

## ECONOMIC SURVEY

**Farming:** Yemen's best farmland is in the highland areas. Cereal crops include wheat, corn, and sorghum. Cotton, grapes, dates, vegetables, coffee, citrus fruits, and other fruits are grown. Goats, sheep, asses, cattle, camels, and chickens are kept. There is some fishing.

**Industry:** Yemen has scanty mineral resources, and though active search for oil is going on, its industry is underdeveloped. Only one in every ten Yemenis works in manufacturing. Small factories produce goods such as paint, textiles, furniture, fruit syrup and other foods, and leather. The port of Aden is a major trading center and also has a large oil refinery.

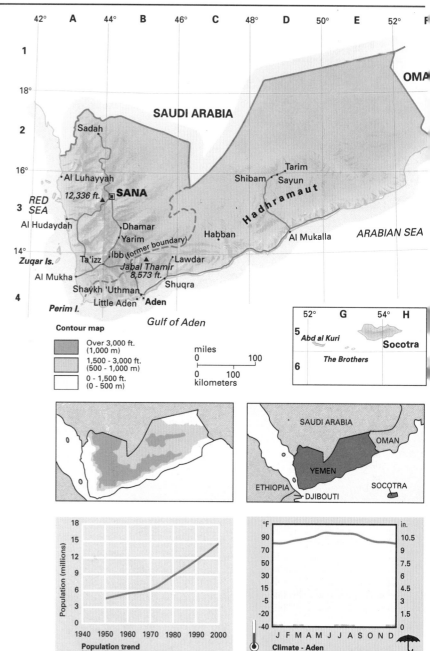

Contour map

Over 3,000 ft. (1,000 m)
1,500 - 3,000 ft. (500 - 1,000 m)
0 - 1,500 ft. (0 - 500 m)

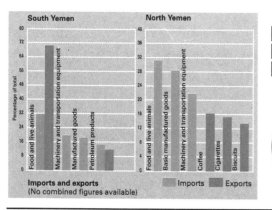

South Yemen — North Yemen

Imports and exports
(No combined figures available)

Imports   Exports

**Age distribution**

Under 15
15 - 60
Over 60

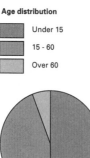

Population trend
No earlier figures available

Climate - Aden

# Former Yugoslavia

**BOSNIA & HERCEGOVINA Area:** 19,741 sq. miles (51,129 km²)
**Population:** 4,397,000 (1992)
**Capital:** Sarajevo (pop. 526,000)
**Official language:** Serbo-Croatian
**Religions:** Islam, Christianity
**Currency:** Dinar

**CROATIA Area:** 21,829 sq. miles (56,538 km²)
**Population:** 4,808,000 (1992)
**Capital:** Zagreb (pop. 931,000)
**Official language:** Serbo-Croatian
**Religion:** Christianity
**Currency:** Dinar

**MACEDONIA Area:** 9,928 sq. miles (25,713 km²)
**Population:** 2,050,000 (1992)
**Capital:** Skopje (pop. 563,000)
**Official language:** Macedonian
**Religions:** Christianity, Islam
**Currency:** Dinar

**SLOVENIA Area:** 7,819 sq. miles (20,251 km²)
**Population:** 1,985,000 (1992)
**Capital:** Ljubljana (pop. 323,000)
**Official language:** Slovenian
**Religion:** Christianity (mainly Roman Catholics)
**Currency:** Tolar

**YUGOSLAVIA Area:** 39,449 sq. miles (102,173 km²)
**Population:** 19,394,000 (1992)
**Capital:** Belgrade (pop. 1,554,000)
**Official language:** Serbo-Croatian
**Religions:** Christianity (mainly Serbian Orthodox Church), Islam
**Currency:** Dinar

## ECONOMIC SURVEY

**Farming:** Farmers grow cereals, cotton, fruit, olives, sugar beet, sunflower seeds, and tobacco. Sheep, pigs, and cattle are raised. But the number of people working on the land is falling rapidly. Forests cover a third of the country, producing timber.

**Mining:** Copper, iron, lead, zinc, and other metals are mined, and offshore wells in the Adriatic Sea yield oil and natural gas.

**Industry:** Since 1945 manufacturing has expanded steadily and now employs half the country's work force. Factories produce cement, steel, paper, cars and car parts, electronic goods such as radios, chemicals, and textiles. Tourism was important until civil war broke out.

**Age distribution**

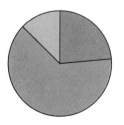

- Under 15
- 15 - 60
- Over 60

This entry covers the five countries that formerly made up Yugoslavia. Much of the region is rugged although inland there are plains drained by the Danube. The climate is Mediterranean on the coast but more extreme inland. Yugoslavia was created in 1918 and after World War II it became a federated communist republic. In 1990 Communism was abandoned and the country began to splinter into its constituent republics, a process accompanied by civil war between some of the ethnic groups.

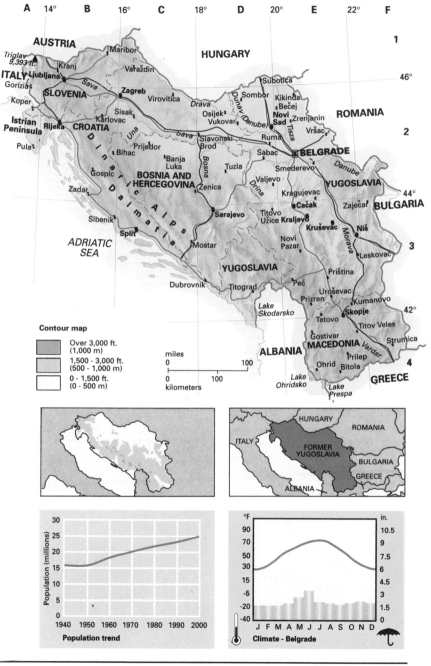

**Contour map**

- Over 3,000 ft. (1,000 m)
- 1,500 - 3,000 ft. (500 - 1,000 m)
- 0 - 1,500 ft. (0 - 500 m)

**Population trend**

**Climate - Belgrade**

# Zaire

**Area:** 905,568 sq. miles (2,345,409 km²)
**Population:** 34,138,000
**Capital:** Kinshasa (pop. 2,654,000)
**Other cities:** Lubumbashi 543,000; Mbuji-Mayi 423,000
**Highest point:** Margherita Peak (in the Ruwenzori Range) 16,762 ft. (5,109 m)
**Official language:** French
**Religions:** Christianity, traditional beliefs, Islam
**Currency:** Zaire
**Main exports:** Copper, coffee, diamonds, oil
**Government:** Single-party republic
**Per capita GNP:** U.S. $260

## ECONOMIC SURVEY

**Farming:** Coffee is the principal cash crop. The main food crops grown are bananas, plantains, cassava, corn, sweet potatoes, rice and yams. Sugarcane, groundnuts (peanuts), beans, and fruit are also grown. Goats, chickens, and pigs are the chief livestock.
**Mining:** Copper is Zaire's leading product. The country is the world's second biggest producer of diamonds, mostly of industrial quality, and there is oil offshore. Other exploited minerals include cobalt, zinc, and manganese.
**Industry:** Zaire makes few manufactured goods. The products of its factories include cement, chemicals, flour, foodstuffs, and soap.

Zaire is Africa's second largest country in area. Most of it lies in the drainage basin of the Zaire River (Congo). There are highlands and plateaus in the south and east along the Great Rift Valley, where Zaire's border passes through lakes Albert (now often called Mobutu Sese Seko), Kivu, and Tanganyika. Tropical rain forest covers most of northern Zaire. North of the forest and in the south are savannas. The climate is hot and humid. The people are almost all Black Africans, with some pygmies and Europeans. About 150 languages are spoken, but Kiswahili and Lingala are used as common tongues. As the Congo Free State, the country was owned by King Leopold II of Belgium from 1884 to 1908, when it became the Belgian Congo colony. It became independent in 1960. There was civil war in the 1960s and futher unrest in the early 1990s.

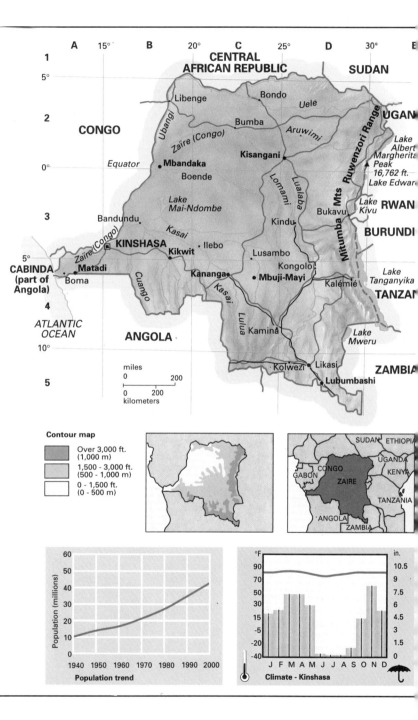

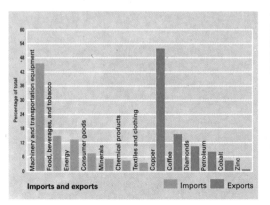

Imports and exports

**Age distribution**

- Under 15
- 15 - 60
- Over 60

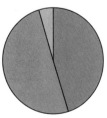

Population trend

Climate - Kinshasa

# Zambia

**Area:** 290,586 sq. miles (752,614 km²)
**Population:** 8,456,000
**Capital:** Lusaka (pop. 870,000)
**Other cities:** Kitwe 472,000; Ndola 442,000
**Highest point:** In the Muchinga Mountains, 6,782 ft. (2,067 m)
**Official language:** English
**Religions:** Christianity, various traditional beliefs
**Currency:** Kwacha
**Main exports:** Copper, zinc, cobalt
**Government:** Multiparty republic
**Per capita GNP:** U.S. $390

## ECONOMIC SURVEY

**Farming:** Nearly three-fourths of the people depend on farming, though soils are poor. Cash crops include sugarcane, coffee, cotton, and tobacco. The main food crops are corn, cassava, millet, sorghum, groundnuts (peanuts), fruit, and vegetables. Cattle, pigs, goats, and chickens are reared.

**Mining:** Zambia is the world's fifth largest producer of copper, which makes up more than 80 percent of its exports. Zambia also has deposits of zinc, coal, cobalt, gold, silver, lead, and vanadium.

**Industry:** Zambia has hydroelectric power (from the Kariba Dam) as well as thermal power stations, but manufacturing is limited to cement, chemicals, and sugar.

Zambia's landscape consists of a high plateau about 3,900 ft. (1,200 m) above sea level, broken by the Muchinga Mountains in the northeast. The vegetation is mainly trees and scrub. In the south and east are the Zambezi and Luangwa rivers. Parts of Lake Mweru and Lake Tanganyika are in Zambia, as is all of Lake Bangweulu. The climate is pleasant, with a short hot season and most rainfall in the north. The people are mostly Black Africans who speak Bantu languages. Zambia was explored by the Scottish missionary David Livingstone, in the mid-1800s. It came under British protection in the 1890s, and was named Northern Rhodesia after the South African politician Cecil Rhodes. From 1953 to 1963 Northern Rhodesia was part of a federation with Southern Rhodesia and Nyasaland. It became independent as Zambia in 1964.

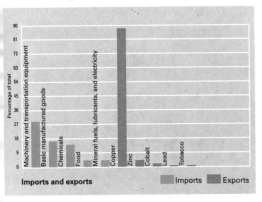

**Imports and exports**

**Age distribution**
- Under 15
- 15 - 60
- Over 60

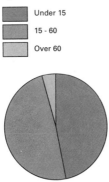

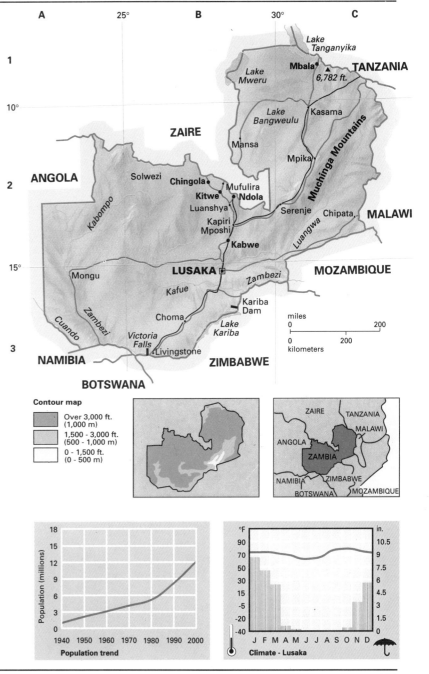

**Contour map**
- Over 3,000 ft. (1,000 m)
- 1,500 - 3,000 ft. (500 - 1,000 m)
- 0 - 1,500 ft. (0 - 500 m)

**Population trend**

**Climate - Lusaka**

see AFRICA, page 14

# Zimbabwe

**Area:** 150,804 sq. miles (390,580 km²)
**Population:** 9,369,000
**Capital:** Harare (pop. 863,000)
**Other cities:** Bulawayo 495,000
**Highest point:** Mount Inyangani 8,514 ft. (2,595 m)
**Official language:** English
**Religions:** Christianity, traditional religions
**Currency:** Zimbabwe dollar
**Main exports:** Tobacco, gold, ferro-alloys, cotton, nickel
**Government:** Multiparty republic
**Per capita GNP:** U.S. $640

Northern Zimbabwe is in a deep trough through which the Zambezi River flows. Lake Kariba, created by the damming of the Zambezi for hydroelectric power, is shared with Zambia. Central Zimbabwe is dominated by the High Veld, a plateau crossing from northeast to southwest. Summers are hot and wet, winters cool and dry. Most Zimbabweans are black Africans speaking Bantu languages. There are also people of European, Asian, and mixed origins. The ruined city of Great Zimbabwe was built in the A.D. 900s. From 1895 Zimbabwe was British-controlled. As Southern Rhodesia, named after the politician Cecil Rhodes, it became a self-governing colony in 1923. In 1965 Rhodesia's white government illegally declared independence. After civil war, true independence with a majority black government was achieved in 1980.

## ECONOMIC SURVEY
**Farming:** Maize is the staple food crop and is also exported. Tobacco is the chief cash crop, followed by citrus fruit, cotton, and sugarcane. Other fruit, tea, coffee, wheat, sorghum, millet, soya beans, sunflower seeds, and groundnuts (peanuts) are grown. Cattle are reared on large farms for meat and milk, and goats, sheep, and chickens are kept.
**Fishing:** Fish farming in the lakes provides trout, prawns, and bream.
**Mining:** Minerals include gold, coal, nickel, asbestos, tin, iron ore, chrome ore, and copper.
**Industry:** Goods include chemicals, textiles, clothing, foods, furniture, and wood and metal products.

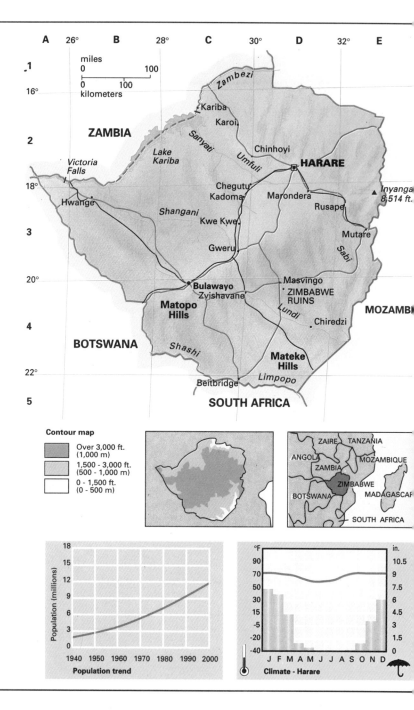

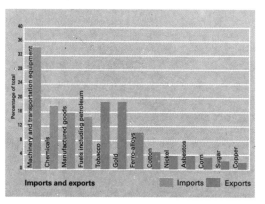

**Imports and exports** — Imports / Exports

**Age distribution**

- Under 15
- 15 - 60
- Over 60

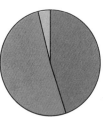

**Population trend**

**Climate - Harare**

# Former and Alternative Country Names

The following list gives old and alternative country names that may be used in books, newspapers, and other publications. It also describes the areas covered by former territories, whose names may still be encountered in fiction and non-fiction.

**Abyssinia,** an old name for Ethiopia

**Aden Protectorate,** a British territory which is now part of Yemen

**Afars and Issas,** a former name for Djibouti

**Aotearoa,** the Maori name for New Zealand

**Basutoland,** the former name for Lesotho

**Bechuanaland,** the former name for Botswana

**Belgian Congo,** a former name for Zaire

**Burma,** the former name for Myanmar

**Byelorussia, Byelarus,** other names for Belarus

**Central African Empire,** a former name for Central African Republic

**Ceylon,** the former name for Sri Lanka

**Commonwealth of Independent States (C.I.S.),** an alliance which includes all the republics of the former U.S.S.R. apart from the three Baltic States

**Congo (Kinshasa),** a former name for Zaire

**Dahomey,** a former name for Benin

**Dutch East Indies,** a former name for Indonesia

**Ellice Islands,** a former name for Tuvalu

**Formosa,** a former name for Taiwan

**French Equatorial Africa,** a vast territory which was divided into Central African Republic, Chad, Congo, and Gabon

**French Indochina,** a former territory which included Cambodia, Laos, and Vietnam

**French Somaliland,** a former name for Djibouti

**French West Africa,** a vast territory which was divided into Dahomey (now Benin), Guinea, Ivory Coast, Mali, Mauritania, Niger, Senegal, and Upper Volta (now Burkina Faso)

**Gilbert Islands,** a former name for Kiribati

**Gold Coast,** a former name for Ghana

**Guiana, British,** a former name for Guyana

**Guiana, Dutch,** a former name for Surinam

**Holland,** a name often used for The Netherlands, although North Holland and South Holland are only two provinces of the country

**Honduras, British,** a former name for Belize

**Italian Somaliland,** a territory which now forms part of the Somali Republic

**Ivory Coast,** another name for Côte d'Ivoire

**Kampuchea,** a name once used for Cambodia

**Khmer Republic,** a former name for Cambodia

**Kirghizia,** another name for Kyrgyzstan

**Malagasy Republic,** a name once used for Madagascar

**Moldavia,** a former name for Moldova

**New Hebrides,** a former name for Vanuatu

**Nyasaland,** a former name for Malawi

**Pakistan, East,** a former name for Bangladesh

**Persia,** a former name for Iran

**Portuguese Guinea,** a former name for Guinea-Bissau

**Rhodesia, Northern,** a former name for Zambia

**Rhodesia, Southern,** a former name for Zimbabwe

**Ruanda-Urundi,** a former Belgian territory which was divided into Rwanda and Burundi

**Russian Federation,** another name for Russia

**St. Kitts-Nevis,** an alternative name for St. Christopher-Nevis

**Siam,** a former name for Thailand

**South Arabia, Federation of,** the name of a territory which now forms part of Yemen

**South-West Africa,** a former name for Namibia

**Soviet Union,** see Union of Soviet Socialist Republics

**Spanish Guinea,** a former name for Equatorial Guinea

**Spanish Sahara,** a former name for Western Sahara

**Tadzhikistan,** an alternative for Tajikistan

**Tanganyika,** the name of an African country which, after it united with Zanzibar, became known as Tanzania

**Trucial States,** a former name for the United Arab Emirates

**Union of Soviet Socialist Republics (U.S.S.R.),** a former country which comprised Russia, Moldova, Belarus, Ukraine, Estonia, Latvia, Lithuania, Georgia, Armenia, Azerbaijan, Kazakhstan, Tajikistan, Turkmenistan, Uzbekistan, and Kyrgyzstan; it spanned Europe and Asia and was the world's largest nation; it was also known as the Soviet Union.

**United Arab Republic,** the name of a union between Egypt and Syria which existed between 1958 and 1961

**Upper Volta,** a former name for Burkina Faso

**West Bengal,** a former name for Bangladesh

# MAP INDEX

In this index, all place names are followed by the page number and then the map reference code. Country names and page numbers that are printed in **bold** type indicate main maps. The following abbreviations have been used: I. = Island, Is. = Islands, Mt. = Mount, Mts. = Mountains.